Terrorism and international law

The proliferation of terrorist activity has provoked an increase in the body of law, at both national and international level, which has sought to counter and prevent it. The bodies involved in this process range from the UN Security Council to government legislatures. This book is the first to address in one volume the wide variety of responses to terrorism as they exist in both international and domestic contexts. It also represents the first ever comprehensive collection of documents concerning terrorism to be found in the laws of the UK and France, as well as in international law.

Terrorism and International Law comprises contributions by fourteen well-known authorities in the area of international, French and UK law, and is divided into four main sections: international cooperation against terrorism, the French and British responses to terrorism, the limits of state action and a documentary supplement. The contributors have sought to show how international and domestic law can be used together to combat the multi-faceted problems which terrorism raises. The issue of human rights is also discussed, with particular reference to the jurisprudence of the European Commission and Court of Human Rights. The documentary section of the book provides coverage of international treaties, UN resolutions, UK and French legislation, case-law and official statements relating to terrorism.

This book provides an invaluable source of commentary and reference material in the area of terrorism and international and domestic law which will be useful for the practitioner, diplomat, student and teacher.

Rosalyn Higgins has been a Professor of International Law at the London School of Economics and is currently a member of the International Court of Justice in The Hague. **Maurice Flory** is Emeritus Professor of International Law at the University of Aix-en-Provence.

Books published under the joint imprint of LSE/Routledge are works of high academic merit approved by the Publications Committee of the London School of Economics and Political Science. These publications are drawn from a wide range of academic studies in the social sciences for which the LSE has an international reputation.

Terrorism and international law

Edited by Rosalyn Higgins and
Maurice Flory

London and New York

First published 1997
by Routledge
11 New Fetter Lane, London EC4P 4EE

Simultaneously published in the USA and Canada
by Routledge
29 West 35th Street, New York, NY 10001

Typeset in Times by
Keystroke, Jacaranda Lodge, Wolverhampton
Printed and bound in Great Britain by
Mackays of Chatham PLC, Chatham, Kent

British Library Cataloguing in Publication Data
A catalogue record for this book is available from the
British Library

Library of Congress Cataloging in Publication Data
A catalogue record for this book has been requested

ISBN 0-415-11606-6

Contents

Contributors

Jacques Borricand is a Professor at the University of Aix-Marseille, where he teaches criminal science. He is the Director of the Institut de Sciences Pénales et de Criminologie in Aix-en-Provence and also Director of the Laboratoire sur la Délinquance et les Déviances. He has published several works and numerous articles, and has worked abroad and organised a number of conferences. He is a consultant for the Council of Europe.

Jacques Bourrinet is a Professor at the University of Aix-Marseille III, Jean Monnet Chairholder in European Economic Integration, Director of the Centre of International and European Study and Research, and Member of the European University Council for the Jean Monnet Project Brussels. His publications include 'Des mythes et des réalités' in G. Feuer (ed.) *Les relations Communauté européenne – Etats-Unis* (ed., 1987); *Les Etats ACP face au marché unique européen* (1994); 'L'accord relatif aux sauvegardes' in Th. Flory *La Communauté européenne et le GATT* (1995); *Les relations extérieures de l'Union européenne* (in collaboration with L. Balmond) (1995); 'Les insuffisances socioéconomiques de l'Etat-Nation moderne et les impératifs de son insertion dans un processus d'intégration économique régionale' in C. Philip and P. Soldatos (eds) *Au-delà et en deçà de l'Etat-Nation* (1996).

Yves Daudet graduated from the University of Paris and became Professor at the universities of Bordeaux and Aix-Marseille. His different postings include the Caribbean, Morocco, Ivory Coast and Mauritius. He is currently Professor of International Law at the University of Paris I (Panthéon-Sorbonne). He is a member of the editorial board of *Annuaire Français de Droit International*. Among various publications, he is the editor of five books dealing with recent activities of the United Nations.

Maurice Flory was born in 1925. He was Professor of International Law at the University of Rabat (Morocco) 1952–56 and then at the University of Aix-Marseille 1956–93. He was Cultural Counsellor of the French Embassy in Morocco 1967–71 and also Director of the Centre de recherches et d'études sur les Sociétés méditerranéennes, Aix (Centre national de la recherche scientifique), 1971–84. He has remained Emeritus Professor at the University of Aix-Marseille since his retirement in 1993. He is the author of *Le statut des Gouvernements réfugiés et le cas de la France Libre* (1952); *Souveraineté des Etats et coopération pour le développement* (1974); *Droit international du développement* (1977); *L'Organisation des Nations-Unies* (1956–95).

David Freestone is Legal Adviser, Environment, at The World Bank, Washington, DC. Prior to this appointment he held, and still retains, a Personal Chair in International Law at the University of Hull. In 1985 he founded and is now Editor-in-Chief of the *International Journal of Marine and Coastal Law*. His current research has been in international and marine environmental law and his recent books include *International Law and Climate Change* (ed. with Robin Churchill, 1991) and *The Precautionary Principle and International Law* (ed. with Ellen Hey, 1996).

Claude Gueydan is Lecturer in Law at the University of Aix-Marseille III, where he is also Assistant Director of the Institut International du Droit de l'Audiovisuel. He specialises in European law and media law. His recent publications include *Grands textes de droit communautaire et de l'Union européenne* (Dalloz, 1996), with Louis Dubois; 'La règlementation et le contrôle des campagnes électorales radiotélévisées en France', in *Les campagnes électorales radiotélévisées*, ed. G. Drouot (Economica 1995); *Publicité et audiovisuel*, ed. with C. Debbasch (Economica 1993); and 'La politique migratoire de la Communauté économique européenne', in *Liberté de circulation des personnes en droit international*, eds M. Flory and R. Higgins (Economica 1988).

Rosalyn Higgins was Professor of International Law at the University of London from 1981 to 1995. She has written on international legal theory, immunities from jurisdiction, United Nations law, and the United Nations. Her publications include *UN Peacekeeping* (4 vols, 1969–1981) and *Problems and Process: International Law and How We Use It* (1994). She is now a Judge at the International Court of Justice.

Patrice Jean has since 1968 been *maître de conférences* at the Faculty of Law of the University of Aix-Marseille. Originally specialising in constitutional law, in recent years he has concentrated on human rights. His recent publications include 'Le contenu de la liberté de circulation' in *Liberté de circulation des personnes en droit international*, eds M. Flory and R. Higgins (Economica 1988); *Aide humanitaire internationale: un consensus conflictuel?*, ed. M. Domestici-Met (Economica 1996).

Henri Labayle was born in 1954. He is Professor of Public Law at the University of Pau, Dean of the Faculty of Bayonne and Jean Monnet Chairholder in European Law. He has written on human rights, law of aliens, European law, terrorism and international law (AFDI 1986). His recent publications include 'The third pillar of the European Union', *Revue* *de sciences criminelles* 1995; and *Cooperation in the fields of justice and home affairs* (Dalloz, forthcoming).

Leonard Leigh is Professor of Criminal Law at the University of London (London School of Economics). He was formerly Lecturer and Reader in Law at the LSE. He was a member of the Canadian Government Task Force on Securities Regulation from 1974 to 1978. His major publications include *Control of Commercial Fraud* (1982) and *Police Powers in England and Wales* (2nd edn, 1985).

Glen Plant practises as a consultant and barrister. He graduated in Jurisprudence from New College, Oxford, and holds an MA from the Fletcher School of Law and Diplomacy, a PhD from London University and the Hague Academy's Diploma in International Law. He has served as a legal adviser in the UN and in the Foreign and Commonwealth Office (which he represented at the negotiations leading to the terrorism treaty of which he writes in this volume) and has taught at London and Durham Universities and the Fletcher School.

Thierry Renoux and **André Roux** are Professors at the University of Aix-Marseille. They are specialists in constitutional and international law and they teach in the Faculty of Law and in the Institut d'Etudes Politiques d'Aix en Provence. They work in the field of the protection of human rights. Together they have written *L'administration de la justice en France* (PUF 1994) and *La Cour de justice de la République* (PUF 1995).

Thierry Renoux is the author of *Le Conseil constitutionnel et l'autorité judiciaire* (Economica 1984); *L'indemnisation publique des victimes d'attentats* (Economica 1988); and *Code constitutionnel* (Litec 1995).

André Roux has written *La protection de la vie privée* (Economica 1983) and *Droit méditerranéen de l'environnement* (Economica 1988).

David Schiff is Senior Lecturer in law at the LSE, where he has been teaching since 1973. Currently his major research interests are miscarriages of justice, and law, freedom and obligation. Recent publications on these themes include 'Miscarriages of Justice: A Systems Approach' (58 *Modern Law Review* 1995, with R. Nobles) and 'Freedom According to Law' (*LSE on Freedom*, ed. Eileen Barker, LSE Books 1995).

Preface

Everyone has his own idea of the notion of terrorism. The idea conjures up the threat or use of violence outside of wartime and most usually against non-military targets, for the achievement of political ends. The phenomenon has long been with us, as the memory of the murder of Archduke Ferdinand testifies. But in the last twenty years it has taken on new dimensions. Whereas the early aerial hijackings were the work of individuals, organized groups, seeking political goals, began to finance and mastermind various acts of terror. These still included hijacking, but extended also to kidnappings, the sending of explosive devices through the post, car-bombings, the placing of bombs on airplanes, the planting of bombs in diverse locations, the shooting of people in airports, the throwing of grenades into places of recreation.

At different moments particular forms of terrorism have waxed and waned. Hijacking is perhaps less prevalent than previously. And with the recent release of many of the hostages taken in the Middle East, it seemed that the phenomenon of kidnapping might be receding. But we know that some hijackings and kidnappings still occur; and we know also that terrorist bombing is a very real and present phenomenon in many countries.

There exists already a certain literature on terrorism, whether written from a legal or political perspective. But this volume breaks new ground in several ways. Above all, it presents an Anglo-French perspective on the problem of terrorism. Part II of this book shows how two close allies, each liberal democracies and each facing the same threat, address the problem. There is much that is similar – but, strikingly, also much that is not the same in their handling of the problem, reflecting the cultural and political differences between the two countries. The response to the problem of terrorism illuminates what is similar and what is dissimilar in the political and legal life of France and the United Kingdom.

At the same time, and exactly because each country is a member of the United Nations and also of the European Union, both France and the United Kingdom can avail themselves of such assistance as is offered by the mechanisms of international cooperation. Issues about the competence to act in varying circumstances are delineated for both countries by the international law principles of jurisdiction. The European dimension has afforded a particular opportunity for effective cooperation in a problem that transcends national boundaries. Indeed, terrorism can strike offshore and not just within national land territory. All these elements are the subject of Part II.

Whatever national measures can be devised, whatever possibilities for international cooperation exist, constraints are still placed upon States in how they choose to protect themselves and their citizens. Both France and the United Kingdom are parties to the European Convention on Human Rights, which requires that even suspected terrorists be afforded the basic human rights guaranteed in that instrument. This necessarily has an impact upon their detention and their trial, among other things. The rights of the victims of terrorism – and the position of the State in relation to those victims – is a traditionally neglected topic: but the impact of terrorism upon ordinary individuals must be at the heart of our concern. And specific assistance may be sought from the international community in the battle. All of these elements are addressed in Part IV.

The study begins with a reminder that terrorism has important non-legal dimensions and that other disciplines may bring useful analysis. In so far as the contribution of international law is concerned, this is shown to be in general international law and also in special action within the United Nations.

The intention of this book is thus to look at a particular problem – terrorism – but in doing so to illustrate the public law and political possibilities within two countries which have much in common, but are yet intensely different. It concludes by providing documents that illustrate these intertwined themes. The reader will find in the Annexes the texts of the leading instruments on terrorism, the French and British position in relation thereto, and – for the first time – the legislation and caselaw of each country as it relates to the phenomenon.

Certain topics are addressed more than once – for example, the question of a definition of terrorism and also the provisions of the European Convention on Terrorism. But these matters arise in different contexts, with different aspects receiving attention. In any event, the editors thought these diverse perspectives not uninteresting.

This study has emerged from a happy and fruitful collaboration of the University of Aix-Marseille and the London School of Economics. With the moral and financial encouragement of the cultural section of the French Embassy in London, assisted by a grant to conclude the project from the STICERD at the LSE, each side has established a team of researchers centred on, but going beyond, its own university. As has been true of all previous collaborative ventures between Aix and LSE,[1] the teams have comprised public lawyers in the widest sense of that term. Two conferences, and extensive work between and since, have permitted the completion of this book.

Each author has retained his or her freedom of opinion. It will be seen that there is not a unanimity of opinion on all the points discussed. None of the authors (including the editors) necessarily agree with certain arguments advanced by their colleagues.

This collection of work was completed in 1992 and for the most part reflects the law at that time. The editors take this opportunity to acknowledge with warm appreciation the research work undertaken by Danesh Sarooshi in connection with the many drafts of the Annexes. The Annexes show the current parties to the leading terrorism treaties. They also include reservations made by France and the United Kingdom. The reader will also find the internal law of each country as it relates to these instruments; and case law thereunder.

Finally, the editors wish warmly to express their appreciation to Routledge for the interest they have shown in this unusual project and the helpful suggestions they have advanced.

Rosalyn Higgins   Maurice Flory
The Hague   *Aix-en-Provence*

NOTE

1   See e.g. M. Flory and R. Higgins (eds), *Liberté de circulation des personnes en droit international*, Economica (1988).

Part I
Introductory

1   The economic analysis of terrorism

Jacques Bourrinet

Until the end of the 1960s, leaving aside some scattered references, there was no systematic economic analysis of crime.

It has been suggested that the fact that all criminal activity was judged to be 'immoral' inhibited scientific analysis of the phenomenon, as economists' reference models were characterized by a puritanical rigidity. It was G. Becker's article 'Crime and punishment: an economic approach',[1] which opened the way for economic research into the problems of criminality. The 'economic' aspect of criminality was approached by analysing the allocation of time and of externalities (the beneficial or harmful effects of one economic agent's activity on other economic agents, beyond his own intention).

It should be recalled that the concept of 'crime', used at the theoretical level to draw up an economic definition, is very broad. For most authors, the concept covers all possible contraventions of the law, whatever their degree, and this produces a very large range of 'crimes', from various forms of tax evasion to premeditated murder, from illegal parking to rape.[2]

In reality, the economist shies from making any moral judgement here, as in all other areas of economic theory. He thus distinguishes criminal activities from lawful activities on the basis of the type of risk involved: criminal activities are those which involve a particular type of risk for those who indulge in them (loss of liberty and the imposition of a punishment).

The starting-point of economic analysis is that contravention of the law results from the choice of the individual who thereby seeks to maximize his hope of utility or of gain. Thereafter, the usual economic calculations seem to apply to participating in illegal activities. According to this analytical outline, the individual will contravene the law and accept the risk of being punished if he hopes to get more satisfaction than he would obtain by devoting a comparable amount of time and resources to lawful activities.

However, the economist acknowledges that the aggregate supply of crime, like individual supply, is sensitive to the likelihood of arrest and of sentencing as well as the severity of the punishment. It is also recognized that if education plays an integrating role by developing the preference for honesty, it will affect the aggregate supply of crime, independently of income.

The economist sees the problems which crime presents on the social level in the same way as those posed by any negative externality. It is desirable to minimize the loss resulting from crime and from crime prevention – that is to say, for a given amount of expenditure to seek the most efficient methods of reducing the social loss caused by crime.

The theoretical hypothesis above has begun to receive some empirical confirmation, and this has allowed analysis to progress on to highly topical aspects of the subject, amongst which one can surely count terrorism.

Terrorism is a form of violent political behaviour, which, for political reasons, seeks first of all to create fear in the community or a substantial part thereof.[3] It is different from revolutionary action in that its immediate objective is intimidation in the short term rather than the overthrow of the government in power. It is therefore a form of political extortion and the main objective of the policies for eradicating terrorism must be, for the economist, to aim at changing the benefits and costs structure so that the return to lawful behaviour appears to all agents to be the optimal solution.

However, the discussion on terrorism does not always lead to a clear description of the behaviour of terrorists or governments. It often takes an emotional or philosophical form which leads to very noble conclusions, but their practical nature and their theoretical justification remain limited. In this context J.D. Lafay[4] quotes the conclusion of an excellent article in which B. Netanyahu states: 'Terrorism is a phenomenon that tries to evoke one feeling: fear. It is understandable that the one virtue most necessary to defeat terrorism is therefore the antithesis of fear: courage.'

Terrorism is not a new phenomenon, and it has manifested itself in different forms in many eras (the European anarchists of the end of the nineteenth century did not hesitate to talk of 'propaganda by the fact' to describe their bloody attacks), but because of its scale and frequency it has without doubt become one of the plagues of modern society.

According to the statistics of the American State Department,[5] between 1968 and 1982 almost 8,000 terrorist acts took place. These included 540 international hostage-takings, carried out by 188 terrorist groups and involving 3,162 victims, with 20 per cent of them being killed or wounded. During the last few years, the annual rate of terrorist acts has varied between 600 and 850, that is around two per day. These acts are greatly concentrated in the USA and the countries of Western Europe. Despite the progress achieved by the United States in the fight against terrorism, terrorism remains highly effective (at least partial success in three out of every four cases).

Moreover, developments in technology have considerably changed the nature and forms of terrorism; this has significantly enlarged its sphere of action, for the weapons available become ever more sophisticated. One of the most formidable today is the computer virus which can harm the largest of companies and even the most powerful of States! Present-day social and economic organization, in which social interdependence is continuously growing, increases the opportunity for terrorist action. Finally, due to advances in methods of communication, terrorist acts can benefit immediately from extensive publicity throughout the world.

Modern terrorism is thus endowed with a very specific nature, as to its scale, its ever changing methods linked to advances in technology, and its internationalism in respect of its methods as well as its objectives. Economic analysis may be used to attempt to bring some light to this phenomenon.

At the theoretical level, economic analysis considers that the relations which build up between terrorists and governments involve a special type of negotiation; game theory and other analytical tools particular to economics can then be used to bring to light the various parties' strategies, to identify the bargaining phases and to evaluate the realistic bases for agreement.

First, the type of rationality of the opposing parties (terrorists and government authorities) will be examined, and then an attempt will be made to identify the specific mechanisms of negotiation between the parties.

THE 'RATIONALITY' OF THE OPPOSING PARTIES

The 'rationality' of the terrorists

Terrorists are often presented as being madmen or fanatics, with whom it would be impossible to conduct a dialogue or to enter into serious negotiations. Consequently, the traditional analyses often give psychotic or psycho-sociological explanations for the violence in order to describe and understand the terrorists' behaviour.

The economist considers that fanaticism does not deny to behaviour a sort of rationality and that agents will endeavour to achieve their objectives at minimum cost, even in the specific case of terrorism.

This general hypothesis, on which economic analysis depends, is supported by a certain number of findings:

The number of terrorist missions which are totally suicidal is small

The majority of terrorists intend, whilst in the service of their cause, to protect their life. There are generally (in 62 per cent of cases, according to some CIA statistics) previously drawn up escape plans or withdrawal plans, in case of developments unfavourable to the terrorists. It can also be noted that actions which carry high risk, such as the hijacking of an aeroplane or the seizure of official buildings, are appreciably less frequent than less risky actions such as placing a bomb or an assassination. Furthermore, the possibility of these different forms being substituted for one another remains, in the short term, high.

Most terrorist groups pursue specific objectives which fall within the framework of a political struggle

M. Stohl[6] has analysed many cases of terrorism in which very close negotiations, which took into account the political context of the terrorists' demands, have successfully resulted in peaceful solutions to hostage-taking.

Terrorists work out a tactic for each operation

Certain studies[7] have shown that terrorists decide on the tactics to adopt according to different factors such as risk, time and the likelihood of confrontation with the authorities.

The presence of relatively regular cycles of terrorist action

The existence of cycles constitutes important evidence of the existence of systematic influences on behaviour. The research of Im *et al.*,[8] amongst others, has used spectrum analysis to reveal an overall cycle of twenty-eight months for all the terrorist acts in the world.

The traditional approach analyses any act of political violence by reference to unseen causes and considers the confrontation between terrorist and State to be entirely ideological in nature. In contrast to this, the hypothesis of a certain rationality in terrorist behaviour (which is the basis of all economic analysis of the phenomenon) is justified as much by the fact that it may be empirically tested as by its valuable findings. The difference between the two approaches and their complementary nature are highlighted in all the economic texts. J.D. Lafay has produced a very complete study of this point.[9]

The 'rationality' of authorities confronted with terrorist action

The economist can concentrate on two essential aspects of this rationality. First, there is the absolute refusal of any negotiation with terrorists, a position of principle more or less officially adopted by numerous States. Second, in the case of bargaining starting between government representatives and terrorists, one must try to identify the rationale which underpins the authorities' decisions.

Is the refusal of any bargaining rational?

In theory, the best attitude of the authorities to dissuade persons from embarking upon terrorist action is the prior commitment never to negotiate with terrorists. It is thereby intended to avoid making the terrorists' illegal activity either constructive or profitable. Various States (the USA and Israel in particular) have officially chosen this strategy, thus hoping to dissuade terrorists from starting any action involving their nationals or national interests.

But such a strategy is only optimal if terrorists are effectively dissuaded from starting any action, or if their essential aim is to obtain concessions from a country. If terrorists start an action despite one or more governments declaring their refusal to negotiate, the authorities' room to manoeuvre will be reduced to zero, and those responsible in the government(s) will be placed in a position of total passivity in the face of the terrorist action.

In fact it is easy to demonstrate that the precommitment by governments never to negotiate with terrorists cannot be totally dissuasive. It will not have any effect on actions where the objective is solely or mainly to attract media attention. Neither would it have any effect on actions which are not aimed at opening negotiations, or on actions where the terrorists do not believe the official declarations of refusal to negotiate and instead make their own estimation of the real likelihood of entering into bargaining.

It may therefore be in the interests of a government which has declared its precommitment not to negotiate to go back on its initial undertaking. And in practice even the most intransigent of governments are frequently driven to this change of strategy. Israel, on different occasions, has been obliged to accept notable exceptions to its policy of absolute refusal to negotiate with terrorists; for example, amongst others, the Maalot affair (May 1974) when ninety school-children were taken hostage; or the exchange in May 1985 of three Israeli soldiers for the freedom of 1,150 Arab prisoners.[10]

If negotiation therefore remains the most frequent outcome, it is appropriate to identify the rationale on which the authorities will rely despite the many constraints which characterize this type of situation.

What can be the authorities' 'rationality' during negotiations entered into with terrorists?

Two main objectives are generally considered by economists as the basis of a government anti-terrorist policy: the terrorists' anticipated benefits should be reduced, and their anticipated costs increased.

It is according to these objectives that the rationality of authorities during negotiations with terrorists can be analysed.

Many of the powers at public authorities' disposal can be used to try to reduce the anticipated advantages for terrorists. Certain studies[11] even go as far as to suggest systematic manipulation of news information in order to deprive any terrorist group of the benefits of worldwide 'live' media interest, an increasingly widespread objective. However this approach does not seem to be very realistic. It assumes that governments exercise very tight control of the means of news communication or that they can rely on strict self-discipline by all media in order to increase the efficiency of their anti-terrorist policy.

When it comes to increasing the anticipated costs for terrorists, most research highlights governments' narrow room for manoeuvre. Any attempt by government in a Western democracy to modify its position in this respect will come up against rigid legal, institutional and administrative constraints, not to mention the vicissitudes of public opinion.

In sum, although the general principles of the authorities' rationale in the course of negotiations with terrorists may be clearly set out by the economist, the mobilization of techniques to put it into effect comes up against many constraints. These constraints are in danger of obscuring government 'rationality' every bit as much from the opposing party (the terrorists) as from the public.

Having taken some cognizance of the 'rationality' of terrorists and of governments confronted by violent actions, we can now analyse the mechanisms of negotiation which may be used by the two parties when a terrorist incident occurs.

THE MECHANISMS OF NEGOTIATION BETWEEN THE PARTIES

These mechanisms fit in with the strategy of the parties. It should be recalled that individuals have various possibilities for expressing their social discontent. Certain are legal, others illegal. Economic analysis presents these forms as interdependent – the choice of one or other category of action being dependent upon a comparison of costs and benefits. These choices and comparisons vary according to the age and social status of the agents as well as the political regime or economic situation of the country or region considered.

During the last few decades, the number of terrorist acts seems to have greatly increased, particularly those which have led to hostage-taking in order to present political demands directly to governments or to the public – thereby avoiding the legal process. We shall therefore consider this category of terrorist action, which, by its objectives, places negotiation with governments at the centre of the action.

In analysing this phenomenon, the economist will consider the specific mechanisms of this type of negotiation in relation to the 'rationality' of the agents, by identifying its phases and determining the costs/benefit ratio and its evolution during the negotiation.

Identification of the phases of the negotiation

Once the negotiation between terrorists and government has started, the final concessions made to the terrorists and the length of negotiation appear, to the economic analyst, to depend closely on the costs borne by the two parties. Such bargaining with terrorists constitutes one of the rare cases where one can observe all the phases in the process of negotiation.

Conceptually, the terrorist incident can be divided into five consecutive phases:[12]

- Phase 1 involves the start of the terrorist act and placing a certain number of hostages under the threat of various weapons.
- Phase 2 is about the drawing up of demands by the terrorists and the transmission of these demands to those responsible in the government.
- Phase 3, which is the longest, is that of bargaining. It can involve injuries being inflicted on some hostages. The government may seek the release of some hostages as a precondition during the negotiations. The terrorists may respond by the selective release of hostages. Other persons may be substituted for some of the hostages. The terrorists may set time limits for the satisfaction of their claims but then let them expire without acting.
- Phase 4 marks the culmination of the bargaining. At this stage some of the terrorists' requirements may have been partially or totally accepted. Or, on the contrary, the bargaining may have led to a lack of agreement and one of the parties may put an end to the incident in a violent manner.
- The fifth and last phase covers the time comprised between the acceptance of the terms of the agreement and the end of the incident, as marked by the terrorists' departure and the release of the hostages. The time between the acceptance of the agreement and the release of the hostages can be particularly long in certain cases, and this will increase the overall duration of the terrorist incident.

The meticulous breaking down of the mechanism of negotiation allows the relations to be better defined and introduces a large number of variables into the econometric models.

The terrorist incident is analysed as a recurrent process: some variables which are considered as endogenous in the first phases may become exogenous in the latter phases. Before phase one, the terrorists can decide on the choice of weapons and the type of hostage-taking which they intend to carry out – a choice which is, in principle, no longer possible once the terrorist operation has started. During the first phase the terrorists must also fix the number of hostages which they intend to capture.

Inherently, any decision taken in one of the phases, either by the terrorists, the government, or both parties together, has vital consequences for the following phases.

The relations between costs and benefits during the bargaining phase

The terrorists systematically draw up precise demands of what they want in return for the release of their hostages. They may ask for money, or the liberation of certain prisoners, or the distribution of propaganda to confirm their political objectives. They can be presented as seeking the highest net return. This net return is calculated on the basis of the difference between the concessions of the government and the costs of negotiation.

The government representatives are also concerned by the highest net return when they make their offers of concessions in return. For as long as the incident continues, the government evaluates the bargaining and the costs of the wait. These costs include in particular the publicity given to the terrorists, the raising of money, and the prejudicial effect of an apparent inefficiency on the part of the government.

After an appraisal of the costs of negotiation, the terrorists wish to be granted the maximum number of their demands, whereas the government wishes to make as few concessions as possible.

Despite all the complexity surrounding negotiations with terrorists, the information available allows a certain number of hypotheses to be tested – concerning the costs of bargaining, the requirements of the terrorists and the length of the incident. These three variables are highlighted in differing degrees in economic works on the subject. Some models, such as that of John G. Cross,[13] emphasize that both the terrorists and the officials are seeking to maximize – without taking time into account – the difference between their benefit, which depends on demands (or concessions), and the costs of bargaining which they are supposed to be suffering. Each party aims at maximizing its respective differences, and it is considered that the length of the terrorist incident can be calculated on the basis of the difference between the current demands and concessions, divided by the rate of concession of the opposing party.

In deciding upon their demands (or concessions) for each phase, the terrorists (or governments) may concentrate on more or less important elements, at the price of a longer incident and the concomitant increase in costs. The incident will end when the demands are equal to the concessions.

On the whole, the amount paid and the length of the negotiation appear very sensitive to the costs supported by the two parties, terrorists and governments.

A number of empirical studies succeed in establishing the following three hypotheses:

1 The increases in (or the lowering of) the costs of bargaining for the terrorists lead them to reduce (or increase) their demands because of the costs incurred by the waiting period. In the same way, the increases in (or lowering of) the costs of bargaining for the government lead it to increase (or reduce) its concessions.
2 The increases (or reductions) in the costs of negotiation will reduce (or increase) the length of the incident.
3 The 'bluff', in the sense of an improbable demand aimed at frightening

the opponent by deluding him, often backfires on the party who practises it. When terrorists are obliged to go back on over-ambitious initial demands, the ransoms finally paid tend to be smaller, *ceteris paribus*.

However, one should not be tempted to accept an over-simplistic economic view, for it appears that this theoretical analysis of the mechanisms of negotiation between the two parties comes up against two types of limitation.

First, there is a lack of sufficiently detailed information available to proceed with the necessary empirical verifications, though one must acknowledge that some countries (e.g. USA, Israel) have made considerable efforts to assemble data.

Second, it must be stated that the real-life situations of bargaining between terrorists and governments never correspond to the relatively simple structure analysed by the theory.

For example, terrorists often draw up multiple demands. In the same way, there is frequently an element of bluff, as terrorists extend time limits which they themselves have fixed. Fear can often change the way an incident will develop, once terrorists, hostages or officials are killed or wounded. Likewise, before the final result, which may be a negotiated agreement or an armed attack, other negotiations may result in partial solutions leading for example to the preliminary release of some hostages by the terrorists.

Even the most sophisticated of theoretical models will not entirely take into account such complex phenomena which in addition remain considerably uncertain on many points.

This statement sets the limits of economic analysis. It does not put into question its usefulness.

***

Economic analysis of terrorism comes within the framework of the general theoretical movement aimed at applying the methods of analysis of the economy to all social problems.

The economist's approach may appear unsatisfactory in so far as he considers the form of utility curves (individual and group choices) as the data, and does not take into account some elements which appear fundamental.

However, by his analysis and his empirical studies the economist can reveal certain limits and can bring to the fore certain criteria which could guide public opinion; in this sense his contribution should not be ignored.

In the absence of empirical figures, it cannot be confirmed, *a priori*, that the economic approach is less effective than that developed by the other social sciences. Moreover, it should be recalled that the economic approach does not aim to replace the approach of the other specialists of human sciences, but rather that its purpose is to complete their analysis.

NOTES

1 G. Becker, 'Crime and punishment: an economic approach', *Journal of Political Economy* 78 (1968).

2 F. Jenny, 'La théorie économique du crime: une revue de la littérature', *Vie et sciences économiques*, 73 (April 1977).

3 R. Kirk, 'Political terrorism and the size of the government: a positive institutional analysis of violent political activity', *Public Choice* 40(1) (1983).

4 *Time*, 14 April 1986, quoted in J.D. Lafay, 'L'analyse économique du problème terroriste', *Analyses de la SEDEIS*, 69, May 1989.

5 S.E. Atkinson, T. Sandler, J. Tschirhart, 'Terrorism in a bargaining framework', *Journal of Law and Economics*, 30 April (1987).

6 M. Stohl (ed.) *The Politics of Terrorism*, New York: Marcel Dekker (1979).

7 E. Mickolus, *Transnational Terrorism: a Chronology of Events 1968–1979*, Greenwood: Westport (1980).

8 E. Im, J. Cauley, T. Sandler, 'Cycles and substitution in terrorist activities', *Kiklos* 40(2) (1987).

9 J.D. Lafay, *op. cit.* note 5.

10 H. Lapan, T. Sandler, 'The political economy of terrorism. To bargain or not to bargain: that is the question', *Americain Economic Review* 78(2) (May 1988).

11 E.g. B. Frey, 'Fighting political terrorism by refusing recognition', *Journal of Public Policy* 7(2) (1988).

12 *Ibid.*

13 J.G. Cross, *The Economics of Bargaining*, New York: Basic Books (1969).

2 The general international law of terrorism

Rosalyn Higgins

It is instructive to examine international law as it applies to terrorism from the particular perspective of the United Nations. In the first place, while much of the legal effort in the fight against terrorism has in recent years been conducted outside of the United Nations, what we may term the international diplomatic history of the topic began within the United Nations. The identification of the issues and the shape of the legal debate were formed within that institution, as were many of the institutional mechanisms for the international community's response. Second, this perspective interestingly illustrates the operational techniques which the United Nations has at its disposal – with its strengths and weaknesses. The marshalling of an international law strategy on terrorism is a story of committees and their reports, of resolutions, of drafting treaties, and of calls for State action. It is also the story of a United Nations that was itself changing against the background of extraordinary world events. Finally, it has been of the essence of this problem that the issue of terrorism has not been self-contained: its essential character is such that it can only be understood by studying its interface with a variety of other international law topics with which the United Nations has also been concerned.

There is a preliminary theoretical question. Does the theme of 'terrorism' really constitute a distinct topic of international law? Should it command a place in introductory courses on international law in the same way as such topics as 'law of the sea' or 'recognition' or 'treaties'? Or should it be reserved as a topic for special study at graduate level? Put differently, is there an international law of terrorism; or merely international law about terrorism? Is our study about terrorism the study of a substantive topic, or rather the study of the application of international law to a contemporary problem?

Of course the answer one gives depends in part upon one's philosophical approach to international law. Whether one regards terrorism – or development, or the environment – as new international law, or as the application of a constantly developing international law to new problems – is at heart a jurisprudential question. My own view is that terrorism is not a discrete topic of international law with its own substantive legal norms. It is rather a pernicious contemporary phenomenon which both presents complicated legal problems and affords an interesting opportunity to see the efforts made within the United Nations to respond to these problems.

DEFINING TERRORISM

Underlining all the initial efforts of the United Nations to address the problem of terrorism has been a debate about whether the concept of terrorism should, and could, be defined. On the one side were those who contended that normative responses to prohibited conduct could not be devised without agreement as to what conduct was indeed prohibited. In particular, what uses of force, by whom and in what circumstances, were to be considered as 'terrorism', thus triggering certain legal consequences? On the other side were those who responded that agreement upon definition was doomed to failure, and that it was better to proceed pragmatically with building up agreed norms that were relevant to different aspects of the overall problem. Intellectually, the former view is clearly right. There will always be room for controversy as to whether normative community responses are or are not to be invoked on a given occasion, if it is unclear whether the triggering conduct is or is not terrorism. At the same time, the pragmatic response was the only possible one, because there simply was not the consensus to identify what acts did or did not constitute terrorism. That was certainly true in the 1970s, when the United Nations began to address this problem, and when the Cold War was at its height. Even in today's vastly improved climate at the United Nations, the definition of terrorism would still present enormous problems. Even though there would now be a greater consensus between the West and Eastern Europe as to what constituted terrorism, the gap of perception between the first and third worlds has perhaps not narrowed so much. Furthermore, the difficulties of definition are objective and not just subjective. The technical problems of definition are prodigious.

The problem of definition, and the related question of whether it is more sensible to proceed pragmatically in the absence of a definition, is by no means unique to the topic of terrorism. The understanding of the meaning and scope of the term 'minorities' has been important both for the UN Commission on Minorities and Non-Discrimination (whose work programme has entailed the study of minority issues) and for the Committee under the International Covenant on Civil and Political Rights (which has to interpret and apply Art 27 of the Covenant which guarantees minority rights). Neither body has in its work succeeded in agreeing upon a definition.[1] Both proceed as best they can, by identifying such consensus as exists within the general subject area. Again, the International Law Commission decided not to proceed with a definition of an international watercourse (or an international drainage basin). It recently adopted draft articles on the matter, having deliberately turned away from early definitional problems. (By contrast, and having previously set the matter aside for some years, the General Assembly did succeed in December 1974 in adopting a resolution specifically on the 'Definition of Aggression'. This detailed resolution is rather specific, though its need to address so many facets of the problem has led to a text that is, to an extent, all things to all men.[2])

In 1972 the General Assembly established an Ad Hoc Committee on Terrorism. Early discussions on agreeing a definition revealed that some regarded certain types of action as characterizing terrorism; others emphasized the relevance to any definition of a prohibited target; others pointed to the purposes of the action undertaken; while yet others thought that the characteristics of the perpetrator were a key factor in any definition. Thus 'hostage taking, aircraft piracy, sabotage, assassination, threats, hoaxes, indiscriminate bombings or shootings' have been viewed by some[3] as acts of terrorism. But at the same time it is apparent that not every assassination, threat, or shooting, by whomsoever, is to be characterized as terrorism; the killing of one soldier on the field of battle by another is not 'terrorism'; the threat by one State that it will assist another if that other is attacked is not 'terrorism'; the shooting of a person in a store during a robbery raid is not 'terrorism'. It is apparent that while these acts *can* constitute terrorism, the definitional answer depends on other factors too. Terrorism cannot be defined by reference alone to the acts committed.

Nor can it be defined by reference alone to the targets. We have all come to share a perception that acts against aircraft, or against kidnapped hostages, constitute 'terrorism'. Civil aircraft and individuals should be able to go about their business without the fear of detention or other violence. But what does the status of the target add to our understanding? Aircraft and individuals have no special 'protected' status – it is simply self-evident that it is intolerable for them to be the target of attacks. Diplomats, and non-combatants in warfare, do have a special status, conferred on them by international treaties. They too are not to be harmed. But even then is every harm to them 'terrorism'? Is the parading for international news cameras of beaten allied airmen by Saddam Hussein really 'terrorism'? Is the German bombing of Coventry or the Allied bombing of Dresden in World War Two really 'terrorism'? Are these acts not rather violations of the relevant laws of war – their legal character depending not at all on any additional description as 'terrorism'?

Purpose or motive is obviously a key element in our understanding of terrorism. We surely all share the sense that for a terrorist, 'the object is to use intense fear or anxiety to coerce the primary target into behaviour or to mold its attitudes in connection with a demanded power (political) outcome'.[4] But it will be seen that here purpose is coupled with method, to give us our sense of 'terrorism'. And again, was the Allies' threat to Saddam Hussein – undoubtedly calculated to cause 'fear or anxiety' – that force would be used after 15 January 1991 if he did not withdraw from Iraq, really to be characterized as 'terrorism'?

If a State uses rockets to coerce another State, that may be lawful or unlawful, depending on all the circumstances. But we do not usually describe it as 'terrorism'. If rockets are launched by an individual, we are apt to speak of 'terrorism'. Is terrorism something that is perpetrated only by private persons or can States engage in 'terrorism'? If a government kills those demonstrating against it, is this unlawful killing, or is it 'terrorism'? Again, does an individual have to be acting from ideology to be a terrorist? Or are mercenaries to be described as terrorists?

The answer to all of these questions leads to yet other difficulties and problems, and to profoundly divergent views. The view of most Western and many third world States was that attempts to define terrorism were doomed to failure and were therefore to be strongly resisted. When it reported to the General Assembly in 1979, the Ad Hoc Committee on International Terrorism avoided any attempt at a definition.[5]

If the West was nervous that a definition of terrorism could be used to include 'state terrorism', the third world was nervous that any definition which emphasized non-State actors would fail to differentiate between terrorism properly so called, and the struggle for national liberation. The Secretary General was asked to report to the General Assembly on the possibility of convening an international conference 'to define terrorism and to differentiate it from the struggle of peoples for national liberation'.[6] It is clear from his Report, submitted in 1989,[7] that the problems about definition had not disappeared with the improved East–West situation, and that differences remained about the usefulness of a definition. Thus Mexico used the occasion to point out that although it had participated positively in all the international measures to contain terrorism, it none the less believed that:

> the basic problem which has arisen in tackling the question of terrorism is the lack of a single criterion determining the fundamental component elements of the definition of the term. Only the adoption of such a criterion would make it possible to establish mechanisms to help eliminate the practice of terrorism.[8]

Syria favoured the calling of a conference to differentiate terrorism from action by national liberation movements.[9] But other countries not only maintained their reservations about the possibility of reaching agreement on definition, but regarded with the greatest suspicion the counterpoising of terrorism and action for national liberation. Quite simply, they regarded the proposal for a conference as providing an unacceptable opportunity for action directed towards national liberation to be regarded as an 'exception to' the prohibition against terrorism. Israel spoke of it as an attempt 'to legitimize and justify terrorism by distinguishing between "permitted" and "forbidden" terrorism. . . It is a cynical and false distinction'.[10] Norway too replied that '[t]he assumption that there is a need specifically to differentiate terrorism from efforts to bring about national liberation could be taken to imply that terrorist acts may be justified in certain cases'.[11]

It will be seen that the Israeli and Norwegian response implies a definition in which methods and target define the offence. Spain, speaking on behalf of the Twelve, emphasized that their view remained that 'however legitimate a cause may be, it can never justify resort to acts of terrorism'. A conference to differentiate terrorism from the struggle for national liberation 'would only contribute to the false idea, which the Twelve have always opposed, that there is a link between terrorism and the exercise of the right of self-determination'.[12] European countries had in fact already set their faces against motive as an 'excusing' factor in their approach to the problem of the political exception to the requirement to extradite. Wishing to ensure that political motivation or objectives did not excuse an offender from being extradited for trial on 'political offence'[13] grounds, it was agreed in the European Convention on Extradition[14] that certain types of activity should not be considered 'political offences' under the Convention. Thus in that instrument there was a negative definition of what constituted a 'political offence' – and that negative definition was by reference to *specified conduct*. In the matter of extradition there was a given international law starting-point that had to be dealt with – the widely accepted prohibition on extradition afforded by the motive/character of an offence being 'political'. It was to escape this that the device was reached – essentially illogical, but operationally effective – of agreeing to determine the motive/character of an offence by reference only to the type of conduct at issue. Being locked into no such comparable Council of Europe constraint, the Twelve saw no reason to go down a similar path. There was no point in offering a definition based on prohibitive conduct – it was better to avoid definitions all together.

This has remained the position in the United Nations. It has proceeded, as we shall see, in a different fashion. The elements widely regarded as constituent elements of any definition (should such a definition have been thought desirable) have in fact been used differently. Prohibited conduct, and prohibited targets especially, have in fact had an important role to play in the United Nation's work on terrorism – but not as elements in a definition of the offence as such. In the meantime, a fine balancing act continues to carry along as wide a consensus as possible. The General Assembly resolution of 1989 makes reference to the inalienable right to:

> 'self determination and independence of all peoples under colonial and racist regimes and other forms of alien domination and foreign occupation' and it upholds 'the legitimacy of their struggle, in particular the struggle of national liberation movements'.[15]

At the same time it condemns as 'not justifiable' all acts of terrorism, 'wherever and by whomever committed'.[16] It also called for the safe release of all hostages, wherever and by whomever they are being held. As for the question of a definition, while there is clearly no consensus on the desirability of pushing ahead on this, the 1989 resolution – adopted without vote – 'recogniz[es] that the effectiveness of the struggle against terrorism could be enhanced by the establishment of a generally agreed definition of international terrorism'.

The question of terrorism, like so many other questions, has been affected by the extraordinary changes in East–West relations in the last seven years. For years the causes of terrorism were on the agenda at the United Nations, to be sympathetically considered alongside efforts to control the phenomenon. In the early 1980s the mood began to change. The first shift in mood came when the Soviet Union was for the first time exposed to international terrorism, when members of their diplomatic staff were kidnapped in the Middle East. United Nations resolutions now began, for the first time, to include a clause which would make clear that terrorism was never to be excused by motive. Whatever the underlying circumstances that had led to such acts, whatever the cause they were seeking to promote, they were unlawful. This trend in United Nations resolutions has been accelerated by the ending of the Cold War. When, under Gorbachev, the Soviet Union withdrew its longstanding military and financial support for radical Middle East groups, the way was opened for consolidation of the view within the United Nations that terrorism was to be regarded as unlawful, regardless of circumstances. Thus by 1989 the General Assembly was able to adopt a resolution,[17] without vote, in which it:

1. *Unequivocally condemns, once again* as criminal and not justifiable, all acts, methods and practices of terrorism wherever and by whomever committed . . .

3. *Calls upon* all states to fulfil their obligations under international law to refrain from organizing, instigating, assisting or participating in terrorist acts in other states, or acquiescing in or encouraging activities within their territory directed towards the commission of such acts . . .

This blanket condemnation of terrorist practices as 'not justifiable' and as 'criminal . . . wherever and by whomever committed' followed a pre-ambular clause that had reiterated the right of self-determination. The implication is clear: the right to self-determination, which continues to be an important part of United Nations policy, cannot justify acts of terror. Although the United Nations had moved to a clear decoupling of legitimate objectives from terrorist measures, the underlying causes of terrorism remained of interest in a different sense. If those underlying causes could no longer serve to justify the terrorist acts, the United Nations still had a legitimate interest in removing the preconditions for the flourishing of terrorism. Thus the 1989 resolution continued to call for States

> . . . to contribute to the progressive elimination of the causes underlying international terrorism and to pay special attention to all situations, including colonialism, racism and situations involving mass and flagrant violations of human rights and fundamental freedoms and those involving alien domination and foreign occupation, that may give rise to international terrorism and may endanger international peace and security.[18]

THE SECURITY COUNCIL

Against this background of general concern by the General Assembly with the question of terrorism, the Security Council has been seized of certain specific issues in which notions of terrorism have played a part. There is a certain lack of consistency as to when acts will or will not merely be classified as unlawful by reference to the specifications governing them, but also classified as 'terrorism'. After the invasion of Kuwait by Iraq in August 1990, the Security Council ordered mandatory sanctions and ultimately authorized the use of force against Iraq. Saddam Hussein detained foreign civilians who had been in Iraq and in Kuwait at the relevant period. By resolution 666 the Security Council determined that this hostage-taking was unlawful, but did not characterize it as terrorism.

Iraqi 'acts of violence against diplomatic missions and their personnel in Kuwait' in September 1990 were also condemned by the Security Council, but without any reference to 'terrorism'.[19] The same was true of the holding of third party nationals against their will.[20] But after the hostilities, in the celebrated resolution 687, we see for the first time the reference to the International Convention against the Taking of Hostages, 'which categorises all acts of taking hostages as manifestations of international terrorism'.[21] Reference was also made to threats by Iraq 'to make use of terrorism against targets outside Iraq'. These preambular provisions were reflected in the list of public undertakings that Iraq was required to give in return for the ceasefire. Operative paragraph 32 required Iraq:

> to inform the Secretary General that it will not commit or support any act of international terrorism or allow any organisation directed towards commission of such acts to operate within its territory and to condemn unequivocally and renounce all acts, methods and practices of terrorism.

Iraq accepted the conditions of the resolution as a whole.

Operationally, this somewhat incidental invocation of 'terrorism' achieved nothing. Exactly the same results – that is to say, the identification of violated norms and the insistence upon a public renunciation of such behaviour – could have been achieved by pointing to the prohibition against hostage-taking and the harming of persons abroad by the agents of the State.

The judgment of the International Court in the case of *Nicaragua v United States*[22] is a striking example of how relevant subject-matter can be dealt with without invocation of 'terrorism'. In that case many of the claims advanced by Nicaragua against the United States were of a category frequently included in the concept of 'terrorism'. Thus, among other things, Nicaragua charged that the United States was 'recruiting, training, arming, financing, supplying and otherwise encouraging, supporting, aiding and directing military and paramilitary actions in and against Nicaragua . . .' and 'killing, wounding and kidnapping citizens of Nicaragua'.[23] These claims were articulated as substantive charges, each reflected in prohibitive norms of international law; and the Court dealt with them as such. From beginning to end of this long case (over 550 pages) there is no use made of the concept of State terrorism. This is all the more striking as for jurisdictional reasons the Court was precluded from applying the United Nations Charter. But it still found sufficient in customary international law to deal with both the substance of what conduct is or is not permitted in what circumstances; and with the attendant questions of US responsibility, or the lack of it, for prohibited acts where they were carried out by those it financed and encouraged. Almost the only reference to terrorism is in the factual references to US legislation whereby aid was conditional upon the recipient country not 'aiding, abetting or supporting acts of violence or terrorism in other countries'.[24]

Recently the Security Council has been concerned with a matter at the heart of the concept of terrorism – aircraft destruction. On 21 December 1988, Pan Am flight 103 was destroyed by a bomb as it flew over Lockerbie, Scotland. All on board lost their lives. On 19 September 1989, UTA flight 772 was destroyed over Téneré in the Chad desert, killing all on board. During 1991, as a result of prolonged investigations, the United States Attorney General and the Lord Advocate of Scotland reported that there was sufficient evidence to issue warrants of arrest for two named Libyan nationals, said to be members of the Libyan Intelligence Service. Listed among the charges is 'the commission of terrorism'.[25] France also reported to the United Nations that the judicial inquiry into the attack on UTA flight 772 'places heavy presumptions of guilt for this odious crime on several Libyan nationals'.[26] The letter referred to 'this terrorist act'. The demands made of Libya were the following:

- The Advocate General of Scotland, stating that the two accused persons were believed to be in Libya, asked for their surrender for trial in Scotland.
- An indictment of the District Court of the District of Columbia, USA, referred to both the deaths of US citizens and the destruction of an American aircraft.

- The United States sought the surrender of the two accused for trial.
- The United Kingdom and the United States issued a joint declaration stating that Libya must: surrender for trial all those charged with the crime and accept complete responsibility for the acts of Libyan officials; disclose all it knows of the crime, including the names of those responsible, and allow full access to all witnesses and evidence; pay appropriate compensation.

For its part France sought the cooperation of Libya and called upon it to produce all the material evidence in its possession; to facilitate access to all documentation by the French authorities; and 'to authorize the responsible Libyan officials to respond to any request made by the examining magistrate responsible for judicial information'.

The United States, the United Kingdom and France issued a tripartite text on terrorism.[27] It stated, *inter alia*, that the responsibility of States begins whenever they take part directly in terrorist actions, or indirectly through harbouring, training, providing facilities, arming or providing financial support, or any form of protection. The tripartite text continued by noting that such States are responsible for their actions before the individual States and the United Nations.

Libya informed the Security Council that it opposed terrorism and that it had assigned judges to investigate the incidents. It was also willing to cooperate with the other countries concerned, and to that end had asked to receive UK and US files. It had also indicated the willingness of Libyan investigators to travel to these countries. Libya complained that it had been rebuffed in these tangible expressions of its commitment to the fight against terrorism, and that its actions and offers of compensation had met only with a renewed demand for the surrender of the two accused persons.

The Security Council passed a resolution[28] which referred to the 'requests addressed to the Libyan authorities', without mentioning in terms that the requests included a call for the accused to be surrendered for trial in Scotland or in the United States. It 'strongly deplored the fact that the Libyan Government has not yet responded effectively to the above requests to cooperate fully in establishing responsibility for the terrorist acts referred to above against Pan Am flight 103 and UTA flight 772'. In paragraph 3 the Security Council:

> Urges the Libyan Government immediately to provide a full and effective response to those requests so as to contribute to the elimination of international terrorism

and in paragraph 5:

> Urges all states individually and collectively to encourage the Libyan Government to respond fully and effectively to those requests.

The Security Council decided to remain seized of the matter.

Before proceeding to a legal analysis of these matters, reference must be made to the Montreal Convention of 1971 for the Suppression of Unlawful Acts against the Safety of Civil Aviation. All the States concerned, including Libya, are parties to this Convention. There is no doubt that the destruction of the two aircraft were 'Convention violations' by reference to the prohibited acts listed in Article 1. This provides:

> 1. Any person commits an offence if he unlawfully and intentionally:
>
> > (a) performs an act of violence against a person on board an aircraft in flight if that act is likely to endanger the safety of that aircraft; . . .

Article 4(2) provides that each contracting State shall take such measures as may be necessary to establish its jurisdiction over the offences listed in Article 1, 'in the case where the alleged offender is present in its territory and it does not extradite him'. Article 7 provides that:

> The contracting state in the territory of which the alleged offender is found shall, if it does not extradite him, be obliged, without exception whatsoever and whether or not the offence was committed in its territory, to submit the case to its competent authorities for the purpose of prosecution.

Against this background, the position of Libya may be understood to be the following: it has, as it is required to have under Article 5 of the Montreal Convention, the power to exercise jurisdiction over the accused persons. It has, as it is required to do under Article 7, submitted the case to the competent authorities. Those authorities are independent, and will decide for themselves whether the evidence warrants prosecution. They have not been assisted by the refusal of the United States and the United Kingdom to turn over the files. There is no reason why the accused should be surrendered to the United States or the United Kingdom. In the first place, they are Libyan nationals, and it is unusual in many countries for nationals to be subject to extradition. There is, in any event, no extradition treaty between Libya and these two countries. Libya could, under Article 8 of the Convention, still choose to extradite, but is not obliged to do so. Its obligation is to institute procedures itself, which it has rapidly done.

There is a certain strength to this argument. But, from the perspective of the United States and the United Kingdom, the legal arguments must not lose sight of the realities. The perceived reality is that any action carried out by the named persons was almost certainly done on the instructions of Colonel Gaddhafi. The courts of Libya are regarded as having the appearance of independence, but in fact operate within the framework of the Government's overall grip on the country. And it is only by pressure to hand over the accused that they may possibly be brought to trial.

There are many other elements that require attention. Libya makes the point that the matter should not at all be before the Security Council. The

Montreal Convention has its own procedures, which should be followed. Article 14 provides that any dispute about the interpretation or application of the Convention should be submitted to arbitration. If arbitration cannot be agreed within six months of a request by one side, either party may refer the dispute to the International Court of Justice. Libya declares that if the United States, the United Kingdom or France are dissatisfied with its application of the Convention in respect of the Lockerbie or UTA affairs, it should agree to arbitration – and failing that, must accept a reference to the International Court of Justice.

The Western powers appear to be taking the view that the situation is not determined by the Montreal Convention. The issue was stated by the United Kingdom representative[29] not to be one concerning a dispute between two or more contracting parties about the interpretation or the application of the Montreal Convention. It was rather 'concerned with the proper reaction of the international community to the situation arising from Libya's failure to respond effectively to the most serious accusations of state involvement in acts of terrorism'.

The unarticulated premise seems to be this. The Montreal Convention is not addressed to the problem of state-sponsored terrorism. Article 5, which stipulates the bases for jurisdiction which a State may – and must – assume, is predicated upon quite different assumptions. One sees from its terms that it is directed towards aviation offences which occur in its own territory, or in respect of a nationally registered aircraft, or in respect of an aircraft landing in its territory with the offender still on board (Art 5(1)). Even Article 5(2) – which requires measures to be taken to establish effective jurisdiction over persons on one's territory – appears to underline that the Convention is directed at rather different circumstances, because there is already territorial jurisdiction over one's own nationals, without anything further requiring to be done. Even if the Convention could be said to apply to a national who engaged in terrorism abroad, and then returned home, it is arguable that it was never directed to the case of nationals who acted under the orders of the State concerned. That is – as the UK representative put it – an act of State terrorism. The individual then is to be surrendered both as the representative of the State, but also to be accountable for his own acts of murder and terrorism, albeit outside of the framework of the Montreal Convention.

JURISDICTION

International law prescribes certain rules for the taking of jurisdiction over persons and events.[30] Broadly speaking, a State has jurisdiction to apply its law to persons and events within its own territory (though foreign diplomats may be entitled to certain immunities from jurisdiction). States may extend their jurisdiction to nationals abroad, but are not obliged to do so, and may in any event defer to a competing territorial jurisdiction. The protective principle allows a State to assert jurisdiction over events outside of its territory, directed at its physical security, currency and official marks. Two rather more controversial heads of jurisdiction are relevant to terrorism: the passive personality principle, said by some to have been authorized by the Permanent Court of Justice in the *Lotus Case*[31] to allow jurisdiction over persons causing harm to one's nationals abroad. The passive personality principle – always uncertain and never really consolidated in general international practice since the somewhat ambiguous pronouncements of the Permanent Court – has been the focus of renewed interest in the context of terrorism. The United States, and to some extent France also, have in their legislation asserted an entitlement to take jurisdiction over persons harming their nationals abroad through acts of terrorism.[32] And in various international instruments on various facets of the subject, the passive personality principle undoubtedly has a role. Finally, States may assert universal jurisdiction over a small number of offences universally considered to be offences *erga omnes* – harming not only those against whom they are directed, but the international community generally. Slave-trading, piracy and war crimes are offences cited in this category. Contrary to popular belief, terrorism is not subject to universal jurisdiction – some degree of connection with the event is required.

Broadly speaking, there have been two major jurisdictional problems in connection with terrorism. The first has been that terrorist offences have often occurred in locations (such as aircraft over international seas) that make the operation of the normal rules of jurisdiction uncertain. The second is that even when it has been clear who may assert jurisdiction, there has not always been the political will to do so. The terrorist can often instil fear that if he is arrested, or imprisoned after trial, further violence will occur against the citizens of the country concerned. It has been the task of the United Nations, in the series of international instruments for which it has had initial responsibility, to try to address each of these problems.

The phenomenon of hijacking (later to be regarded as one of the offences that would generally be classified as a 'terrorist' offence) started to become prevalent at the beginning of the 1960s. The first non-unilateral efforts to deal with the phenomenon were made in the 1963 Convention on Offences and Certain Other Acts Committed on Board Aircraft (known as the Tokyo Convention). Its jurisdictional provisions are strangely constructed. Article 4(3) provides that 'This Convention does not exclude any criminal jurisdiction exercised in accordance with national law', while Article 4 deals with jurisdiction only in a very indirect manner, incidental to the question of interference in flight:

> A contracting state which is not the state of registration may not interfere with an aircraft in flight in order to exercise its criminal jurisdiction over an offence committed on board except in the following cases:

(a) the offence has effect on the territory of such state;
(b) the offence has been committed by or against a national or permanent resident of such state;
(c) the offence is against the security of such state;
(d) the offence consists of a breach of such rules or regulations relating to the flight or manoeuvre of such aircraft in force in such state;
(e) the exercise of jurisdiction is necessary to ensure the observance of any obligation of such state under a multilateral international agreement.

Jurisdiction in relation to specified offences became a more central element of subsequent 'aircraft treaties'. Not only was it necessary to define who had jurisdiction over events outside of national territory, and where various interests collided, allowing overlapping jurisdiction, but it had rapidly become apparent that all too often States wished not to exercise jurisdiction, for fear of reprisal. The new Conventions sought to ensure that those with prime jurisdictional competence (i.e. those where the plane arrived and where the hijacker was present) would either proceed to exercise criminal jurisdiction, or extradite the offender to States having other permitted jurisdictional competence. Thus in the Hague Convention of 1971 for the Suppression of Unlawful Seizure of Aircraft,[33] States undertook to make the offence punishable by severer penalties and to establish its jurisdiction when the offence is committed on board an aircraft registered in the State, or on board an aircraft which lands in the State. The Convention neither provided for, nor excluded, jurisdiction on the basis of the nationality or passive personality principles. But each State undertook 'to establish its jurisdiction over the offence in the case where the alleged offender is present in its territory and it does not extradite him',[34] pursuant to extradition provisions specified elsewhere.[35]

This technique of *aut punire aut dedere* has come to be the classic formula of such treaties for ensuring that there is the broadest possibility for the offender being brought to trial. In the Montreal Convention of 1971 for the Suppression of Unlawful Acts Against the Safety of Civil Aviation,[36] the *aut punire aut dedere* principle was provided for in the strongest and most unequivocal language – but the basis for the exercise of jurisdiction remained essentially the same as in the Hague Convention, except that it was more directly provided for. Again, nationality and passive personality jurisdiction is neither required nor prohibited, but 'The Convention shall not exclude any criminal jurisdiction exercised in accordance with municipal law'.[37]

The other 'terrorist' conventions – those concerning the taking of hostages, and harm to internationally protected persons – have followed the same path. The offence is described in one article, then States are required to establish jurisdiction in a variety of circumstances. In the Protected Persons Convention[38] jurisdiction is to be established where the crime is committed within a State's territory or on board a registered ship or aircraft; where the offender is a national (nationality principle); and 'when the crime is committed against an internationally protected person ... who enjoys his status as such by virtue of the functions which he exercises on behalf of that state'.[39] He must be brought to trial or extradited. In the Hostages Convention there is a broadly based jurisdiction which includes nationality and passive personality jurisdiction.[40] In a strongly worded provision, Article 8 requires the State in whose territory the offender is found, 'without exception whatsoever and whether or not the offence was committed in its territory', to submit the case for prosecution unless it extradites him.

For the moment the *aut dedere aut punire* principle remains treaty based. But the pattern is becoming sufficiently clear, and the ratifying parties sufficiently substantial, for the question soon to be asked, whether, as a matter now reflective of general international law, the *aut dedere aut punire* principle applies to terrorist offenders.

STATE TERRORISM

The international legal foundation of the concept of terrorism began with the phenomenon of violent offences by individuals directed against civilians (or against the military in non-combat situations) in order to make political protests to, or to secure certain political behaviour by, States. Later, the existence of the legal phenomenon of State terrorism was suggested. Sometimes this was used to describe the financing, training and encouraging of persons who engaged in such acts. On other occasions, the phrase 'state terrorism' was used simply as a pejorative description of action that was disapproved of – such as certain colonial policy, or an invasion of another country. The former phenomenon was simply an unlawful act under international law, engaging the responsibility of the State. It has long been clear that a State is internationally responsible for unlawful acts that harm other States, or the nationals of other States. It is a matter of the law of State responsibility that this occurs not only when the foreign national is directly harmed, but when the harm is indirectly caused through the active encouragement of such acts.[41] Classically, the encouragement was of such acts by one's own nationals – for example, riots against foreigners, or the ransacking of embassies. But even if the support is given to such harmful acts when perpetrated by foreigners against yet other foreigners, the principle is the same: the responsibility of the State indirectly supporting such acts is engaged, and one really has no need of the separate language of 'terrorism' to make the legal point. And *a fortiori*, nothing is gained – save at the crude political level – by classifying political acts of which one disapproves as 'terrorism'. If those acts are in any event unlawful – such as invasion, or oppression of a certain people – they do not need the name 'terrorism' to describe the offence. But the term has become part of the political vocabulary, used on the one hand to describe

States like Libya and Syria, which have been believed to have trained, financed and facilitated those who have caused violent acts around the world (including in aircraft) in support of certain political ends. On the other hand, it has been used by those who have seen the United States as engaging in unacceptable political or military activity in such places as Grenada: this activity has then been termed 'terrorism'.

CONCLUSIONS

The impression of the term 'terrorism' being a term of convenience is emphasized by the work of the International Law Commission. In the Draft Code on the Peace and Security of Mankind, initially under study by the ILC in 1954, 'terrorist acts' formed part of the definition of the concept of aggression. Aggression was defined, *inter alia*, as 'the undertaking or encouragement by the authorities of a state of terrorist activities in another state'. After a prolonged period of inattention, the Draft Code came under renewed consideration from 1985–1991. The text was almost completed in 1990[42] – by which stage terrorism was the subject of a separate article in the Draft Code. But then the Draft Code itself is widely regarded by many writers (including this one) as a compendium of elements of existing international law, and not as a 'real' topic itself.

The concept of aggression, as ultimately defined in General Assembly resolution 3314 of 1974, does not contain any reference to terrorism as such. But some of the component elements that we have come to associate with state terrorism (including the sending of armed bands to the territory of another, or allowing one's territory to be used as a base for violence against another state) are to be found within the definition.

We may conclude thus:

The term 'terrorism' has no specific legal meaning. It covers compendiously the following:

1 Offences by States against diplomats.
2 Offences by States against other protected persons (e.g. civilians in times of war).
3 Offences by States, or those in the service of States, against aircraft or vessels.
4 The offence of State hostage-taking.
5 The offence by States of allowing their territory to be used by non-State groups for military action against other States, if that action clearly includes prohibited targeting (i.e. against civilians), or prohibited means of force.
6 Action by non-State actors entailing either prohibited targets or prohibited means.
7 Connivance in, or a failure to control, such non-state action. This engages the indirect responsibility of the State, and is subsumed under 'State terrorism'.

Item (6) above does not at first sight come within the scope of international law, which is largely concerned with the norms that govern the behaviour of States. But it has become a matter for international legal concern because of the concept of 'international crimes' and the possibility, under international law, of international jurisdiction over them. That being said, although all acts by private persons using prohibited means, or directed against prohibited targets, may loosely be termed 'terrorism', not all such acts give rise to universal jurisdiction. Certain major offences against persons protected by the 1949 Geneva Conventions do give rise to such jurisdiction. In *that* context we could say 'terrorism is a crime which allows of universal jurisdiction'. But as we have seen above, the aircraft offences, deemed 'criminal' as a term of approbation, still do not give rise to universal jurisdiction. Put differently, although individuals may be said to bear criminal responsibility for a range of activities coming within the general scope of the term 'terrorism', only a very few of them (war crimes, crimes against humanity) give rise to universal jurisdiction. But most of them do allow of the possibility of trial within various national jurisdictions, because of broadly based (even if not universal) jurisdiction permitted under international law.

'Terrorism' is a term without legal significance. It is merely a convenient way of alluding to activities, whether of States or of individuals, widely disapproved of and in which either the methods used are unlawful, or the targets protected, or both. International law generally, and the mechanisms of the United Nations specifically, have sought painstakingly over the years to specify exactly what is prohibited, and to provide wide possibilities for jurisdiction over such events and persons. None of that activity has in fact required an umbrella concept of 'terrorism', over and above the specific topics of hostages, aircraft, protected persons etc. The term is at once a shorthand to allude to a variety of problems with some common elements, and a method of indicating community condemnation for the conduct concerned.

NOTES

1 See the proposal of Capotorti, 'Study on the Rights of Persons belonging to Ethnic, Religious and Linguistic Minorities', E/CN.4/Sub.2/384, 1 Nov. 1979; and of De Schenes, E/CN.4/Sub.2/1985/31, at 30 (1985).
2 General Assembly resolution 3314 (XXIX), 14 Dec. 1974.
3 This was part of an answer given by a US official in Legislative Initiatives to Curb Domestic and International Terrorism: 'Hearings before the Subcommittee on Security and Terrorism of the Senate Committee on the Judiciary', 98th Cong., 2nd Sess. III (1984).
4 Paust, 'A survey of possible legal responses to international terrorism: prevention, punishment and cooperative action', 5 *Georgia Journal of International and Comparative Law* (1975) 431.
5 GAOR 34th session, Supp. No. 37 (A/34/37) 1979.
6 In General Assembly resolution 42/159, 7 Dec. 1987.

7 A/44/456/Add.1, 10 Oct. 1989.
8 *Ibid.*, p. 9.
9 *Ibid.*, p. 15.
10 *Ibid.*, p. 8.
11 *Ibid.*, p. 11.
12 *Ibid.*, p. 13.
13 On the concept of political offence see M. Garcia-Mora, 'The nature of political offence' 48 *Virginia Journal of International Law* (1962) 1226; M. Defensor-Santiago, *Political Offences in International Law* (1977); G. Gilbert, 'Terrorism and the political offences exemption reappraised' 34 *ICLP* 695; L.C. Green, 'Terrorism, the extradition of terrorists and the "political offence" defence', 31 *German Year Book of International Law* (1988) 337.
14 359 UNTS 274.
15 General Assembly resolution 44/29, 4 Dec. 1989.
16 *Ibid.*
17 General Assembly resolution 44/29, 6 Dec. 1989.
18 *Ibid.*, para. 6.
19 S/RES/667, 16 Sept. 1990.
20 S/RES/670, 25 Sept. 1990.
21 S/RES/687, 8 Apr. 1991.
22 *Case Concerning Military and Paramilitary Activities in and against Nicaragua*, Merits, ICJ Rep. (1986) 14.
23 *Ibid.*, p. 19.
24 Special Central American Assistance Act, 1979, S 536(g). *Ibid.*, p. 69.
25 Letter of 20 Dec. 1991 from the UK to the Secretary General of the UN, S/23307.
26 Letter of 20 Dec. 1991 from France to the Secretary General, S/23306.
27 Issued on 27 Nov. 1991 and annexed to S/23309, 20 Dec. 1991.
28 S/23422, 21 Jan. 1992.
29 Sir David Hannay, 33033rd Mtg. 21 Jan. 1992, SC Press Release S/5348.
30 See Mann, 'The doctrine of jurisdiction in international law', 111 *Hague Recueil* 1, and 'The doctrine of international law revisited', 186 *Hague Recueil* 9; Jennings and Watts (eds) *Oppenheim's International Law* (9th edn) pp. 456–98. There is a vast literature on this topic.
31 PCIJ Series A, No. 10 (1927) 92.
32 s.1203, 18 USC, Pub. L. No. 98–473, Ch.9, and s.2002(a) 98 Stat. 1976, 2186.
33 UNTS (1973) 106.
34 Art. 4.
35 Art. 8.
36 947 UNTS 177
37 Art. 5.
38 Convention on the Prevention and Punishment of Crimes against Internationally Protected Persons, including Diplomatic Agents, GA res. 3166 (XXVIII) 1973.
39 *Ibid.*, Art. 3.
40 International Convention Against the Taking of Hostages, A/RES/146, 1980, Art. 5.
41 See ILC Draft Articles on State Responsibility, which elaborate how, although a state is not normally responsible for the acts of private persons (Art. 11(1)), they may become attributable to the state by virtue of Arts. 5–10.
42 A/CN.4/430, 1990.

3   International law: an instrument to combat terrorism

Maurice Flory

The profusion of international law texts on terrorism has produced some excellent studies of the topic.[1] They underline the limitations of international law as an effective weapon in the fight against terrorism, though it be unanimously decried as a crime. The diversity and complexity of terrorist activities complicates the task; and despite a number of existing classifications, there is still no generally accepted, comprehensive legal definition of terrorism.

This paper is concerned with the role of international law. It is thus necessary to exclude at once purely domestic manifestations of terrorism. The villainous abductions carried out by the Italian Mafia fall within the realm of Italian law, and it is for the national authorities to take legal action. Politically motivated terrorist operations may also fall within the realm of domestic law: the responsibility for prosecuting and punishing the agents of terrorist attacks carried out by Corsican and Breton liberation movements ultimately belongs to the French Government, for example. International law is concerned only with cross-border terrorism and in cases in which the victim's State does not refrain from legal proceedings.

Organized crime and political terrorism are not easily distinguished. The former often resorts to political justifications; the latter often relies on hired men. As an incident develops, one type can often evolve towards the other and the distinction is further blurred. In spite of the inherent difficulty in separating these two forms of terrorism, only political cross-border terrorism will be taken into account here as that is what concerns international law. The other forms mainly concern domestic criminal law, and at times – in the case of a fugitive for example – the temporary assistance of the neighbouring countries' security forces.

Political terrorism is more than a serious criminal act. It also carries a message. Through the use of threat or blackmail it calls for attention. The choice of a particular victim is never a coincidence. By carrying out attacks in public places like a busy street, a train station, an airport or a department store, terrorists seek to pressure governments through the creation of a widespread climate of public fear. Individual attacks often target diplomats or public figures as representatives of the State; media personalities to impact on public opinion; academics and scientists to denounce intellectual patronizing and cultural colonialism; or again industrialists, seen as representing economic imperialism.

States facing this problem have two means of action: criminal repression of terrorists, or a political approach which depends on diplomacy and co-operation. These two methods rest on different philosophical grounds. The former is more technical in nature, relying on criminal legislation and legal procedures known to the domestic legal system. It focuses on establishing that a criminal act has taken place, and then prosecuting it – without any undue concern about the context. The latter approach more readily opens the debate, taking into account not only the isolated act but also its environment and its message. It amounts to a form of dialogue which quickly bypasses the individual authors of the act and leads to State level. This process is often obscured by two complications: the dialogue may impede efficient State repression of criminality by creating the appearance of complicity; moreover, intervention will be guided by individual States' national interests, which may jeopardize any attempt at genuine international cooperation.

Over the last three or four decades these two approaches to the problem of terrorism have led to a deadlock. On the one hand, lack of a precise and accepted definition of terrorism has curtailed the exercise of the legal approach. Conversely, the need for consensus among concerned countries has frustrated any resort to political means. The eradication of long-standing obstacles since the end of 1991 may lead to promising improvements in the future role of law, however.

THE LEGAL APPROACH TO TERRORISM

The first means of action overlooks the causes of terrorism and focuses on the criminal act and its perpetrators. Any form of discussion with the actors or their sponsors is disregarded. The approach limits itself to a purely formal denunciation of criminal acts. It may be a satisfying legal analysis in and of itself, but the results it secures are not those expected, as the required conditions for its success are lacking.

The required conditions

This approach requires an agreed definition of what an act of terrorism is. The internationalization of terrorism should result in its global repression by means of greater legal assistance among States. As pointed out by Judge Guillaume, terrorist acts should be criminalized in every State. Criminal procedures should be revised accordingly; courts' territorial jurisdiction should be more readily recognized, even when attacks are carried out by non-nationals outside their home territory; finally, terrorists should be arrested, prosecuted and tried and, failing that, extradited.[2]

How can we then promote an international criminal law which, in spite of the successive efforts following the two world wars, has so far remained at an early stage of development, and when most countries still consider terrorism as an exclusively national issue? This role appears to rest with the United Nations, as it brings together almost all States and is therefore best suited to advancing a universal rule. It also has a number of qualified bodies in which to do so (the Sixth Commission of the General Assembly; the International Law Commission; specialized committees, etc.). Nevertheless, it appears that until now, the United Nations has been unfit to assume this capacity because of its members' conflicting interests. For example, the Sixth Commission was unable to reach an accepted definition of terrorism. Upon request from the UN General Secretary on 23 September 1972, the General Assembly added a new matter to its agenda. The title itself is illustrative of the difficulties undermining the initiative:

Measures to prevent international terrorism which endangers or takes innocent human lives or jeopardizes fundamental freedoms, and study of the underlying causes of those forms of terrorism and acts of violence which lie in misery, frustration, grievance and despair and which cause some people to sacrifice human lives, including their own, in an attempt to effect radical changes.

This initiative generated an intense activity, including a Report of the Secretary General of 2 November 1972 on resolution 3034 XXVII, setting up a Special Committee of thirty-five members on international terrorism which produced two reports in 1973 and 1979. In addition, repetitive resolutions are voted by the General Assembly, either periodically or on the spur of a particularly bloody event (e.g. A.38/130 in 1983; A.40/61 and 40/85 in 1985; 42/159 in 1987), or by the Security Council (S.579 on 18 Dec. 1985). Even the International Court of Justice did not, in the Iran hostages case, take the opportunity to attempt to establish a definition.

This inability to establish a common ground is clearly evidenced in the title of the above-mentioned item on the General Assembly's agenda. The General Assembly – dominated by a majority of third world countries, and the Security Council – divided in two blocks, cannot agree on how best to confront terrorism. Moreover, the third world and Eastern countries clearly reject a formal definition of terrorism.[3]

However, as one moves from the universal context to a more homogeneous community, success is more readily achieved. Europe leads the way. The Strasbourg Convention of 27 January 1977 has succeeded in defining terrorism. The Convention does not contain a definition *per se*, but a list of what are considered to be terrorist acts appears in section 1. In particular, the Convention classifies political terrorism as an ordinary criminal act for the purposes of extradition – and it is this technique which is generally preferred to local prosecution.[4]

The same approach is used in other agreements which deal with the issue in a precise sphere. In this way, the terrorist act is more easily defined, notably the Conventions dealing with the repression of aircraft hijack (the 1963 Tokyo, the 1970 Hague and the 1971 Montreal Conventions).[5]

Accordingly, there is no universally accepted definition of terrorist action in international law. Existing definitions are either limited in scope to particular facets of terrorism, or approved by only a limited number of States. Criminals are given the possibility of finding refuge in States which do not subscribe to the accepted definition. The definitions do not take into account the political aspects of terrorism – they simply emphasize its particularly odious criminal character. This disregard for the political coloration of terrorism might seem to suggest that States wish to operate an effective extradition system to the detriment of asylum.[6] The suspect's extradition or prosecution should be made automatic, by application of the principle of *aut dedere aut judicare*, but in reality, States have retained a good measure of discretion which often results in the non-application of the rule which they otherwise pretend to support. In other words, the same conventions which reduce terrorism to a crime also include protection clauses and sufficiently ambiguous language to allow States to resort conveniently to protection clauses when they see fit. This has inspired Guy de Lacharrière to say, 'Judging by their conduct at the level of the creation of law, States are authors or accomplices of ambiguity in international law'.[7]

The consequences of this deficiency

The international community's failure to define terrorism is political, not technical. States which are frustrated, disempowered, victims of economic and social wrongs, or which are portraying themselves as such, refuse to embrace a purely formal or factual definition of terrorism. Without overtly commending it, these States implicitly excuse terrorism, often perceived as a last resort weapon for the powerless. They are disinclined to sign, let alone ratify, a definition which would restrict their freedom of action and might result in condemning militants who are often the object of public admiration. An example of this was in World War Two, when resistance fighters were seen as terrorists by the Germans, while considered heroes by the Allies.

Failure to build a transnational mechanism to suppress international terrorism may result in provoking unilateral responses by the victim States. In the absence of effective measures sanctioned by international law, the victim State often breaches the law itself under the pretence of self-defence, by resorting to methods sometimes similar to the ones it denounces.[8]

How can we possibly escape this vicious circle? Are we not compelled to go beyond the first approach and forced to look at terrorism differently?

TAKING THE POLITICAL MESSAGE INTO ACCOUNT

Apart from not being appreciated by victim States, this second approach presents the added difficulty of opening a dialogue, sometimes a real negotiation, with persons or organizations which it is embarrassing to identify. Even a remote contact may appear to legitimate their cause, which is not a result desired by victim States.

This impression, however, is quickly dismissed by further analysis. The fact that a terrorist act is inexcusable should not preclude a political assessment of the situation. Exploring the political depth of a given terrorist manifestation does not in the least suggest the approval of what remains a criminal act. However, recognizing the political dimension of terrorism will influence the handling of the problem. In one way or another the terrorists' message must be addressed, and therefore the political dimension of the act committed must be acknowledged. This approach accounts for a better appreciation of the act, and does not necessarily favour terrorists – as they may, as a result, be condemned by a greater number of States or by the international community through the United Nations.

This approach assumes however the presence of an identifiable political message, endorsed by a foreign State or somehow linked to another State's policy. Most terrorism today falls within the ambit of this hypothesis (Palestine, Arab terrorism, Ireland, Central American guerrillas). On the contrary, the approach does not easily apply to terrorist activity aimed at challenging the economic order, conducted by isolated individuals or small groups – such as 'Red Brigades' or 'Baader-Meinhof' – over which States have practically no means of control apart from repression.

Moreover, this approach requires a change in behaviour by victim States. They must look at the political motive behind the condemned act. Indeed, in the secrecy of diplomacy or intelligence services, most States already acknowledge this political dimension. It therefore appears possible to treat the two aspects of terrorism simultaneously and also distinctively. The criminal act must be prosecuted, and the political issue thoroughly appraised.

Considering the political issue is already a response. It is a sufficient indication that the message has been received and taken seriously. Victim States themselves will obviously refuse to deal with those whom they consider criminals: That is why the resort to other procedures such as inquiries, mediation or conciliation may be useful. The particular method used will depend in the end on the type of underlying political conflict. The classic case involves territorial claims and peoples' right to self-government, or ethnic minority self-administration (such as the Palestinians, Kurds, Armenians or Irish). Another type of conflict which has resulted in international terrorism is related to North–South relations, a conflict between opulence and misery: a modern international version of hunger revolts. In that conflict lies the terrorism of tomorrow – according to some third world leaders whose rhetoric is designed to mobilize public opinion and to make a scapegoat of the West. In spite of their rich petrol resources, both Khomeini's Iran and Saddam Hussein's Iraq have resorted to a similar discourse which has induced waves of terrorism sponsored by religious groups.

This second approach has not, until recently, sustained a spectacular development, as the required concerted State action to examine this complex political problem was not possible. Victim States which occasionally undertook the task on their own failed, or found only temporary solutions which by no means resolved the issue.

International solidarity strengthened

Recent events in the Middle East allow us to complete the analysis. In fact, we are witnessing the end of a particularly cruel period of terrorism, which, in addition to the known arsenal of terrorists, saw the multiplication of hostage-takings to a point where it became routine. The release of Terry Anderson at the end of 1991 after 2,454 days of captivity marks the end, we hope, of one of the most sinister episodes of international terrorism.

A close look at the process which led to this result confirms the need to resort to both legal and political approaches. On the legal front, the numerous attempts (though technically faulty) constituted a starting-point. Clearly, they underlined the international community's abhorrence of terrorist action, denounced as a criminal act by a number of legal conventions formulated from the 1930s until now. Though subject to legal criticism, and lacking some important ratifications, these conventions, along with several resolutions voted by the United Nations and a number of regional institutions, nevertheless provide a legitimate basis for the fight against terrorism, while waiting for more concerted action by the international community. One cannot fail to notice that hostage-taking, which public opinion views as particularly cowardly and iniquitous, has not resulted in any legal proceedings apart from the United States' action before the International Court of Justice, whose judgment of the case was particularly disappointing.[9] The long sufferings of the hostages in Lebanon have not resulted and will probably not result, in the near future, in the prosecution of the authors or the instigators of these crimes. Criminal law did not solve the crisis. The positive results were instead achieved by interventions taken in full awareness of the political context, helped by a favourable climate.

The demise of the Soviet Union and the triumph of democracies have modified the traditional power struggle. States that sponsor terrorism have found themselves lacking if not an ally, at least a counterweight which cripples the West's ability to react effectively. The defeat of Iraq further showed that the United Nations (given the unprecedented collaboration of Russia and the USA) could effectively adopt Chapter VII coercive measures. Syria, siding with the Americans in the Gulf expedition, could no longer promote nor tolerate terrorism in the Lebanon which is under its close control. Libya itself is now forced to accept judicial inquiries into terrorist activities which it is suspected of having instigated. Terrorist groups are now deprived of both territorial asylum and political accomplices on which they used to rely.

Finally, one must observe that despite its insistence on divorcing the Gulf operation from the Palestinian issue,[10] the United States has nevertheless indicated its preference for a global solution to the Middle East problem through a peace conference. Accordingly, they demonstrated their resolve to confront, at last, the fundamental issues behind the Palestinian conflict – one of the most chronic sources of terrorism.

It was in this promising climate that the UN General Secretary has turned to intense, secret diplomatic activity. It appears that in the case of the hostages in Lebanon, they were freed in exchange for Arab prisoners being released by Israel. The existence of political negotiation conceals the criminal character of the act. It is closer to a formal exchange of prisoners of war following a ceasefire than to anti-terrorist action. Tainted by a quest for efficiency, the result is less than satisfying. If the exchange of prisoners at the end of hostilities is an acceptable practice, taking innocent foreigners as a bargaining counter is not. As has been said, such a practice takes us back to the Middle Ages. This model disregards law and justice and will not lead to a lasting reduction in terrorism.

The return to the law

From this example, can we possibly work out how the law should be brought into play? In the case of the Lebanon, it seems unlikely. The hand was already dealt and it was essential not to waste the trump cards that remained. However, things could change in the future if existing rules of law are applied, insufficient though they may be.[11] Advantage should be taken of the current promising climate, which may not last, to complete them.

With respect to hostage-taking, the State on whose territory it occurs must be presumed responsible and carry the burden of establishing its innocence. Exonerating Lebanon and Iran may lead to dangerous claims of exemption. A working group made up of forty government representatives met in Geneva in November 1991 and approved a 'draft declaration on the protection of people against forced disappearance'. The declaration – which is to be submitted to the UN General Assembly – denounces the systematic practice of abduction as a crime against humanity. According to the draft of Article V:

> besides the appropriate penal sanctions, abductions will engage the civil liability of authors and of the State or government authorities which have organised, agreed or tolerated this practice, without prejudice

to the international liability of this State, according to principles of international law.

In addition, it is clearly stated that no circumstances may be invoked as justifications.[12] Victim States can initiate judicial inquiries – as was done by the US Attorney General William Barr, who disclosed that two Libyan security agents were to be charged in relation to the attack on the Pan Am flight bombing which killed 270 people in Lockerbie in December 1988. Facing a hostile environment, the Libyan Government finally started judicial proceedings and accepted the presence of British and American observers to monitor the honesty and efficacy of the proceedings. Furthermore, international organizations, leagues for human rights and the victims' families would be allowed to send observers and attorneys. Libyan authorities have agreed to collaborate fully with Scottish and American investigations. Later, a government communiqué indicated that while refusing to hand over the suspects, the Libyan authorities had agreed to let a neutral international commission conduct the inquiry.[13] At the same time, after the charging of Libya government officials by a French judge, the French President declared that his country would adopt the same course of conduct in relation to the bombing of a UTA DC10 over Niger on 21 December 1988, killing 170 people.[14] Thus, Libya admitted the principle of '*judicare*'. The United States, convinced that it could not rely on the justice of a terrorist State, claimed the '*dedere*'. Its claim was supported by Security Council resolution 731, of 21 January 1992. Libya sought interim measures before the International Court of Justice alleging that it could not legally extradite nationals and that it was Libya's prerogative to judge them. Libya also asked the Court to order protective measures. On 14 October 1992, the Court rejected Libya's application on the grounds that Article 25 of the UN Charter gives priority to Security Council decisions. Accordingly, resolution 731 applied, plus resolution 748 which decided an embargo in case of non-compliance.

Any contradiction between the legal action and the political issue must vanish if we are to progress in the fight against terrorism. Although it is difficult to reach, this objective is none the less possible. First it implies an agreed definition – simple and at the same time practical – and encompassing all the various forms of terrorism. Second, the failings of the *aut dedere aut judicare* rule must be reviewed so as to strengthen its application.[15] Finally, States must show a political willingness to react, and overcome the tendency to excessive caution caused by diplomatic calculation and speculation as to the future. This tendency was evoked by Jean-Paul Kauffmann, a personal witness of the UTA tragedy:

> Preoccupied more with law than justice, and obsessed by the question of Kuwait, the American and British governments paid little attention to the hostages in the Lebanon, their first true prisoners of war . . .[16]

Simultaneously, the political debate which is at the heart of the terrorist question must be chiefly conducted by the international community – since it is the international community which disposes of various means of action through the United Nations or regional organizations.[17]

This is more or less what happened with the hostages in Lebanon. The end of bipolarism, the demise of the Iraqi sanctuary, the rallying of Syria and through Syria of Lebanon, and the opening of a peace conference, created a favourable political climate in which negotiations for the release of the hostages were possible. From now on, we must go further and secure convictions of the terrorists, if we can identify them. This task is far from easy as is shown by a statement of ex-hostage J.P. Kauffmann, nine months before the release of the last hostages in Lebanon:

> We were abducted because our governments supported Saddam Hussein... Having lived with and observed my abductors for three years, I know that they and their chiefs have recently become enthusiastic followers of him who they once despised ... the time has come to ask ourselves who really are the torturers of those who languish silently in Beirut jails. Of whom are they the prisoners? The Iranians? These days they proclaim themselves to be guardians of the peace! The Syrians? They are our allies! Saddam Hussein? Our abductors have mistrusted him for too long... So one must come to the conclusion that these people act solely out of self-interest ...[18]

If this pessimistic conclusion is probably true today, there remains the fact that at the outset there were links to particular States and governments, and throughout the tragedy there was an identifiable territorial authority. To resolve the issue one must assemble sufficient collective will amongst the victim States.[19] That is what has now happened in the case of Libya. In order to achieve success, it is imperative that the political dimension of these atrocities should not be buried. If the peace efforts under way were to fail, it is foreseeable that Arab terrorism and, more specifically, Palestinian terrorism will flourish anew.[20]

NOTES

1 For general studies on the topic, see: Guillaume, G., 'Terrorisme et droit international', *RCADI* (1989), III, t. 215, p. 287 with complete bibliography; Labayle, H., 'Droit international et lutte contre le terrorisme', *AFDI* (1986), p. 105; Patrnogic, J. and Meriboute, Z., 'Terrorisme et droit international', *Études polémologiques*, 38 (2) 1985, p. 133.
2 Guillaume, *op. cit.* note 1, p. 325.
3 Resolution A 46/51 of 9 Dec. 1991 on the measures aiming at the elimination of international terrorism considers that: 'the adoption of a definition of international terrorism which meets general approval would render the fight against terrorism more efficient'. On the other hand, this resolution reflects the ongoing contradictions within the UN by condemning all forms of terrorism, whilst at the

same time affirming the legitimacy of the fight of people submitted to colonial regime and other forms of domination.

4 Vallée, C., 'La Convention européenne des droits de l'homme', *AFDI* (1976), p. 756.

5 Guillaume, G., 'La Convention de la Haye de 1970 pour la répression de la capture illicite d'aéronefs', *AFDI* (1970), p. 35; 'Le terrorisme aérien et les sommets des sept pays industriels, les déclarations de Bonn (1978) et de Venise (1987)', *RF de droit aérien et spatial*, Oct.-Dec. (1989), p. 494.

6 Labayle, *op. cit.* note 1, p. 120.

7 de Lacharrière, G., *La politique juridique extérieure*, Economica, (1983), p. 103.

8 See Yves Daudet's contribution in this collection. See also Labayle, *op. cit.* note 1, p. 134.

9 ICJ 24 May 1980; Ph Breton, 'L'affaire des otages américains devant la CIJ', *JDI* 4 (1980), p. 787; Zoller, E., 'L'affaire du personnel diplomatique et consulaire des EU à Téhéran', *RGDIP* (1980), p. 973.

10 By opposition to the French position which has always claimed a link between the two questions.

11 See Labayle, *op. cit.* note 1, p. 108; Patrnogic and Meriboute, *op. cit.* note 1, p. 136.

12 The efforts by this working group led on 17 Dec. to the General Assembly's res. 46/125 which notes with satisfaction that the declaration project will be submitted for approval to the 48th session of the Human Rights Commission.

13 *Le Monde* 5 Dec., 16 Dec. and 18 Dec. 1991.

14 *Le Figaro* 16–17 Nov. 1991.

15 See Labayle, *op. cit.* note 1, p. 123.

16 Kauffmann, J.P., 'Qui sont les bourreaux de Terry Anderson?', *Le Monde*, 16 Dec. 1991.

17 'That the means used by terrorists forbid leniency and therefore justify severe punishment, it would have been preferable to admitting that terrorism has become the contemporary form of political delinquency. We should have accepted it, without necessarily showing indulgence', Labayle, *op. cit.* note 1, p. 122.

18 Kauffmann, *op. cit.* note 16.

19 For a criticism on the States' behaviour, see a letter by Mrs Marie Seurat, widow of Michel Seurat, the researcher abducted in Beirut on 11 May 1985, and executed by the Islamic Djihad on 5 March 1986. This letter, addressed to the French Ministry for Foreign Affairs, underlines the complete disregard showed by the French Government to her request to bring home the deceased's body. She insists on the 'absent-mindedness, ignorance or indifference of the public authorities'.

20 See Kauffmann: 'too often we forget that this conflict began with the 1982 Israeli invasion of Lebanon. This military occupation was soon followed by the first abduction of the American University's director on July 19, 1982', *op. cit.* note 16.

Part II
Cooperation against terrorism

4 International cooperation against terrorism and the development of international law principles of jurisdiction

*David Freestone**

The increase in the use of political terrorism over the last twenty-five years has evoked legal responses at both the national and the international level. The main thrust of the legal response of the international community has been the conclusion of conventions – at regional and global level – which seek to regulate, harmonize and/or extend the claims to criminal jurisdiction of the contracting States.[1] In general, the conventions have been responses to particular problems such as hijacking or attacks on diplomats, but there is now a sufficient number of such conventions for it to be possible to isolate trends and perhaps to draw some conclusions about the way they have influenced the development of the customary international law on jurisdiction. The purpose of the present paper is to examine the general principles of international law which provide the framework within which the jurisdictional rules operate and then to examine some of the methods which the multilateral conventions have used to meet the problems posed by the disparate jurisdictional systems of States and the constraints of customary international law. The chapter will begin however with a brief review of the principles – accepted by international law – upon which the criminal jurisdiction of States is predicated,[2] and an examination of the international law dimensions of extradition and deportation, which are the main procedural means by which an offender – or more precisely a fugitive offender (such as a transnational terrorist) – may be brought before national courts.

PRINCIPLES OF CRIMINAL JURISDICTION

Primarily criminal jurisdiction rests in the State where the offence was committed. This *territorial principle* is a firmly established concomitant of the concept of State sovereignty, and for a number of reasons is regarded as the most fundamental form of jurisdiction.[3] The doctrine of ubiquity permits States themselves to determine the criteria by which territorial jurisdiction is applied. Some States require the criminal acts themselves to take place within their territory;[4] some accept that jurisdiction may be based simply on the effects felt within their territory.

Therefore, and paradoxically, even the territorial principle often operates extra-territorially in that States may claim jurisdiction according to this principle over crimes committed by individuals who have never physically set foot in their territory.

Other principles of jurisdiction operate more obviously extra-territorially. The *nationality principle* entitles a State to exercise personal jurisdiction over crimes committed by its nationals wherever they may physically have been committed.[5] The principle of *flag State jurisdiction* permits States to exercise criminal jurisdiction over crimes committed on board ships or aircraft registered with them. Writers dispute whether this is a variant of territorial or personal jurisdiction.[6] However, with the increased significance of such offences, it is probably more sensible to accept – as does the Council of Europe Committee on Crime Problems[7] – that this is best seen as an autonomous ground for jurisdiction.

The *protective principle* confers on States the right to try offences which threaten their security, institutions and other fundamental national interests.

The principle of *universality* has been described by Brownlie as:

> a principle allowing jurisdiction over acts of non-nationals where the circumstances, including the nature of the crime, justify the repression of some types of crime as a matter of international public policy.[8]

For those offences for which this universality is recognized, the very widest net of jurisdiction is possible, allowing trial of foreign offenders for offences committed abroad usually without any link other than the fact of physical custody of the offender.[9] For this reason the principle – in its simplest guise of custody jurisdiction – has been utilized by an increasing number of international treaties, notably the counter-terrorism conventions discussed in more detail below. It is perhaps important to stress that universality does not automatically accrue to all offences created by international law,[10] but there is increasing doctrinal support for the view that universal jurisdiction over hijacking has now passed into customary law.[11]

The *representational principle* is similarly derived from international treaty arrangements. This principle, identified by the Council of Europe Committee on Crime Problems, 'refers to cases in which a State may exercise extraterritorial jurisdiction where it is deemed to be acting for another State which is more directly involved, provided certain conditions are met.'[12] Although similar to the universality principle, the crucial feature of the representational principle appears to be that the decision to prosecute is taken in the context of an international agreement or other arrangement.[13]

The final principle, the *passive personality principle*, is derived from the nationality not of the perpetrator of the offence (as in the nationality principle above), but from that of the victim. It has traditionally been regarded by commentators as at the fringes of customary international law, and Anglo-Saxon writers have been particularly vocal in condemning its legality.[14] Its legality was challenged by France before the Permanent Court of International Justice in the 1927 *Lotus Case*,[15] but the Court did not find it contrary to international law. It has moreover been utilized by an increasing number of national legal systems and international treaty arrangements.[16]

EXTRADITION AND DEPORTATION

Of equal practical significance to the issue of whether a state legal system may exercise criminal jurisdiction over an alleged terrorist offender is the question of how an offender who is situated in another country may be brought before the criminal courts of the State willing to try him or her. As will be discussed below, in the absence of express agreement international law does not permit one state to exercise executive jurisdiction in the territory of another. Unless therefore the offender surrenders voluntarily, the only legal means by which such an individual may be brought before the criminal court of the seeking State is for the fugitive offender to be either deported or extradited by the foreign authorities. The two processes are very different. Extradition is the formal surrender of a fugitive criminal to a requesting State – usually under the terms of a bilateral or multilateral treaty – whereas deportation is the summary expulsion of an alien.

Extradition

Although Grotius argued in 1626 that States were under a general obligation to surrender up or try foreign offenders within their territory – the *aut dedere aut judicare* principle[17] – the modern system of extradition depends upon an often 'ad hoc' network of bilateral treaties, some still dating from the nineteenth century, supplemented by an increasing number of modern 'single crime' multilateral conventions covering issues from genocide to apartheid and drug smuggling, as well as terrorist offences.

State practice is notoriously diverse on extradition, but there are some common features. This is largely because, as Shearer suggests, nineteenth-century extradition treaty-making practice was based on that of France.[18] Commentators have been generally agreed for some years that there is a pressing need for modernization and harmonization of extradition procedures at global level.[19] The Council of Europe European Convention on Extradition (1979) makes a useful start in this direction, but the fact that the United Kingdom only recently became a party, and with not insignificant reservations,[20] highlights the difference in approach between civil law and common law countries which a unitary convention would need to address.

There is certainly no single procedural system for extradition. Once a request for extradition has been made by the authorities of one State to another, extradition becomes a matter for the domestic law of the requested State. Common law systems will not generally entertain such a request in the absence of a bilateral treaty nexus between the two States, while civil law countries may or may not impose such a prerequisite: note for example the contrast between the English Extradition Act procedure of 1870 and the French Extradition Law of 1927, each described below.[21] Similar national differences emerge in relation to the next hurdle: the offence must be an 'extraditable offence' – that is it must be an offence covered by the extradition laws of both States. English law requires that for an offence to be 'extraditable' it must be listed in the treaty with the requesting State – the 'enumerative' method. Other States adopt an 'eliminative' method – whereby all offences punishable by an agreed degree of severity (usually a maximum penalty) are extraditable.[22] The eliminative approach also sidesteps the 'dual criminality' requirement. Dual criminality is the general requirement that the extraditable offence be a crime in both the requesting and requested State. In practice this requirement does not usually depend upon what the criminal offence is called in each legal system, provided that the relevant conduct is a criminal offence in each State.

Once it has been established that the relevant offence is extraditable, the 'speciality principle' leads naturally from this. The speciality principle requires that a fugitive should not be tried other than for the specific offence for which extradition was granted, without being first given the opportunity to leave the country again.[23] Trial in breach of the speciality principle will usually be in breach of international treaty obligations, though national laws do vary as to the extent to which a fugitive offender is able, of his or her own volition, to raise this as a defence in domestic proceedings. The courts of the extraditing State will be highly reluctant to allow such a plea made prior to extradition taking place, for this would be imputing bad faith into the foreign (*ex hypothesi*) friendly requesting State. After extradition the law of the receiving State may not permit such a plea to be made.

There are two broad exceptions to this whole process. The first relates to nationals; the second to political offenders. The rationale for the exclusion of nationals from extradition has its roots in 'nineteenth-century national chauvinism'[24] and developed at a time when standards of criminal justice varied widely. In modern times it is the civil law countries which, claiming extensive extra-territorial jurisdiction on the nationality principle, have maintained a refusal to extradite nationals. Common law countries have not generally maintained such a position and have on occasion even waived general reciprocity in order to allow the extradition of nationals to countries which would not do likewise.[25]

The exclusion of political offenders from extradition also has its roots in nineteenth-century practice. The first such exclusion is found in a Belgian treaty of 1934,[26] and it can now be found in the overwhelming majority of extradition treaties and national extradition laws. The two main limbs of the 'political offence' exclusion can be seen clearly in Article 3 of the European Convention on Extradition which allows contracting States the option of refusing extradition for a 'political offence' or 'an offence connected with a political offence' (i.e. criteria relating to the nature of the offence itself), or in circumstances where:

> the requesting state has substantial grounds for believing that a request for extradition for an ordinary criminal has been made for the purpose of prosecuting or punishing a person on account of his race, religion, nationality or political opinion or that that person's position will be prejudiced for any of these reasons [i.e. criteria relating to the circumstances of trial].

The latter limb has been called the 'humanitarian exclusion' and can be found in a number of other treaties including Article 5 of the European Convention on the Suppression of Terrorism, discussed further below (pp. 54–5). Important as such safeguards appear to be, they may in fact be of limited utility to the individual fugitive, for courts have again had difficulty utilizing provisions of this kind because of the fact that making such a finding involves casting a major aspersion on the objectivity and fairness of the criminal justice system of another State, and the *bona fides* of the requesting authorities.

Equally difficult is the 'political offence' exception. There is no international law definition of such an offence and State practice varies widely on the variety of factors – some subjective, some objective – which may be taken into account by national courts in deciding whether a crime may be classified as 'political'. It is even possible to discern crude foreign policy considerations in some decisions.

Deportation

In contrast to extradition, deportation is an executive, not a judicial, procedure, based on a State's right to exclude or expel undesirable aliens. International law does however impose certain restrictions on this right. General customary international law requires minimum standards of conduct in the handling of deportation,[27] and treaty law has developed other restrictions in relation to issues such as the legitimate circumstances of deportation[28] and the grounds which may be invoked.[29] Nevertheless it appears that deportation in response to a prior request from another State is not contrary to international law. Because it is an executive procedure it avoids all the technical difficulties of extradition. In many States, including the United Kingdom, the use of deportation as a method of 'disguised extradition' is a flagrant and probably illegal misuse of an administrative procedure.[30] Even so, such arguments do not appear to outweigh its 'convenience in practice' and a study in 1978 found deportation to be a much more widely used method of bringing offenders to trial than extradition.[31]

PRINCIPLES

These jurisdictional rules operate, however, within a framework of international law principles, and it is worth adumbrating the most important of these:

1 The principle of sovereign equality of States

Jurisdiction is a crucial aspect of State sovereignty. Inter-State relations on the basis of equality depend upon a mutual recognition of each others' jurisdictional rights.

2 The principle of territorial integrity (in Art. 2(4) UN Charter)

At its most obvious level this means that the exercise of enforcement jurisdiction within the territory of another State will be a violation of territorial integrity,[32] unless of course that exercise is sanctioned by agreement, as for example, in the case of the Irish Government agreement in October 1979[33] to permit UK helicopters to fly ten kilometres into Irish airspace. This is obviously an example of enforcement jurisdiction rather than prescription, but by analogy it may be presumed that the unilateral promulgation of a law authorizing the domestic authorities of one State (e.g., the UK) to exercise enforcement jurisdiction even without the act of enforcement in another State (e.g., Ireland), would in itself constitute a threat to the territorial integrity of Ireland and thus engage international responsibility. Apart from such a case it is difficult to see how the simple *promulgation* of a claim to extra-territorial jurisdiction would conflict with this principle.

3 Non-intervention in the internal affairs of another State

This is codified in the 1970 UN General Assembly resolution on friendly relations[34] (now accepted as a definitive interpretation of the UN Charter):

> No State . . . has the right to intervene, directly or indirectly, for any reason whatever, in the internal or external affairs of any other State . . .

> Every State has an inalienable right to choose its political, economic, social and cultural systems without interference in any form by another State.

It has often been argued that certain types of extra-territorial jurisdictional claims conflict with this principle – notably those arising from the US anti-trust legislation.[35] It seems, however, a less-easy proposition to sustain in relation to claims of extra-territorial criminal jurisdiction over terrorist offences. In normal conditions it is more difficult to argue that a unilateral claim to jurisdiction in relation to a criminal offence committed in another State, or over an offence committed by that other State's national (which will be concurrent with that other State's jurisdiction), constitutes an intervention in the internal affairs of that other State, unless of course the act prescribed is not an offence in that other State.[36]

By the same token, a State may well feel inhibited from protesting at the assertion of extra-territorial jurisdiction over offences committed in its territory or by its nationals if those offences were terrorist offences directed (*ex hypothesi*) at the political, economic, social or cultural system of another State. This does raise the question (returned to below at pp. 58–9) as to whether silence in the face of an assertion of extra-territorial criminal competence constitutes acquiescence for the purpose of the evolution of customary law. Does the promulgation of a law claiming jurisdictional competence constitute a claim for these purposes, or does a trial (or even a conviction or sentence of punishment) have to take place?

THE MULTILATERAL CONVENTIONS

This section will examine the way in which jurisdictional issues have been handled by the major multilateral conventions negotiated at global and regional level in response to terrorist acts with an international, or transnational, dimension.[37] The first manifestation of post-war terrorism with a transnational character was the increase in offences on aircraft – notably hijacking. The main hijacking and aircraft conventions are well known, so this discussion will only refer to their main features.

The 1963 Tokyo Convention[38] was, of course, concerned with the whole range of problems associated with offences on board aircraft. It based its case on existing principles. It stressed the primacy of the jurisdiction of the State of registration, and although the Convention does not actually provide that hijacking should be regarded as 'air piracy', this was clearly the intent. This was recognized by the United Kingdom implementing legislation – the UK Tokyo Convention Act (1967) – which included Articles 15–17 of the Geneva Convention on the High Seas (1958) as a Schedule, and by section 5 of the 1982 Consolidation Act which specifically uses the term 'air piracy'.

Article 4 provides supplementary jurisdiction, phased in non-obligatory terms, which appears to sanction executive jurisdiction over aircraft in flight according to the territorial, passive personality, and protective principles. It seems to have been reservations by various States about these aspects of the Tokyo Convention regime (rather than simple lack of interest) which delayed the entry into force of the Convention until 1969. It may be significant that the Convention reached the required number of ratifications in 1969 – a year in which there was a large increase in the number of aircraft hijackings (an increase maintained in the following year).[39]

A much more innovative stance was taken by the Hague Convention (1970)[40] which provided a more purpose-built regime for hijacking. The approach of this convention seems to have been used as a model for the later conventions. It will be recalled that its principal methods were the following:

1 It defined 'hijacking' as an offence, which it obliged contracting States to make punishable by severe penalties (Arts. 1 and 2).
2 It established the principle of 'extradite or submit for prosecution', which in this modified sense will be called *aut dedere aut judicare* (Art. 7). This sought to provide a tighter jurisdictional net, a 'no hiding-place' approach, so that an offender who avoided extradition for one of the traditional reasons did not escape submission for trial.
3 It greatly extended the jurisdictional competences of State Parties, in that Article 4 obliged States to establish their jurisdiction:
   • as the registering State;[41]
   • as the State where an aircraft lands with an offender aboard;
   • as the State of place of business or residence of lessee in case of leases without crew.

In addition, Article 4(2) obliged States to establish jurisdiction where the offender was in their territory and they did not extradite him. Custody jurisdiction – known in customary international law as *universality* jurisdiction – has traditionally only been recognized in relation to a few offences, such as piracy or slave-trading, although in recent years it has been claimed in relation to a growing number of offences, including war crimes and genocide.[42] As indicated above, there is a well-known controversy as to whether this Article established a form of universality jurisdiction. On the basis that it is only binding on contracting parties to the Hague Convention it has been called *quasi-universal*, but it is worth pointing out that the Hague Convention now has over 140 parties, which places it among the most widely ratified conventions.

The importance, or additional importance, of this issue is that the principle of Article 4 – whether we call it universality or quasi-universality – is also used in the Montreal Convention for the Suppression of Unlawful Acts against the Safety of Civil Aviation.[43] Here the Hague model is used quite clearly:

• defined offences are set out (Art. 1);
• the *aut dedere aut judicare* principle (Art. 7) is used; and
• there are similar obligations in relation to jurisdiction (Art. 5).

One must be sceptical as to the extent to which these conventions actually reduced the flood of hijacking in the late 1960s and early 1970s (the worst two years were 1969 and 1970). They seem rather to be symptomatic of a generally stronger, more united, stance taken by the States most affected: increased airport security, threats of boycotts like the Bonn Declaration of 1978 of non-cooperating States.[44]

Like other 'copycat' crimes there are obvious fashions in terrorist crimes.

The 1970s saw a slight decrease in hijacking but an increase in the number of kidnappings, and often murder, of prominent politicians, diplomats and industrialists. The 1980s saw an increase in the use of remote controlled bombs, such as that which exploded on a Pan-American 747 flight over Lockerbie in Scotland in December 1988, killing 270 passengers and crew.[45] The methods used for the aircraft conventions were applied virtually *en bloc* to the conventions drafted in response to these offences.

Both the Convention on the Prevention and Punishment of Crimes Against Internationally Protected Persons, Including Diplomats (1973) (hereafter the IPP Convention)[46] and the UN Convention Against the Taking of Hostages (1979) (hereafter the Hostages Convention)[47] use the same model – setting out defined offences followed by the obligation to establish extended jurisdiction and the modified *aut dedere aut judicare* obligation. Indeed, Article 5 of the Hostages Convention uses the identical terminology to the IPP Convention; it reads as follows:

1. Each State Party shall take such measures as may be necessary to establish its jurisdiction over any of the offences set forth in article 1 which are committed:
(a) in its territory or on board a ship or aircraft registered in that State;
(b) by any of its nationals or, if that State considers it appropriate, by those Stateless persons who have their habitual residence in its territory;
(c) in order to compel that State to do or abstain from doing any act; or
(d) with respect to a hostage who is a national of that State, if that State considers it appropriate.

2. Each State Party shall likewise take such measures as may be necessary to establish its jurisdiction over the offences set forth in article 1 in cases where the alleged offender is present in its territory and it does not extradite him to any of the States mentioned in paragraph 1 of this article.

3. This Convention does not exclude any criminal jurisdiction exercised in accordance with internal law.

The same model too is used by the 1980 International Atomic Energy Authority Convention on the Physical Protection of Nuclear Material.[48] Article 7 sets out new offences to be created by the parties, however the jurisdictional clause (Art. 8) is noteworthy because it requires the establishment of jurisdiction over the relevant offences according to the territorial and the national principle, and then by paragraph 2 of that Article states:

Each State shall likewise take such measures as may be necessary to establish its jurisdiction over these offences in cases where the alleged offender is present in its territory and it does not extradite him pursuant to article 11 to any of the States mentioned in paragraph 1.

All three of these UN Conventions have provision for cooperation in the supply of evidence (often a vital aspect of extra-territorial jurisdiction) and include fair treatment provisions. The Hostages Convention 1979 also has what has been called a 'political asylum' clause (Art. 9), which itself appears to be modelled on a similar provision (Art. 5) in the 1977 European Convention on the Suppression of Terrorism.[49]

The same general approach is also taken by the most recent of the counter-terrorist conventions – the 1988 IMO International Convention for the Suppression of Unlawful Acts Against the Safety of Maritime Navigation,[50] which is discussed in detail below by Dr Plant in Chapter 5. By this stage the approach has virtually become a formula, and although the Convention does include some very particular and unusual provisions the general jurisdictional approach has become predictable. This too defines the offences with which it is concerned (Art. 3), establishes the *aut dedere aut judicare* principle (Art. 10(1)), and extends jurisdictional competence over the listed offences (Art. 6).[51]

Before leaving these conventions something should be said about the procedures they establish for extradition. The law of extradition is a notoriously complex and technical area,[52] nevertheless some consideration must be paid to aspects of it here because the principle of 'extradite or try' is a key idea behind the conventions' jurisdictional approach. For extradition to take place it is of course necessary to fulfil the requirements of national extradition law. Most national systems will not permit extradition unless the request satisfies the dual criminality principle. This requires that the extraditable offence be a crime in both requesting and requested States. This rule applies in both its substantive and procedural aspects. *Substantively* this is done by requiring each contracting State to make the relevant offences punishable under its national law (and incidentally extradition treaties are deemed to be amended where this is necessary and/or possible). *Procedurally* the problem is more difficult because of the differences between national jurisdictional rules. One State may, for example, request extradition according to a principle of jurisdiction which is not recognized by the requested State (e.g. the passive personality principle). The UK would traditionally not recognize such a request. Here the UN conventions use a similar formula to try to minimize this difficulty. For example Article 10(4) of the Hostages Convention reads:

> The offences set forth in article 1 shall be treated, for the purpose of extradition between States Parties, as if they had been committed not only in the place in which they occurred but also in the territories of the States required to establish their jurisdiction in accordance with paragraph 1 of article 5.

This 'jurisfictional' device is designed to allow States to extend their jurisdictional network without necessarily having to accept the more controversial principles of jurisdiction. The territorial principle is obviously one which all States accept, and this treaty device seeks to extend the territorial network to the territories of all the States Parties. It provides the most obvious example of what the Council of Europe's Committee on Crime Problems has called the 'representational' principle.[53]

So, to take a hypothetical and perhaps controversial example, a request by Germany to the United Kingdom for the extradition of an offender over whom Germany seeks to exercise jurisdiction according to the passive personality principle (i.e. where a German national has been the hostage) will be deemed to be based upon the territorial principle (i.e. will be deemed to have been committed in Germany), and will thus be recognizable by the UK courts. It should be noted that Article 5(1)(d) (see p. 51 above) does confer discretion on States as to whether or not to espouse jurisdiction under the passive personality principle by the use of the phrase 'if that State considers it appropriate'. However that discretion appears to be conferred only on the State with primary jurisdiction – not that State which exercises 'representational' jurisdiction, which appears to be obliged to accept any form of jurisdiction legitimately exercised under the Convention for these purposes. This does incidentally appear to be the interpretation put upon these provisions by the British Government, for the UK Taking of Hostages Act (1982) appears to extend to such a situation.[54]

THE REGIONAL CONVENTIONS

The regional conventions do not follow this pattern quite so faithfully. Both the Organization of American States (OAS) Convention (1971) and the European Convention for the Suppression of Terrorism (1977) (hereafter the 'Terrorism Convention') take the important steps of removing or restricting the political offence exception – thus addressing what is perceived to be a major impediment to the extradition of terrorists. Article 2 of the OAS Convention requires that the listed offences:

> Kidnapping, murder and other assaults on life or personal integrity of those whom the State has to give special protection according to international law, as well as extortion in connection with those crimes, shall be considered 'common crimes of international significance regardless of motive'.

This deprives terrorist offenders of the protection of the political offence exception. The Convention also has an 'extradite or try' clause: 'if extradition is refused because the person sought is a national' or for some other 'legal or constitutional impediment', then there is an 'obligation to prosecute as if the act had been committed in its territory' (Art. 1). But there is no obligation on States Parties to extend their national criminal jurisdiction in order to meet this obligation. Under Article 8 Contracting States simply accept the obligation 'to endeavour to have the criminal acts contemplated in this Convention included in their penal laws, if not already so included'. The Terrorism Convention (1977)[55] uses a mixture of the techniques which have been discussed. It seeks to establish the closest kind of jurisdictional net both quantitatively (in the sense of the number of offences which it covers) and also qualitatively, in that its drafters obviously felt able to address some of the issues which the global conventions ignore. In Article 1 it lists the 'terrorist offences' covered by the Convention; these are:

(a) an offence within the scope of the Convention for the Suppression of Unlawful Seizure of Aircraft, signed at The Hague on 16 December 1970;
(b) an offence within the scope of the Convention for the Suppression of Unlawful Acts against the Safety of Civil Aviation, signed at Montreal on 23 September 1971;
(c) a serious offence involving an attack against the life, physical integrity or liberty of internationally protected persons, including diplomatic agents;
(d) an offence involving kidnapping, the taking of a hostage or serious unlawful detention;
(e) an offence involving the use of a bomb, grenade, rocket, automatic firearm or letter or parcel bomb if this use endangers persons;
(f) an attempt to commit any of the foregoing offences or participation as an accomplice of a person who commits or attempts to commit such an offence.

The regime of the Convention can also be extended, at the option of the Contracting States, to any serious offence involving violence against life, physical integrity or liberty of a person, or against property if the offence creates a collective danger for persons.[56]

Having defined the offences covered by the regime, the Convention deprives those accused or convicted of such offences of the opportunity of using the political offence exception to extradition (Art. 1), and establishes the by now familiar, modified principle of *aut dedere aut judicare*.[57] It also requires Contracting States to extend their domestic jurisdiction so as to be able to try offenders found in their territory whom they do not extradite.[58]

Two aspects of these obligations justify closer examination: first, the elimination of the political offence exception, and second, the obligation to extend jurisdiction to meet the *aut dedere aut judicare* obligation.

The political offence exception

It is Article 1 of the Terrorism Convention which obliges parties to remove the political offence exception in extradition proceedings relating to persons charged with the listed offences. The effect of this restriction of the political defence is however restricted by two other provisions: Articles 13 and 5, which will be considered in turn.

First Article 13, which permits parties to enter a reservation permitting them to reject a request for extradition on the grounds that it is a political offence, notwithstanding that it is a listed offence. This seems to negate one of the main objectives of the Convention and has come in for a great deal of vigorous criticism.[59] It was included so as not to deter those States which felt themselves unable to renounce the political offence exception unequivocally – most obviously Ireland. It has been utilized by some five out of the fourteen parties. The right of reservation is however itself subject to two further provisions:

1 the requirement of reciprocity in Article 13(3);
2 the obligation on a reserving State when deciding whether to invoke its reservation to take into account the following factors:
   • that it created a collective danger to the life, physical integrity or liberty of persons; or
   • that it affected persons foreign to the motives behind it; or
   • that cruel or vicious means have been used in the commission of the offence.[60]

Second, the important provision of Article 5 – included apparently at the instigation of the United Kingdom – also permits a State to refuse extradition of an offender in relation to a listed offence if the requested State has substantial grounds for believing that the request for extradition for an offence mentioned in Articles 1 or 2 has been made for the purpose of prosecuting or punishing a person on account of his race, religion, nationality or political opinions, or that that person's position may be prejudiced for any of these reasons. This has been called the 'political asylum' proviso, to distinguish it from the 'political offence' exception. It concentrates on the circumstances of the likely trial or punishment, rather than the motives or circumstances of the offence itself. This is an important human rights clause, but in so far as it presumably involves judicial or political determination of the lack of impartiality or discriminatory behaviour of the judicial system of another State (*ex hypothesi* a friendly State), the courts and the executive may find it difficult to apply.

Extended jurisdiction

The second issue to consider arises from Article 6(1) which requires that:

Each Contracting State shall take such measures as may be necessary to establish its jurisdiction over an offence mentioned in article 1 in the case where the suspected offender is present in its territory and it does not extradite him after receiving a request for extradition from a Contracting State whose jurisdiction is based on a rule of jurisdiction existing equally in the law of the requested State.

Lowe and Young[61] pose the problem of a State which has passed legislation conferring extra-territorial jurisdiction upon itself in order to meet the obligations of the Convention, then being faced with the suggestion that these extra-territorial assertions of jurisdiction have themselves to be taken into account in determining the reciprocity of interest for the purposes of Article 6 – a form of rolling extra-territorial claim.

Perhaps this explains the unusual way that the Terrorism Convention, has been implemented in the United Kingdom by the use of both fiction and double fiction. Under the Suppression of Terrorism Act (1978), a scheduled offence committed within a Convention country is deemed to have been committed in the United Kingdom – a fiction.[62] In addition, an offence committed outside another Convention country, but according to a principle which is accepted in that Convention country (provided that the offender is a national of a Convention country), is also deemed to be committed within the United Kingdom – a double fiction.[63] By the use of this method of implementation the United Kingdom has rather neatly avoided addressing this issue. This is presumably deliberate, for the UK courts already have wide jurisdiction over some of the listed offences under, for example, the Aviation Security Act.[64] The object of this clause was probably to maximize jurisdiction without forcing States to accept new principles. Despite these innovatory features the Terrorism Convention is still based on the same model as the wider conventions, and cannot be said to have been a great success. It has attracted criticism from many sides of the political spectrum,[65] and it was slow to receive wide ratification within the Council of Europe.

The Terrorism Convention was however the subject of a most unusual and interesting arrangement negotiated under the auspices of the European Community: the 1979 Dublin Agreement.[66] Under this agreement, negotiated outside EC law and which would therefore be governed by international law, the EC Member States agreed to apply the regime of the Terrorism Convention between themselves without reservation – despite the fact that not all the EC States were parties to that Convention. Indeed Denmark, which was a party, had made a reservation under Article 13 (reserving the right to allow the political offence exception), and Ireland had not even signed the Convention.

Under the Dublin Agreement, if EC members wished to reserve the political exception in extradition between themselves, they were required to lodge a reservation to that effect with the Irish Foreign Ministry (Art. 3). The Agreement specifically permits Ireland (Art. 3(3)), as a non-signatory to the Terrorism Convention, to refuse extradition on the grounds that it accepts the obligation to try domestically. This unusual, if not actually unique, arrangement required ratification by all nine of the then members of the EC in order to come into force: it remains not in force.

The Dublin Agreement was hailed in some quarters as the first step in the creation of a European judicial area. This originated from a French proposal of 1977. The exact form this judicial area would take has not always been clear, but it has encompassed proposals including a European Terrorist Court, or a Criminal Chamber of the European Court of Justice in Luxembourg which would hear all terrorist cases where extradition is involved, or cases referred to it by Member States reluctant to extradite a terrorist offender.[67]

There have also been calls for a common system of extradition between Member States of the EC. The EC has concluded some agreements – notably the TREVI arrangements which are the main forum for cooperation on a practical and operational level against terrorism and other serious crimes.[68] The working party of senior officials which produced the Dublin Agreement also produced in 1980 a draft convention concerning cooperation in criminal matters, which was never opened for signature.[69] Internal EC politics appear to have prevented this idea from progressing,[70] although it has been kept alive by the Legal Affairs Committee of the European Parliament which in 1982 produced a report arguing the case that the EEC Treaty itself provides a legal basis for the conclusion of such arrangements under Community law.[71] In 1984 the draft treaty on European union provided for the establishment of a 'Homogeneous Judicial Area',[72] but this concept was not accepted by the Single European Act in 1986. Since then, discussions have centred on the issue of police cooperation (see Chapter 6). The 1992 Treaty on Political Union[73] includes 'Provisions on Co-operation in the Spheres of Justice and Home Affairs', under which Member States declare that they regard a number of areas as 'of common interest'. These include 'judicial co-operation in criminal matters' (Art. A(6)) and 'police co-operation for the purposes of preventing and combating terrorism . . . in connection with the organisation of a Union wide system for exchanging information within a European Police Office (EUROPOL)' (Art. A(8)).

CONCLUSIONS

For a number of reasons, it is notoriously difficult to establish clear State practice in the area of criminal jurisdiction. These reasons include the complexity of the subject-matter, the lack of coordination and agreement between States as to the precise meaning and extent of the key concepts, and the accumulation of significant evidence of protests, etc. Doctrine too is notoriously diverse in the area. This inevitably renders the task of establishing the exact content of international customary law particularly difficult. It will be recalled that Article 38 (1)(b) of the Statute of the International Court of Justice talks of 'international custom as evidence of a general practice accepted as law'. In the North Sea continental shelf cases[74] the International Court of Justice developed what has become seen as a classic formulation of the requirements for the establishment of a rule of custom, namely: evidence of a uniformity or consistency of practice; evidence of a generality of practice; evidence of duration of that practice over time (although if the first two have been established, the short passage of time will not in itself be an obstruction); and (arguably the most significant in the establishment of new rules) evidence of the psychological element – *opinio juris sive necessitasis* – the 'conception that the practice is required by, or consistent with, prevailing international law'.[75] Brownlie points out that in approaching the latter question the International Court of Justice has either been willing to assume the existence of *opinio juris* on the basis of evidence of general practice, doctrine or previous judicial decisions, or has adopted a more rigorous approach, calling for 'more positive evidence of the recognition of the validity of the rules in question in the practice of states.'[76] In three cases in particular the International Court of Justice has adopted the later approach: the *Lotus Case*,[77] the *North Sea Continental Shelf Cases*[78] and the *Nicaragua Case*.[79] The classic formulation of this approach is in the North Sea cases in which the Court required:

> evidence of a belief that this practice is rendered obligatory by the existence of a rule of law requiring it. The need for such a belief, i.e. the existence of a subjective element, is implicit in the very notion of *opinio juris sive necessitatis*.[80]

There is a particular tension in seeking to establish general practice and *opinio juris* from treaty-making practice. On the one hand the existence of a treaty laying down general rules might be taken to be an explicit recognition that existing rules of custom do not already oblige the contracting parties to act in the way the treaty requires;[81] on the other hand the treaty may simply be seen as an instrument of coordination codifying and declaring existing custom (i.e. a so-called 'law-making' treaty). Once a treaty has achieved a wide membership then the debate changes – for it can be argued that the rules it contains have become general practice and passed into customary law. Such an argument would be subject to the 'persistent objector' principle – that a State, by persistent objection, may contract out of a custom in the process of formulation. Brownlie argues that 'evidence of such [persistent] objection must be clear and there is probably a presumption of acceptance which is to be rebutted'.[82]

If States make reservations to treaty provisions establishing general rules, then persistent objection is clear, but it is more difficult to argue that the existence of reservations *per se*, or even the acceptance of the right to make reservations, undermine what Brownlie calls the 'probative value' of such treaty provisions.[83] The number of States that need to be party to a treaty for a debate to begin about the emergence of general practice from 'law-making' treaties is also controversial; so also is the position of States which are not parties to such treaties. Nevertheless, logic suggests that it should be easier to establish the existence of a permissive rule (i.e. a rule allowing States to take such action if they wish) than an obligatory rule (i.e. a rule requiring or prohibiting certain conduct). The late Professor Michael Akehurst wrote:

... if other States do not protest against the conclusion or execution of such treaties, one is entitled to infer that there is a permissive rule of international law authorising such action.[84]

It is therefore a daunting task to draw conclusions from this necessarily brief examination of the jurisdictional principles espoused and utilized by the international conventions against terrorism. Such conclusions will inevitably be tentative. Nevertheless it must be recognized that international legal responses to terrorism through multilateral treaty-making represent a significant pattern of international cooperation, which has provided both an opportunity and an impetus for some important intergovernmental work at both a practical and a theoretical level.

At the very least, the conventions against terrorism provide a significant quantity of evidence of what the States Parties regard as acceptable jurisdictional claims. Further than this it can be argued that the conventions, which not only establish networks of jurisdiction between States Parties but also extend these networks to nationals of non-parties, do constitute evidence of the development of customary international law. The very number of States Parties to the counter-terrorism conventions does add to such arguments. On 1 January 1993 there were 145 parties to the Tokyo Convention and 150 to the Hague and 149 to the Montreal Conventions.[85] This is probably as near universal adherence as is feasible. At the same date the IPP Convention had 83 and the Hostages Convention 72 parties. While these latter figures do not approach universal adherence, they do demonstrate a general support within the international community. Thus jurisdictional concepts found in all these treaties can be argued to reflect a significant pattern of State practice amounting to evidence of custom. Arguments in relation to concepts or jurisdictional principles which are to be found in some of these agreements may have to be argued on a case-by-case basis. Three principles of jurisdiction could particularly be argued to have been developed by these conventions.

First, the *passive personality principle*. In the past this has been condemned by common law writers, such as Brierly,[86] as contrary to international law. The principle is still not free from controversy, and the counter-terrorist conventions deal gently with it – either in the discretionary jurisdiction paragraphs, or with phrases such as 'if the State considers it appropriate'. Indeed not all the relevant conventions contain reference to it, but the Tokyo Convention, the IPP Convention, the Hostages Convention and now the 1988 IMO Convention and its Protocol all permit its use. In addition, the implementation of these conventions and other counter-terrorist measures by a number of States, including those such as the United States and France[87] with a history of opposition to the concept, make it difficult to maintain the argument that the principle is *per se* contrary to international law.[88]

Second, the *representational principle*. As discussed above, this principle, not included in the traditional doctrinal texts, is explained on page 14 of the Council of Europe Committee on Crime Problems Report on Extra-territorial Criminal Jurisdiction as referring to:

> cases in which a State may exercise extraterritorial criminal jurisdiction where it is deemed to be acting for another State which is more directly involved, provided that certain conditions have been met.

As indicated above, this principle appears to have found its main form in the counter-terrorism treaties, and examples can be seen in the texts of bilateral arrangements such as the Anglo–Irish criminal jurisdiction arrangements as well as in the multilateral treaties discussed above and in the national implementing legislation.

Third, the *universality principle.* There has been a long-standing controversy over the issue of whether hijacking is subject to the principle of universality – or custody – jurisdiction under customary international law, or whether such jurisdiction is 'quasi-universal', in the sense that international law only permits such jurisdiction to be exercisable within a treaty nexus. There is already strong, and growing, doctrinal support for the view that universality jurisdiction for hijacking is already customary. The very wide adherence to the hijacking conventions – Tokyo, The Hague and Montreal – suggests that for hijacking at the very least the right to try on the basis of universality has now moved into the realm of customary law.

It is probably still true to say that 'terrorism' is not itself a crime triable according to the universality principle, if only because of the intrinsic difficulty of defining 'terrorism'.[89] It would not however be true to say that terrorist *offences* are not so triable, for there is a wealth of treaty-making practice to gainsay that. Indeed, in relation to the core of offences which are covered by those multilateral conventions which have achieved wide adherence – such as hijacking and hostage-taking – it might be argued that this general pattern of treaty practice, which includes custody jurisdictional provisions within its obligatory forms of jurisdiction (and which seeks to extend its ambit to the nationals of signatories and non-signatories alike), suggests that not simply hijacking, but also a wider core of 'terrorist offences', are subject to jurisdiction according to this principle under customary international law. The readiness with which the 1988 IMO Conference on Maritime Safety was prepared to accept this principle in relation to the offences it proscribes might perhaps support such an argument.

The exact content of this core of offences would be controversial, but might perhaps include those offences listed in Article 1(a)–(d) of the Terrorism Convention (see p. 54). Whether this argument is accepted or not, it is clear that the universality principle itself is widely accepted. We appear to be at the beginning, or even in the midst, of a piecemeal but still quite radical change in the customary law limits of this kind of jurisdiction.

The main contribution which this network of counter-terrorist treaties has made to the development of general customary international law must surely be in the development of jurisdictional mechanisms and rules which will inevitably come to be applied in relation to other issues of transnational criminal jurisdiction.

NOTES

* The author is pleased to acknowledge the invaluable research assistance of Paul Arnell in preparing this paper for publication and the Research Fund of the University of Hull Law School in facilitating that assistance. The themes in this chapter are also explored by the author in A.V. Lowe and C. Warbrick (eds) *The United Nations and the Principles of International Law: Essays in Memory of Michael Akehurst* (Routledge, 1994), pp. 137–59.

1 At a global level note particularly:
(1963) Tokyo Convention on Offences and Certain Other Acts Committed on Board Aircraft. UKTS 126 (1969), Cmnd. 4230. Entered into force 4 Dec. 1969.
(1970) Hague Convention for the Suppression of Unlawful Seizure of Aircraft. UKTS 39 (1972), Cmnd. 4965; (1971) ILM 133. Entered into force 14 Oct. 1971.
(1971) Montreal Convention for the Suppression of Unlawful Acts Against the Safety of Civil Aviation. UKTS 10 (1971), Cmnd. 5524. Entered into force 26 Jan. 1973; and its 1988 Protocol for the Suppression of Unlawful Acts of Violence at Airports Serving International Civil Aviation.
(1973) UN Convention on the Prevention and Punishment of Crimes Against Internationally Protected Persons, Including Diplomatic Agents. Misc. 19 (1975), Cmnd. 6176. Entered into force 20 Feb. 1977.
(1979) UN Convention Against the Taking of Hostages. (1979) 18 ILM 1456. Entered into force 4 June 1983.
(1980) IAEA Convention on the Physical Protection of Nuclear Material. Misc. 27 (1980); (1979) 18 ILM 1419. Entered into force 8 Feb. 1987.
(1988) IMO International Convention for the Suppression of Unlawful Acts Against the Safety of Maritime Navigation and its Protocol on the Suppression of Unlawful Acts Against the Safety of Fixed Platforms Located on the Continental Shelf. (1988) 3 IJECL 317.

At a regional level note:
(1971) OAS Convention to Prevent and Punish Acts of Terrorism Taking the Form of Crimes Against Persons and Related Extortion that are of International Significance. Entered into force 16 Oct. 1973.
(1977) European Convention on the Suppression of Terrorism. ETS No. 90; UKTS 93 (1977). Entered into force 4 Aug. 1978.

2 There is an enormous literature on this. A brief but highly contemporary assessment can be found in *Extraterritorial Criminal Jurisdiction*, Report of the European Committee on Crime Problems, Council of Europe, Strasbourg, 1990. For a more detailed discussion see M. Akehurst, 'Jurisdiction in international law' (1972–3) 46 *British Yearbook of International Law* 145. For a discussion in relation to terrorism see Freestone, 'Legal responses to terrorism' in J. Lodge (ed.), *Terrorism: a Challenge to the State* (1981) pp. 195–224, at 201ff.

3 See e.g. G. Williams, 'Venue and ambit of the criminal law' (1965) 81 *Law Quarterly Review* 276.

4 These in turn recognize jurisdiction based on the initiation of offences within their territory (the 'subjective' territorial approach) and/or on the completion of such offences (the 'objective' territorial principle).

5 This principle is regarded as a fundamental form of jurisdiction by civil law countries, but has not, until recently, been widely accepted by common law countries. A relatively large number of UK statutes now utilize this; see J.D.M. Lew, 'The extraterritorial jurisdiction of the English courts' (1978) 27 *International and Comparative Law Quarterly* 168.

6 See e.g. the extended discussion in D.P. O'Connell, *The International Law of the Sea* (Vol. II) (Clarendon, 1984), pp. 746ff.

7 *Op. cit.* note 1.

8 Brownlie, *Principles of Public International Law* (4th edn) (Clarendon, 1990), pp. 304–5. He thinks that hijacking and offences related to traffic in narcotics are 'probably' subject to universal jurisdiction.

9 Art. 10 of the Harvard Research Draft Convention on Jurisdiction, with Respect to Crime (1935) 29 *American Journal of International Law* Supp. 443, does recognize jurisdiction for offences other than piracy, on the basis of simple custody jurisdiction specifically to prevent offenders escaping punishment:

(a) when committed in a place not subject to its authority but subject to the authority of another state, if the act or omission which constitutes the crime is also an offence by the law of the place where it was committed, if surrender of the alien for prosecution has been offered to such other state or states and the offer remains unaccepted, and if prosecution is not barred by the lapse of time under the law of the place where the crime was committed. The penalty imposed shall in no case be more severe than the penalty prescribed for the same act or omission by the law of the place where the crime was committed.

(b) when committed in a place not subject to the authority of any state . . .

10 This point is made by Brownlie, *op. cit.* note 8. E.g., Art. VI of the Convention on the Prevention and Punishment of the Crime of Genocide only permits trial 'by a competent tribunal of the State in the territory where the act was committed, or by such international penal tribunal as may have jurisdiction with respect to those Contracting Parties which shall have accepted its jurisdiction' (UKTS 58 (1970) Cmnd 4421; 78 UNTS 227). For this reason, the judgment of the Jerusalem Court in *Attorney-General of the Government of Israel* v *Eichmann* ((1961) 36 ILR 5 at para. 22) that genocide is triable under customary international law according to universality is probably mistaken.

11 See e.g. Brownlie, *op. cit.* note 8; Akehurst, *op. cit.* note 2; D.R. Harris, *Cases and Materials on International Law* (4th edn), (Sweet & Maxwell, 1991), pp. 275–86.

12 These conditions include 'a request from another State to take over criminal proceedings, or either the refusal of an extradition request from another State and its willingness to prosecute or confirmation from another State that it will not request extradition'. The Committee found this principle embodied in the 1972 European Convention on the Transfer of Proceedings in Criminal Matters, *op. cit.* note 2, at p. 14.

13 An interesting bilateral example would probably be the Anglo-Irish reciprocal legislation: Criminal Law Jurisdiction Act, 1976 (Eire) and the Criminal Law Jurisdiction Act, 1975 (UK). The Irish bill was referred to the Supreme Court by the President [1977] IR 129. This legislation was the result of an Anglo-Irish Commission which reported in May 1974 (Cmnd 5627). See also A. McCall-Smith and P. Magee, 'The Anglo-Irish law enforcement report in historical and political context' [1975] *Crim LR* 200–214. Further multilateral examples are highlighted below.

14 See e.g. J.L. Brierly, *Law of Nations* (6th edn), Waldock (ed.) (Clarendon, 1963), pp. 299–304; also 'The Lotus Case' (1928) 44 *Law Quarterly Review* 154, 161.

15 *France* v *Turkey* (1927) PCIJ Reps Series A, no. 10.

16 The controversial nature of this principle is often recognized by the conventions which will be considered here by qualifying the obligation to claim such jurisdiction with phrases such as 'if that State considers it appropriate' (see e.g. the Hostages Convention, Art. 5(1)).

17 *De Jure Belli ac Pacis*, 1625, Bk 2, c. 21.

18 L.A. Shearer, *Extradition in International Law* (Manchester University Press, 1971), pp. 16–19.

19 Shearer, *ibid.*, and M.C. Bassiouni, *International Extradition and World Public Order* (Sijthoff/Oceana, 1974).

20 (1957) European Treaty Series, no. 24; (1991) UKTS 97, Cmnd 1762. For the reservations and declarations of all the States Parties including the UK see SI 1990/1507, Schs 3 and 4.

21 See L. Leigh, 'Extradition and terrorism: the British view', Chap. 9, and H. Labayle, 'Extradition and terrorism: the French view', Chap. 10, this volume. Note further that Art. 4 of The Netherlands Constitution prevents extradition in the absence of a treaty, and Germany will only extradite on the basis of reciprocity (Art. 4(1) of Law of 23 Dec. 1929).

22 Shearer in 1971 found that after 1945, of the fifty extradition treaties registered with the UN, thirty-three adopted the eliminative method in preference to enumeration; this compares with 80 out of 163 earlier treaties, *op.cit.* note 18, p. 135.

23 Bassiouni, *op.cit.* note 19, pp. 314–21; and Shearer, *op.cit.* note 18, pp. 27ff.

24 Freestone, 'Legal responses to terrorism' in J. Lodge (ed.), *Terrorism: a Challenge to the State*, *op. cit.* note 2, pp. 209ff.

25 See e.g. D. Schiff, 'Astrid Proll's case' [1979] *Public Law* 353–71.

26 Convention pour extradition des malfaiteurs, 1834 (1833–4) 84 *Consolidated Treaty Series* 461.

27 State responsibility may arise for an expulsion which is conducted in an arbitrary manner, e.g. by the use of unnecessary force, or by the mistreatment of the alien. See e.g. the *Boffolo Claim* (*Italy* v *Venezuela*) 10 RIAA 528; *Dr Breger's Case* 8 Whiteman 861. See also Goodwin-Gill, *International Law and the Movement of Persons Between States* (Clarendon, 1978), *passim*, who suggests substantive and procedural limitations on State rights to expel.

28 Notably under the European Convention on Human Rights. See D.J. Harris, M. O'Boyle and C. Warbrick, *Law of the European Convention on Human Rights* (Butterworths, 1995), at pp. 73–80.

29 Free movement of persons is one of the 'Four Freedoms' of the European Community: see Title III, Art. 48–73 EEC. Note the restrictions on the use of grounds of 'public policy, public security or public health' in Directive 64/221/EEC (OJ Spec. edn 1970 (II) p. 402). There is now an extensive jurisprudence of the European Court of Justice on this issue.

30 See *R* v *Secretary of State for Home Affairs, ex p. Soblen* [1963] 1 QB 837. The UK courts indicated that evidence that Soblen was being deported to the USA from Britain in response to a prior request (for a non-extraditable offence) would indicate bad faith. However the plea of Crown privilege prevented Soblen from having access to government papers which might establish this. See P. O'Higgins, 'Disguised extradition: the Soblen case' (1964) 27 *MLR* 521.

31 A.E. Evans, 'The apprehension and prosecution of offenders: some current problems' in A.E. Evans and J.F. Murphy (eds), *Legal Aspects of International Terrorism* (Lexington Books, 1978), pp. 493–521. Evans found that in the years 1960–77, twenty States requested extradition of eighty-seven persons from

twenty-one states, but only six were granted, whereas 145 deportations were made by twenty-eight states to twenty-five destinations.

32   E.g., after Adolf Eichmann, former Head of the Jewish Office of the German Gestapo, was abducted from Argentina by a group of Israelis, now known to be from the Israeli Secret Service (Mossad), the Argentine Government lodged a complaint with the UN Security Council, that:

> ... having examined the complaint that the transfer of Adolf Eichmann to the territory of Israel constitutes a violation of the sovereignty of the Argentine Republic ... incompatible with the Charter of the United Nations, ...
>
> (2) Requests the Government of Israel to make appropriate reparation ...

After a reported apology from Israel, agreement was reached between the two governments, which issued a joint communiqué on 3 Aug. 1960 that they regarded the incident as 'closed'.

The Israeli trial court in *Attorney-General of the Government of Israel* v *Eichmann* (1961) 36 ILR 5 (at para. 41, citing the English case *Ex p. Elliott* [1949] 1 All ER 373) found 'an established rule of law that a person being tried for an offence against the laws of the State may not oppose his trial by reason of the illegality of his arrest or of the means by which he was brought within the jurisdiction of that State'.

It is however unclear whether as a matter of international law the obligation to make reparation for a violation of territorial sovereignty such as that involved in the Eichmann case includes an obligation to return the offender. In the *Lawler Incident* (McNair, *Law Officers' Opinions* (Vol. 1), (Cambridge University Press, 1956), at p. 78) the British Law Officers found such a duty, but in the *Savarkar Case* (Scott, *Hague Court Reports* 275, 279) the Permanent Court of Arbitration refused the return of a fugitive who had been illegally handed over to the UK authorities as a result of a mistake by a French policeman. J.E.S. Fawcett, 'The Eichmann Case' (1962) 38 *British Yearbook of International Law* 181, suggests some important limitations on the right to demand the return of a fugitive in such circumstances which are particularly germane for the present discussion, namely ... 'that the State [demanding reconduction] is the *forum conveniens* for his trial, and that it declares an intention to put him on trial. If these conditions are not satisfied, then the State must accept reparation in another form, since otherwise the interests of justice would be defeated'.

33   Concluded after the murder of Lord Mountbatten in Aug. 1979. For general discussion see J. Lodge and D. Freestone, 'The European Community and terrorism' in Y. Alexander and K. Myers (eds), *Terrorism in Europe* (Croom Helm, 1982), pp. 79, 91.

34   General Assembly Declaration on Principles of International Law Concerning Friendly Relations and Co-operation among States in Accordance with the Charter of the United Nations. G A res. 2625 (XXV), 24 Oct. 1970. The resolution was adopted by the General Assembly without a vote.

35   See e.g., the general discussion in A.V. Lowe, *Extraterritorial Jurisdiction* (Grotius, 1983) pp. xv–xxii.

36   See e.g. the specific exception in s 1(1) of the UK Tokyo Convention Act 1967.

37   The present writer prefers the term 'transnational' in this connection to distinguish the analysis from the writings of those who argue that 'international terrorism' is a carefully orchestrated conspiracy instigated by 'Communists' (see e.g. 'Editors' Introduction' in *Terrorism in Europe, op.cit.* note 32) or maverick statesmen such as Colonel Gaddhafi of Libya.

38   See note 1.

39 For a compilation of all aircraft hijack incidents between Jan. 1960 and July 1977 see A.E. Evans and J.F. Murphy, *op. cit.* note 30, pp. 68–147.

40 See note 1.

41 It was understood at the Hague Conference that aircraft need not be registered in a Contracting State for the Convention to apply.

42 In relation to war crimes it was claimed by the UN War Crimes Commission, (1949) 15 *War Crimes Reports* 26. The Israeli court claimed universality jurisdiction over genocide in *Attorney-General of Israel* v *Eichmann* (1961) ILR 5, but this claim does involve a controversial interpretation of Art. VI of the 1948 Genocide Convention (see para. 22 of judgment). Note also such claims in 1961 Single Convention on Narcotic Drugs, 520 UNTS 204, and Convention on the Suppression and Punishment of Apartheid, (1974) 13 ILM 50.

43 See note 1.

44 (1978) 17 ILM 1285. In the declaration the Group of Seven industrial nations threatened to cease all flights to and from States that did not extradite or prosecute alleged hijackers and/or return hijacked aircraft.

45 Similar incidents included the bombing of a French UTA plane over Niger in 1989 and the destruction of an Air India aircraft over the Atlantic in 1985, see *Keesing's Record of World Events* 1989, p. 36910, and 1985, p. 33987 respectively. The Lockerbie incident spawned the unprecedented UN Security Council demand that those alleged to have planted the bomb be handed over to the UK or the US, as well as the imposition of sanctions, see Security Council resolutions 731 (1992) and 748 (1992), cited in (1992) 31 ILM 750 750. The issue remains unresolved.

46 See note 1.

47 See note 1.

48 See note 1.

49 1977, ETS no. 90. The Convention is discussed further below.

50 And its protocol. See note 1.

51 Art. 6 is worth reproducing:

1 Each State Party shall take such measures as may be necessary to establish its jurisdiction over the offences set forth in Article 3 when the offence is committed:

(*a*) against or on board a ship flying the flag of the State at the time the offence is committed; or

(*b*) in the territory of that State, including its territorial sea; or

(*c*) by a national of that State.

2 A State Party may also establish its jurisdiction over any such offence when:

(*a*) it is committed by a stateless person whose habitual residence is in that State; or

(*b*) during its commission a national of that State is seized, threatened, injured or killed; or

(*c*) it is committed in an attempt to compel that State to do or abstain from doing any act.

3 Any State Party which has established jurisdiction mentioned in paragraph 2 shall notify the Secretary-General of the IMO. . . .. If such State subsequently rescinds that jurisdiction it shall notify the Secretary-General.

4 Each State Party shall take such measures as may be necessary to establish its jurisdiction over the offences set forth in Article 3 in cases where the alleged offender is present in its territory and it does not extradite him to any of the States Parties which have established their jurisdiction in accordance with paragraphs 1 and 2 of this Article.

5 This Convention does not exclude any criminal jurisdiction exercised in accordance with national law.

52 On extradition generally see M.C. Bassiouni, *International Extradition and World Public Order* (A.J. Sijthoff, 1974) and Shearer, *op. cit* note 18.

53 See note 2.

54 The Taking of Hostages Act, 1982 provides in s 1:

A person, whatever his nationality, who, in the United Kingdom or *elsewhere*, –

(*a*) detains any person ('the hostage'), and

(*b*) in order to compel a State, international organisation or person to do or abstain from doing any act, threatens to kill, injure or continue to detain the hostage, commits an offence. [emphasis added]

S 3(4) reads:

(4) For the purposes of the [Extradition] Act of 1870 any act, wherever committed, which –

(*a*) is an offence under this Act or an attempt to commit such an offence, and

(*b*) is an offence against the law of any State in the case of which that Act is applied. . .

shall be deemed to be an offence committed within the jurisdiction of that State.

55 See note 1. For a more extended discussion see Freestone, *op. cit.* note 2, p. 211ff, and Freestone, 'The EEC and common action on terrorism' (1984) *Yearbook of European Law* 207, 211ff.

56 Art. 2. Note that both Arts. 1 and 2 include attempts to commit, participation as an accomplice in, and participation as an accomplice in attempts to commit such offences.

57 Art. 7.

58 Art. 6.

59 See e.g. P. Wilkinson, 'Problems of establishing a European judicial area', Report to *Conference on Democracy against Terrorism in Europe: Tasks and Problems* (Strasbourg, Nov. 1980) AS/Pol/Coll/Terr (32)6) p. 4.

60 These are in fact the terms of the 1974 resolution of the Council of Europe Committee of Ministers.

61 A.V. Lowe and J.R. Young 'Suppressing terrorism under the European Convention: a British perspective' (1978) 305 *Netherlands International Law Review* 305, 330.

62 Suppression of Terrorism Act 1978, s 4(1).

63 *Ibid.*, 4(3).

64 The Aviation Security Act 1982 consolidates a considerable proportion of aviation security-related legislation, including the Hijacking Act 1971.

65 See e.g., P. Wilkinson, *op. cit.* note 57, and *contra* J.J.A. Salmon, 'La Convention européenne pour la répression du terrorisme: un vrai pas en arrière' [1977] *Journal des tribunaux* 497 (24 Sept 1977) and G. Soulier, 'European integration and the suppression of terrorism' [1978] *Review of Contemporary Law* 21.

66 Cmnd 7823. cf. M.C. Wood, 'The European Convention on the Suppression of Terrorism' (1981) 1 *Yearbook of European Law* 307 and Freestone, *op. cit.* note 54.

67 cf. Freestone, *op. cit.* note 54.

68 See House of Commons Parliamentary Papers, 'Practical police cooperation in the European Community', HC 363, 1989–90.

69 Apparently as a result of Dutch opposition – ostensibly because of certain technical provisions of the Convention – but *Le Monde* reported that this was in fact in retaliation for French blocking of Dutch proposals for the desalination

of the Rhine. As a result of the failure of the 1980 draft, it was reported that France refused to ratify the Terrorism Treaty or the Dublin Agreement. See further J. Kelly, 'Problems of establishing a European judicial area', Report to *Conference on Democracy against Terrorism in Europe*, Strasbourg, November 1980, AS/Pol/Coll/Terr(32) 8.

70 Mention should also be made of another EC arrangement concluded after the Libyan Embassy siege which one presumes covers attacks by diplomats rather than against them. On 11 Sept. 1984 the EC Foreign Ministers in Dublin concluded a set of measures 'to combat terrorism and abuse of diplomatic immunity' (*The Times*, 1 Sept. 1984 and (1983–4) HC 499–iii, 51).

71 Report drawn up on behalf of the Legal Affairs Committee on the European Judicial Area (Extradition), Rapporteur A. Tyrrell, EP Doc 1–318/82. For an extended discussion see Freestone *op. cit.* note 54.

72 Art. 46 of the Draft Treaty provided:
    In addition to the fields subject to common action, the coordination of national law with a view to constituting a homogeneous judicial area shall be carried out in accordance with the method of co-operation. This shall be done in particular:
    – to fight international forms of crime, including terrorism.
    For further comments see e.g. D. Freestone and J.S. Davidson in J. Lodge (ed.), *European Union: the EC in Search of a Future* (Macmillan, 1984) pp. 125 et seq.

73 Text in *OJC* 191, 29 July 1992.

74 *FRG* v *Denmark*; *FRG* v *The Netherlands* [1969] ICJ Reps 3.

75 Hudson, quoted in Brownlie, *op. cit.* note 8, p. 7.

76 *Ibid.*

77 See note 15.

78 See note 73.

79 *Nicaragua* v *US* (Merits) [1986] ICJ Reps 14.

80 [1969] ICJ Reps 44 (para. 77), cited in *Nicaragua Case, ibid.*

81 Schwarzenberger, e.g., argues that the early development of custom was from networks of bilateral treaties laying down principles which passed into custom; see G. Schwarzenberger, *A Manual of International Law* (5th edn) (Stevens & Sons, 1967) p. 32.

82 *Op. cit.* note 8, p. 10.

83 *Ibid.*, p. 13.

84 M. Akehurst, 'Custom as a source of international law' (1974–5) 47 *British Yearbook of International Law* 1, 45.

85 Source: M.J. Bowman and D.J. Harris, *Multilateral Treaties* (University of Nottingham, 1993 Suppl).

86 E.g. J.L. Brierly, 'The Lotus case' (1928) *Law Quarterly Review* 154, 161–2.

87 US legislation s. 1203, 18 USC, Pub.L. No. 98–473, Ch. 9, and 2.2002(a) 98 Stat. 1976, 2186, and France; see Chap. 8. For a wider discussion see C.R. Blakesley, 'Jurisdictional issues and conflicts of jurisdiction' in M. Cherif Bassiouni (ed.), *Legal Responses to Terrorism: US Procedural Aspects* (Martinus Nijhoff, 1988), pp. 131–79.

88 Whether the principle may only be utilized in relation to certain offences would require an examination of State practice outside the scope of this chapter.

89 See Higgins, Chap. 2, in this volume.

5 Legal aspects of terrorism at sea

*Glen Plant**

INTRODUCTION

On 7 October 1985, four armed men claiming to represent the Palestine Liberation Front took control of the Italian-flag cruise liner *Achille Lauro* on the high seas about thirty miles off Port Said and held the crew and passengers hostage. They had boarded her in port in Genoa posing as legitimate passengers. They demanded the release of fifty Palestinian prisoners held in Israel and threatened to blow up the ship if intervention were attempted, and to start to kill the passengers if their demands were not met.[1] Subsequently a Jewish American passenger, Mr Klinghoffer, was shot dead and his body thrown overboard. Several days later the four men gave themselves up to the Egyptian authorities, following negotiations between them, with the aid of an intermediary, while the ship was lying off Port Said. These negotiations resulted in an offer to the terrorists of a safe conduct to Tunisia in return for their leaving the ship without further violence.

On 11 October an Egyptian civilian aircraft was intercepted by US military aircraft over the Mediterranean Sea and instructed to land at an airforce base in Sicily. Four Palestinians on board were detained by the Italian authorities and subsequently indicted and convicted in Genoa for offences related to the hijacking of the ship and the death of Mr Klinghoffer.[2] Italy, which had apparently not been consulted about the interception operation, refused a request from the United States for their extradition.[3] The President of the UN Security Council condemned the attack in a statement on behalf of all its Members.[4]

Before the 1980s ships were not generally regarded as high-risk terrorist targets. This was not because security in ports or on ships was better than in airports and on aircraft – favourite terrorist targets in the past. On the contrary, although a number of countries, including the United Kingdom and France, operated fairly efficient port security systems (notwithstanding the lack of international standards), security in the maritime field was probably less tight than in the aviation field worldwide. The more important factors precluding attacks upon ships in preference to aircraft were the relative invulnerability of shipping targets, for example to bomb threats, their larger scale and the greater difficulties of effecting escape from them to a safe haven arising from their slower speeds and limitation to one plane of operation.

Nevertheless, the *Achille Lauro* incident underlined the possibility of further serious terrorist attacks against ships and led to a rapid inter-national response. This essentially took two forms: 1. the negotiation, fol-lowing an American initiative in the International Maritime Organisation (IMO), and adoption in September 1986 of a set of global standards for port security – the Measures to Prevent Unlawful Acts against Passengers and Crews on Board Ships; and 2. the negotiation, once the Measures were in place, of a *dedere aut iudicare*-type convention to cover ships – the Convention for the Suppression of Unlawful Acts against the Safety of Maritime Navigation, adopted in Rome in March 1988.

The Measures were regarded, at least by the United States, as the more important of the two reactions, largely because it is in port rather than on board a ship at sea that terrorist threats against ships will be most easily prevented, but also because conventions of the type mentioned are rarely if ever enforced in practice and appear to have a more symbolic than practical role. Largely at US insistence, therefore, serious negotiations on the Convention did not commence until the measures were in place. This chapter will, however, concentrate on the Convention, because it raises a number of interesting questions of international law.

A key resolution on terrorism, resolution 40/61, adopted by consensus by the UN General Assembly in December 1985, shortly after the *Achille Lauro* incident, included a paragraph requesting the IMO to recommend appropriate action.[5] Italy then put forward a proposal, later co-sponsored by Austria and Egypt, to negotiate a convention against maritime terrorism. Negotiations on the basis of drafts prepared by the three co-sponsors were conducted under the auspices of the IMO.

The political interest of Italy and Egypt – especially in improving their relationships with the United States following this damaging incident (Egypt had apparently not taken the action required of it under the Hostages Convention (for explanation see p. 71) – was clear. The interest of the third co-sponsor, Austria, a land-locked State with few maritime interests, was less obvious, except perhaps that it was a general concern to combat terrorism, of which Austria had been a recent serious victim with the bomb attack on Vienna Airport in 1985. The United Kingdom also acted as a sort of unofficial co-sponsor in the sense that, as the host State of the IMO, it felt it was incumbent on itself to play a particularly supportive role. Moreover, the unwritten political agenda, as far as the co-sponsors were concerned, was that solutions should be sought which were acceptable to the United States, as the United States (as well as Israel) felt itself to be a particular victim of the incident and took a strong interest in the Convention. It followed that a 'maximal' approach was taken so as to cover the maximum numbers of ships and geographical areas where terrorist attacks might take place without at the same time impinging on matters and areas of obvious domestic concern to the States Parties. Most importantly, the list of ('terrorist') offences covered is maximized so as to cover, in particular, all of the facts of the *Achille Lauro* incident, and the list of bases of jurisdiction is likewise maximized so as to give each of the States which were 'victims' of that incident the possibility of seeking extradition of the offenders in any future similar situation. These lists are longer than in any of the previous anti-terrorist treaties (see pp. 269–98). The attitude of most Western States has consistently been that terrorist acts should be condemned wherever and by whomever committed, regardless of the underlying causes.

The Convention has to date received sixteen ratifications (as of 30 June 1992),[6] including those of Austria, France, Italy and the United Kingdom, but not yet those of Egypt, Israel and the United States (although the US administration has taken preparatory steps towards obtaining the advice and consent of the Senate). It, and the Protocol, entered into force on 1 March 1992. It seems surprising that a co-sponsor and the two States most interested in the impact of the Convention have not yet ratified four years after the Convention was adopted – even taking into account the delaying effect of cumbersome constitutional processes – especially when the number of ratifications falls only two short of those necessary to bring it into force. In the United Kingdom the Measures and the Convention are enacted internally in Parts II and III of the Aviation and Maritime Security Act 1990.[7]

A second, and opposing, political theme of great importance was the Arab concept of terrorism. The Iran–Iraq War was continuing at the time of the negotiations, and Iran was attacking foreign shipping in and around the Strait of Hormuz. In 1986 the United States had bombed Libya for its alleged support of terrorism. As a result of these matters, attempts were made by some Arab States to introduce references to 'State terrorism', and to make explicit and unnecessary references to terrorism in straits used for international navigation. Arab and African countries, in particular, have also long sought to include in such instruments references to the *causes* of terrorism and to exclude the acts of certain liberation movements from the scope of terrorism. The result was a careful compromise designed to meet the needs of both of these political themes, which is described on pp. 73–4.

An additional peculiar theme of this Convention that is worth noting is the importance attached to the special nature of shipping and the interests of the shipping industry – championed in particular by Greece and Liberia. This had a number of consequences, including the inclusion of preambular paragraph 11, which makes it clear that the normal shipboard disciplinary powers of a master over his crew are not altered by the Convention. The most important consequence, however, was the inclusion of Article 8 concerning a right of delivery of offenders (see pp. 85–6).

The Convention provides that a person alleged to have committed a broad range of acts connected with attacks against ships or persons on board should either be extradited or have his case submitted to the appropriate national authorities with a view to prosecution. States Parties are in some instances obliged and in others permitted to establish their jurisdiction with respect to such matters. In addition, it contains provision for a possible review conference and provisions concerning cooperation, prevention, the transmission of information, the treatment to be accorded to alleged offenders and the power of a master to deliver alleged offenders to the authorities of a State Party other than the flag State.

In addition to the Convention, an optional protocol – the Protocol for the Suppression of Unlawful Acts Against the Safety of Fixed Platforms Located on the Continental Shelf ('the Protocol')[8] – was adopted. This makes similar provision in relation to fixed platforms located on the continental shelf, except that there is no equivalent of the master's power of delivery.

There are in force a number of multilateral conventions concerning international terrorist acts of a type similar to this, which are referred to generally below as 'the precedents' or as 'prosecute or extradite conventions'. The Montreal and Hague Conventions[9] (the 'aviation precedents') provide for 'prosecution or extradition' of offenders or alleged offenders in cases of serious offences affecting the safety of aircraft in flight. Just prior to the diplomatic conference at which the IMO instruments were agreed, the Montreal Convention was supplemented with a Protocol concerning attacks at airports serving international civil aviation.[10]

No such convention has ever been agreed before in relation to ships or to fixed platforms, but the Hostages, Internationally Protected Persons and Physical Protection of Nuclear Material Conventions – all 'prosecute or extradite' conventions – require States Parties to establish jurisdiction over the offences covered by those conventions whenever those offences are committed (among other places) on board a ship 'registered in that State'.[11] Thus, if and when the IMO Convention comes into force, a State which is party both to it and to one or more of the three above-mentioned conventions might have a choice of conventions when the acts in question take place *on board* (but not simply *against*) a ship *and* that ship is registered in that State. This may give rise to certain questions of conflict of conventions, especially in view of the fact that, while language used in the IMO instruments is frequently borrowed from these precedents, they have been negotiated at different times and in several different fora,[12] and this has resulted in some divergence of language and of substance in comparable provisions (see pp. 91–2 below).

Professor Malvina Halberstram, a member and sometime head of the US delegation to the IMO negotiations, has discussed the application of the law of piracy to the *Achille Lauro* case, as well as the negotiation of the Convention and Protocol up to the second session of the Ad Hoc

Preparatory Committee to the diplomatic conference.[13] It is not the intention of this author to debate the application *vel non* of the law of piracy in such cases, but rather to expand upon the discussion of the two instruments, taking into account the important changes made at the diplomatic conference which finalized them.

ELABORATION OF THE INSTRUMENTS

The negotiation process involved a good deal of informal negotiation as well as discussion in several standing committees of and the creation of an Ad Hoc Preparatory Committee of the IMO. The latter met twice, first in London between 2 and 6 March 1987, and later in Rome between 18 and 22 May 1987 – giving (together with the diplomatic conference itself) a total of only twenty days of formal negotiations. The revised draft produced by the co-sponsors following the first preparatory meeting[14] included for the first time a draft optional protocol relating to fixed platforms, which was intended as a compromise between those States that wished to see platforms included in the scope of the Convention and those that wished to exclude them altogether.

In view of the limited available financial resources, there are no summary records of the diplomatic conference, although a record of the decisions of the conference was kept.[15] In any event, much of the work was conducted in informal consultations on particular draft articles or groups of articles – the provisional results of which were often reflected in conference working papers.

Of the seventy-nine participating States, twenty-four signed the Convention,[16] and twenty-two the Protocol,[17] on 10 March 1988, when they were opened for signature in Rome. Unusually only sixty-nine of the participating States signed the Final Act of the conference,[18] which was unusually important, because it contained a statement representing a compromise between those States that had wished for a reference in Article 4 of the Convention (on geographical scope) to straits used for international navigation, and those which did not[19] (see p. 79 below).

The decision of the IMO Council to establish an Ad Hoc Preparatory Committee rather than referring the preparatory work to the IMO Legal Committee (or to another standing body) was fortunate, since it encouraged the formation of delegations with a broad range of expertise in a variety of legal fields, including in many cases experience of negotiating 'prosecute or extradite' conventions.[20] This is not to deny that the contribution of the Legal Committee and the presence on a number of delegations of those lawyers regularly engaged in IMO legal matters were valuable in ensuring that the adaptation of the accepted language to the maritime field did not violate established IMO practice and concepts of maritime law.

The use of such a committee also introduced an element of flexibility, since there was no feeling that the time-honoured procedures of an established committee needed necessarily to be followed, nor that the solutions suggested by the Ad Hoc Preparatory Committee were in any way sacrosanct: improvisation, the bringing in of recognized experts when necessary, and willingness to explore any possible solution were hallmarks of the negotiations. Emphasis was placed on practicality and pragmatism, involving the adaptation of accepted language from the precedents to the peculiar requirements of the maritime field, rather than rewriting of the law.

The fact that negotiation took place within the auspices of the IMO had some impact on the content of the texts themselves – notably in the inclusion of the standard IMO provision for a review conference (Art. 20 of the Convention and Art. 8 of the Protocol).[21] Its greatest impact, however, was in relation to the political aspects of the negotiations. The IMO is a small, specialized agency of the UN system. It seeks to avoid the alignment of delegations along the lines of political blocs or groupings present in many other inter-governmental organizations and nurtures an 'IMO spirit', which exhorts delegations to an efficient, practical approach to tasks, not generally consistent with the introduction of extraneous political considerations.

THE CONVENTION

The provisions of the Convention will now be considered under five headings: the Preamble; the ships covered by and geographical scope of the Convention (Arts. 1, 2 and 4); the offences covered by the Convention (Art. 3); the 'prosecute or extradite' system (Arts. 5 to 15);[22] and dispute settlement and the final articles (Arts. 16 to 22). The Protocol will be discussed on pp. 89–90 below.

The Preamble

Most of the preambular paragraphs derive from the precedents and were relatively uncontroversial. The Preamble was used, however, to accommodate a compromise concerning two of the important political questions left to be decided by the diplomatic conference.[23] First was the question whether or not there should be some exception from the operation of the Convention for acts carried out for political motives – notably acts of national liberation movements (NLMs). Second was the question whether or not language should be included indicating culpability either of persons acting on behalf of States (so-called 'State-sponsored terrorism') or, indeed, of States themselves (so-called 'State terrorism').

The seventh and eighth preambular paragraphs were agreed as elements of a 'package deal', achieved on the last day of the diplomatic conference, following informal consultations, in which certain Arab delegations on the one hand, and the United Kingdom, United States and certain other Western delegations on the other, played a prominent role. The seventh preambular paragraph recalled and recited operative paragraph 9, and the eighth preambular paragraph operative paragraph 1 of UN General Assembly resolution 40/61 (1985). Operative paragraph 9 of the resolution urged States to contribute to the progressive elimination of the underlying causes of terrorism – listing colonialism, racism and fundamental violations of human rights as examples; operative paragraph 1 unequivocally condemned all acts of terrorism, wherever and by whomever committed. Neither paragraph had appeared in earlier draft texts, but early during the diplomatic conference the Algerian delegation had proposed,[24] with support from several other Arab delegations, the insertion of a paragraph similar to the seventh preambular paragraph as adopted, except that it employed the words 'in particular' in relation to paragraph 9 of the resolution; this might have implied that it was more important than the other provisions of the resolution, including paragraph 1. The compromise solution involved the placing together of the two paragraphs in a manner which gave equal weight to the views of those requiring an unequivocal condemnation of terrorism and those attaching priority to dealing with the political problems which they see as a part of the cause of resort to terrorism. A close examination of the seventh preambular paragraph shows that it merely recalls a paragraph of a non-binding resolution which urges States to contribute to the progressive elimination of the *underlying causes* of terrorism and, in doing so, to pay special attention to situations in which the activities of NLMs are particularly pertinent. It does not suggest that acts of NLMs are in any way exempted from the scope of the Convention.

The 'package deal' also involved the dropping of several related proposals. The President of the Conference was able to announce on the last day of the conference, following two days of informal consultations, that Kuwait was willing to drop its proposal for a new Article 11A expressly providing for a political offence exception[25] (see further p. 87 below). The Saudi delegation did not insist on its proposal to include various references in the text of the Convention and Protocol to 'crimes' committed by governments.[26] Although this proposal had attracted some support, notably from Arab delegations, it aroused strong opposition from other delegations on the ground that governments could not be subject to national criminal law rules and procedures. Before the diplomatic conference the Kuwaiti delegation suggested an alternative preambular reference to State-sponsored acts,[27] but this was also resisted on the ground that it was unnecessary – since the acts covered by the Convention are expressed to be acts committed by 'any person', and this includes, as a matter of course, a person sponsored by a State. It was also objected that inclusion of such a term might have adverse consequences upon the interpretation of the precedents.

In a rather different vein, the eleventh preambular paragraph notes 'that acts of the crew which are subject to normal shipboard discipline are outside the purview of this Convention'. This clause is designed to ensure that disciplinary offences traditionally dealt with by the master will not be interpreted as falling within the description of the conduct constituting the substantive element of the offences. Since references in 'prosecute or extradite' conventions to political intent or to 'terrorism' or 'terrorist' are unacceptable to a number of States, the acts constituting the offences in those conventions must be positively enumerated – and this can never be done precisely enough to ensure the inclusion of all acts desired to be covered and exclusion of acts not desired to be covered.[28] Moreover, proposals to include in the Preamble a provision expressly excluding from the scope of the Convention such acts as football hooliganism and Greenpeace-style environmentalist organizations' seaborne protest operations were not pressed, on the understanding that such acts were to be considered as not included in its scope.[29]

Ships covered by and geographical scope of the Convention (Arts. 1 to 4)

The discussions of the definition of 'ship' for the purposes of the Convention, the exclusion of certain categories of ship from its scope and the Convention's geographical scope were interrelated throughout the negotiations. The decision to include an optional Protocol on fixed platforms, moreover, necessitated consistency between the definition of 'ship' in the Convention and use of the term 'fixed platform' in the Protocol. As many ships and platforms as possible were to be covered by the instruments whenever the offence involved an 'international element' which took the incident in question beyond the scope of matters properly governed by national law alone.

The primary task was to choose between a negative approach to the scope of the Convention – listing ships and geographical circumstances in which it *did not* apply; a positive approach – listing those circumstances in which it *did* apply; and a mixed approach. Several variations on the mixed approach were tried,[30] and the Convention as adopted reflects this approach: Article 1 of the Convention defines 'ship' for the purpose of the Convention; Article 2 lists those ships to which it does not apply; and Article 4 lists the geographical circumstances in which it applies. The Protocol follows a similar pattern (Art. 1).

Definition of 'ship' (Art. 1)

A 'ship' is defined in Article 1 of the Convention as 'a vessel of any type whatsoever not permanently attached to the sea-bed'. It need not necessarily fly the flag of or otherwise have the nationality of a State Party.

In their earliest drafts the co-sponsors included the concept of a 'ship in service', intended to equate to the concept of 'aircraft in flight' used in the Montreal Convention, but there were strong doubts as to whether such a term was appropriate in the case of ships. A ship might, for example, be considered to be 'in service' while conducting a number of acts preparatory to or following upon the completion of a particular voyage, but it is difficult to determine when these begin or end. The omission of the term might, however, have resulted in the Convention being applied to ships not navigating or capable of navigation in a manner introducing an international element into the offence. Article 2(1)(c), therefore, excludes from the application of the Convention a ship 'which has been withdrawn from navigation or laid up'. Opinions differed between the various delegations as to precisely which categories of vessel were covered by this subparagraph, but it was intended that the withdrawal from navigation need not be permanent so long as, at the time of the offence, the vessel is not navigating because for example it is not crewed or has only a maintenance crew or does not have the requisite permissions to navigate.[31]

In their earliest drafts the co-sponsors also employed the term 'seagoing' in relation to 'ship' but this was dropped,[32] because it would have excluded from the scope of the Convention offences involving the international element of a non-sea-going ship being hijacked in coastal or inland waters and forced to sail out onto international waters.

Finally, the diplomatic conference adopted the proposal of a group of delegates who conducted informal consultations on the draft Protocol that the use of the terms 'ship' and 'fixed platform' should be complementary and that 'ship' should be interpreted as widely as possible, so as to include in particular mobile offshore drilling units (MODUs), even when operating attached to the sea-bed.[33] The inherent ambiguity in the terms 'vessel' and 'not permanently attached' suggest that it is legitimate to refer to this decision as a means to interpret the Convention under the terms of Article 32 of the Vienna Convention on the Law of Treaties.[34] It follows that the term 'navigating' used in Articles 3 and 4 should be interpreted to include operations of MODUs.

There is some doubt, however, whether or not the final texts of the two instruments achieved the aim of covering all vessels and platforms. There is doubt in particular as to whether platforms without an 'economic' purpose are included, as well as platforms sitting on, but not attached to, the sea-bed. It is clear, however, that any fixed platforms beyond the continental shelf could not be covered (see p. 89 below).

Ships not covered (Art. 2)

Aircraft used in military, customs or police service were expressly excluded from the scope of the aviation precedents. Some delegations, however, felt it appropriate to include in the scope of the IMO Convention all warships and government-owned vessels, as long as their immunity from enforcement jurisdiction was not affected and they were not actively engaged in hostilities. A proposal to include in the scope of the Convention only such government ships as ice-breakers and research vessels – not easily able to defend themselves – received strong support, and Article 2(1)(a) and (b) (agreed after informal consultations at the diplomatic conference) excludes not only warships but also any 'ship owned or operated by a State when being used as a naval auxiliary or for customs or police purposes' – wording intended to reflect this proposal. The status of fishery protection vessels and of government quarantine vessels is not made clear, but the better view is that they are excluded.

The saving clause, Article 2(2), is not strictly necessary and was added to avoid doubt. It follows the language of Article 32 of the Convention on the Law of the Sea (UNLOSE),[35] and is to be understood to refer to *enforcement* jurisdiction only.

Georgraphical scope (Art. 4)

The provision concerning the geographical scope of the Convention, Article 4, presented great difficulties. After extensive informal consultations, it was decided to take a positive approach to the enumeration of the geographical circumstances in which the Convention was to apply, although earlier drafts involved variations on a mixed approach.[36]

Article 4(1) uses the term 'the ship'. This means a ship as defined in Article 1 and referred to in Article 3 as one in relation to which the acts constituting offences are carried out. The Convention applies in accordance with the provisions of Article 4(1) if the ship 'is navigating or is scheduled to navigate into, through or from waters beyond the outer limit of the territorial sea of a single State, or the lateral limits of its territorial sea with adjacent States'. This text does not reflect the intended meaning wholly accurately, mainly because the diplomatic conference did not have time to check the final text prepared by the Secretariat (see p. 72 above). The intended sense would, perhaps, be better conveyed by either deleting the last three words, which are misleading, or, better still, substituting the phrase 'beyond the outer or lateral limits of the territorial sea of a single State' at the end of the paragraph.

Article 4(2) provides that in cases not covered by paragraph 1, the Convention 'nevertheless applies when the offender or the alleged offender is found in the territory of a State Party other than the State referred to in paragraph 1'.

Reading the two paragraphs of Article 4 together, it can be seen that the Convention applies to all cases of navigation, actual or scheduled, except cases of 'short-range' or 'local' cabotage – that is, when a ship is navigating and scheduled to navigate only within the internal waters or territorial sea (or both) of a single State, whether the flag State or another State. Even in cases within this exception, however, the Convention applies if the offender or alleged offender is found in the territory of a State other than the State in whose waters the cabotage was taking place[37] (a location described below as 'abroad').

The words in paragraph 2 – 'the State referred to in paragraph 1' – refer to 'a single State' as it appears in paragraph 1. Somewhat awkwardly it was found necessary to employ this term 'a single State' in such a way as to give it several meanings. In the context of paragraph 1 it means *any single* coastal State in whose waters the ship is navigating or scheduled to navigate; it also means *all* coastal States in relation to ships navigating or scheduled to navigate exclusively in waters beyond States' territorial waters. In the context of paragraph 2 it means that particular State in the waters of which the ship was or was scheduled to be engaged in short-range cabotage at the time of the offence. If the single term had not been used, the drafting of both paragraphs so as to try to capture each meaning would have been very complicated.

The international elements attracting the operation of the Convention are thus: actual navigation, whether voluntary or not, of a ship in any waters in as much as this is not limited to the territorial sea or internal waters of a single State; or the scheduling of a ship to navigate in this way, even if that schedule is not in the event followed because the hijackers stop or divert the vessel; or the finding of the offender or alleged offender abroad, when neither of the other elements is satisfied. The term 'scheduled', it is true, does not make entirely clear what degree and manner of planning is necessary, but it proved impossible to agree on a less subjective term.[38]

The cabotage exception was problematic. The choice whether or not to include ships engaged in cabotage in the scope of the Convention was complicated by two suggested possible distinctions: the first between so-called 'long-range' cabotage, involving voyages across international waters between the metropolitan territory of a State and its overseas territories or between two such territories, and 'short-range' cabotage between ports on the same or adjacent sea-coasts; and the second between foreign flag ships engaged in short-range cabotage in the waters of a particular coastal State, and domestic ships doing the same.[39] Various compromise solutions were proposed before it was decided to place *all* short-range cabotage (both domestic and foreign) under Article 4(2) and *all* long-range under Article 4(1).

It was decided, furthermore, to describe the geographical elements in the Convention in terms of the location, actual or scheduled, of *the ship* at the time of the offence – rather than of the place where *the offence* took place – although in some earlier drafts these methods had been combined. This approach, however, required a delicate description of the limits of the territorial sea for the purpose of describing the location, actual or intended, of the ship. Since the only crossings of territorial limits envisaged in Article 4(1) are of the limits between, on the one hand, the territorial sea of a particular State and, on the other, either the waters seaward of its territorial sea or the territorial sea of a neighbouring State, a method had to be found of describing the limits of the territorial sea of such a State without including in that description the baseline which divides it from internal waters and from which it is delimited. Various suggestions were considered,[40] and the final version, referring to 'outer' and 'lateral' limits, was included at the last-minute insistence of one delegation.

The 'outer limit of the territorial sea' is a self-explanatory term, found for example in the Geneva Convention on the Territorial Sea and in UNLOSC.[41] Informal consultations had resulted in a formula that avoided use of the term 'lateral limits' – a term not normally used to describe the line of delimitation between the territorial seas of two adjacent States: it is not found in UNLOSC and was criticized by one delegation for, in its view, not accurately describing median lines delimiting the territorial seas of two opposite States where no high-seas waters lie between them. A single delegation, however, was not satisfied with a text that did not refer to 'lateral limits'.

It might appear that delegations omitted to clarify the position of vessels navigating or scheduled to navigate exclusively between the *internal waters* of several States. There was some discussion of international rivers and lakes at the first session, and of the Great Lakes System in particular at the second session, of the Ad Hoc Preparatory Committee. It was intended that such navigation between adjacent internal waters be covered by Article 4(2) of the Convention. Furthermore, the words in paragraph 1, 'into, through or from', were designed to capture instances, not only of ships crossing the limits between adjacent territorial seas or between territorial seas and waters seaward of them, but also those of ships sailing exclusively on the high seas or in other waters seaward of the territorial sea – for example tankers shuttling between off-shore terminals.

As has been mentioned, a number of Arab delegations desired a reference in Article 4 to straits used for international navigation. At least one State bordering a strait, however, was concerned to avoid language which suggested any diminution of the coastal State's sovereignty in the waters of such straits. As part of a package deal to secure general agreement to Article 4 the following statement on straits (proposed by the UK delegation following informal consultations) was included in the Final Act of the conference:

> 23. In relation to Article 4 of the Convention for the Suppression of Unlawful Acts against the Safety of Maritime Navigation, some delegations were in favour of the inclusion in Article 4, paragraph 1, of straits used for international navigation. Other delegations pointed out that it was unnecessary to include them since navigation in straits was one of the situations envisaged in Article 4, paragraph 1. Therefore, the Convention will apply in straits used for international navigation, without prejudice to the legal status of the waters forming such straits in accordance with relevant conventions and other rules of international law.

Almost all instances of navigation in straits are caught by the words of Article 4(1), and the only practical effect on the interpretation of Article 4 which this paragraph might have is the removal from paragraph 2 to paragraph 1 of Article 4 of the rare cases where a ship navigates and is scheduled to navigate exclusively in the waters of a single State which are also waters of a strait used for international navigation. Since the words of Article 4 do not appear to be ambiguous or unclear however, it is to be wondered whether or not this paragraph can be so employed as an aid to interpretation in accordance with the provisions of Article 32 of the Vienna Convention on the Law of Treaties. It is apparently not covered by the terms of Article 31(2) of that treaty, since the failure of some States to sign the Final Act suggests that some, at least, might have disagreed with the statement.

The offences covered by the Convention (Art. 3)

The offences covered by the Convention are listed in Article 3 and substantially reproduce *mutatis mutandis* the offences provided for in the aviation precedents. The principal offences are listed in paragraph 1 and the secondary offences in paragraph 2. To these are added, however, a new principal offence (in Art. 3(1)(g)) of injuring or killing a person in connection with the commission or attempted commission of any of the other principal offences, and a new secondary offence (in Art. 3(2)(c)) of threatening to commit the principal offences set out in paragraph 1, sub-paragraphs (b), (c) and (e). These secondary offences involve unlawfully and intentionally: performing acts of violence against persons on board a ship; destroying a ship or causing damage to it or its cargo; and destroying or seriously damaging maritime navigational facilities or interfering with their operation.

The precise coverage of Article 3 will depend upon the municipal laws of the States Parties, since the exact definition of the offences may differ somewhat under the various systems of criminal law; nevertheless, it does indicate reasonably clearly the acts covered.

The Convention applies whatever the nationality of the offender or alleged offender. A person is not guilty of an offence, however, if he or she is acting 'lawfully' – for example, when exercising police powers. It is not made clear under the laws of which State the lawful nature *vel non* of the act is to be judged, but it is likely that the laws of the flag State will suffice. The act must also be done 'intentionally': this presumably refers to intention as to the commission of the acts constituting the offence, but not necessarily as to the results of those acts.

Principal offences

Sub-paragraph (a) of paragraph 1 makes it an offence unlawfully and intentionally to seize or exercise control over a ship – without more.

Sub-paragraph (f) requires that for an offence to be committed, navigation of the ship must actually be endangered by the listed acts, but for the acts covered by sub-paragraphs (b) to (e) to constitute offences they need only be 'likely to endanger' the safe navigation of the ship in question.[42] The intention in these cases is apparently to exclude acts which are not likely to endanger the *ship* – in the sense either that she is put in danger of sinking or grounding, or that the safety and lives of the passengers and crew or a significant proportion thereof are threatened by acts affecting the ship as an entity – but rather are acts involving isolated individuals which simply happen to be taking place on board her.

Sub-paragraph (e) of paragraph 1, concerning damage to or interference with navigational facilities, was included at the suggestion of New Zealand.[43] All navigational facilities, wherever located, are covered, and an offence is committed whenever a single ship likely to be endangered by such acts – or the *threat* of such acts (Art. 3(2)(c)) – is navigating or scheduled to navigate in the areas covered by Article 4. The term 'maritime navigational facilities' is not defined, and regard might usefully be paid to the interpretation of the equivalent term in the Montreal Convention.[44] It would appear to include, for example, buoys, lights, light-ships and radar beacons, but not normally port or harbour installations. It is unclear whether or not vessel traffic service or ship reporting systems are included.

Sub-paragraph (g) of paragraph 1 was retained largely at the insistence of the US delegation.[45] It is not entirely clear what degree of connection there must be between the injuring or killing and the commission or attempted commission of one of the other principal offences, but it proved difficult to find clearer wording. In cases of injury it seems that the degree of injury suffered need not necessarily be severe.[46]

Secondary offences

Article 3(2)(a) (on attempts) follows the precedents, but Article 3(2)(b) (on complicity) omits to make it an offence (as the precedents do) to be an accomplice of a person who *attempts* to commit one of the offences listed in paragraph 1. That sub-paragraph, in addition, expressly refers to a person who 'abets' the commission of such an offence, as well as to accomplices: certain delegations in whose legal systems the term 'accomplice' does not include an abettor insisted on this. Delegations whose legal systems include abettors among accomplices in general were careful to add the word 'otherwise', and it is unlikely that this addition will be permitted to affect the interpretation of the precedents adversely.

The Hostages Convention provides that a person commits an offence who seizes or detains and threatens to kill, injure or continue to detain another person in order to compel a third party to do or abstain from doing any act as a condition for that person's release (Art. 1(1)). The co-sponsors appear to have been influenced by this and included several references to threats in their preliminary drafts. The second preparatory meeting decided by an indicative vote to retain some references to threats, and the Chairman of the Whole proposed a new paragraph making it an offence to threaten to commit any of the offences set forth in Article 3(1) (b) and (c). At the diplomatic conference there was a large measure of support for its deletion, but this was opposed by some influential delegations. It was important to draft such a provision narrowly enough to include threats proper, but to exclude such offences as fraud, blackmail and bribery not properly covered by conventions of this type.[47] The French delegation asserted, moreover, that consistency with the French penal code required it to be expressed in terms not of a simple threat to carry out the acts in question, but as a threat to do so made in order to compel a person to carry out or refrain from carrying out a particular act.[48] Other delegations were, on the contrary, unable to accept a text which required such a condition. One delegation proposed a compromise text based upon Article 7(1) (e) (ii) of the Convention on the Physical Protection of Nuclear Material.[49] This proved acceptable to the French, but not to a third, delegation. The final wording (in Art. 3(2)(c)) is a compromise wording suggested by the United Kingdom, intended to leave the question whether or not the threat must be accompanied by a condition to national law. It was also decided at the diplomatic conference to add a (very restrictive) requirement that the threat should of itself be likely to endanger the safe navigation of the ship in question and, following indicative votes, to add the offence described in sub-paragraph (e) of paragraph 1 to the principal offences in relation to which the secondary offence may be committed. France, still not content, it appears, declared upon approving the Convention that it did not consider itself to be bound by the dispute-settlement provision, Art. 16, in respect of this paragraph.

The 'prosecute or extradite' system (Arts. 5 to 15)

The 'prosecute or extradite' machinery established by the IMO Convention is essentially the same as that of the precedents, except for the addition of Article 8 concerning the power of delivery. This article derives from the Tokyo Convention,[50] which is not a 'prosecute or extradite' treaty. Except in respect of this exception, changes to the wording of the precedents were minimized, and were not generally intended to import differences of substance.

Punishment (Art. 5)

The text of Article 5, which reproduces Article 2 of the Hostages Convention, was not altered at all during the negotiations. It is considered to cover both the concerns of those delegations which wished to make it clear that it was the right of States to determine what penalties were 'appropriate', and those which wished those penalties to be 'severe'.

Jurisdiction (Arts. 6 and 9)

Article 6 establishes two types of jurisdiction – obligatory and discretionary. Paragraph 1 provides that each State Party *shall* 'take such measures as may be necessary to establish its jurisdiction over the offences set forth in Article 3', when the offence is committed:

(a) against or on board a ship flying the flag of the State at the time the offence is committed; or

(b) in the territory of that State, including its territorial sea; or

(c) by a national of that State.

Paragraph 2 adds that it *may* also establish its jurisdiction over any such offence when:

(a) it is committed by a stateless person whose habitual residence is in that State; or

(b) during its commission a national of that State is seized, threatened, injured or killed; or

(c) it is committed in an attempt to compel that State to do or abstain from doing any act.

The Article is perhaps most closely modelled upon Article 5 of the Hostages Convention, although it lists more grounds for establishment of jurisdiction, especially discretionary jurisdiction, than that precedent, and adds an obligation to notify the Secretary-General of the IMO of the establishment of such discretionary jurisdiction (Art. 6(3)). It concerns only the establishment, and not the exercise, of jurisdiction. Article 9 was thus inserted upon a Dutch proposal to make it clear that the normal rules of international law on investigative and enforcement jurisdiction remain unaffected by the Convention.[51]

While paragraphs 1 and 2 of Article 6 concern the establishment of jurisdiction over offences *ab initio* ('primary jurisdiction'), paragraph 4 provides for the establishment of jurisdiction where the alleged offender is present in a State's territory and it does not extradite him to any of the States establishing jurisdiction in accordance with paragraphs 1 or 2 ('secondary jurisdiction'). Paragraph 3, moreover, provides for notifications which give States the opportunity to know which States have established discretionary jurisdiction; and paragraph 5 is a standard (and superfluous) provision in 'prosecute or extradite' conventions.

The Chairman was obliged to seek indicative votes on contentious points at the second preparatory session and at the diplomatic conference. At the first preparatory session The Netherlands delegation introduced a comprehensive redraft of the article and related provisions – the general effect of which would have been to reduce grounds for jurisdiction to the territoriality and nationality principles.[52] It was not, however, felt appropriate to redraft accepted language in this radical way, and only selective changes were made to the text, which are described below.

Obligatory jurisdiction (Art. 6(1))

Article 6(1)(a) takes into account changes in flag between the time of the offence and the application of the provisions of the Convention. The exact form to be taken by Article 6(1)(b) was left for decision by the diplomatic conference. In earlier drafts both 'territory' and 'territorial sea' were employed, but the final formula (proposed by the Soviet delegation) of 'territory . . . including (the) territorial sea', was agreed following informal consultations. It is not intended to suggest that the territorial sea is identical to land territory, nor to affect the regime of those waters.[53]

Discretionary jurisdiction (Art. 6(2))

Article 6(2)(a) derives from the Hostages Convention. It is necessary because the laws of some States do not permit the establishment of jurisdiction on the ground of habitual residence of a stateless person in that State. There was some opposition to its inclusion, but on the other hand there was also some support for its extension to *all* persons habitually resident in the State in question.

Article 6(2)(b) and (c) make provision for discretionary jurisdiction which can be justified on the basis of the 'passive personality' or the 'protective' principles of jurisdiction. Their inclusion among the grounds for discretionary jurisdiction, following a series of indicative votes, may be seen as a compromise between those who supported the inclusion of obligatory jurisdiction derived from the nationality of the victim or from coercion of a State and those who opposed any sort of jurisdiction on these grounds. Professor Halberstram suggests in her article[54] that their inclusion was a *sine qua non* to the USA.

The question was raised at the diplomatic conference whether the inclusion of grounds for discretionary jurisdiction did or did not merit consequential changes elsewhere (in particular to Art. 10), to reflect the fact that the different States involved in a case might have made different choices between the various grounds for the establishment of such jurisdiction – if establishing it at all. It is not made entirely clear what are the consequences of a request for extradition from a State which has established the relevant discretionary jurisdiction to a State which has not. Professor Halberstram records that, during the preparatory phase of the negotiations, one delegation:

> indicated that it might propose that the prosecute or extradite requirement apply only with respect to requests by states that assert jurisdiction under the mandatory provisions and that it did not apply to requests by states that assert jurisdiction under the optional provisions.[55]

As she explains, this would effectively have rendered Article 6(2) nugatory.[56] Towards the end of the diplomatic conference, moreover, the

Egyptian delegation introduced a proposal to permit States to make reservations with respect to paragraph 2. Even if this had been acceptable to the majority, its drafting would have been exceedingly complicated, and the proposal was not adopted by the hard-pressed conference.[57] There was in the end insufficient time to consider the issue in detail.

Finally, proposals to include the nationality or principal place of business of a 'demise-charterer in possession of the ship',[58] or a 'charterer of a bareboat chartered ship',[59] as a ground for the establishment of discretionary jurisdiction were ultimately defeated by an indicative vote at the diplomatic conference. Opponents feared an excessive proliferation (and thus clashes) of jurisdictions – in this case one based on private law concepts not readily accepted as relevant in the context of a public law convention.

Secondary jurisdiction (Art. 6(4))

A French proposal to restrict the scope of secondary jurisdiction under Article 6(4) to some only of the offences listed in Article 3[60] was withdrawn following an indicative vote at the diplomatic conference. This paragraph (as with its equivalents in the precedents[61]), ought not to be interpreted as imposing an obligation to prosecute only in the event that a request for extradition is received.

Custody and inquiry (Art. 7)

Article 7 is little different from the equivalent provisions in the precedents concerning the taking of measures to ensure the presence of an offender or alleged offender for the purpose of prosecution or extradition; the notification of measures to interested States and international organizations; and the rights of the person in custody. The procedural standard required is, as in the precedents, the national standard. The minor drafting changes are not intended to introduce changes of substance. The Article also reproduces Article 6(4) of the Hostages Convention, which states the existing law codified in Article 36(2) of the Vienna Convention on Consular Relations,[62] and which ensures that laws and regulations are adopted which give full effect to the purposes for which the rights under paragraph 3 are accorded.

The reference to 'territory' in Article 7(1) is intended to include the territorial sea of a State, but this is not to permit a coastal State to interfere with the innocent passage of foreign ships.

Power of delivery (Art. 8)

Article 8(1) of the Convention permits the master of a ship of a State Party to deliver to the authorities of any other State Party any person whom he has reasonable grounds to believe has committed an offence under Article

3. Article 8(3) obliges that other State, unless it considers that the Convention does not apply, to accept delivery and to proceed in accordance with the provisions of Article 7. The receiving State must give reasons for any refusal, and may in turn request the flag State of the ship to accept delivery of the person (Art. 8(5)). The master is also obliged to give the other State as much warning as possible, and to furnish its authorities with all the evidence pertaining to the offence in his possession (Art. 8(2) and (4)). The Article is loosely based upon Articles 9, 13 and 14 of the Tokyo Convention, and was adopted following informal consultations at the diplomatic conference.

The inclusion of a provision containing at least the substance of paragraphs (1) and (3) of Article 8[63] was called for out of a desire to avoid masters of ships which are far from or which never call at home ports (most notably flag of convenience or land-locked State ships) having to detain alleged offenders on board for long periods – a situation for which few ships are equipped.

The major disadvantage of such a provision, however, is the potentially politically sensitive consequences of placing the decision to choose the State of delivery in the hands of a private citizen and obliging that State to take delivery unless it considers the Convention to be inapplicable. Paragraphs 2[64] and 5 were thus added to the early proposed drafts as partial safeguards. Paragraph 4, moreover, is designed to facilitate the coastal State in proceeding further in accordance with the provisions of the Convention.

The appropriateness of such a provision in a 'prosecute or extradite' convention may be questioned. The right, moreover, of the receiving State under Article 14(1) of the Tokyo Convention to refuse to admit a non-national, a permanently resident offender or alleged offender, and to send him or her on to his or her State of nationality or to the State where he or she started their journey is replaced with a mere *permission*, in Article 8(5), to request the *flag State* to take delivery. It is to be wondered why the flag State is preferred to the States of nationality or of original embarcation of the delivered person. The saving for immigration laws in Article 14(2) of the Tokyo Convention is not reproduced, although it was not intended that the coastal State be obliged to consider the delivered person as admitted to its territory under its immigration laws. In addition, in neither Convention is the question of which State should bear the cost of on-delivery by the receiving State clarified.

Finally, it is not made clear whether it is under the law of the flag State or of the the receiving State that the evidence referred to in paragraph 4 must be lawfully in the master's possession.

Prosecution or extradition (Art. 10)

This is the key provision of the Convention. It is identical to Article 8 of the Hostages Convention, except that the first line of paragraph 1 refers to an 'offender' as well as to an 'alleged offender' and the last to 'other offence' instead of 'ordinary offence'. It is not intended, however, to differ in substance from the precedents.[65] Gillian White has written the following about the equivalent provision in the Hague Convention:

> Article 7 was the subject of a considerable controversy at the Diplomatic Conference. A number of States, including both the United States and the Soviet Union, argued that States should be under an obligation in every case either to extradite or prosecute the hijacker. However such a provision would have been unacceptable to many other States who considered that there might be exceptional cases where, perhaps for lack of evidence or for humanitarian reasons, the circumstances would not justify bringing a prosecution. Those States considered that, although cases where proceedings were not brought would be rare, they could not accept a fetter on the discretion enjoyed by their prosecution authorities to decide whether or not to prosecute in the light of all the facts of a case.[66]

Extradition (Art. 11)

Article 11(1) to (4) essentially reproduces Article 10 of the Hostages Convention and the equivalent provisions in the other precedents, and, like them, is not intended to affect any restrictions that might exist in a State's national laws on the extradition of offenders. Three paragraphs have been added however, which do not appear in the equivalent provisions in the precedents.

At the first preparatory session, the question arose of a system of priorities between different States making an extradition request, and the USSR introduced a proposal at the first preparatory session, with some support from The Netherlands, to establish a clear priority in favour of the flag State. This proved unacceptable to many States, for which it would cause difficulties in national law, and the sponsors introduced as a compromise a provision requiring a State Party considering requests for extradition to 'pay due regard' to the interests and responsibilities of the flag State (Art. 11(5)).

Articles 11(6) and (7) arose from the informal consultations conducted by the President of the diplomatic conference in relation to the draft preamble, draft article 11 and a proposed draft article 11A. Kuwait proposed the new draft article to provide for a political offence exception. One of the two alternative texts would have reproduced Article 9(1) of the Hostages Convention.[67] It seems that in view of the 'package deal' achieved by the informal consultations (see pp. 73–4 above), Kuwait did not insist on its proposal, but Article 11(6) and (7) were none the less inserted upon the insistence of another Arab delegation. They reproduce in essence Article 9(1)(b)(ii) and (2) of the Hostages Convention.

Paragraph 7 appears to do no more than state the *lex posterior* rule set out in Article 30 of the Vienna Convention on the Law of Treaties.

Duty to cooperate (Art. 12)

Article 12(1) is intended, like its equivalents in the precedents, to provide a duty to cooperate in supplying evidence – not only in connection with the trial of a case but also in connection with the proceedings leading up to a trial. The words 'assistance in obtaining' were inserted in order to stress that the duty was a continuing one throughout those proceedings.

The first sentence of Article 12(2) replaces the traditional language used in the precedents with language more closely conforming to Article 9(2) of the UN Convention on Torture 1985.[68] The second sentence was added in order to ensure that this change of wording did not result in the omission of an obligation of States not party to treaties on mutual judicial assistance to afford each other assistance in matters covered by the Convention in accordance with their national laws.

Cooperation in prevention of offences (Art. 13)

Article 13(1) is based on Article 4 of the Hostages Convention, but omits a subordinate clause: this omission was made on the understanding that it involved no departure from the substance of the precedent.

The co-sponsors' original version of Article 13(2), moreover, was based on Article 10(2) of the Montreal Convention, but it was replaced (at the suggestion of the Greek and Liberian delegations) with language derived from maritime treaties and felt to be more appropriate in the maritime context.[69] There appears to be little change in substance. The duty to release the vessel is not intended to result in major financial obligations for the port State.

Communication of information (Arts. 14 and 15)

Article 14 was based on and intended to have the same effect as Article 12 of the Montreal Convention. The same is true of Article 15 with respect to Article 13 of the Montreal and Article 7 of the Hostages Conventions. It is the IMO Secretary-General who is required to receive and communicate further the information in question.

Dispute settlement (Art. 16) and final clauses

Dispute settlement (Art. 16)

Article 16 is identical to Article 14 of the Montreal Convention or Article 16 of the Hostages Convention, except for two small drafting changes in paragraph 2 and the addition of the words 'within a reasonable time' in paragraph 1 to bring its language closer to the wording of the Manila Declaration on the Peaceful Settlement of International Disputes.[70]

Final clauses (Arts. 17–22)

The final clauses, except the provision for a revision conference which is standard IMO practice (Art. 20), were largely based on the equivalent provisions in the Hostages Convention.

The only truly contentious points were the numbers of States and the periods of time required before the Convention could enter into force or be denounced. The period of ninety days (specified in Article 18) in relation to entry into force and the period of one year (in Article 19) in relation to denunciation were shorter than the co-sponsors originally suggested. The number of ratifications, etc. required for the purposes of Article 18 (fifteen) was chosen at the diplomatic conference as a compromise solution between one delegation that wished for a minimum of twenty, and all other delegations, that were content with the figure of ten.

THE PROTOCOL

The final text of the Protocol emerged from intensive informal consultations between the representatives of twelve States[71] at the diplomatic conference. It follows very closely the pattern of the Convention. Article 1(1) of the Protocol applies Articles 5, 7 and 10 to 16 of the Convention *mutatis mutandis* to the offences listed in Article 2 of the Protocol – which parallel very closely the pertinent offences in Article 3 of the Convention, where they take place on board or against a platform located on the continental shelf of a State Party. In addition, Article 3 of the Protocol is identical *mutatis mutandis* to Article 6 of the Convention, except that the separate grounds for establishing obligatory jurisdiction based on registry of the ship and location within a State's territory are replaced with a single ground for such jurisdiction, based on the location of a platform on a State's continental shelf. Finally, Article 4 provides that 'Nothing in this Protocol shall affect in any way the rules of international law pertaining to fixed platforms located on the continental shelf'. This is perhaps the nearest equivalent to Article 9 of the Convention.

There is also an equivalent to Article 4(2) of the Convention in Article 1(2) of the Protocol, which was inserted during the diplomatic conference at the suggestion of the US delegation.[72] The Protocol thus applies to all offences against or on board installations located on a State's continental shelf, and to offences against or on board installations in a State's territorial sea or internal waters when the offender escapes abroad. It is noteworthy, especially with respect to narrow-shelf States, that no mention is made of installations in a State's Exclusive Economic Zone or equivalent.

The Preamble and the final clauses (Arts. 5 to 10 of the Protocol) also recall or reflect the provisions of the Convention. The periods of time specified in the final clauses are the same as those in the Convention, but the number of ratifications, etc. required for the Protocol to come into force is only three. The Protocol, however, 'shall not enter into force before the Convention has entered into force' (Art. 6(1)). Consideration of fixed platforms was, of course, very much secondary to that of ships. Indeed, two States[73] signing the Convention in Rome – including one of the co-sponsors of the Convention – declined to sign the Protocol in company with it.

CONCLUDING REMARKS: COMPARISON AND POSSIBLE CONFLICT WITH EARLIER CONVENTIONS

The IMO instruments, like the precedents, adopt a system of jurisdiction based on the principle of *aut dedere aut iudicare* – not one of universal jurisdiction. It is true that they go beyond the precedents in providing for additional offences not previously provided for, and for grounds for the establishment of both primary and secondary jurisdiction broader than the equivalent grounds in the precedents (as well as, of course, in including Art. 8 in the Convention).

Nevertheless, the scheme of the instruments is the same as that of the other global conventions. In particular, they do not displace the political offence exception in relation to the offences listed, or place greater emphasis on extradition in preference to submission for prosecution – as does at least one regional convention, the European Convention on the Suppression of Terrorism.[74]

The European Convention provides that each of the offences listed in Article 1 of that Convention, which include, for example, offences 'within the scope of' the aviation (and other) precedents, shall not, 'for the purposes of extradition between Contracting States', 'be regarded as a political offence or as an offence connected with a political offence or as an offence inspired by political motives'. The description of the offences in Article 1 of the European Convention overlaps to a limited degree with the descriptions of the offences provided for in the IMO instruments,[75] and Article 2 permits further overlap by allowing a State Party 'to apply Article 1 to any other "serious offence involving an act of violence . . . against the life, physical integrity or liberty of a person" and to any other "serious offence involving an act against property . . . if the act created a collective danger for persons"'.[76] Because, however, the European Convention does not provide for a procedure for concerted revision of the list of offences to which the political offence exception will not apply as between States Parties, the anomalous situation is likely to arise that many of the offences within the scope of the precedents will not be subject to such a defence and will be very likely (where the European Convention applies without reservation[77]) to result in *extradition* as between, for example, the United Kingdom and Germany, but most serious offences against or on board ships *will* be subject to such a defence and are not necessarily likely to result in extradition rather than submission for prosecution as between the same two countries. It would seem appropriate to revise the European Convention so as to include new offences 'within the scope' of the IMO instruments in the list in Article 1 of that Convention.

The partial overlap between the provisions of the IMO instruments and of certain of the precedents has been mentioned above (p. 71.). In this respect the absence of certain safeguards previously provided for, notably in the Hostages Convention, and the removal (by Art. 11(5)) of a small degree of the customary freedom of choice of the State holding the offender for extradition or submission for prosecution, might be thought likely to give rise to some conflict of conventions. In practice, in the author's opinion, this will not be the case.

The IMO instruments, like the aviation precedents, do not reproduce the following: the safeguard clause relating to treaties on asylum, appearing in Articles 15 of both the Hostages and the Internationally Protected Persons Conventions; the grounds for exception to the granting of extradition established in Article 9(1) of the Hostages Convention (except to the limited extent provided for by Art. 11(6) of the IMO Convention); and Article 12 of the Hostages Convention, concerning acts of hostage-taking prohibited by the Geneva Conventions of 1949[78] or the Additional Protocols thereto.[79] These omissions will not generally result in instances of submission for prosecution, extradition or granting of asylum which would not occur were such provisions included, including by the UK or France.

The provision on asylum just mentioned was reproduced in the co-sponsors' preliminary drafts of the Convention, but despite one delegation's concerns about possible conflicts of conventions, it was generally agreed that its omission would not affect the application of the laws on asylum. Article 11(6) and (7) of the IMO Convention does, moreover, substantially reproduce Articles 9(1)(b) and (2) of the Hostages Convention,[80] but the reproduction of that Article was not strictly necessary, because the provision of an option of submitting a case for possible prosecution in addition to the option of extradition is itself largely designed to avoid any suggestion of an obligation to extradite in the circumstances envisaged by that article.[81] In addition, the omission of an equivalent to Article 12 of the Hostages Convention produces no conflict of conventions, since, far from excluding certain acts carried out in pursuance of the right of self-determination from the scope of that Convention, it merely permitted alternative legal bases under different instruments for the same obligation to 'prosecute or extradite' when the acts in question were captured by the terms of more than one of the instruments mentioned.[82]

Finally, it should be pointed out that Article 11(5) of the IMO Convention does not establish a binding obligation, but only a discretion, to extradite to the flag State rather than another State, if extradition is the chosen course – nor, incidentally, does it indicate what weight to give to the interests of different flag States when several are involved in a single incident.

The IMO Convention and Protocol are thus two more steps in the process of modification by treaty by the international community of the international law rules governing criminal jurisdiction over foreigners in particular spheres of human activity threatened by terrorist acts. The instruments can be seen as a continuation of a theme: a 'sectoral' approach; the finely balanced *aut dedere, aut iudicare* scheme; and the specific enumeration of offences in preference to attempts to define terrorism or terrorist acts. The bloody attack upon the *City of Poros* tourist ferry in the Gulf of Aegina in July 1988[83] illustrates the continued danger of terrorist acts against ships. It is to be hoped that the IMO Convention will be an effective measure against the proliferation of such acts.

NOTES

*   The opinions expressed are the author's own and do not necessarily represent those of the FCO, which he represented at the diplomatic conference discussed herein.

1   *The Times*, 8 and 10 Oct. 1985, p. 1.

2   *The Times*, 12 Oct. 1985, p. 1. In addition, two of their accomplices were tried and convicted in Italy and four other offenders tried and convicted *in absentia*.

3   *Ibid.*

4   At the 2618th meeting of the Security Council on 9 Oct. 1985, the President issued a statement which, among other things, resolutely condemned 'this unjustifiable act of highjacking as well as other acts of terrorism, including hostage-taking': UN Doc. S/17554, 9 Oct. 1985.

5   UN General Assembly resolution 40/61, 9 Dec. 1985 (operative para. 13).

6   Those of Austria, China, France, the Gambia, Germany (GDR), Hungary, Italy, the Netherlands, Norway, Oman, Poland, the Seychelles, Spain, Sweden, Trinidad and Tobago and the UK. The text of the Convention is contained in IMO Doc. SUA/CONF/15/Rev. 1, 10 Mar. 1988.

7   See G. Plant, 'The Aviation and Maritime Security Act 1990', note in 1991 *Lloyds Maritime and Commercial Law Quarterly*, 44–51. Part II of the Act enacts the Convention quite faithfully, but there are a few changes: see *ibid.* at pp. 48–9.

8   IMO Doc. SUA/CONF/16/Rev. 2. 10 Mar. 1988. This also has thirteen parties.

9   The Convention for the Suppression of Unlawful Acts Against the Safety of Civil Aviation, done at Montreal, 23 Sept. 1971: UKTS No. 10 (1974); the Convention for the Suppression of Unlawful Seizure of Aircraft, done at The Hague, 16 Dec. 1970: UKTS No. 39 (1972).

10   The Protocol for the Suppression of Unlawful Acts of Violence at Airports Serving International Civil Aviation, Supplementary to the Convention for the Suppression of Unlawful Acts against the Safety of Civil Aviation, done at Montreal, 23 Feb. 1988: UKTS Misc. No. 6 (1988); Cmnd. 378.

11   The International Convention against the Taking of Hostages, done at New York, 18 Dec. 1979 to 31 Dec. 1980: UKTS No. 81 (1983) (Art. 5(1)(a)); the Convention on the Prevention and Punishment of Crimes against Internationally Protected Persons, including Diplomatic Agents, done at New York, 14 Dec. 1973 to 31 Dec. 1974: UKTS No. 3 (1980) (Art. 3(1)(a)); and the

Convention on the Physical Protection of Nuclear Material, done at New York and Vienna, 3 Mar. 1980: UKTS Misc. No. 27 (1980) (Art. 8(1)(a)).

12 The Hostages and Internationally Protected Persons Conventions were negotiated in the Sixth Committee of the UN General Assembly, the latter following preparatory work by the ILC, and the Protection of Nuclear Material Convention in the IAEA.

13 M. Halberstram, 'Terrorism on the high seas: the *Achille Lauro*, piracy and the IMO Convention on Maritime Safety' (1988) *American Journal of International Law*, 269–310.

14 The texts are contained in Annexes 1 and 2 to IMO Doc. PCUA 2/2, 20 Mar. 1987.

15 IMO Doc. SUA/CONF/RD/1 to 5, 1, 3 and 10 Mar. 1988.

16 Argentina, Austria, Bahamas, Brazil, Bulgaria, Canada, Chile, Costa Rica, Ecuador, France, Greece, Hungary, Israel, Italy, Jordan, Liberia, Morocco, Norway, Philippines, Sweden, Switzerland, Turkey and USA.

17 The same less Austria and Turkey. The numbers compare favourably with those for the Conventions on Hostages (seven) and Protected Persons (none), but less favourably with the Hague Convention (forty-nine), the Montreal Convention (thirty) and the Montreal Protocol (forty-seven).

18 The Final Act is contained in IMO Doc. SUA/CONF/17, 29 Mar. 1988. The signatories are listed in IMO Doc. SUA/CONF/18, 29 Mar. 1988. Cuba, Guinea, the Holy See, Panama, Qatar and Tunisia sent observers. The PLO also sent an observer. Also present were representatives from the UN, UNHCR, UNIDROIT, the International Chamber of Shipping (ICS) and the Baltic and International Maritime Council (BIMCO).

19 Para. 23 of the Final Act, *ibid*.

20 The Chairman of the Committee of the Whole, Mr Kirsch, for example, had arrived hot foot from chairing the diplomatic conference on the ICAO Protocol in Montreal.

21 This provision has the advantage of obviating the need to convene a diplomatic conference in order to amend either instrument, as was necessary in relation to the Montreal Convention. Any review conference will be held within the structure of the IMO. The 'IMO factor' also ensured that the definition of 'ship' included 'dynamically supported craft' (IMO-accepted terminlogy for hovercraft and hydrofoils).

22 Any reference to an article in this text which does not specify that it is a reference to either a Convention or a Protocol article should, unless it is indicated otherwise, be taken as a reference to the Convention and also, where appropriate, to that article as extended *mutatis mutandis* to the Protocol.

23 See Halberstram, *op. cit.* note 13, pp. 305–8.

24 IMO Doc. SUA/CONF/CW/WP. 13, 3 Mar. 1988.

25 IMO Doc. SUA/CONF/CW/WP. 7/Rev. 1, 3 Mar. 1988.

26 This proposal, also made at the preparatory sessions, was introduced to the diplomatic conference in IMO Doc. SUA/CONF/CW/WP. 14, 3 Mar. 1988.

27 IMO Doc. SUA/CONF/12, Jan. 1988.

28 For a discussion of the virtues and vices of the 'inductive approach' see G. Levitt, 'Is terrorism worth defining?' (1986) XIII *Ohio Northern University Law Review*, 97 at 97 and 108–12.

29 The FRG delegation had suggested in IMO Doc. SUA/CONF/WP. 11, 2 Mar. 1988, that a preambular provision would suffice to exclude such acts.

30 See Arts. 1 and 3 of the co-sponsors' preliminary drafts; IMO Doc. PCUA 1/3, 3 Feb. 1987; and IMO Doc. PCUA 2/2, Annex 1, 20 Mar. 1987; and Arts. 1 and 4 of IMO Doc. PCUA 2/5, 2 June 1987. The three preliminary drafts employed a mixed method. The working group at the first preparatory meeting considered

several variations before recommending a mixed approach in IMO Doc. PCUA 1/WP.13, 5 Mar. 1987. The revised text (PCUA 2/2) similarly contained a definition of 'ship', a negative listing of ships not covered by the Convention in draft Art. 2, and a mixed approach to geographical scope. As late as the diplomatic conference a new approach was proposed by the Bulgarian and Ukrainian delegations omitting a geographical-scope provision and simply providing that the Convention was to apply to the listed offences in relation to any ship, with the exception of those listed in Art. 2 as adopted: SUA/CONF/CW/WP.24/Rev. 1, 4 Mar. 1988.

31 Delegations suggested many examples of types of vessels which might be excluded from the scope of the Convention, although not all delegations would agree that they are in fact all excluded: floating restaurants; light ships; mothballed ships; ships undergoing repairs in port; ships being fitted out for a voyage; ships in the course of reconstruction; ships in port for a substantial period with no planned voyage; ships on trial runs; ships not operating because of lack of a licence to sail, certification or crew; and ships being kept in readiness for commercial operations by skeleton crews.

32 This was done on the assumption that Art. 4 (geographical scope) would be suitably worded.

33 IMO Doc. SUA/CONF/CW/WP.18, 3 Mar. 1988.

34 Vienna Convention on the Law of Treaties, done at Vienna, 23 May to 30 Nov. 1969 and New York, 1 Dec. 1969 to 30 Apr. 1970, UKTS No. 58 (1980).

35 UN Convention on the Law of the Sea, done at Montego Bay, 10 Dec. 1982: UKTS Misc. No. 11(1983); Cmnd. 8941.

36 See note 30.

37 The whole Convention applies and not just parts of it, as in the aviation precedents. Proposals which, if adopted, would have excluded the application of Arts. 5 and 13–15 of the Convention were not pressed at the diplomatic conference.

38 Such terms as 'intends to cross' (IMO Doc. PCUA 1/3, 3 Feb. 1987) or 'in the light of its destination has to cross' would have been more subjective. It is interesting to note that Art. 4(2)(a) of the Montreal Convention refers to 'the place of take-off or landing, actual or *intended* of an aircraft'.

39 Efforts at the second preparatory meeting to accommodate one delegation's desires to include unlawful acts on board or against foreign flag vessels engaged in cabotage on the Great Lakes System led to an arbitrary distinction being made in the draft convention between 'foreign' and 'domestic' local cabotage, which was considered unacceptable by two delegations, including that of France (IMO Doc. SUA/CONF/6/Corr.1, 29 Feb. 1988).

40 Perhaps the best of these was made by The Netherlands delegation in IMO Doc. SUA/CONF/CW/WP.6, 1 Mar. 1988.

41 The Convention on the Territorial Sea and the Contiguous Zone, done at Geneva, 29 Apr. 1958: UKTS No. 3 (1965); and UNLOSC, *op. cit.* note 35, Art. 4.

42 Sub-para. (d) provides that the safe navigation of a ship can either actually be endangered or merely be likely to be endangered. The term 'the safe navigation of the ship' was preferred to alternative proposed wording such as 'safety', 'seaworthiness', 'safety of those on board' and 'capability of the ship to operate'.

43 IMO Doc. SUA/CONF/CW/WP.1, 1 Mar. 1988. France, in particular, opposed it: IMO Doc. SUA/CONF/6, 21 Dec. 1987.

44 The Montreal Protocol refers to 'facilities of an airport' (Art. II(1)(b)). '(A)ir navigation facilities' used by aircraft in flight are already covered by the Montreal Convention, and it may be assumed that the new term in the Protocol excludes them. This new term is undefined but is assumed to include at least

certain public parts of an air terminal, which are arguably the nearest aviation equivalents to harbours and harbour installations.

45 Halberstram, *op. cit.* note 13, pp. 293–5, gives her version of the reasons motivating the US delegation.

46 Lack of support for inserting the word 'severely' was shown by an indicative vote.

47 It was not included in the Montreal Protocol, because the ICAO Sub-Committee charged with the preparation of the draft instrument feared that the differences between the Montreal and Hostages Conventions could 'lead to difficult problems of conflicts of conventions', in particular in determining which one of them was *lex specialis*: Report of the Sub-Committee: ICAO Doc. LC/SC-VIA, Pt II, Montreal, Jan. 1987, p. 11, para. 14.7.

48 IMO Doc. SUA/CONF/CW/WP.17, 3 Mar. 1988.

49 *Op. cit.* note 11. The proposed wording was as follows:
    (c) threatens to commit any of the offences set forth in paragraph 1, sub-paragraphs (b) and (c), with the purpose of obliging a physical or legal person, an International Intergovernmental Organisation or a state to carry out any action or refrain from any such action, if that threat is likely to endanger the safety of maritime navigation.

50 Convention on Offences and Certain Other Acts Committed on board Aircraft, done at Tokyo, 14 Sept. 1963: UKTS No. 126 (1969).

51 IMO Doc. PCUA 1/WP.3, 3 Mar. 1987 (draft art. 6) and earlier undated *aide-memoire* addressed to the co-sponsors after their preparation in April 1987 of their revised draft (PCUA 2/2).

52 IMO Doc. PCUA 1/WP3, *ibid.*

53 The word 'including' is intended to suggest that, but for its presence, the territorial sea would be excluded from the meaning of 'territory'. The identical phrase was also used in Art. II of the International Convention on Civil Liability for Oil Pollution Damage (done at Brussels, 29 Nov. to 31 Dec. 1969: UKTS No. 106(1975)) and Art. 3(1) of the International Convention on the Establishment of an International Fund for Compensation for Oil Pollution Damage (done at Brussels, 18 Dec. 1971: UKTS No. 95 (1976)).

54 *Op. cit.* note 13, pp. 296–302.

55 *Ibid.*, p. 300.

56 *Ibid.*

57 IMO Doc. SUA/CONF/CW/WP.35/Rev.1, 8 Mar. 1988. The equivalent proposal in relation to the Protocol was in IMO Doc. SUA/CONF/CW/WP.38, 8 Mar. 1988. The Egyptian delegation, it appears, had Art. 6(2)(c) of the Convention particularly in mind.

58 Wording included in the final draft of the Convention: IMO Doc. PCUA 2/5, Annex 1, 2 June 1987.

59 Wording proposed by Iran in IMO Doc. SUA/CONF/CW/WP.3, 1 Mar. 1988.

60 IMO Doc. SUA/CONF/CW/WP.16/Rev.1, 3 Mar. 1988.

61 See Halberstram, *op. cit.* note 13, p. 297, and R. Rosenstock, 'International Convention Against the Taking of Hostages: another international community step against terrorism' (1980) 9 *Denver Journal of International Law and Policy*, 169 at 181.

62 Vienna Convention on Consular Relations, done at Vienna, 24 Apr. 1963: UKTS No. 14 (1973).

63 Spain proposed an article of a single paragraph providing for a right of the master of a ship to deliver and an obligation on the coastal State to proceed in accordance with the provisions of Art. 7 (IMO Doc. PCUA 1/WP.10, 3 Mar. 1987). Proposals by Greece and Liberia (IMO Doc. SUA/CONF/CW/WP.12, 2 Mar. 1988) and France (IMO Doc. SUA/CONF/6, 21 Dec. 1987) added a duty on the coastal State to take delivery.

64   Para. 2 derives from proposals by France (IMO Doc. SUA/CONF/6, *ibid.*) and China (IMO Doc. SUA/CONF/CW/WP.20, 3 Mar. 1988).

65   G. White 'The Hague Convention for the Suppression of Unlawful Seizure of Aircraft' (1971) 6 *Review of the International Commission of Jurists*, 38 at 42, and the *Yearbook of the ILC of 1972* (vol. I), pp. 196–210, 218–24 and 241–2.

66   White, *ibid.*, p. 42.

67   Interestingly, Argentina made a proposal to the opposite effect which attracted little support: IMO Doc. SUA/CONF/CW/WP.2, 1 Mar. 1988.

68   Convention against Torture and Other Cruel, Inhuman or Degrading Treatment or Punishment, done at New York, 4 Feb. 1985: UKTS Misc. No. 12(1985).

69   IMO Doc. PCUA 1/WP.7, 3 Mar. 1987. The language was derived from two treaties: Art. 7(1) of the International Convention for the Prevention of Pollution from Ships, done at London, 8 Oct. to 2 Nov. 1973: UKTS Misc. No. 26 (1974); and Part A, Reg. 19(f) of the Annex to the Safety of Life at Sea Convention, done at London, 1 Nov. 1974 to 1 July 1975: UKTS No. 46 (1980).

70   The Manila Declaration on Peaceful Settlement of International Disputes, adopted as UN General Assembly resolution 37/10 (1982). The words were added upon a Bulgarian proposal: IMO Doc. PCUA 1/WP.16, 5 Mar. 1987.

71   Australia, Canada, China, Denmark, FRG, Iran, Italy, Netherlands, Norway, Spain, UK and USA.

72   IMO Doc. SUA/CONF/CW/WP.9, 2 Mar. 1988.

73   Austria and Turkey.

74   The European Convention on the Suppression of Terrorism among Member States of the Council of Europe, done at Strasbourg, 2 Jan. 1977: U.K.T.S. No.93 (1978).

75   See Michael C. Wood, 'The European Convention on the Suppression of Terrorism' (1981) Y.B. European L. 307, 318.

76   *Ibid.*, pp. 319–320.

77   France having (unlike the UK) reserved the right to refuse extradition in accordance with Art. 13(1) of the European Convention is more likely to opt for prosecution of such an alleged offender whose extradition is requested by the UK, whereas the UK is more likely to comply with a French request for extradition of such an alleged offender in its custody than itself to commence prosecution proceedings.

78   Conventions for the Amelioration of the Condition of the Wounded and Sick of Armed Forces in the Field, The Amelioration of the Condition of Wounded, Sick and Shipwrecked Members of Armed Forces at Sea, Relative the the Treatment of Prisoners of War and Relative to the Protection of Civilian Persons in Time of War, done at Geneva, 12 Aug. 1949: U.K.T.S. No.39 (1958).

79   Additional Protocols I and II to the Conventions, *ibid.*, done at Geneva, 10 June 1977. U.K.T.S. No.19 (1977).

80   Art. 11(6) is, however, not expressed in mandatory terms, and it cannot be read, as Rosenstock (*op. cit.* note 61, p. 183) suggests Art. 9(1)(b)(ii) of the Hostages Convention can with a view to the provision concerning the International Committee of the Red Cross Art. 6(5) of the Hostages Convention), since this is not reproduced in the IMO Convention.

81   Rostenstock, *supra*, at pp. 181–183.

82   *Ibid.*, pp. 183–185. See also Libyan proposal CW/WP.15/Rev.1, 4 Mar. 1988.

83   *The Times*, 12 July 1988, p. 1.

6 Cooperation between Member States of the European Community in the fight against terrorism

Claude Gueydan

During the last two decades European cooperation in the fight against terrorism has often been mentioned as a vital necessity in the light of the acceleration in international trade. It should however be recognized that cooperation like this concerns areas of law which touch the very heart of our countries' so-called sovereign powers. It is not easy to separate cooperation between States against terrorism from worldwide collaboration against crime. The terrorist – not usually over-concerned with the methods used to achieve his desired goals – will in fact take advantage of all the weaknesses which exist in the legal systems and police organizations of each country. These issues generate feelings which are difficult to overcome, and attempting to address them can provoke some very powerful objections. Additional problems then arise which cannot be resolved in the short term.

The continent of Europe has become an area of very active circulation in people and goods. The prospect of the creation of a large internal market and of European union, the growth and modernization of methods of transport, together with a continuing increase in the flow of trade, all result in problems of security. Europe is in fact a fragile, sensitive zone, where terrorism may result in extensive damage to life and to the economy. It is a region rich in industrial sites which are difficult to make completely secure. Dense urbanization facilitates movement of illegal immigrants and territorial divisions between countries prevent groups of organized criminals or terrorists from being pursued as effectively as is necessary.

Europe is also an area where people persecuted in their own countries can find a welcome, refuge and asylum. The relative economic prosperity attracts a growing number of different groups of people. The liberalization of Eastern Europe has added new movements of population to the usual influx from the South and from Africa. Terrorist groups take advantage of this immigration by infiltrating some of their members whenever they can; we have seen that diplomatic and consular staff posted to our countries have occasionally, particularly in France and the United Kingdom, been involved in assisting terrorism.

Europe is the arena preferred by international terrorism as, during 1983–1986, nearly 40 per cent of the 3,000 terrorists offences committed took place on European soil.[1]

International organization of the fight against terrorism is made even more difficult because of diversification in the types of subversion. In fact, terrorism exists in various forms.[2]

To combat terrorism, the States of Europe have put into place at national level organizations which are often complex, and which involve several ministries (e.g. in France the Ministry of the Interior and the Ministry of Defence) and various services. The complexity of these national organizations is not a sign of inefficiency.[3] The fight against terrorism requires several levels of information, of specialization and of response backing each other up or complementing one another. It is the same at the international level, where countries have, to start with, put into place a series of bilateral or multilateral cooperation agreements with the countries sharing their borders.[4]

These agreements, although necessary, have proved to be inefficient in combating modern forms of terrorism. They have not always been satisfactorily applied, due to the existence of differing national policies. Moreover, nearly all of them include safeguard clauses which allow countries to refuse totally or partially to cooperate when an issue or matter could undermine national interests.[5]

In order to stimulate regional cooperation, various informal or ad hoc intergovernmental groups have been created either during the course of international meetings or in response to a sudden increase in terrorist acts. Above all they make it possible to coordinate decisions at operational level and to facilitate the transmission of sensitive information. Their work is often confidential.[6]

In all the systems for combating terrorism reviewed above, each country retains the power within its own territory to specify appropriate laws for the resolution of the problems which it encounters. Confronted with practical limits, with an increase in new forms of terrorism and at times under pressure from public opinion, the countries have agreed to attempt to harmonize their national laws by entering into multilateral European Conventions within the framework of the Council of Europe or the European Community.

The systems provided for by the Convention applying the Schengen Agreement or by the Treaty of Maastricht pave the way for a regulatory regime which will be much more independent of national legislation and national rights.

In a Europe without borders, the advent of a European system of law and order implies that terrorists perceive themselves as being up against a 'bastion' of unvarying regulation within a wide area, and that they cannot take advantage of more permissive legislation in one country to protect their possible fall-back positions. It also assumes that each Member State accepts that its rights be limited to such restrictions as are 'necessary in a democratic society' within the meaning of the European Convention on Human Rights.[7]

Furthermore, a series of multilateral conventions has been drawn up within the framework of the Council of Europe and put before the twenty-seven Member States, and from time to time other countries, for signature and ratification. All these conventions concern criminal law in general; only one specifically mentions terrorism.

This set of conventions was prepared by committees of the Council's experts, at the request of certain Member States or of study groups. They form a legal arsenal capable of improving the fight against terrorism.[8]

A European Committee on Crime Problems (ECCP) has been created within the framework of the Council of Europe. The various conventions hand over responsibility to the Committee for ensuring that they are applied, and if necessary, for facilitating the amicable settlement of any difficulty in their operation.[9] The ECCP is composed of qualified individuals from the various Member States; it can resolve any problems encountered in the interpretation of the conventions and can also draft proposals – addressed to the Committee of Ministers – for the amendment or completion of any clause of a convention currently in force.

To complete this set of conventions, the Convention for the Protection of Human Rights and Fundamental Freedoms of 1950 should be mentioned, as well as the supervision of its application by the Court and by the European Commission on Human Rights.[10]

These treaties, drawn up from time to time, according to the opportunities and wishes of the moment, always include limitation clauses allowing a country to refuse to cooperate. This element of flexibility in the conventions is necessary on account of the geographical area concerned and the disparity of Member States' legal systems.[11] These many restrictions make it all too easy for countries which are parties to the conventions to avoid the necessary obligations. The grounds for a refusal to cooperate, which are practically the same in all the conventions, envisage the case where the measure sought is contrary to the fundamental principles of the legal system of the country, or where it risks undermining sovereignty, law and order, or other essential interests of the country, or where it is based on considerations of race, religion, nationality or political opinion.

Even though they do not refer specifically to terrorism, all these conventions make it easier to prosecute and sentence those who commit offences of a terrorist nature. There is, however, a particular convention in this field – the European Convention for the Suppression of Terrorism. This was signed at Strasbourg on 27 January 1977.[12] It has been ratified by twenty-two Members of the Council of Europe, including all twelve Member States of the European Community. This convention was drafted in response to the increase in the number of terrorist threats in Europe during the mid-1970s. It combines in a single legal document several areas of cooperation which until then were covered by various rarely applied agreements.[13]

The first area of cooperation concerns extradition. Articles 1 and 2 of the Convention list the offences which countries party to the Convention will no longer consider as 'political offences'. Among those listed are in particular: the unlawful seizure of aircraft; serious offences such as an attack against the life, physical integrity or liberty of internationally protected persons; offences involving kidnapping, the taking of a hostage or serious unlawful detention; and offences involving the use of a bomb, grenade, rocket, automatic firearm or letter or parcel bombs, if this use puts people in danger.

On assessing the nature of an offence, the country in question undertakes to take into account the following points: whether the offence has presented a collective danger to life, to physical integrity or liberty of persons; whether it has affected persons disassociated from the factors which motivated it; and whether cruel and vicious means have been used in carrying it out. The main interest of this Convention lies in the fact that the criteria above for determining which offences constitute acts of terrorism are specifically listed. In relation to all such offences, this ought to make the extradition of offenders and accomplices easier between countries which are party to the Convention. Moreover, contrary provisions in any previous treaties on this subject are modified by the new Convention.

Another area of cooperation concerns maximum mutual assistance in criminal proceedings relating to the offences defined in Articles 1 and 2 of the Convention. Contracting States not wishing to extradite the author of an offence are under an obligation to take all necessary measures to establish that their courts have jurisdiction to deal with the matter and to start proceedings in accordance with the appropriate national criminal procedure.[14]

Finally, where no amicable settlement has been reached under the aegis of the European Committee on Crime Problems, an obligatory procedure is specified in Article 10 for resolving disagreements between countries party to the Convention, in relation to its interpretation or its application.[15]

The positiveness of the system thus established has been called into doubt because ten countries, on ratification of the Convention, issued a reservation based on Article 13. This is the case for the Republic of France which reserves the right to refuse extradition in connection with any offence which it considers as political or inspired by political motives. In addition, the French Government accompanied its ratification with a declaration specifying that the application of the Convention should not result in undermining the right of asylum, and that it must respect the fundamental principles of French criminal law and the French Constitution.[16] This reservation has been criticized. During the debate on ratification in the French Parliament, M. Foyer stated that recourse to a reservation was an extremely serious matter, and that, quite apart from any legal analysis, he could see little political point in ratifying a Convention which would not be binding in any case.[17] One certainly cannot dispute that, by use of reservations and unilateral declarations, large parts of the system of protection have become excluded.[18]

France's ratification of the Convention ten years after signing it, and not long after the wave of bloody terrorist attacks in Paris in September 1986, was considered to be more of a psychological or political gesture towards public opinion than a real desire to be bound by a restricting and solemn international agreement. Certain authors consider that the agreement is marked by ambiguity: 'the Convention forms part of a general tendency to self-persuasion by European societies, in which they insist that their fears and impotence in the face of terrorist violence are being screened by a legal shield'.[19]

For others, the ratification is the result of a development in doctrine and caselaw in respect of terrorism: according to this, it is implicitly admitted that 'an offence can no longer be accepted as being political in nature when the criminal acts committed are so serious that the alleged political end cannot justify the use of methods considered unacceptable'.[20]

One must qualify one's appraisal of the system of conventions organized within the framework of the Council of Europe: to those who 'pose the question of the usefulness of these multilateral conventions, which often create quite a stir, and of which the contents leave an impression of emptiness',[21] it should be pointed out that the system at least exists and that the fight against international terrorism in the world today calls for modern and efficient methods and the establishment of a common policy in respect of crime.

Moreover, this system of conventions is just the limited product of a much more ambitious programme, that of the European Judicial Area, which was first conceived in the context of the European Economic Community.[22]

The powers of the Community do not extend to the field of criminal law. It therefore became traditional to use the framework of the Council of Europe as well as bilateral agreements to develop cooperation in this field. After 1970, matters progressed with the setting up of European Political Cooperation, which in turn led to the institutionalization of the European Council in 1974. Many initiatives were to develop within this new framework.

POLITICAL AND INTER-GOVERNMENTAL COOPERATION IN COMBATING TERRORISM

The European Communities started to concern themselves with combating terrorism several years after the United Kingdom entered the Common Market. It was in fact the British Government, under pressure from IRA terrorism, which proposed to the European Council in Rome on

2 December 1975 a resolution concerning the study of problems linked to the maintenance of law and order. This initiative was accepted and resulted in a first programme of cooperation in the fight against international terrorism and organized crime. The programme was adopted by the Ministers of the Interior of the nine countries during their meeting in Luxembourg in June 1976. However, it was above all at a meeting in London on 1 June 1977 that ministers decided to adopt a series of practical measures. These included the exchange of information on terrorist activities, techniques to be adopted in order to face up to terrorist acts, control of arms trafficking, exchange of police personnel, and the protection of the safety of civil aviation.[23]

The spectacular increase in terrorist operations in Europe – particularly the kidnapping of M. Schleyer, the President of the German employers' federation, and the hijacking of a Lufthansa Boeing – brought about an awareness of the need for greater cooperation, and indeed the need to draw up a minimum number of common rules. At the signature of the two European Conventions on extradition and on the suppression of terrorism, the French Government made a political statement, refusing to participate in the cooperation required by the conventions on the grounds that there was too much disparity, and no real cohesion, between the nineteen countries who were adherents at that time. President Valéry Giscard d'Estaing therefore put forward the idea of a 'European judicial area' within the more restricted framework of the European Economic Community, at the European Council held in Brussels in December 1977.[24] This project fits into the dynamic of European union and was in fact aimed at stimulating the process of integration which had been blocked since the Tindemans report had been set aside several months before.[25] The President proposed that a new step toward the organization of a European Union be taken. He stated that the Treaties of Paris and Rome had laid the foundations of an economic area, but that the people of Europe realized that European integration must not be limited to this. The President considered that the construction of European union ought to encompass a new concept, that of a judicial area. He suggested that the nine Member States put in place the first element of a single Judicial Area by the adoption of a convention for automatic extradition, and appropriate guarantees, in the case of particularly serious crimes regardless of their motives.

The project presented on this occasion listed five areas of cooperation in relation to crime: the drawing up of a convention on extradition; the improvement of mutual assistance in criminal matters; the establishment of a procedure for the transfer within Europe of criminal proceedings; recognition of the international validity of criminal judgments; and the establishment of a procedure for the transfer of prisoners.[26] These propositions were not particularly innovative, as a legal document already existed in respect of a number of the points, in the form of a Council of Europe convention. The development and application of these proposals within the framework of the Community was to be just as difficult; the question of the creation of a European Judicial Area touches the very heart of national sensitivities.

The European Council of April 1978 decided to increase the cooperation of the Nine in protecting their societies against terrorist violence, and to ask the Ministers of Justice to make some concrete proposals.

Since July 1976, a group of civil servants from the various Ministries of Justice had already been working on drafts of the convention on the prevention of serious crime. The assassination of President Aldo Moro by the Red Brigades in May 1978 led to an increase in the work of the experts, whilst the nine Member States stepped up their declarations on terrorism.[27] The 'incantatory' quality of these declarations requires no further proof, for they did not result in a single agreement legally binding at Community level. Are these declarations not really intended simply to convince public opinion that politicians at the highest level are concerned at the rising tide of terrorism?

The only concrete, though limited, result of this work has been the Agreement concerning the Application of the European Convention on the Suppression of Terrorism, signed in the name of political cooperation by the Ministers of Justice of the nine Member States, at a meeting in Dublin on 4 December 1979.[28]

This agreement, first proposed by Belgium, had the aim of making the Strasbourg Convention of 27 January 1977 applicable between the Member States of the EEC, without some Member States (France fell into this category at the time) having to become a party to the Convention. In short, it was a matter of nine countries doing what it was impossible to achieve with twenty-one. The two documents are similarly organized. By way of exception to the traditional principle of non-extradition of political criminals, Member States are forbidden to refuse extradition on the grounds of the political nature of an offence when the offence figures on a list of particularly serious offences. In the case of extradition being refused, the Member State concerned is under an obligation to take criminal proceedings before the competent authorities by virtue of the principle *aut dedere aut judicare* (transfer or prosecute), already evoked by other conventions binding on France. The method of reserves is also similar to that of the Strasbourg Convention.

For France, the ratification of the Dublin Agreement was for a long time dependent upon the outcome of a second draft agreement on mutual assistance in criminal matters, proposed within the context of the European judicial area. The text of this latter Convention had been presented to the Conference of Ministers of Justice held in Rome on 19 January 1980. The Netherlands refused to sign this second agreement as it considered that it was more appropriate to deal with mutual assistance in criminal matters within the framework of the Council of Europe. As a result, the talks came to a standstill and the draft agreement was withdrawn. Faced with the successful ratification of the European Convention on the Suppression of Terrorism by the Member States of the Council of Europe, and with the upsurge in international terrorism from 1986 onwards, the French Government felt unable to remain isolated for much longer and decided in 1987 to ratify the Strasbourg and Dublin agreements at the same time.

The Dublin Agreement had still not been ratified by all the Member States of the EEC, and was not in force, as at the beginning of 1993;[29] it is today practically without interest, due to the success of the ratification of the European Convention on the Suppression of Terrorism.

A relaunch of the French project of a European judicial area was however proposed by M. Badinter at the Conference of Ministers of Justice of the Ten on 25 October 1982. The first draft of the European Convention on Mutual Assistance in Criminal Matters was improved to reinforce the protection of human rights and was completed by the proposal to create a 'European Criminal Court'. It would be obligatory to open proceedings in this Court against those accused of offences whenever extradition had been refused and the country in question was not competent to take proceedings itself.

These last proposals were not accepted, due to opposition from Belgium, The Netherlands and the United Kingdom. This set-back tolled the death-knell of the French idea of a European judicial area, and the debates on ratification of the Treaty of Maastricht clearly show the present obstacles to starting a process of legal integration in this field. Is it necessary to wait for the next upsurge of terrorism to progress further? Will the intentions of the Member States of the European Community regarding criminal matters one day become binding legal agreements?

A second revival of cooperation in criminal matters was proposed by Italy in 1985, when it held the Presidency of the Community. The group of experts in the field of judicial cooperation was reactivated on this occasion and proposed various new texts.[30]

All these new Conventions had been prepared by the Working Party on Judicial Cooperation and were presented for signature within the framework of the Conference of Ministers of Justice of the twelve Member States of the Community. This 'Conference' should not be confused with that of the *Council of Ministers* of the EEC which, on the same day, brings together the same Ministers of Justice but which has a different sphere of activity and a different agenda.[31]

The limits of the collaborative framework chosen to develop European criminal law have been clearly shown. This cooperation – on the fringes of the treaties establishing European union – in fact remains marked by the desire to work solely within an inter-governmental system.[32] The legal documents drawn up are international treaties, autonomous in relation to European Community law: the settlement of differences, when provided for, does not refer to a legal settlement or even to a possible interpretation by the Court of Justice of the European Community but instead to an arbitration procedure.[33]

European political cooperation, although established in the EEC system by the Single European Act of 17 and 28 February 1986, thus results in a system of extra-community cooperation under the pretext that the powers concerned are outside the sphere of the EEC.

It was also within the context of political cooperation that the European Council in Rome of 1 and 2 December 1975 accepted the British Prime Minister's proposal that those ministers responsible for matters of domestic security (depending on the country, the Minister of the Interior and/or the Minister of Justice) meet on a regular basis to discuss questions which arise during the performance of their responsibilities, and particularly in the field of public law and order.

The Ministers' first conference took place in Luxembourg on 29 June 1976. It was named 'TREVI' in memory of a famous fountain in Rome and by the contraction of the words 'Terrorism', 'Radicalism', 'Extremism' and 'International Violence'. The conference – an instrument of intergovernmental cooperation in police affairs – set up certain bodies: to start with, four groups of experts were given the responsibility of preparing work and drawing up proposals.

- The TREVI 1 Group is in charge of combating terrorism. This group set up a communications network which allows information to be transferred rapidly and safely by liaison officers on exchange between the partners.
- The TREVI 2 Group is in charge of exchange of information relating to the maintenance of law and order, the training of police staff and technical aspects of operations.
- The TREVI 3 Group was created in 1986 in order to coordinate strategies regarding the fight against organized crime and the traffic of narcotics. The Secretary General of Interpol has the status of an observer in this group, which should make coordination between the two organizations easier.
- The TREVI 1992 Group was created in 1989 to study the consequences of the removal of controls at borders within the EC.

The studies and the conclusions of these four working parties are sent to a committee of ministerial civil servants made up of the Director Generals, or the heads of Police Divisions, of the relevant ministries. The Committee draws up propositions which are then submitted to ministers. To respond to the criticisms of the European Parliament, a member of the Commission has, since the June 1991 meeting in Luxembourg, participated in the work of the ministers.[34] The meetings of these various authorities take place every six months. According to experts, this TREVI conference has proved to be a meeting place which is useful both politically and technically.[35] However, because of the secret nature of its activities it is not possible to determine with any certainty exactly how efficient it is.

At its meeting in Luxembourg on 28 and 29 June 1991, the European

Council requested the ministers responsible for domestic security to prepare a report on the creation of a European Office of Police (EUROPOL). This project had been proposed by the German Government which wanted the creation of an equivalent of the Federal Police (FBI) of the United States. The report, drawn up in the context of the TREVI Conference, was submitted to the European Council at Maastricht. It provides for setting up the first body to be specialized in the matter of drugs, the European Drugs Unit (EDU). A ministerial agreement for the creation of this centre and its situation is in the course of preparation.[36] The EUROPOL Office, which was taken up in the Treaty of Maastricht, has been made concrete since 4 September 1992 by the formation of a team of fifteen police officers, under German presidency, working in the headquarters of the Schengen system (SIS) in Strasbourg. It has the task of preparing and defining methods of action, which are initially to be limited to a system of information exchange working in collaboration with the similar structure in the SIS.[37]

One should also mention the creation in 1980 of an informal working party on coordination in the field of the suppression of terrorism. Twice a year, this group brings together those who are in charge of combating terrorism in each of the Member States of the Community. The cooperation by Member States within the framework of this group makes it possible for experiences drawn from real events to be judged and compared, and for dialogue in the technical field to be improved so as to increase the efficiency of operational forces in combating terrorism.[38]

The ministers responsible for immigration hold meetings parallel to those of TREVI. The challenges posed by the problems of immigration may be relevant to the fight against terrorism. Within this framework, a convention on the crossing of the Community's external borders was submitted to the Member States for signature. The aim of this convention is to ensure that the Member States apply uniform rules for controls at external borders on persons visiting the country for a short period of time. The standardization of the formalities in respect of visas by the introduction of a sole visa would also be able to simplify the visits of non-EEC travellers to many Member States. This convention is at present blocked by the dispute between the United Kingdom and Spain regarding Gibraltar.[39] The ministers have also provided for a Centre for Information, Research and Exchange on Cross-border Movements and Immigration (CIREFI).[40]

The surprising complexity of the mechanisms for cooperation put into place during the last two decades should once again be stressed. The increase in the number of structures, one superimposed on another, is not in itself an organizational development likely to encourage efficiency and reliability. An objective assessment of the system which has been created is even more tricky.

THE USE OF THE LEGAL SYSTEM OF THE COMMUNITY IN THE SUPPRESSION OF TERRORISM

The EEC treaties do not prohibit Member States from entering into any international convention which would allow them to develop collaboration in areas not covered by these treaties; Article 5 of the Treaty of Rome however requires the Member States to 'ensure fulfilment of the obligations arising out of this Treaty', and further, to 'abstain from any measure which could jeopardise the attainment of the objectives of this Treaty'. If an agreement between Member States contravenes European Community Law, the Commission, as Guardian of the Treaties, may request an opinion from the Court of Justice, and after having served notice may take proceedings against the States in contravention. It should however be recognized that is not always politically practical for the Commission – which is subject to many criticisms and pressures – to use an unwieldy procedure such as this.

The various problems posed by the suppression of terrorism are not altogether unconnected with certain powers of the Community. In the field of the free movement of goods, Article 223 paragraph 1(b) of the EEC Treaty expressly provides that 'any Member State may take such measures as it considers necessary for the protection of the essential interests of its security which are connected with the production of or trade in arms munition and war material'. This Article essentially applies to the movement of arms, munitions and military equipment, and permits derogation from the general principle of the free circulation of products. It therefore remains the rule that the Member States have competence in this field. However, Article 223 specifies several limitations: 'such measures shall not adversely affect the conditions of competition in the common market regarding products which are not intended for specifically military purposes'. Moreover, the derogation is only admissible if it is 'necessary', and the interest protected must be 'essential' to the security of the Member State. The words used imply a strict interpretation of this Article.[41]

In respect of the matters covered by Article 223, we have seen above that there exists a European Convention, concluded in 1978 within the framework of the Council of Europe, on the control of the Acquisition and Possession of Firearms by Individuals. In this same field, the Council of Ministers adopted a Directive on 18 June 1978 concerning the control of the acquisition and the possession of arms.[42] This Directive fits in with the prospect of abolition of border controls within the European Community as from 1 January 1993, and it was therefore formulated on the basis of Article 100A. Here again is a field where a directive of the Community and a convention of the Council of Europe are superimposed one on the other; this situation is not an isolated case.[43] Certain observers speak of a competition between the two organizations, even a race to stake out the territory and protect competing prerogatives. Member States will one day have to find a solution to this situation which does not make for ease in understanding and applying the rule of law.

Relations and cooperation between the European Community and the Council of Europe could be based on Article 230 of the EEC Treaty. This allows the Community to establish '*all* appropriate forms of cooperation' with the Council of Europe. A wide reading of this Article makes it possible for this cooperation to include all the questions arising from a uniform and reasoned application of the conventions dealing with terrorism and organized crime within the EEC.[44] But, as we have seen above, governments generally prefer to resort to the mechanism of an (EEC) Member State's implementation of an existing convention established within the framework of the Council of Europe.

Furthermore, Article 220 of the EEC Treaty specifies:

> Member States shall, so far as is necessary, enter into negotiations with each other with a view to securing for the benefit of their nationals:
> – The protection of persons and the enjoyment and protection of rights under the same conditions as those accorded by each State to its own nationals.[45]

The concepts of 'protection of persons' and 'enjoyment and protection of rights' referred to in this Article could apply to EC nationals who are the victims of terrorist activities. However, Article 220 does not refer to the adoption of secondary legislation but to 'negotiations', which implies that the final outcome of the process, which is essentially diplomatic in nature, is to be an international treaty. In fact there is nothing in law which prohibits an international agreement adopted within this framework from referring back to secondary legislation for the organization and adoption of practical implementation of the cooperation thus entered into. Only the lack of political will and the existence of very strong national sensitivities prevent us from realizing the achievements possible here.

However, criminal offences may have consequences in European Community law – for example the decision of the Court of Justice in the case *Cowan*,[46] which surprised a good number of observers. In this case, a British tourist, the victim of an attack in Paris, requested compensation from France under the provisions of the French Code of Criminal Procedure. Faced with the French authorities' refusal to grant compensation, Mr Cowan took the case before the Tribunal de Grande Instance of Paris (the court of first instance), which asked the Court of Justice of the EC to settle a preliminary point. The Court held in its judgment of 2 February 1989 that:

> although in principle criminal legislation and the rules of criminal procedure, among which the national provision in issue is to be found, are matters for which the Member States are responsible, the Court has consistently held (see *inter alia* the judgment of 11 November 1981 in

the Case 203/80 *Casati* [1981] ECR 2595) that Community law sets certain limits to their power. Such legislative provisions may not discriminate against persons to whom Community law gives the right to equal treatment or restrict the fundamental freedoms guaranteed by Community law.[47]

And the EC Court held that the provisions of the French Code of Criminal Procedure in question were not compatible with the principle of non-discrimination between European Community nationals which is contained in Article 7 of the Treaty of Rome.

Here again, we have seen that there exists a Council of Europe Convention – that of 1983 on the compensation of victims of violent crime. What use is this Convention (outside of the wider geographical field where it could be applied) in respect to relations between Member States of the Community, since according to the decision of the Court they are nevertheless bound to compensate victims of offences who are Community nationals in the same way as their own nationals?

The introduction of free circulation of persons, the unhindered movement of capital, freedom to provide services, the easing of restrictions on the right of residence and the suppression of border controls within the Community may therefore have some effect upon the policy of the Member States in respect of crime.

To harmonize their policy regarding the fight against terrorism, the Member States may still use Articles 100, 100A and 235 of the EEC Treaty. Article 100 allows the Council of Ministers, acting unanimously on a proposal of the Commission, to issue directives for the approximation of such laws as 'directly affect' the establishment or functioning of the Common Market. The term 'directly affect' when applied to the field of criminal law appears to reserve the scope of Article 100 to the harmonization of legislation in respect of economic offences. The Court of Justice, consulted in 1976 by the Commission on a draft directive concerning the prevention and punishment of economic offences, recommended using instead the procedure of Article 235.[48] This procedure concerns actions of the Community which 'prove necessary to attain . . . one of the objectives of the Community'.

In spite of the requesting of an opinion, the draft on economic offences came to nothing. It is therefore difficult to imagine recourse being made to this procedure in combating terrorism. The concept of 'necessary action' in Article 235 could however easily be given a wide interpretation in this field. However, national parliaments are particularly avaricious of their prerogatives in the criminal field, and no government can overlook this factor. The unanimity required for decision-taking in relation to Articles 100 and 235 does not help matters either. It is not the same for Article 100A, which allows a vote in the Council by qualified majority and the use of the cooperation procedure with the European Parliament. That the scope of Article 100A is restricted to the progressive creation of an area without internal frontiers does not seem to us to create an obstacle, since as we have seen, it is precisely the building of the large internal market which causes considerable worry to those responsible for the security services in our countries.

It is not possible to dismantle the barriers between Member States within the Community and at the same time to refuse to cooperate in respect of the supervision of frontiers. This is what certain Member States have to face up to; it will surely generate further ambitious projects.

The Council's Directive of 28 June 1990 concerning the right of residence, supplemented by a Directive of the same date concerning the right of residence of salaried and non-salaried workers and by a Directive concerning the right of residence of students,[49] have completed the many Community agreements on freedom of movement for persons. However, the abolition of checks and formalities imposed on citizens crossing frontiers within the Community still poses several difficulties; and these checks have not been totally removed as at 1 January 1993.

Questions regarding the right of asylum can also be relevant to the fight against terrorism. After lengthy preliminary work, the ministers of Member States with responsibility for immigration signed in Dublin, at their meeting of 15 June 1990, a Convention determining the Member State responsible for examining an application for asylum made in one of the Member States of the European Community.[50] This Convention determines, by use of common selection criteria, which State has jurisdiction to consider the first request of a refugee. A procedure for exchange of information on those seeking asylum is also provided for, by means of a Centre for Information, Research and Exchange on Asylum (CIREA).[51] As at 1 January 1993, this Convention has still not been ratified by certain Member States and therefore cannot enter into force.

The matter of asylum is also considered in the Treaty on European Union signed in Maastricht on 7 February 1992. The Treaty contains under Title VI provisions on cooperation in the fields of justice and home affairs. The idea of 'home affairs' in fact came from the contraction of the original expression, which provided for inter-governmental cooperation between Ministers of the Interior (Home Office Ministers) and Ministers of Justice.[52] Even if the word 'inter-governmental' was not included in the final document, the use of the term 'cooperation' clearly shows the limits of the exercise envisaged. Article K2 of the Treaty of Maastricht also specifies that this cooperation shall not affect the exercise of 'the responsibilities incumbent upon Member States with regard to the maintenance of law and order and the safeguarding of internal security'. And Article K4 expressly provides for the Council's vote on these matters to be unanimous.

Also in the Treaty of Maastricht, areas of cooperation envisaged referred to in Article K1 points 1 to 6 are: asylum policy; rules governing the crossing of the external borders of Member States; immigration policy and conditions of residence in Member States' territory by third country nationals; the combating of drug addiction and fraud; and judicial cooperation in civil matters.

Points 7 to 9 of the same Article refer to judicial cooperation in criminal matters; customs cooperation; police cooperation in order to prevent and combat terrorism; unlawful drug trafficking; and other serious forms of international crime.

Finally Article K1 refers to the creation of the European Police Office (EUROPOL) which, as we have already seen, was also being studied by the TREVI Group and inter-governmental cooperation. This office would be, in a manner of speaking, an office centralizing information on delinquents and on crimes, and would operate as the Community's central office of INTERPOL, replacing the national INTERPOL offices.

The methods of action provided repeat the procedures used within the framework of political and inter-governmental cooperation prior to this new Treaty, that is to say, as we have seen: collaboration, adoption of common positions, common action and conclusion of conventions.

The only possible way to go further in the process of legal integration is provided for by a combination of the procedures of Article K9 of the Treaty of Maastricht and of the new Article 100C of the EEC Treaty. Within this framework, the Council, under certain conditions, would be able to use a qualified majority vote from 1 January 1996 onwards. However, this Article K9 procedure is not applicable to the areas of cooperation of interest to us in this chapter – that is to say, those areas mentioned in points 7 to 9 of Article K1, as listed above.

The new Article 100C, added to the EEC Treaty by the Treaty of Maastricht, gives the Council of Ministers, ruling unanimously until January 1996 and thereafter by a qualified majority, the power to determine the non-EC countries whose nationals must possess visas when crossing the external borders of the Member States. This Article has the effect of putting the Member States' policy regarding visas under Community control. However, the scope of this new Article is very much limited by the fact that a unanimous decision is necessary (para. 1), that other Conventions on the same subjects remain in force for so long as they are not replaced by directives (para. 7), and that this new power must not undermine the performance of obligations incumbent on Member States for the maintenance of law and order and the protection of national security (para. 5).

The force of the Community legal order would however apply to Article 100C, as it is an integral part of the EEC Treaty. An appeal to the Court of Justice could therefore control derogations by Member States; the restriction of the powers of each Member State regarding the justification of law and order measures stated by the Court of Justice in *Rutili* could apply here. In its judgment[53] the Court held:

... the concept of public policy must, in the Community context and where, in particular, it is used as a justification for derogating from the fundamental principles of equality of treatment and freedom of movement for workers, be interpreted strictly, so that its scope cannot be determined unilaterally by each Member State without being subject to control by the institutions of the Community;

Accordingly, restrictions cannot be imposed on the right of a national of any Member State to enter the territory of another Member State, to stay there and to move within it, unless his presence or conduct constitutes a genuine and sufficiently serious threat to public policy.

Once more the Court applied the general principles taken from the Council of Europe Convention on Human Rights, stating:

... the restrictions on the powers of Member States in relation to the control of foreigners are a specific demonstration of the more general principle embodied in articles 8, 9, 10 and 11 of the Convention for the Protection of Human Rights and Fundamental Freedoms signed in Rome on 4th November 1950 and ratified by all the Member States, and of article 2 of Protocol n° 4 to the same Convention, signed in Strasbourg on the 16th September 1963, which specifies in identical terms that a breach of the rights guaranteed by the articles referred to on the grounds of the requirements of law and order and public safety, should not go beyond what is necessary to protect these requirements in a democratic society.

Since the acceleration in the construction of the single market and the gradual abolition of internal frontiers, the zone of prosperity constructed by the twelve Member States has posed new security problems. This has led the officials of the Member States to draw up programmes of cooperation which herald the arrival of a more structured European policy on crime. These programmes were included in the Treaties of Schengen and of Maastricht. The difficulties in ratifying and implementing these Treaties illustrate the complexity of the issues concerned. Apart from the problem of extradition, the fight against terrorism raises the issue of visas, of the unification of checks at external frontiers, of asylum, of immigration etc.

THE SCHENGEN AREA

Faced with the refusal of certain States, including the United Kingdom, to cooperate further in regard to police matters, a draft bilateral agreement was prepared in secret by Chancellor Kohl and President Mitterrand during a Franco-German summit at Fontainebleau, on 17 June 1984. This draft led to the signature on 13 July 1984 of the Sarrebruck Agreement on the gradual abolition of checks at the Franco-German border.[54]

The three Benelux countries, interested by the process which had been started, wanted to join the system, and this led to the signing at Schengen on 14 June 1985 of a new agreement on the gradual abolition of checks at their common borders.[55] This agreement is almost exclusively concerned with the problems of nationals of Member States crossing common internal borders. The measures envisaged permit a simple visual surveillance of tourist vehicles crossing common borders at a reduced speed, and the reduction to a minimum of the stopping time for vehicles in the other categories of road and rail transport. The parties to the agreement also undertake to reinforce cooperation between their police authorities in respect of crime prevention and control.[56]

The implementation of this Convention suffered several delays, due to the process of German unification. The necessity of completing the implementation finally led to the conclusion of the Convention Applying the Schengen Agreement on 19 June 1990, again in Schengen. This document of 142 articles was signed by the five original Member States. These States were joined by Italy on 27 November 1990, then by Spain and Portugal on the 15 June 1991, since when Greece has acquired the status of an observer pending becoming a full member.[57]

The new Convention provides for the total abolition of checks at internal frontiers and envisages the harmonization of the rules on crossing external borders, visa policy, the movement of foreigners, narcotics and arms, and requests for asylum.

Regarding cooperation in the relation to police and to security, the Convention breaks new ground by providing for a very novel system divided into four elements.[58]

The first element, mentioned in Article 40, deals with trans-frontier observation. An officer of one Member State, after making a request for judicial cooperation, may receive authorization to continue to watch and follow in another country a person suspected of having taken part in an extraditable offence. The specific offences in question are notably: murder; assassination; abduction; hostage-taking; destruction by explosives, etc. The agents conducting the observation can neither question nor arrest the person under observation, nor can they use their authorized firearm. The officers authorized to conduct trans-frontier observation are also specified, and, in France, for example, they include officers of the national police and the gendarmerie as well as customs officers.

The second element concerns, under Article 41, the right to pursue across borders persons caught in the act of committing offences or of escaping. Taking into account the urgency of the matter, the officers of a Member State may continue their pursuit whilst using all possible means to inform the authorities of the country being crossed. The limits of time and area in respect of this right of pursuit are to be fixed by each Member State. The officers conducting the pursuit, who must wear a uniform or armbands and be identifiable, have the right to question the person pursued only under exceptional circumstances and in cases of urgency, and the formal arrest is carried out by officers of the Member State where the pursuit took place. The officers in hot pursuit can only use their authorized firearm in legitimate defence, and they must give an account of their mission to the authorities of the Member State affected by the pursuit.

Despite the restrictions on the exercise of the right of pursuit contained in the Convention itself, it is easy to imagine that the authorization of foreign police staff to enter, in uniform, the territory of a neighbouring country in order to continue an assignment which had been started elsewhere amounts to a real revolution. The gap thus opened in the sacrosanct principle of the sovereignty of Member States is the consequence of the change in attitudes of those responsible in Europe for these issues in the last ten years.[59]

The third element deals with mutual assistance in criminal policy. This includes, in Articles 48 to 91, a mechanism for judicial cooperation; the application of the principle of *non bis in idem*; extradition; the transfer of the enforcement of criminal judgments; and provisions on narcotics, firearms and ammunition. This cooperation supplements or enhances the law of the conventions otherwise developed within the framework of the Council of Europe.

Finally, the fourth element concerns the putting into place of a Schengen Information System (SIS) to facilitate the transfer of data on wanted persons. This centrally computerized data system, a databank on a European scale, can be consulted by each of the Member States. Each Member State of the new organization must appoint an authority of that Member State capable of exercising independent control over the national part of the databank and of verifying that the data included are not prejudicial to the rights of individuals. The level of protection of data of a personal nature respects the principles of the Council of Europe Convention of 28 January 1981.[60]

The Schengen Convention also provided for the putting into place of a special institutional mechanism. This is comprised of an Executive Committee, composed of one minister for each Member State, which checks that the agreement is being properly applied and which rules by unanimous decision. This Committee has created many subordinate bodies for the preparation of its decisions in the various areas of cooperation concerned.

The Convention specifies in its Article 134 that the provisions of the Convention are only applicable in so far as they are compatible with European Community Law. This constitutes a safeguard in the case of a blatant contradiction between the Convention and Community law. The only reservation that one might have is that as the Court of Justice is not competent to interpret the text of this Convention, there is no guarantee that the text will be interpreted uniformly throughout the whole of the area concerned, nor of it being compatible with the legal system of the Community.

Due to decisions in the Schengen area being taken on the basis of unanimity, the cooperation entered into remains inter-governmental in nature. The legal processes used consist of progressively harmonizing the national laws concerned, in conformity with the principles and the chosen methods of cooperation. A great deal of progress has been made. Schengen heralds a new era as the challenges of terrorist threats have made it possible for very strong links to be created between European democracies.[61] Some examples are the cooperation which has been established for several years now between Spain and France for dealing with Basque terrorism, or between Germany and France in cases concerning the Bader group or Action Directe. The time when offences committed by terrorists will no longer be treated specially and when such offences will be considered ordinary crimes is perhaps closer than we think. The reactions of the general public and of the media, shocked by the attacks carried out, may lead to even closer cooperation between the governments concerned.

However, the Schengen system has been strongly criticized in Community circles and by certain national authorities. The European Parliament tends to consider the Convention applying the Schengen Agreement as merely a 'testing ground' for the implementation of Community regulation in the field. Noting large gaps in the areas of police cooperation, crime prevention, judicial cooperation, extradition and the transfer of the enforcement of judgments, the Parliament proposes that this exercise in inter-governmental cooperation be submitted to the supervision of the Court of Justice of the European Communities.[62] This proposal, though logical within the dynamic of the Community, has little chance of being accepted. It is not to be ruled out that, with the Treaty of Maastricht coming into force, for the Court to specify certain concepts and apply principles drawn from the interpretation of the European Convention on Human Rights, as has already happened on several occasions.[63]

The reactions noted at the European Parliament in Strasbourg indicate a certain vexation at seeing advanced co-operation being developed without any link with the EEC system and without the control of Community bodies. In several resolutions,[64] the Parliament condemns the violation of democratic principles and of international conventions on human rights by States anxious to act in secret and without parliamentary control. The Parliament also requested that all members of the inter-governmental conference negotiating the Treaty on European Union should ensure that questions of mutual assistance in criminal matters fell within the exclusive competence of the Community. On this point, the Parliament obtained partial satisfaction in the Treaty of Maastricht, in that the new power in the area of law and internal affairs does address these issues; decisions are however required to be taken unanimously.

Certain of these criticisms are excessive. If it is true that the first Schengen Convention of 1985 was ratified in France by a simple decree, the

Convention of 1990 applying the Schengen Agreement was the subject of a long debate on ratification in the national parliaments. Moreover, in France, the matter was referred by M. Pierre Mazeaud and sixty-three deputies to the Conseil Constitutionnel, which decided on 25 July 1991 that the Agreement was not contrary to the Constitution.[65]

Furthermore, for the Schengen Agreement to be implemented, a series of decisions is required to harmonize the legislative provisions in force in Member States, and at that time national parliaments will be able once again to come to a decision on which modifications are necessary or desirable.[66]

Reactions within the Member States were equally strong. In France for example, the Senate created a Control Commission responsible for the implementation and the functioning of the Convention applying the Schengen Agreement. In its first report,[67] this Commission noted in particular the immense complexity of the system put into place and the fact that national parliaments had not been consulted sufficiently on all the consequences of sensitive issues such as visas, asylum, mutual assistance in respect of policing or the Schengen Information System.

During the debate on ratification in The Netherlands, the Dutch Parliament obtained the right of veto over decisions by the Schengen Executive Committee:[68] the measures proposed by this Committee must be submitted to the Parliament before their formal adoption. This new mechanism adds a parliamentary control prior to the minister's vote in the Executive Committee. Although satisfying as a matter of principle for national public opinion, this initiative may result in legal difficulties stemming from a mixture of concepts and the lengthening of procedures. The national parliament would in fact be given a double control. Before the Committee takes a decision, the parliament would give the minister power to negotiate; but how can the confidentiality of these instructions and the room for manoeuvre necessary in any negotiations be assured? When a new point arises or there is a development in the negotiating positions, would not the minister have to run a shuttle between the Committee and parliament? Would not the parliament become the *de facto* negotiator of the inter-governmental agreement? And if one takes the other parliaments into account, is it possible or reasonable to conduct negotiations with two or three thousand participants? Then again, after the Committee has taken a decision, the same parliament would be called upon to approve national legislation, where this is required.

The greatest difficulties lie ahead. Certain Member States have in fact large gaps – legislative weaknesses on important points in the areas of cooperation mentioned. The report of the Control Commission of the Senate highlights these. Germany for example will have to review its law on the right of asylum, Belgium will have to resolve the question of visiting visas issued by honorary consuls, Italy and The Netherlands will have to adopt a law on the protection of computerized data of a personal nature so as to introduce a level of protection equivalent to that which exists in France, and so on.

***

The system of mutual assistance in criminal matters, in place for some thirty years in Western Europe, is extremely complex and does not seem to have resulted in the development of easily understood and precisely defined rules.

In order to face up to inadequate security, States have multiplied the number of agreements, organizations and methods. If the goal appears evident, the rules established are complex. Is it important? In the matter of combating terrorism, political decisions often take precedence over the purely mechanical application of the rule of law.

At institutional level one could describe two institutional systems, juxta-posed and overlapped by a third, without the division of tasks between these systems having been precisely or definitely determined. The first system is that of the EEC. The process of integration in the Community seems to have run out of steam when one looks at the areas of internal and legal affairs where decisions are taken on a unanimous basis. However the rule of law may also be clarified in the light of the caselaw of the Court of Justice. The *Cowan* case allows us to mark out certain paths, and judicial cooperation between the European Court and the national courts will perhaps permit further progress.

When one wishes to achieve a more ambitious policy, one reaches the second system, that of the Schengen Area, where the partners are fewer. However here the effort to integrate is only envisaged at the cost of abandoning any resolution of disputes by an integrated legal mechanism.

These first two institutional systems could one day be superimposed on one another and blend into one single system. On this point the position of the United Kingdom is of capital importance and any future progress is dependent on it. These two systems in a way represent the theory of a Europe at two speeds.

The Council of Europe forms the third system. This uses the classic tech-niques of international public law. The number of conventions signed by various partners and the many reserves or declarations on interpretation ensure neither the transparency of the system nor its efficiency. However the system of the Council of Europe serves as a reference and a model for the two other systems. Unfortunately the entry of the countries of Eastern Europe does not make it possible at present to achieve cohesive positions in relation to mutual assistance in criminal affairs.

Behind these three systems there are the countries with their dreams, their ideas, their policies, their doctrine – more or less rigid – and their ambitions. Future progress depends on a change in these. The declarations of a political nature are extremely numerous and one should mention high up the list the 'Final Document of the Copenhagen Meeting' of 29 June 1990 and the 'Paris Charter for a New Europe' of 21 November 1990.[69] These documents, adopted during meetings of the Conference on Safety and Co-operation in Europe (CSCE), are of fundamental importance. In fact the undertaking, taken within the enlarged framework of this Conference, to protect the democratic order against acts of terrorism refers us back to questions of principle and augers well for the future of this cooperation.

NOTES

1   In this respect see the report of X. de Villepin to the Senate on 'La ratification de la Convention européenne pour la repression du terrorisme', *Sénat* 346, 1 July 1987.
2   Cf. G. Soulier 'Lutte contre le terrorisme', in M. Delmas-Marty (ed.) *Raisonner la raison d'Etat, vers une Europe des droits de l'homme* (PUF, 1989), p. 29f.; J.L. Thebaud 'Terrorisme et démocratie', *Esprit* 3 (1989) 99; D. Rouard 'Les nouvelles routes de la mafia' *Le Monde* 26, 27, 28, 29 Jan. 1993; M. Garicoix 'Les policiers ont découvert une fabrique d'armes de l'ETA' *Le Monde* 17 Feb. 1993.
3   E. Plenel 'Police et terrorisme', *Esprit* 11 (1986) 7.
4   Some examples of agreements of this type:
    - the Member States of Beneiux signed the Traité d'extradition et d'entraide judiciaire en matière pénale (27 June 1962); the Traité sur l'exécution des décisions judiciaires en matières pénales (26 Sept. 1968); the Convention concernant la coopération administrative et judiciaire dans le domaine des réglementations se rapportant à la réalisation des objectifs de l'Union économique du Bénélux (29 Apr. 1969); and Traité Bénélux sur la transmission des poursuites (11 May 1974).
    - Holland and the FRG signed, on 30 Aug. 1979, the agreement concerning the application of the European Convention on Mutual Assistance in Criminal Matters of 1959.
    - France and the FRG concluded an agreement on 13 July 1984 at Sarrebruck relating to the gradual suppression of controls at the Franco-German border.
    - France and Italy signed the Paris agreement of 13 Oct. 1986 which created a committee for mutual assistance in the fight against terrorism, traffic of narcotics and organized crime.
    - France and Spain signed the agreement of Aiguablava (Costa Brava) of 29 May 1987 concerning police cooperation.
    - The UK and France signed the Franco-British administrative arrangement of 19 May 1989 and the protocol of 25 Nov. 1991, on the policing, mutual assistance in criminal matters, civil safety and mutual assistance, concerning the fixed link across the Channel.
5   Cf. G. Siegele 'Le terrorisme' in *La prévention du crime et le traitement des delinquants*, Huitième Congrès des Nations Unies à la Havane. Doc.A/CONF. 144/G/ République fédérale d'Allemagne, juillet 1990, p.34: '. . . Le terrorisme moderne qui, de nos jours ignore les frontières entre les Etats, pour autant qu'elles soient même encore tangibles, ne peut être combattu et endigué efficacement que par la coopération internationale. . . l'efficacité de la coopération internationale sera conditionnée au plus haut point par la question de savoir si les conventions internationales adoptées contre la violence terroriste seront

mises en vigueur effectivement et si les accords conclus pourront être approfondis . . .'.

6 Cf. P. le Jeune 'La politique européenne de lutte contre le terrorisme', thèse de Doctorat de Droit, Lyon 1991; C. Joubert and H. Bevers 'La police et l'Europe, in *Revue de science criminelle* (1992), 712.

Some examples of inter-governmental working groups: the Cross-Channel Intelligence Conference or Cross Channel Group; the Berne Club, set up in 1979; the Quantico Group (after the name of the town in the USA where it was created); the Vienna Club or the Club of Five, created in 1979; International Criminal Police Organisation (ICPO), created in Vienna in 1923, and leading to the creation of Interpol, the headquarters of which have been situated in Lyon since 1984.

7 Cf. Soulier *op. cit.* note 2, p. 32.

8 Amongst these conventions the following should be mentioned: the European Convention on Extradition signed in Paris on 13 Dec. 1957, completed by two additional Protocols signed in 1975 and 1978; the European Convention on Mutual Assistance in Criminal Matters, signed in Strasbourg on 20 June 1959, completed by an additional protocol signed on 17 Mar. 1978; the European Convention on the International Validity of Criminal Judgments, signed at The Hague on 28 May 1970; the European Convention on the Transfer of Proceedings in Criminal Matters, signed in Strasbourg on 15 May 1972; the European Convention on the Control of the Acquisition and Possession of Firearms by Individuals, signed in Strasbourg on 28 June 1978; the European Convention on the Compensation of Victims of Violent Crimes, signed in Strasbourg on 24 Oct. 1983.

9 See e.g. Art. 10 of the Second Additional Protocol to the European Convention on Extradition; Art. 65 of the European Convention on the International Validity of Criminal Judgements; or Art. 17 of the European Convention on the Control of the Acquisition and Possession of Firearms by Individuals.

10 On the application of this convention refer to the study by Jean, Chap. 12 in this book.

11 See A. Decocq, 'Les conventions européennes sur le terrorisme', *Notes et etudes de l'Institut de Criminologie*, 14 (July 1990) 35.

12 Council of Europe, European Treaty Series 90.

13 On the application of this convention, refer to the study by Labayle, Chap. 10 in this book.

14 The rule *aut dedere, aut judicare* appears in many other international conventions, notably in the Montreal Convention of 1971 on the Safety of Civilian Aircraft.

15 For a detailed analysis of the Convention, see C. Vallee 'La Convention européenne pour la répression du terrorisme', *Annuaire français de droit international* (1976), 756.

16 Decree No. 87–1024 of 21 Dec. 1987, publishing the European Convention on the Suppression of Terrorism, *Journal officiel de la République Française (JORF)*, 22 Dec. 1987, p.14954.

17 Cf. J. Charpentier, 'Vers un espace judiciaire européen', *Annuaire français de droit international* (1978), 927.

18 Cf. J.A. Frowein, 'Reservations to the European Convention on Human Rights' in *Mélanges en l'honneur de G.J. Wiarda*, 1988, p. 193.

19 H. Labayle and R. Koering-Joulin 'Dix ans après . . . De la signature (1977) à la ratification (1987) de la Convention européenne pour la répression du terrorisme', *Jurisclasseur périodique* 33–7 (Sept 1988), I: 3349.

20 R. de Gouttes 'De l'espace judiciaire pénal européen à l'espace judiciaire pénal pan-européen' in *Mélanges Levasseur* (Litec, 1992), p. 9.

21 See the report of Jacques Foyer to the Assemblée Nationale, on the ratification of the European Convention on the Suppression of Terrorism. Assemblée Nationale No. 784, 21 May 1987.

22 Cf. Charpentier, *op. cit.* note 17.

23 See *Bulletin CE* 6–1977, point 2.3.31.

24 Cf. E. Grabit 'Recherches sur la notion d'espace judiciaire européen'. Phd thesis, (Universitaires de Bordeaux, 1988).

25 See Suppl. 1/76 to *Bulletin CE*.

26 See Charpentier, *op. cit.* note 17 and Gouttes, *op. cit.* note 20.

27 Within the scope of political cooperation during this period, the European Council made declarations on terrorism in Dec. 1975, July 1976, Dec. 1977, Apr. 1978. Numerous other declarations were made in respect of the wave of terrorist attacks of the 1980s. The Foreign Office Ministers of the twelve Member States also publish declarations of the same type during their regular meetings.

28 Coopération politique: Accord de Dublin, *Bulletin CE* 12–1979, p. 99. See also: Assemblée Nationale Française, projet de loi 632, 10 Apr. 1987; report by *op. cit.* note 21; and report by *op. cit.* note 1.

29 The Dublin Agreement had only been ratified by Belgium, France, Italy and Holland.

30 The Convention between the Member States of the European Communities on Double Jeopardy, signed on 25 May 1987; the agreement relating to the application between the Member States of the European Community of the Convention of the Council of Europe of 1983 on the Transfer of Sentenced Persons, signed on 25 May 1987; the agreement between the Member States of the European Communities on the Simplification and Modernization of Methods of Transmitting Extradition Requests, signed on 26 May 1989; the agreement on the Transfer of Proceedings in Criminal Judgments signed on 6 Nov. 1990; the Convention between the Member States of the European Community on the Enforcement of Foreign Criminal Sentences, signed on 13 Nov. 1992.

31 See the agenda of the 1533th session of the Council, held on 13 Nov. 1991 in Brussels. This agenda makes no mention of the agreement on the enforcement of foreign criminal sentences, *Bulletin CE* 11–1991, point 1.7.9., p. 117.

32 See E. Decaux, 'La politique étrangère et de sécurité commune' in Montchrestien (ed.) *Les accords de Maastricht et la constitution de l'Union européenne* (CEDIN, 1992), p. 105.

33 See, e.g., Art. 5 of the Dublin Convention which refers to the arbitration procedure provided for in Art. 10 of the European Convention on the Suppression of Terrorism.

34 Cf. *Bulletin CE* 6–1991, point 1.4.10.

35 See in this respect: J. Montreuil, 'La coopération policière européenne' in *Mélanges Levasseur*, *op. cit.* note 20, p.67; Joubert and Bevers, *op. cit.* note 6, p. 713; and R. Schmidt-Nothen, 'La coopération policière en Europe', *Revue internationale de politique criminelle* (Sept.–Oct. 1989), 5.

36 *Bulletin CE* 12–1992, point 1.5.13.

37 See E. Inciyan, 'Une Europe de la sécurité' in *Le Monde*, 6 Sept. 1992, p. 8, and *Bulletin CE* 6–1992, point 1.5.14.

38 See Le Jeune, *op. cit.* note 6.

39 See *Bulletin CE* No. 12–1992, point 1.5.12.

40 See *Bulletin CE* No. 6–1992, point 1.5.13.

41 See in this respect J. Verhoeven, 'Article 223' in V. Costantinesco *et al.* (eds) *Traité instituant la CEE - Commentaire article par article* (Economica, 1992), p. 1400.

42 *Official Journal of the European Communities (OJEC)* No. L.256, 13 Sept. 1991.

43 Cf. in relation to television where for the Council of Europe there exists a European Convention on Transfrontier Television (1989) and for the EEC, a Directive of 3 Oct. 1989 concerning the coordination of certain legislative, statutory and administrative provisions of the Member States on television broadcasting activities. It is the same in respect of recognition of diplomas.

44 See H.P. Furrer, 'La contribution du Conseil de l'Europe à la construction européenne' *Les organisations internationales contemporaines: crise, mutation, développement; XXIe colloque de la Société Française pour le Droit International*, Strasbourg, 21–23 May 1987 (Pédone, 1988), pp. 281–312.

45 It was within the framework of Art. 220 EEC that the Member States adopted the Brussels Convention of 27 Sept. 1968 on the Jurisdiction and the Enforcement of Judgments in Civil and Commercial Matters. *OJEC*, No L.229, 31 Dec. 1972, p. 32

46 *Cowan* [1989] ECR 195.

47 *Ibid.* at 221–2.

48 See I. Keersmacker, Report to the European Parliament, Doc. Séance 531/76 of 2 Feb. 1977, p. 19. The opinion of the ECJ was not published.

49 See *OJEC* L.180, 13 July 1990, p. 26.

50 See *Bulletin CE*, 6–1990, point 2.2.2.

51 See *Bulletin CE*, 6–1992, point 1.5.13.

52 See M.F. Labouz, 'Les accords de Maastricht et la Constitution de l'Union européenne' in Montchrestien (ed.) (CEDIN, 1992), p. 182.

53 *Rutili* [1975] ECR 1, paras. 27–33.

54 Published in *JORF*, 3 Aug. 1984, p. 2565.

55 Schengen Agreement, published in *JORF*, 5 Aug. 1986, p. 9612.

56 See B. Neel, 'L'Europe sans frontières intérieures, l'accord de Schengen' 10 *Actualité juridique (droit administratif)* (1991), 659; H. Blanc, 'Schengen: le chemin de la libre circulation en Europe' 351, *Revue de marché commun* (1991), 722.

57 See *Bulletin CE* 6–1991, point 1.4.11.

58 See Joubert and Bevers, *op. cit.* note 6, p. 715 and Montreuil, *op. cit.* note 35, p. 69.

59 See 'Les systèmes de police et la coopération policière en Europe: comparaisons, tendances, défis', Colloque de l'Ihesi, Paris, 1–4 Dec. 1992.

60 Convention for the Protection of Individuals with regard to Automatic Processing of Personal Data.

61 See H. Labayle and D. Simond, 'Terrorisme et harmonisation juridique en Europe, éléments pour une problématique', *Journées d'études du SGDN* (Secrétariat Général de la Défense Nationale, 1990).

62 See resolution of the EP of 19 Nov. 1992. *OJEC* C. 337, 21 Dec. 1992.

63 See esp. the decision of the CJEC of 15 May 1986: 222/84 *Johnston* [1986] ECR 1651.

64 See resolution of EP of 23 Nov. 1989 (*OJEC* C.323, 27 Dec. 1989, p.98) and resolution of EP of 15 June 1990 (*OJEC* C.175, 16 July 1990, p.170).

65 Decision of the Conseil Constitutionnel 91–294 DC of 27 July 1991, *JORF*, 25 July 1991, p. 10001.

66 Following the general election of Mar. 1993, the new French Government pointed out that the conditions necessary for the implementation of the Schengen Treaty had still not been met and that it would therefore postpone implementation until the next year or thereafter.

67   See Villepin, *op. cit.* note 1.
68   See C. Chartier 'Les députés et sénateurs néerlandais ont obtenu un droit de veto sur l'application des accords de Schengen', *Le Monde*, 25 June 1992, p. 8.
69   See J.D. Vigny, 'Le document de la réunion de Copenhagen', 9 *Revue universelle des droits de l'homme*, (1990), 305–12.

Part III
French and British responses

7 Managing terrorism the British way

David Schiff

Introduction

Just as the international community adopts common practices to control or prevent terrorism, so individual States respond to terrorism by amending their domestic laws to achieve a certain level of control or prevention.[1] Nowadays international cooperation often provides the impetus for the invocation of domestic legal changes,[2] since it is recognized that each country is equally at risk from terrorism and equally entitled to adopt measures against terrorism, and that a uniform approach has a number of advantages. One of the practical advantages of such a uniform approach is that, in being consistent with international law and cooperation, it allows matters such as the extradition of terrorist suspects to run smoothly, rather than suffering from the problems that have been experienced in adapting the principles of the political offence exemption to extradition[3] to the conditions of modern terrorism. Another practical advantage is that a uniform approach is more likely to conform to other international agreements, such as human rights conventions and practices, which attempt to restrain the domestic response to terrorism. The upholding of such human rights standards is not only right in principle and part of a State's international obligations, but also restrains over-reaction by the State, which in practice may often prove to be counter-productive.[4]

The domestic response to terrorism will thus operate as part of the international community's collective or regional response, within the constraints set out as internationally agreed limitations on the exercise of coercive powers by the State. However it is also the case that each country's legal response to terrorism will to some extent be determined by the particular form of terrorism operating within their jurisdictions: the particular political conflicts that engender the terrorism; the recent historical events; the degree of public support for the terrorists, among other things. These factors are inevitably likely to affect the choice of mechanisms adopted by the State as a response to terrorism, whether mainly reactive or preventative. Each individual State will, in being confronted with the particular threats to its authority, react uniquely. What amounts to sound preventative action in one country may be counter-productive in another. Even the definitions or basic legal concepts around which the State organizes its response to terrorism may need to be the particular response of the individual State, rather than a prototype for all States. In these terms the organizational problems of cooperation between States in preventing or controlling terrorism are multiplied within the State, where organizational problems inevitably arise with counter-terrorist measures. This is so because counter-terrorism, in adopting abnormal rules that are distinct from the normal rules of, say, the criminal process, creates organizational needs to reconcile or harmonize these exceptional norms within the normal, constitutionally posited rules. Without such reconciliation and harmonization, counter-terrorist measures are destructive of constitutions, that is the public law framework of the legitimate exercise of authority.

Legal fictions are adopted in order to recognize the need for a State's unique response to issues such as terrorism, of which the notion of a 'margin of appreciation' is a classic example.[5] States may take such measures as are individually consistent with their particular make-up and needs. States may also, within their jurisdictions, create regional differences. In surveying some recent examples of the British State's response to terrorism – and in particular that terrorism that arises out of political conflicts having internal origins (namely those that involve Northern Ireland) – particular attention will be focused on organizational questions. Organizational disunity itself becomes a problem of counter-terrorist measures. And the piecemeal way of dealing with organizational disunity raises difficulties in achieving a rational and unitary approach, or a consistent set of counter-terrorist policies.

What will be undertaken here is a brief account of some recent examples of Britain's response to terrorism arising out of its own internal conflicts in Northern Ireland. What will be highlighted in this account are the problems of adopting a rational approach to counter-terrorist strategy, how such a rational approach is disrupted by problems of organizational unity, and the politics of counter-terrorism. In the politics of counter-terrorism, political rationality – meeting the needs of specific interest groups – takes priority over other objectives.[6] Here one will often find that symbolic gestures prevail. Such gestures will be less easy to justify to the inter-national community, although they may appear to be highly significant within the State. The interplay of rational, organizational and symbolic approaches will be described.

Background

Northern Ireland, comprising six counties, was adopted as part of the United Kingdom following the Anglo-Irish Treaty of 1921, which arranged the partition of Ireland. What was then created in the southern part of Ireland was the Irish Free State, which later became the independent Irish

Republic.[7] This state of affairs was not a happy compromise for many of the parties involved,[8] and emergency powers have been in continual force from the inception of Northern Ireland;[9] the system of political authority has broken down and since 1972 has been replaced by direct rule from London. The recent 'troubles' in Northern Ireland were precipitated by a civil rights campaign in 1968–69 in which the minority Catholic community[10] protested about the serious levels of discrimination against them in the areas of local government, housing and employment. The British army was initially deployed in Northern Ireland in 1969 to restrain violence between the two communities, but soon itself became the target for the Irish Republican Army (IRA). The IRA and other nationalist/Catholic paramilitary organizations have been actively engaged in terrorism since 1970; their violence has been aimed at both security forces and economic targets in Northern Ireland and, on occasions, in mainland Great Britain and sporadically in Europe. Active loyalist/Protestant paramilitary organizations have also developed who largely aim their violence at members of the Catholic community. The levels of violence have been high, averaging between 100 and 300 deaths annually.[11]

For Northern Ireland after direct rule in 1972, the Northern Ireland (Emergency Provisions) Act 1973 was passed. That Act set the pattern for emergency powers operating solely in Northern Ireland but not the rest of the United Kingdom. Its main provisions included the power of internment (preventative detention without trial), special non-jury courts (the 'Diplock Courts'), proscription of terrorist organizations, special powers of arrest and search, and amended rules of evidence at trial. The current legislation is the Northern Ireland (Emergency Provisions) Act 1991. In Northern Ireland these emergency powers operate and are supplemented by the Prevention of Terrorism (Temporary Provisions) Act 1989 which operates in the whole of Great Britain (including Northern Ireland). It is the latter general legislation which will be considered first, after a brief look at the legal concept of terrorism currently operating in Britain.

Terrorism

The Northern Ireland (Emergency Provisions) Act 1991[12] does include a general interpretation of the term terrorism. However, rather than rely on such a general interpretation the Act uses the concept of a 'scheduled offence' and a list of offences which count as scheduled offences to clarify what terrorism is. This list is assumed to be exhaustive of the offences that a terrorist is likely to commit, although it clearly includes offences which may be committed by those with no terrorist motivation. What follows from this list of scheduled offences in Northern Ireland is the system of trial (trial without a jury), restrictive conditions for granting bail, different rules of evidence at trial particularly in respect of confessions and offences of possession, among other things.[13] The greatest practical significance of the concept of scheduled offence is that it permits differentiation for the purpose of organizing the separate system of non-jury trial for all terrorist offences. The principal justifications for such a system are the fear of intimidation of jurors and the possibility of partisan juries in a divided society.[14] The list of scheduled offences is very wide in order to catch all the terrorist activity in Northern Ireland: the list includes homicide; arson; serious offences against the person and property; various explosives and firearm offences; robbery; aggravated burglary; intimidation; blackmail; membership of proscribed (illegal) organizations; and numbers of other offences. In a society with a high level of terrorist activity, the relationships between ordinary crime and criminals and terrorism and terrorist organizations becomes blurred, necessitating – if a list concept such as scheduled offences is used – a long list of offences. Such a list concept is used in the European Convention on the Suppression of Terrorism 1977, but without the apparent need for such a broad list of offences.[15]

Many of the uses of the word terrorism in the Emergency Provisions Act 1991 assume that it is to be understood as having some substantial meaning apart from being the general word to unify a list of offences. This is particularly important in relation to the new offence in section 27 of the Emergency Provisions Act 1991 of directing a terrorist organization. For a substantive definition of terrorism, the Prevention of Terrorism (Temporary Provisions) Act 1989[16] section 20 can be used, as well as the general interpretation section 66 of the Emergency Provisions Act 1991. This is the definition which has remained unaltered, despite the changing scope of the Prevention of Terrorism Acts, since 1974. Terrorism is defined as 'the use of violence for political ends and includes any use of violence for the purpose of putting the public or any section of the public in fear'. It is this loose definition which will operate, or be taken to apply, whenever the word 'terrorism' appears in the Prevention of Terrorism Act 1989 and in the Emergency Provisions Act 1991 – for example where arrest powers in these statutes are authorized for terrorism in general rather than some more specific offence. The danger of such a loose definition is of course in not being limited to specific serious offences, that it may be used over-extensively, thereby trivializing the fight against terrorism which needs to be limited to the exceptional.

The Prevention of Terrorism Act 1989: A rational approach?

The advent of a bombing campaign in Great Britain by the IRA in the 1930s was the precursor to the enactment of the Prevention of Violence (Temporary Provisions) Act 1939. One response to the events in Northern Ireland of the early 1970s spilling over onto the mainland of Great Britain – particularly the Birmingham Pub Bombs[17] – was the speedy passage[18] through Parliament of the Prevention of Terrorism Act 1974. It was clearly modelled on the 1939 Act. It was ready for implementation and conceived of as occupying the same rational space for fighting the serious but containable threat of the IRA. That rational space was for legislation dealing with emergencies (such as wartime emergency provisions) with a temporary, crisis-management objective. The 1974 Prevention of Terrorism Act was not modelled on the emergency provisions then operating in Northern Ireland[19], which contained more extensive powers, were more fully developed and less containable. Although the 1939 Act had two primary thrusts – expulsion orders to remove people from Great Britain,[20] and arrest powers for questioning[21] – the 1974 Prevention of Terrorism Act added a third – to provide for the proscription of the IRA and the possibility of the proscription of other 'terrorist' organizations.[22] Where have these relatively straightforward legislative responses to the terrorist threat emanating from the political conflicts in Northern Ireland led to in the latest Prevention of Terrorism Act, that of 1989?

In 1954, fifteen years after its passing, the Prevention of Violence (Temporary Provisions) Act 1939 was repealed.[23] In contrast, fifteen years after 1974, the 1989 Prevention of Terrorism Act has (despite its continued designation as temporary) become permanent. The 1974 Prevention of Terrorism Act incorporated its temporary status by the requirement of half-yearly renewal by statutory instrument,[24] and the 1984 Prevention of Terrorism Act required annual continuation by statutory instrument with an overall time span of five years.[25] The 1989 Prevention of Terrorism Act contains no fixed repeal date, although it remains subject to annual renewal by order.[26] The Preamble to the 1974 Prevention of Terrorism Act talked of 'An Act to proscribe organisations concerned in terrorism, and to give power to exclude certain persons from Great Britain or the United Kingdom in order to prevent acts of terrorism, and for connected purposes'. The 1976 and 1984 Prevention of Terrorism Acts Preambles talk only of reenactment, with amendments, of the previous Acts. The Preamble to the 1989 Prevention of Terrorism Act indicates its more extensive scope:

> An Act to make provision in place of the Prevention of Terrorism (Temporary Provisions) Act 1984; to make further provision in relation to powers of search under, and persons convicted of scheduled offences within the meaning of, the Northern Ireland (Emergency Provisions) Act 1978; and to enable the Secretary of State to prevent the establishment of new explosives factories, magazines and stores in Northern Ireland.

As optimal choice for countering terrorism on mainland Britain (remembering the continuing but separate Northern Ireland Emergency Provisions legislation),[27] the number of powers in each of the succeeding Prevention of Terrorism Acts has been increasing, although none of the original powers has been lost; so we have increase and amendment, but not subtraction (despite both official and unofficial calls for various repeals).[28] In 1989 the main increase in powers provides for those extending investigative powers and attacking the financial basis of terrorism (Part III). With the 1989 Prevention of Terrorism Act we have an incremental increase in powers as a response to the continuing threat of Northern Ireland terrorism on mainland Britain, together with the threats of international terrorism and the recognized permanency of those threats. We have the unitary political aim to do something about those threats by increasing the armoury of powers available to tackle them.

Part I of the Act re-enacts proscription and the variety of offences that create the unlawful status of an organization, such as offences of belonging to, supporting or assisting such an organization. The two proscribed organizations in Great Britain (as opposed to the larger number proscribed under the Emergency Provisions Act 1991) remain the IRA and the INLA (Irish National Liberation Army). The regional difference is represented by the different lists of proscribed organizations under the respective Prevention of Terrorism Act 1989 and the Emergency Provisions Act 1991 (containing a list of some ten organizations in Sched. 2). Although the different lists are justified by the greater quantity of terrorism in Northern Ireland, and the active role of loyalist or Protestant paramilitary organizations as well as the larger number of active nationalist or Catholic para-military organizations, a lack of organizational unity is the consequence. Such disunity has obvious dangers; since there are examples of loyalist/ Protestant para-military organizations operating on the mainland, especially in Scotland, an appearance can be given of non-evenhandedness. Since 1984 there have been no prosecutions in the United Kingdom for the main (non-public order) offences under Part I: their retention is mainly symbolic, in that 'It is impossible to deproscribe these two organisations'[29] – principally because of the public's perception of such a change.[30] This is not the case in Northern Ireland where a number of prosecutions occur annually. However, proscription is one of the key elements in the new offences in Part III of the Act, of contributing to or assisting in the retention or control of the resources of a proscribed organization – and hence the arguments for and against proscription[31] take on additional organizational problems. In addition, Part III clearly applies to those organizations proscribed under the separate Northern Ireland provisions, as it does to other non-proscribed organizations whose activities can be classified as terrorist within the meaning given by the definition in section 20 (see p. 128 above). So, for example, an organization not proscribed, such as Sinn Fein, might have its funding investigated, and thereafter possibly have its funds forfeited and even perhaps its bankers prosecuted, if the factual test of its funds being used for terrorism were seen to be satisfied.[32] The financial relationship between Sinn Fein and the IRA becomes investigable under these new powers. The increasing range and complexity of the anti-terrorist powers in the Prevention of Terrorism Act 1989 make a unitary response less feasible, as the powers feed off each other and create their own organizational problems.

Part II of the Act re-enacts the executive exclusion order power with the codes of practice relating to the making of representations and removal directions now located in Schedule 2. This change in form characterizes the recognition that the practice of exclusion is nearly wholly outside judicial control,[33] or at least that the safeguards in the legislation are at best procedural rather than substantive. It cannot be claimed that those who become the subjects of exclusion orders (often to prohibit their entry into one part of the UK)[34] are deprived of the 'normal' rights to a fair trial of the case against them, resulting in Viscount Colville's view of the exclusion order power in the 1984 Prevention of Terrorism Act: 'This power is the most draconian in the present Act'.[35] Viscount Colville believes that the exclusion order power 'certainly should not be re-enacted on a permanent basis'.[36] In contrast to the first five years of the 1980s, where the total number of exclusion orders in force averaged close to 250, the second half of the decade has seen that number halved.[37] The re-enactment of Part II represents the continuing aim that elements of the fight against terrorism involve security-sensitive information which cannot be deliberated upon either openly or before a judicial forum, and that the freedom of some citizens to move about or reside in one part of the United Kingdom can be curtailed by executive fiat on the basis of that information.[38]

Part III of the Act enacts the new prong of counter-terrorism which reflects not only a national but also an international initiative, to attack the financial basis of terrorist organizations. Whereas Parts I and II of the Act, as presently formulated, operate only in the context of terrorism arising out of the political conflicts in Northern Ireland, Part III has a broader ambit. Inviting contributions for, or giving or lending money for a proscribed organization has been an offence since 1974,[39] and it has been recognized for some time that terrorist organizations have been financed not only by individual contributions but also by extortion, protection rackets and other criminal activities.[40] However, the small number of charges under the former provisions (s. 10 of the Prevention of Terrorism Act 1984)[41] well illustrates the limits of the effectiveness of those counter-terrorist measures. So the new provisions are designed to go much further. Section 11 of the Prevention of Terrorism Act 1989, modelled on section 24 of the Drug Trafficking Act 1986, makes it an offence to assist in the retention or control of terrorist funds, and section 12 enforces disclosure about such funds irrespective of the privileged nature of that information. These are coupled with wide investigative powers under section 17 and Schedule 7, which, in respect of privileged information, probably go even further than those sanctioned by the Police and Criminal Evidence Act 1984 and other relevant legislation.[42] Section 13, again modelled on the Drug Trafficking Act 1986, enacts wide forfeiture provisions. Overall it can be expected that these relatively new provisions, which contain considerable problems of interpretation and impose onerous burdens on bankers and others, will have far-reaching effects. They are enacted with the primary target of attacking the financial bases of terrorism – after international consultation – with the experience of the Drug Trafficking Act 1986 and the mechanisms set up to operate it, and following the development of recent initiatives to this end in Northern Ireland.[43]

Part IV of the Act re-enacts the general arrest powers in respect of acts of terrorism[44] and their use as port and border controls.[45] The port powers as now particularized in Schedule 5 permit detention for examination by an examining officer for up to twelve hours (without direct suspicion) to determine '. . . whether that person appears to be a person who is or has been concerned in . . . terrorism . . .',[46] followed by a second twelve-hour period where the examining officer has reasonable suspicion of such involvement,[47] with the possibility of detention up to forty-eight hours at the behest of the examining officer and up to seven days with the permission of the Secretary of State.[48] This regime of powers has been upheld by the European Commission of Human Rights, despite the random nature of the first examination provision.[49] However in *Brogan and Others* v *United Kingdom*[50] the period of extended detention under the general arrest powers (and equally applicable to the port powers) was held to contravene Article 5(1)(c) of the European Convention on Human Rights that:

> Everyone arrested or detained in accordance with the provisions of paragraph 1(c) of this Article shall be brought promptly before a judge or other officer authorised by law to exercise judicial power . . .

The Court considered that the requirement of promptness was relatively inflexible and that the shortest period of detention that applied to one of the four applicants in this case, namely four days and six hours, was beyond the limits of promptness. The Prevention of Terrorism Act 1989, re-enacts the offending provisions of the Prevention of Terrorism Act 1984, using recourse to a derogation notice of an emergency under Article 15(1) of the Convention as the means of avoiding any change in the law following the European Court's ruling.[51] Whether such a derogation notice rather than a change in the law consonant with the Court's decision would be upheld by the European Court should a case come before it on this issue is open to some doubt.[52] But, in the context of the rational actor, this response represents a continuing unitary theme: that anti-terrorist measures need to accumulate to achieve success, cannot be reduced and may be only minimally amended.

Part V of the Act, apart from the more extensive investigative powers that it enacts, and other miscellaneous matters, re-enacts the criminal offence of omitting to disclose information about terrorism.[53] That offence, which was not initially included in the Prevention of Terrorism Act 1974 and only appeared in the Prevention of Terrorism Act 1976 following a back-bench amendment, has not been without its critics, including Viscount Colville who clearly favours repeal.[54] Prosecutions for this offence on the mainland are very limited and convictions negligible.[55] It remains as one of the list of existing provisions which appear to have potential rather than real significance. It is worth noting, for example, that despite the fact that the executive powers of internment have not been employed since 1975, they remain on the statute book.[56]

Part VI of the Act concerns solely the addition of further provisions for Northern Ireland. The inclusion of Part VI is the first occasion when the Prevention of Terrorism Act and the Northern Ireland (Emergency Provisions) Acts are integrated at this formal statutory level. Section 21 contains the wide emergency power for police or army in Northern Ireland to control the movement of any person who happens to be at a 'place of search' – which includes domestic accommodation – where a search for munitions is in operation. What is significant is that it becomes clear that those who have a responsibility for security in Northern Ireland are involved in the processes of creation of all anti-terrorist legislation. In a similar vein, section 22 amends the rules relating to remission for those who are imprisoned for more than five years for a terrorist offence in Northern Ireland: that such an amendment is included in the Prevention of Terrorism Act rather than some amending Northern Ireland (Emergency Provisions) Act breaches the containability advantage of the separate mainland anti-terrorist legislation.[57]

This short account of some of the provisions of the 1989 Prevention of Terrorism Act has attempted to illustrate some of the rational and unitary explanations for the increased scope and range of the Act, resulting in a statute now containing nine schedules and of seventy-two pages in length, compared to the 1974 Prevention of Terrorism Act with three schedules and fourteen pages. It has also demonstrated some of the organizational problems of how the Act relates to the more extensive powers in Northern Ireland, and how some of its provisions are now of more symbolic than real importance, their continued existence being based more on the reassurance of public opinion.

The Elected Authorities (Northern Ireland) Act 1989 and the Broadcasting Ban 1988: Symbolic gestures?

The Elected Authorities (Northern Ireland) Act 1989[58] sets out to counter terrorism by amending the democratic process of elections in Northern Ireland. The core of the Act is the requirement that local election candidates in Northern Ireland, or candidates for election to the Northern Ireland Assembly, are not validly nominated as candidates unless they have made a declaration against terrorism, and that persons nominated 'shall be conclusively presumed to have made a declaration'.[59] The declaration is set out in Schedule 2:

> I declare that, if elected, I will not by word or deed express support for or approval of –

(a) any organisation that is for the time being a proscribed organisation specified in Schedule 2 to the Northern Ireland (Emergency Provisions) Act 1978; or

(b) acts of terrorism (that is to say, violence for political ends) connected with the affairs of Northern Ireland.

Such a declaration is primarily aimed at Sinn Fein candidates.[60] Provisional Sinn Fein have achieved some success in local council elections in the 1980s and one of their leaders, Gerry Adams, was elected to Parliament as member for West Belfast.[61] Sinn Fein is not a proscribed organization under either the Prevention of Terrorism Act 1989 or the Emergency Provisions Act 1991, but the IRA is. The Elected Authorities Act 1989 is, according to Richard Needham MP (Under-Secretary of State, Northern Ireland Office), not meant to 'restrict the freedom of electors to vote for whomever they choose'; rather the aim is to enshrine

the principle that elected office carries with it certain basic political responsibilities, one of which is that expression of support for, or approval of, terrorism or organisations actively engaged in perpetrating terrorism are not compatible with the acceptance of office in democratic local government.[62]

For a period up until 1974 Sinn Fein was a proscribed organization in Northern Ireland, but de-proscription at that time was considered important as part of the political strategy of trying to draw the Catholic community into the democratic processes in Northern Ireland. By sections 18,19 and 21 of the Offences Against the State Act 1939, treasonable or other organizations can be proscribed in the Republic of Ireland and membership made a serious offence. The IRA is proscribed but certainly not Sinn Fein whose candidates are regularly elected to public office at both local and national level. In Northern Ireland the electoral successes of Sinn Fein coupled with their avowed policy of using 'the ballot box in one hand and the Armalite in the other', and the disquiet of Unionist local councillors at having to share the council chamber with those who they believe are either involved themselves in terrorist acts or are the apologists for the terrorists, inevitably led to a reaction. The first stages of that reaction were the attempts to exclude Sinn Fein councillors from participation in council work. These attempts failed.[63] The next stage was a discussion paper issued by the Northern Ireland Office in October 1987 entitled 'Elected Representatives and the Democratic Process in Northern Ireland'. That discussion paper, which clearly favoured a declaration against terrorism in preference to either outright proscription for Sinn Fein or extended disqualification, or some form of oath of allegiance, did not meet with universal approval.[64]

The wording of the declaration will, nearly inevitably, be interpreted to cover too little or too much because of the impractical character of the legal stipulation. The declaration talks of 'word or deed' and 'express support for or approval of'. Consider whether a councillor who attended an IRA funeral of a constituent would have done the deed that amounts to approval of a proscribed organization. Consider the reaction in the council chamber to a discussion of events such as those in Gibraltar when three unarmed IRA suspects were shot dead. At what point does criticism of the actions of the security forces amount to approval of 'acts of terrorism'?

The breach of the declaration provisions of section 6 of the Act are clearly formulated to impose an objective standard: 'if his words or actions could reasonably be understood as expressing support for, or approval of . . .'. They impose restraint on private as well as public expressions where they are 'likely to become known to the public'. They cover expressions made abroad and those made at times that would otherwise be privileged (as in the Northern Ireland Assembly). The mechanism of enforcement of the declaration is through proceedings in the High Court for disqualification from office for a period of five years[65] following a determination that a person is in breach of the declaration. Since any person entitled to vote has standing to apply to the High Court to attempt to bring about disqualification, it can be anticipated that that Court may from time to time become the forum for politically motivated actions, out of which different political groups would hope to make political capital.

The choice to restrict Sinn Fein in this way, rather than to proscribe it or leave it unrestricted is clearly legally problematic as illustrated above, and close to the boundaries of legitimate democratic practice.[66] Despite this, it could still be seen as a rational choice. It goes hand in hand with the recent broadcasting restrictions which applied to Sinn Fein and which attempted to impose a partial muzzle on their use of the media. Also it follows the change in the electoral process resulting from the political conflicts in Northern Ireland brought about in the Representation of the People Act 1981 to disallow IRA prisoners from standing for Parliament, after the electoral success of Bobby Sands.[67]

The broadcasting ban issued in October 1988 by the Home Secretary required the main broadcasting authorities not to broadcast:

> any words spoken, whether in the course of an interview or discussion or otherwise, by a person who appears or who is heard on the programme in which the matter is broadcast where (a) the person speaking the words represents or purports to represent an organisation specified in para 2 below, or (b) the words support or solicit or invite support for such an organisation . . .

The organizations referred to include proscribed organizations under the current Prevention of Terrorism Act and Emergency Provisions Act, and 'Sinn Fein, Republican Sinn Fein and the Ulster Defence Association'.[68] The exceptions to this ban are words spoken by or in support of a parliamentary, local or European candidate, or words spoken in the course of parliamentary proceedings. The technical difficulties of the wording of this ban leave it open to numerous interpretations.[69] Clarification from the Home office suggested that the ban restricted direct reporting of someone speaking on behalf of Sinn Fein, but did not restrict a voice-over of someone speaking their words whilst the audience are watching the picture of the representative of Sinn Fein. This ban, which did not go so far as to make Sinn Fein an illegal organization as such, tends to be justified in either one of two ways. Either it is an attempt to deny those who wish to excuse or justify terrorist activity the oxygen of publicity, by restraining them from directly addressing the public and having an unproblematic media platform, or it is a restriction resulting from the offensiveness of their comments especially following a terrorist atrocity. Both of these reasons have been given by members of the Government and by academic commentators.[70] The first reason has a potential claim to being part of a rational policy to counter terrorism; the second does not. And of course the real casualties of such a ban are the public, who in being impeded in making their judgements on the basis of all the evidence, suffer a restriction of their freedoms.

If the approach of the Electoral Authorities Act 1989 and the broadcasting ban to defeating terrorism is optimal, then it rests on the premise that strategy for countering terrorism must operate not only at a security level but also at a political level. As a rational approach, the declaration provision in the Elected Authorities Act 1989 and the media restrictions of the broadcasting ban are meant to remove the camouflage from those whose actual aims are non-democratic (the violent overthrow of the existing order). On the other hand it might be that these examples have more to do with the politics of appeasing certain interest groups in Northern Ireland and encouraging them into political dialogue by symbolic action, than actually furthering the fight against terrorism.

The arrest powers of the Prevention of Terrorism Act 1989, section 14 and the Emergency Provisions Act 1991, sections 16–18: organizational unity?

It is not possible here to go through the main provisions of the Emergency Provisions Act 1991, whose history since 1970 is extensive, and all of whose powers have been subject to detailed and lengthy review and debate. One example will be concentrated on, namely that of arrest powers, since they represent significant updating from the 1973, 1978 and 1987 Emergency Provisions Acts, and because they are closely associated with an equivalent set of powers in the Prevention of Terrorism Act 1989.

The powers of arrest contained in section 14 Prevention of Terrorism Act 1989 are, principally, those enacted in the Prevention of Terrorism Act 1974. In 1974, as far as the mainland was concerned, the regime of police powers for arrest, detention and questioning had not been consolidated into the Police and Criminal Evidence Act 1984. So, whereas in 1974 police powers of arrest for questioning, or detention for questioning, were either non-existent or piecemeal or at least problematic,[71] in 1989 a clear regime of police powers, permitting detention up to a maximum of ninety-six hours subject to periods of review by various authorities, was in operation for arrestable offences.[72] In 1974, some of the necessity for enacting a specific regime of arrest powers in relation to terrorism was thought to be the inadequacy of the general arrest powers that were then in operation. Whether or not they satisfied the need to arrest those suspected of terrorism, they were certainly seen to be inadequate for the purposes of investigating terrorism. Detention for questioning was the key investigative advantage of the then newly enacted Prevention of Terrorism Act 1974 arrest powers and their linked port examination powers.[73] In the debates preceding the enactment of the Police and Criminal Evidence Act 1984, the argument in favour of the importance of an investigative power to detain for questioning leant on the usefulness of such a power in the fight against terrorism. But in relation to serious crimes, rather than just terrorism, the desire to balance greater investigative powers with better safeguards for individual suspects was clearly evident. The Prevention of Terrorism Act 1989 has failed to bring the regimes of the Prevention of Terrorism Acts and the Police and Criminal Evidence Act together, even though this sequence of legislative history would suggest such an outcome.[74] Hence the period of extended detention beyond forty-eight hours permitted by section 14(5) Prevention of Terrorism Act 1989, up to a seven-day maximum, is subject to no periods of review – it operates quite separately from the safeguards adopted in the Police and Criminal Evidence Act 1984. Part of the reason for this lack of cohesion (the importance of which has been proved by recent events[75]), might be illustrated by looking at the relationship between the Prevention of Terrorism Act 1989 arrest powers and the regime of powers for arrest and detention which operate in Northern Ireland under the Emergency Provisions Acts.

A number of arrest powers were contained in the Northern Ireland (Emergency Provisions) Act 1978, namely sections 11, 13 and 14. A range of powers has appeared to be necessary in order to authorize arrest by different enforcement agencies (the army as well as the police) and for differing purposes (e.g., the s. 11 power was primarily linked to the executive power of internment). Section 13 most closely resembled the Prevention of Terrorism Act arrest power; however, despite amendment, some differences remain – as now re-enacted in sections 16–18 of the Emergency Provisions Act 1991.

The 1980s have seen a significant increase in the use of the Prevention of Terrorism Act power rather than those under the Emergency Provisions Acts, as well as some attempt to use ordinary criminal investigative powers for less serious 'terrorist' offences.[76] In conjunction with the policy of 'criminalizing' the offences of the terrorist in Northern Ireland, goes the policy of reducing the separateness of the emergency provisions that operate to segregate and politicize the legal system in Northern Ireland. Use of the Prevention of Terrorism Act arrest power serves both purposes. In particular, after the British Government withdrew its notice of derogation under the European Convention on Human Rights in 1984, that had up until then applied to Northern Ireland's separate emergency provisions, the fight against terrorism could be seen to operate equally and uniformly under the Prevention of Terrorism Act applying to the whole of the United Kingdom. Notwithstanding the advantages that flow from the more general use of the Prevention of Terrorism Act arrest power in Northern Ireland, organizational problems have been created and as a consequence decisions taken which have spawned new inadequacies.

If we look closely at the reasons given for the latest derogation notice issued in December 1988 in order to avoid altering the existing regime of arrest powers under the Prevention of Terrorism Act, following the ruling in *Brogan and Others* v *the United Kingdom*,[77] we can see that they apply much less forcefully, if at all, on the mainland as opposed to Northern Ireland. It would appear that objections to a form of judicial scrutiny authorizing periods of extended detention come from the Northern Ireland judiciary.[78] So, the following argument can be presented. If the British Government had not withdrawn its notice of derogation in 1984 in order to pursue a policy of normalization, and if the Prevention of Terrorism Act arrest power had not been adopted for more comprehensive use in Northern Ireland, partly in order to pursue the same policy, then the likelihood of an unreformed Prevention of Terrorism Act arrest power in the 1989 Act and a notice of derogation applying for the first time to the whole of the United Kingdom would have been greatly reduced.

Sequential decisions, from past to future, that appear good enough at the present time, are characterized in the changes that surround the recent history of section 14 Prevention of Terrorism Act 1989 and its relationship to the emergency arrest powers of the Emergency Provisions Act 1991. Factored decision-making, with different interests pressing on different branches of the State's organization, coalesce in producing the artificiality of a state of emergency in the whole of the United Kingdom, brought about by a decision of the European Court of Human Rights.

Conclusion

A leading academic commentator who has been influential in helping to construct Britain's response to terrorism has surmised that:

A careful study of the British response to terrorism, both in Northern Ireland and internationally, shows that a well-defined and consistent approach has been adopted by successive governments since the mid-

1970's. The underlying principles that inform the British policy, recently succinctly reiterated by the Home Secretary, are: (i) a firm political will to uphold the rule of law and democratic government and to defeat terrorism; (ii) absolute refusal to surrender to terrorist extortion and demands; (iii) determination to act in accord with domestic and international law; (iv) treatment of convicted terrorists as common criminals with no special privileges, pardons, or amnesty; (v) the promotion of national and international measures to combat terrorists by minimising their rewards and maximising their costs and losses.[79]

This conclusion cannot be supported by an analysis, as has been presented here, of the rationale of the major legal provisions as they have evolved to counter terrorism. The combination of rational, organizational and political approaches that have pressed themselves on the changing legislative framework to counter terrorism have produced a range of responses which cannot easily be described as 'well-defined and consistent', nor as wholly upholding 'the rule of law and democratic government' nor 'in accord with domestic and international law'. And what is often characteristic of these responses to terrorism is that they are legally imprecise, leaving wide areas of discretion to those whom they empower.

The momentum of the British management of terrorism at the specific level of legislative enactment and executive order, rather than at the more general level of political programme and propaganda, demonstrates how such exceptional powers are destructive of constitutional restraints on the exercise of power. When faced with the serious levels of violence arising out of the political conflicts in Northern Ireland, and despite the weight of national and international[80] pressure and machinery aimed at supervising the counter-terrorist measures, a rational and unitary approach is lost under the competing needs of maintaining organizational unity and satisfying political demands. Too many of the provisions currently authorized have lost their effectiveness, or been proved at some level to be counter-productive; too many retain their status as, at best, symbolic gestures – less products of rational policy-making than increasingly irrational, dramaturgical or emotional responses. It is feasible, on the basis of the evidence presented here, to argue that the time has come to restart the process of countering terrorism in Britain, and to make a complete break from the prevailing models derived from 1922, 1939, 1973 and 1974.[81] It might be that cooperation within Europe may present such an opportunity. Within Northern Ireland it is recognized by many commentators that counter-terrorist measures are to a greater or lesser extent part of the range of problems that underlie terrorism. A new set of counter-terrorist initiatives are not in themselves going to solve the social, economic, religious and political conflicts in Northern Ireland, but they may well facilitate the climate in which serious political dialogue, rather than terrorism, has a greater chance of flourishing.

NOTES

1 No attempt will be made here to distinguish phrases such as 'counter-terrorism', 'anti-terrorism', etc., such as is done by other writers, e.g. E. Morris and A. Hoe, *Terrorism: Threat and Response* (Macmillan, 1987).

2 Such as with proposals emanating from the 'informal' TREVI Group in Europe since the late 1970s. E.g., the bulk of the new set of rules operating in Part III of the Prevention of Terrorism (Temporary Provisions) Act 1989 and Part VII of the Northern Ireland (Emergency Provisions) Act 1991 to attack the financial basis of terrorism, seem to have had such an impetus. For an analysis of common action within the EU, see D. Freestone, 'The EEC Treaty and common action on terrorism', *Yearbook of European Law* (Clarendon Press, 1984) pp. 207–29; J. Lodge and D. Freestone, 'The European Community and terrorism: political and legal aspects' in Y. Alexander and K. A. Myers (eds), *Terrorism in Europe* (Croom Helm in association with the Centre for Strategic and International Studies 1982), pp. 79–101.

3 This exemption was propounded in English law in s. 3 Extradition Act 1870. See generally C. Van den Wijngaert, *The Political Offence Exception to Extradition* (The delicate problem of balancing the rights of the individual and the international public order) (Kluwer, 1980); and more particularly, D. Schiff, 'A note on extradition and terrorism', *Alberta Law Review* (1983) 21 436–46.

4 A classic example of this was the effect of the introduction of internment (preventive detention) in Northern Ireland in Aug. 1971. Following the introduction violence escalated; the number of deaths linked to terrorism in Northern Ireland in 1972 (well over 450) was at least three times as many as in 1971.

5 In the jurisprudence of the European Court and Commission of Human Rights the notion of a 'margin of appreciation' or 'measure of discretion' has been applied to a number of the protected rights, but particularly those incorporated in Arts. 8–11 of the European Convention, including privacy and the freedoms of thought, expression and association. These rights are some of those most under threat from counter-terrorist provisions. It is equally applicable to other rights, such as those of liberty and security under Art. 5, as recently considered by the European Court in *Brogan and Others* v *UK* (1989) 11 EHRR 117 (discussed on p. 132).

6 For a clear statement of this model of state decision-making, see G.T. Allison, *Essence of Decision: Explaining the Cuban Missile Crisis* (Little, Brown and Co., 1971), Ch. 5 'Model III: governmental politics'.

7 The whole of Ireland had been under British rule since the twelfth century.

8 This is well illustrated by P. Foot in his polemic *Ireland: Why Britain Must Get Out* (Chatto & Windus, 1989). See also, J. Darby, *Conflict in Northern Ireland: the Development of a Polarised Community* (Gill & Macmillan, 1976); M. Farrell, *Northern Ireland: the Orange State* (2nd edn) (Pluto Press, 1980); P. Bew, P. Gibbon and H. Patterson, *The State in Northern Ireland, 1921–1972* (Manchester University Press, 1979). As for the future, see J. McGarry and B.O'Leary, *The Future of Northern Ireland* (Clarendon Press, 1990).

9 The Civil Authorities (Special Powers) Acts (Northern Ireland) 1922–43.

10 The 1.5 million population of Northern Ireland is approximately 60 per cent Protestant and 40 per cent Catholic.

11 See Helsinki Watch Report, *Human Rights in Northern Ireland* (1991) Ch. 3.

12 Hereafter referred to as the Emergency Provisions Act 1991. The general interpretation section is s. 66.

13 See Pt I: 'Scheduled Offences' Emergency Provisions Act 1991.

14 Despite these serious problems there are nevertheless a good number of

arguments supporting the return to jury trial: see S.C. Greer and A. White, *Abolishing the Diplock Courts* (Cobden Trust, 1986).

15 It is worth noting that one of the continuing problems with the extradition arrangements between Britain and Ireland, despite the Irish Extradition (European Convention on the Suppression of Terrorism) Act 1987 being modelled on the European Convention, is that some of those who it is alleged have committed terrorist crimes in Northern Ireland are not being extradited, and are gaining the protection of the political offence exemption from extradition, because their crimes are not within the list of offences for which the political offence exemption does not apply in the European Convention on the Suppression of Terrorism's list. See generally, G. Gilbert, 'The Irish interpretation of the political offence exemption', *International and Comparative Law Quarterly* 41 (1992) 66–84; C. Campbell, 'Extradition to Northern Ireland: prospects and problems', *Modern Law Review* 52 (1989) 585–621.

16 Hereafter all of the Prevention of Terrorism (Temporary Provisions) Acts will be referred to as the Prevention of Terrorism Act 1974 or 1976 or 1984 or 1989.

17 See B. Gibson, *The Birmingham Bombs* (Barry Rose, 1976).

18 Passing all its parliamentary stages between first presentation on 27 Nov. 1984 and Royal Assent on 28 Nov. 1984.

19 Principally at that time the Northern Ireland (Emergency Provisions) Act 1973.

20 Ss 1–3. The Act also included the executive power to make registration orders and prohibition orders – the latter designed to prohibit entry into Great Britain.

21 S. 4. The Act used the words '. . . pending the determination of the question whether he is such a person' – namely a person concerned with acts of violence in relation to Irish affairs. The time limits for detention were 48 hours plus a further five days with the authorization of the Secretary of State – exactly the same time limits as enacted in the Prevention of Terrorism Act 1974 and retained since then.

22 S. 1(3).

23 The Act was originally designed to last for no longer than two years, see s 5(2).

24 S. 12.

25 S. 17.

26 S. 27.

27 Now the Emergency Provisions Act 1991.

28 An official example being Viscount Colville's *Review of the Operation of the Prevention of Terrorism (Temporary Provisions) Act 1984, (Cm 264) (1987)*. As an example of an unofficial call, see C. Scorer and P. Hewitt, *The New Prevention of Terrorism Act: the Case for Repeal* (National Council for Civil Liberties, 1985).

29 Colville, *ibid.*, p. 46.

30 'The most dangerous would be a perception that the leading merchants of Irish terrorism were no longer disapproved . . .' *ibid.*

31 See C. Walker, *The Prevention of Terrorism in British Law* (2nd edn) (Manchester University Press, 1992), Ch. 5.

32 Ss 11–13. Sinn Fein is usually described as the political wing of the IRA.

33 On exclusion orders, see D. Bonner, *Emergency Powers in Peacetime* (Sweet & Maxwell, 1985), pp. 191–209.

34 The equivalent of the 1939 Act's prohibition order. See, e.g., C. Walker, 'Members of Parliament and executive security measures', *Public Law* Winter [1983] 537, dealing with the order against Gerry Adams of Sinn Fein.

35 *Op.cit.* note 27, p. 40.

36 *Ibid.*

37 See Viscount Colville, *Report on the Operation in 1988 of the Prevention of Terrorism (Temporary Provisions) Act 1984* (HMSO, 1989), table 11, p. 21.

38 There are inevitably implications for the free movement of persons within the EU and the corresponding need to share security-sensitive information.

39 Prevention of Terrorism Act 1974, s.(1)(b).

40 See, e.g., J. Adams, *The Financing of Terror* (New English Library, 1986), Ch. 7 'The IRA mafia'.

41 See Colville, *op. cit.* note 27, p. 47.

42 Police and Criminal Evidence Act 1984, ss 8–14 and Sched. 1; Criminal Justice Act 1988, Part VI; Drug Trafficking Offences Act 1986.

43 See J. Adams, R. Morgan and A. Bambridge, *Ambush: the War between the SAS and the IRA* (Pan, 1988), p. 37.

44 S. 14. These arrest powers are considered in detail in Walker, *op. cit.* note 30, Ch. 7, and Bonner, *op. cit.* note 32, Ch. 4(2).

45 S. 16 and Sched. 5.

46 Sch. 5, s. 2(1).

47 Sch. 5, s. 2(4).

48 Sch. 5, s. 6.

49 *McVeigh, O'Neill and Evans* v *UK* (1981) 5 EHRR 71.

50 *Op. cit.* note 5.

51 The derogation was dated 23 Dec. 1988.

52 This has already been argued by D. Bonner, 'Combatting terrorism in the 1990s', *Public Law* Autumn [1989] 448–51. The European Commission of Human Rights admitted a challenge to the derogation notice by the British Government under Art. 15(1) of the European Convention, in an application brought by P. Brannigan and P. McBride, *Guardian*, 2 March 1991, p. 7.

53 S. 18.

54 *Op. cit.* note 27, Ch. 15.

55 *Ibid.*, p. 50.

56 Now Pt IV and Sch. 3, Emergency Provisions Act 1991.

57 See Pt 6.

58 Hereafter referred to as the Elected Authorities Act 1989.

59 S.7(3) Elected Authorities Act 1989.

60 Sinn Fein being the political wing of the IRA, and PSF (Provisional Sinn Fein) being the political wing of the Provisional IRA. Since 1986 a group calling itself Republican Sinn Fein has also come into being.

61 See generally L. Clarke, *Broadening the Battlefield: the H Blocks and the Rise of Sinn Fein* (Gill & Macmillan, 1987); P. Bishop and E. Mallie, *The Provisional IRA* (Corgi, 1987); P. Arthur and K. Jeffery, *Northern Ireland Since 1968* (Basil Blackwell, 1988). Sinn Fein has also achieved some electoral success in the Irish Republic.

62 H.C. Debs, Standing Committee A, col. 7, 15 Dec. 1988.

63 See *In Re Curan and McCann's Application* [1985] 7 NIJB 22 and *Re French and Others' Application* [1985] 7 NIJB 48.

64 See B. Thompson, 'Protecting the democratic process', *Public Law* Spring [1988] 18–24. Previous support for such a proposal came from P. Wilkinson, 'Maintaining the democratic process and public support' in R. Clutterbuck (ed.), *The Future of Political Violence* (Macmillan, 1986), Ch. 17.

65 S. 8, Elected Authorities Act 1989.

66 See H.F. Rawlings, 'Introduction', *Introduction to Law and the Electoral Process* (Sweet and Maxwell, 1988).

67 For a clear view against this provision, see C. Walker, 'Prisoners in parliament – another view', *Public Law* [1982] 389–94.

68 Legal challenges to this ban have been unsuccessful, see *R* v *Secretary of State for the Home Department, ex parte Brind* [1990] 1 All ER 469 and [1991] 1 All

ER 720. Also see the critical commentaries, B. Thompson, 'Broadcasting and terrorism' *Public Law* Winter [1989] 527–41; J. Jowell, 'Broadcasting and terrorism, human rights and proportionality', *Public Law* Summer [1990] 149–56; B. Thompson, 'Broadcasting and terrorism in the House of Lords', *Public Law* Autumn [1991] 347–53.

69 This clearly adds to the problems of broadcasters not knowing, in many instances, whether or not they will be in breach. The consequence is thought to be a 'chilling effect', making broadcasters very wary about how they can report on or make programmes about Northern Ireland.

70 H.C. Deb., vol. 138, cols 893–903, 19 Oct. 1988; and P. Wilkinson, *op. cit.* note 62.

71 See L.H. Leigh, *Police Powers in England and Wales* (2nd edn) (Butterworth, 1985), Ch. II 'The development of police powers'.

72 Police and Criminal Evidence Act 1984, ss. 40–44.

73 The rules of the common law governing questioning of suspects and the extent to which such questioning was or was not authorized were unclear, and only moderately clarified by the 'quasi-law' of the 1912 and the 1964 versions of what was known as the Judges' Rules.

74 This was even more significant in Northern Ireland with the introduction of the Criminal Evidence (Northern Ireland) Order 1988, which among other things reversed the traditional right to silence by permitting the failure of a suspect to give evidence to be taken into account along with other evidence of guilt. See S. Greer, 'The right to silence: a review of the current debate', *Modern Law Review* 53 (1990) 723–4.

75 Particularly the now notorious miscarriage of justice cases where these extended arrest powers were first used, namely the 'Birmingham Six', 'Guildford Four' and 'Maguire Seven' cases: see, C. Mullin, *Error of Judgement: the Truth about the Birmingham Bombings* (Chatto & Windus, 1987); R. Kee, *Trial and Error (The True Events Surrounding the Convictions and Trials of the Guildford Four and the Maguire Seven* (Hamish Hamilton, 1989).

76 This is well illustrated by G. Hogan and C. Walker, *Political Violence and the Law in Ireland* (Manchester University Press, 1989) pp. 46–58.

77 *Op. cit.* note 5.

78 See H.C. Deb. vol. 146, cols 53–68, 30 Jan. 1989.

79 P. Wilkinson, 'British policy on terrorism: an assessment' in J. Lodge (ed.), *The Threat of Terrorism* (Harvester Wheatsheaf, 1988) p. 50.

80 A recent example of international supervision is the Helsinki Watch Report, *Human Rights in Northern Ireland* (1991).

81 Civil Authorities (Special Powers) Act (Northern Ireland) 1922; Prevention of Violence (Temporary Provisions) Act 1939; Northern Ireland (Emergency Provisions) Act 1973; Prevention of Terrorism (Temporary Provisions) Act 1974.

8 France's responses to terrorism

Jacques Borricand

By its nature, terrorism threatens the very existence of society, in particular democratic society and quite rightly there has been talk of there being a 'terrorist drama'.[1] By systematic recourse to methods which create terror among populations in order to achieve his aims, particularly political ones, and thus influence history, the terrorist adopts the principle according to which the end justifies the means.

At the end of the last century, anarchism had already led the French legislator to react with the law of 28 July 1894. This policy was subsequently extended by ignoring the political nature of the crime whenever a serious offence was at issue. This is the lesson of the Gorguloff judgment of the Court of Cassation on 20 August 1932: murder, by its very nature and whatever the motives, constitutes a common law crime. Shortly afterwards, the statutory order of 29 July 1939 hardened the repression by restoring the death sentence for breaches of State security.

But it is mainly after the 1960s that the terrorist problem grew to its full extent: taking of hostages, aircraft hijackings and murder of diplomats upset the international community and in particular Western Europe.

In France in the 1970s, the doctrine of 'sanctuary' was developed: it consisted in protecting national territory and national interests by keeping them neutral in the eyes of terrorist groups, so that it was obvious that France was keen to keep itself aloof from conflicts in which they were involved. Apart from some regionalist problems, then, France was relatively safe from terrorism.

The 1980s saw a notable reorientation of French anti-terrorist policy, confronted as it was by the more and more murderous activities of 'Action Directe', by the upsurge of Corsican and Basque separatists, and abroad by the kidnapping of French citizens by more extreme Islamic groups. After a brief hesitation in 1981, a policy of repression was developed from 1982 onwards (dissolution of the Front de Libération National Corse (FLNC) and a change of attitude towards the Basque separatist movement ETA), and this policy was reinforced from 1986 to 1988, though today one can clearly detect some redefinition (in the words of Roland Dumas, 'the page has to be turned'[2]).

This upsurge in terrorism led to the setting up of a specific scheme, exceptional to common law. This scheme requires international solidarity in order to ensure a more powerful response. But before such a scheme can be implemented, the difficult question of the notion of terrorism must be solved.

THE NOTION OF TERRORISM

In order to define this notion in domestic law, it is essential to explain first the problem in international law. The concepts developed by the latter have indeed been projected into national law.

In international law

It is noteworthy that international documents referring to terrorism refrain from giving any definition of it, as is shown by the International Law Commission's Draft Code of Crimes against the Peace and Security of Mankind (see Art. 2 para. 6) or the Strasbourg European Convention on terrorism.[3]

Before the war

The only legal instrument which gives a definition of terrorism is the Geneva Convention of 16 November 1937 for the Prevention and Punishment of Terrorism, which never came into force. Paragraph 2 of the first Article stated that:

> in the present Convention, the expression 'acts of terrorism' means criminal acts directed against a State and intended or calculated to create a state of terror in the minds of particular persons, or a group of persons or the general public.

This attempt at a definition has been much criticized and quite rightly so.[4] Indeed, defining terrorism by the terror it causes is a tautology; speaking of criminal facts is remarkably vague, since the notion of crime varies from one State to another; and lastly, classing as terrorism only those acts that are directed against a State, that is acts directed against a structure consisting at once of a population, a territory and a government endowed with sovereign power, is a very restrictive idea, since in most cases only one of these elements is the target of a terrorist attack.

After the war

From 1954, the International Law Commission elaborated, within the United Nations, a Draft Code of Crimes against the Peace and Security of Mankind, among which acts of terrorism are mentioned.

In March 1973, the representatives of the Ministers of the Council of Europe had asked for a study to be carried out on some legal aspects of terrorism. On 16 May 1973, the Consultative Assembly of the Council of Europe (recommendation 703) condemned 'international terrorist acts which, regardless of their cause, should be punished as serious criminal offences involving the killing, kidnapping or endangering of the lives of innocent people'. In the face of 'the disappointing response of the international community', it considered 'a joint action among Member States of the Council of Europe all the more necessary', and hoped for 'effective sanctions against terrorism'.

These efforts were crowned with success, for they led to the signature in January 1977 of the European Convention on the Suppression of Terrorism, ratified in France by the law of 16 July 1987 (Art. 689(3) of the Code of Criminal Procedure).[5]

The merit of this text is to make, for the first time, an express reference to terrorism. In this perspective, it pays considerable attention to the extradition of terrorists, by identifying two categories of offences. The first one, dealt with in the first article, comprises offences which, 'for the purposes of extradition shall not be regarded as a political offence'. First of all, this refers to offences controlled by the Hague Convention and the Montreal Convention, and by the texts relating to the protection of diplomatic agents. Secondly, as a general rule, the first article lists a very broad range of offences, such as kidnapping, the taking of a hostage or unlawful detention, the use of bombs, of firearms, etc. The second category of offences comprises offences which a State may not regard as political ones: according to Article 2, these are 'any act[s] of violence, other than one covered by article 1, against the life, physical integrity or liberty of a person'.

The general nature of the terms used in this text thus makes it possible to include in the notion of terrorism acts which were not previously qualified in that way, such as anarchism.

But the Strasbourg Convention goes further than the preceding conventions in that its first article mentions offences which are never to be considered as political. As a result of the mandatory nature of this provision, the wording now seems to deny the terrorist act any political qualification. But in the second article, States are allowed full scope to accept or dismiss this qualification as a political offence.

Thus, examining the legal instruments presently in force in international law proves to be disappointing. Drawing up a restrictive list of acts possibly excluded from extradition is evasive, since none of the above-mentioned texts qualifies such acts as acts of terrorism. It has been possible to speak of 'the undetectable act of terrorism'.[6] This can be explained, because 'we have a series of preconceived ideas about acts of terrorism which are far from always being the case',[7] and there is a tendency to use this classification slightly at random.[8] It is significant that, during the Occupation in

France, the same individuals were regarded as terrorists by some, and as Resistance fighters by others; that during the Algerian war the Algerian rebel who exploded a bomb in a café was regarded as a terrorist, whereas the drunkard who throws a Molotov cocktail in a public place is not regarded as such. More recently, at the time of the Munich attack in 1972, need I remind you that the raid by the Fedeyine was described as a terrorist act, whereas much more murderous Israeli bombings in retaliation against Arab villages were not treated in the same way by the press?

This ambiguity in the notion of terrorism probably explains why the French legislator was slow to define it.

In national law

Curiously, it is only with the law of 9 September 1986 that the legislator decided to incriminate terrorist offences. The legislator had the choice of two methods: either to create a new offence as was done, for example, in German legislation, or merely to list certain pre-existing offences and subject them to a more severe special regime whenever they are committed in certain circumstances. The legislator chose the second method, as the Spanish legislator had done in 1984. According to the new Article 706–16 of the French Code of Criminal Procedure

> when they [the offences] are linked to a collective or individual undertaking whose intention is to seriously disturb public order by intimidation or terror, they are prosecuted, investigated and judged according to the rules of this Code subject to the provisions of the present Title.

That shows that terrorist behaviour presupposes at the same time an objective fact – a specifically defined offence – and a subjective fact – the motive of intimidation or terror.

The objective fact: a specifically defined offence

In the list of Article 706–16, it is possible to distinguish three kinds of offences.

1. Offences involving an act of violence against a person:
   - wilful homicide (murder and assassination) with the exclusion of parricide and infanticide (Arts 295–8; Arts 301, 303 and 304 Penal Code);
   - intentional violence resulting in unintentional mutilation, disability or death (Arts 310 and 311 Penal Code);
   - intentional violence against minors up to fifteen years of age either regularly or resulting in mutilation or disability (Art. 312 Penal Code);
   - kidnapping, detention and hostage-taking (Arts 341–4 Penal Code);

- kidnapping a minor by fraud or violence (Arts 354 and 355 Penal Code);
- threatening any attempt against the life of a person or against property (Art. 305 Penal Code);
- Aircraft hijacking (Art 462 Penal Code).

2. Offences comprising attempts against property:

These are offences which, because of their effect on personal safety, constitute a public danger:

- defilement of monuments or objects of public use committed by means of fire or explosives (Art. 257 para. 3 Penal Code);
- destruction committed in the course of burglary either against a magistrate, juror, lawyer or witness, or in any case by means of fire or explosives (Art. 434 paras 2 and 3, and Arts 435–7 Penal Code);
- aggravated burglary, committed by two or more persons, at night or with violence (Arts 379 and 382, para. 3 Penal Code);
- extorting money (Art 400, para. 1 Penal Code);
- using any means to derail a train or to cause a collision (Arts 16 and 17 of the law of 15 July 1845 on the railways).

3. Acts penalized as accessory to offences:

- criminal conspiracy (Arts 265–7 Penal Code);
- making or possessing murderous or incendiary devices (Art. 3 of the law of 19 June 1871 which repealed the order of 4 Sept. 1870 on the making of weapons of war); sale or export of gunpowders (Art. 6 of the law of 3 July 1970); acquiring or possessing such substances (Art. 38 of the statutory order of 18 April 1939);
- making, possessing, stocking and transferring biological weapons (Arts 1 and 4 of the law of 9 June 1972 on biological or toxin-based weapons);
- possessing a stock of weapons of the first or fourth category (Art. 31 of the statutory order of 18 April 1939), carrying and transporting such weapons (Art. 32 of the same statutory order).

A reasonable further provision adds to the above-mentioned offences any others directly connected to them by cause and effect. And of course where logical connections such as that are made, proceedings can be joined and competence extended.

Although logical, the inclusion of connected offences is noteworthy, since in the case of a political offence, they would not be treated in this way. The 1986 legislator reasoned quite differently, in order to extend to a greater number of offences the exceptional rules he had created (e.g. centralization of prosecutions – for which see below).

The subjective fact

One must stress the comprehensive nature of the list set out in Article 706–16 which contrasts sharply with the more precise one of Article 689–3 of the Code of Criminal Procedure.

To the objective criterion, consisting of the aforesaid precise list, is to be added a subjective one relating to offences 'linked to a collective or individual undertaking whose intention is seriously to disturb public order by intimidation or terror'. This rather ponderous and tautological wording addresses the context of the motive, and after that its characteristics.

The context of the motive

The motive of intimidation or terror must inspire the authors not so much of the basic offence, but rather of the enterprise ('the undertaking') which is its framework, its context or its underpinning, and of which it is the expression. The concept of undertaking, criticized by some, is nevertheless familiar to lawyers (see Art. L.84 or Art. 405 Penal Code). The Littré dictionary defines the undertaking as follows: 'any formed intent which is put into execution'. During the parliamentary debates, the Minister of Justice, M. Chalandon, confirmed this definition and made it clear that the legislator did not intend to limit the role of the judge to a pure and simple identification of the goal sought after, and that he should have to ascertain the existence of a 'formed intent or concerted plan materialized by coordinated efforts with a view to the aim to be achieved.'[9]

Thus

> the notion of undertaking excludes any idea of improvisation; it presupposes preparations and a minimum of organization. The following factors might thus be taken into consideration: setting up a plan of action, gathering material means, drawing up a contingency plan, or drafting a press release.[10]

In brief, the undertaking presupposes some premeditation and organization from which chance is excluded.

The law then provides for the undertaking to be 'individual or collective'. Most often the undertaking will be collective, and moreover it might constitute a criminal conspiracy as defined in Articles 265 *et seq.* Penal Code. But it is easy to imagine an undertaking which is individual. The case of a terrorist acting on his own is not a purely theoretical assumption.

The characteristics of the motive

According to the text, the motive underlying the undertaking is seriously to disturb public order by intimidation or terror.

Serious disturbance of public order is not a very precise notion, though it evokes the 'serious act' of the Strasbourg Convention (parcel bombs, car bombs, etc). Simply put, it amounts to a feeling of permanent insecurity which may haunt the public.

Intimidation consists in paralysing other people's initiatives.

Terror finally, has two meanings according to the *Petit Robert* dictionary. First, 'an extreme fear which deeply distresses and paralyses', and second, 'a collective fear which one imposes on a population in order to crush its resistance'. Is the latter definition appropriate to our understanding of this term? According to Professor Pradel, 'the act of terrorism is thus one which creates a collective fear in the population in order to make it yield'.[11] In our opinion, one must go further.

First of all, it seems desirable to understand political terrorism in a much broader way than the 1937 Geneva Convention. The terrorist act may indeed be directed not only against a State, but also against a policy, a regime, the organization of a society, a philosophy, a religion. Anarchism and nihilism obviously come into this definition. But terrorism, even if generally trying to achieve change in existing structures, may equally be aimed at securing their continuance.

More and more, the terrorist act is intended to demonstrate the fragility of a certain social and political order, mainly that of democratic countries. In this perspective, it attacks the State, its symbols or the representatives of certain economic power[12] or political power.[13] It often gains sympathy from one part of public opinion or the press by presenting the authors of terrorist action as victims of a decadent society. Sometimes the terrorist aggression is somehow theatrical in nature, due to the dialogue that the terrorist intends to establish with the representatives of the State through the mass media or through creating 'People's Courts' charged with judging the guilty parties of the 'system'.

These different characteristics work towards giving the terrorist act an unexpected importance, turning terrorists into spokesmen who can lay down conditions to States and scoff at their discord. Through publicity, they are thus empowered to put forward ideas which they want to be acknowledged or to see prevail. This is why terrorist aggression will almost always appear unselfish. Exceptionally, it might express itself in the making of material profit, when that is aimed at serving a worthy cause.[14]

To sum up, the terrorist act appears as an *act of violence committed by an individual with a political, ideological, social or even religious aim.*[15]

But this factor is not sufficient to characterize the terrorist act. Thus, acts of armed violence, committed with a political intention on the occasion of a conflict, are not necessarily terrorist *acts*. To be qualified as such, they need to be *out of all proportion to the sought-after result*. This is indeed the case for aircraft hijackings, for the taking of innocent hostages, for damage to persons and property on an unsuspected scale. Here we come close to the criteria used by national legislations to deprive some particularly reprehensible acts of the benefit of extradition. Thus the French law of 10 May 1927 is directed at 'acts of odious barbarity and of vandalism forbidden by the laws of war' (Art. 5).

This characteristic reminds one of the principle of proportionality, which forbids the committing of acts without military necessity. The idea stems from a distinction between civil and military objectives. This appeared in the statutes of the Nuremberg International Military Court where Article 6(b) enumerated amongst war crimes 'the destruction without motive of towns and villages or devastation which is not justified by military requirements'.[16]

These two factors confer a certain specificity on the terrorist offence. For Professor Pradel, it would seem to constitute a particular form of political offence, even if, obviously, the law does not allow the distinction between a political offence and a common law offence.[17]

We do not share this opinion. On the contrary, it seems to us that the offence of terrorism is a common law offence, as is crime against mankind. This offence 'is a common law crime committed in certain circumstances and for some precise grounds according to the text which defines it'.[18] The similarity between these two types of offence is striking. Crimes against mankind are 'inhuman acts and acts of persecution which have been committed systematically in the name of a State following a policy of ideological hegemony'.[19]

Theoretical writers have rightly pointed out that Crimes against Mankind are a common law offence 'with a motive of attempting murder in the course of executing State policy'.[20] In the same way, terrorist offences are common law offences which are subject to particular regulations because of certain grounds or motives.[21]

The new draft Penal Code makes wide use of the provisions of the 1986 law. But unlike the 1986 law which did not create an offence under the heading of acts of terrorism, Book Four defines 'a new category of offences, by describing as terrorist acts various acts dealt with elsewhere in the Penal Code' whenever they come within a particular context. Amongst other things, this leads to an aggravation of the sentences enforced. Terrorist acts are those offences defined as being linked 'to an individual or collective undertaking whose intention is seriously to disturb public order by intimidation or terror'.

Article 421–1 thus defines as terrorist acts a certain number of offences, such as wilful attempts against the life of a person, attempts against freedom of movement, thefts or destruction by explosives, when they are connected with a terrorist undertaking – the definition of which is identical to the one of the present Article 706–16 of the Code of Criminal Procedure. Article 421–2, however, establishes a totally independent terrorist offence which has been termed 'ecological terrorism'.

At the same time, the new Penal Code maintains a regime departing from common law in ways which we will examine now.

THE REGIME APPLIED TO THE TERRORIST ACT

Aware of the increasing perils of terrorism and in order to attempt to reduce them, the legislator has established a regime departing from common law practice.[22] The special standing in common law of the terrorist act appears in the methods both of prosecution and of punishment.

The prosecution of the terrorist act

An escalation of terrorism was experienced in France during the 1980s: the assassination of General Audran in 1985, of Georges Besse in 1986, and Basque and Corsican activism.[23] At the same time, various terrorist movements in the Middle East, such as Hezbollah, increased the threat. This increase in terrorist activity led the legislator to develop a response both at the national and international levels.

At the national level

The efforts resulted in a double action, on the part of both police and judiciary, the common denominator of which is a process of centralization and the consummation of which at the political level was the creation of a 'Secrétariat d'Etat à la Sécurité Publique' (Junior Minister of Public Security).

Police action

Under the aegis of the Ministry of the Interior, a vast number of departments contribute towards the fight against terrorism. The endeavour is directed along three lines: intelligence, coordination of all means and services, and the development of targeted actions enabling terrorists to be brought quickly before the courts.

In the forefront are the Security Branch of the police force, 'Renseignements Généraux' (RG), and the counter-espionage services, 'Direction de la Surveillance du Territoire' (DST). In addition to these departments there are others, such as the Department of Security and Defence and the Intelligence Service, 'Direction Générale de la Sécurité Extérieure' (DGSE). In a more targeted way, the border police, the gendarmerie (military police force), the city police and of course the Criminal Investigation Department contribute to the collection of information.

In order to ensure the coordination between these different departments, the anti-terrorist action unit, Unité d'Action Anti-Terroriste

(UCLAT) was created. The police force of Recherche, Assistance, Intervention, Dissuasion (RAID) is at the disposal of this unit, which is in contact with the Préfet of Corsica and the Sous-préfet of the Basque country.

An anti-terrorist committee had been set up at the Elysée in 1982. A series of unfortunate mistakes led to its disappearance in 1984.

On the other hand, the inter-departmental committee of anti-terrorist collaboration, Comité Interministériel de Liaison Anti-Terroriste (CILAT), was created. It brings together representatives of the Ministry of Justice, the Ministry of Foreign Affairs, the Ministry of Defence, the Chief of Police for Paris and DGSE, with the aim of drawing up plans for the fight against terrorism.

Finally, during an international colloquium held in Paris in October 1989, judge Boulouque suggested the creation of a terrorism surveillance committee, formed of elected representatives, lawyers, researchers and security professionals to study the evolution of political violence on a permanent basis.[24]

Judicial action

The prosecution of terrorist offences can be achieved through two means, either by application of the European Convention of Human Rights or by resorting to the 1986 law.

1. Referring to the European Convention: In accordance with the European Convention, Article 689–3 of the Code of Criminal Procedure provides that

> anybody in France may be prosecuted and tried by the court, who committed outside the territory of the Republic:
> – one of the criminal offences defined by articles 295 to 298, 301, 303, 304, the first and third paragraphs of article 305, articles 310 and 311, the third (2°) and fourth (3°) paragraphs of article 312, articles 341 to 344, 354 and 355 of the Penal Code, when these offences are committed, or where the law so provides attempted, against a person entitled to international protection, including diplomatic agents;
> – one of the criminal offences defined by articles 341 to 344 and 355 of the Penal Code, or any other criminal offences involving the use of bombs, grenades, rockets, automatic firearms, letter or parcel bombs, insofar as such use poses a danger to the public, and when this criminal offence is linked to an individual or collective undertaking intending seriously to disturb the public order by intimidation or terror.

This text implements the well-known system of universal competence which enables the court of the country of arrest to judge the above-mentioned offences irrespective of where those offences were committed, and of the nationality of the offender or the victims.[25] The examining magistrate could have proceeded with the formal charging of a suspect (Art. 80 para. 3 Code of Criminal Procedure), and possibly have issued one of the four warrants at his disposal (Art. 122 Code of Criminal Procedure), if there had been serious and consistent indications of guilt, which does not seem to have been the case.

2. Resorting to the law of 1986   A specific regime, exceptional to common law, has been set up by the law of 1986 in Article 706 Code of Criminal Procedure.[26] The 'Conseil Constitutionnel' (Constitutional Council) was invoked and pronounced that the rules, exceptional to common law, embodied in the new law were justified by the specific nature of terrorism but that they could not be extended to other types of offence without the principle of equality being undermined.[27]

The law of 1986 is original on two accounts. On one hand it centralizes procedures in Paris. On the other, it provides for changes in the procedure for questioning suspects.

i Centralization of procedures

From 1983, the eighth division of the 'Parquet' (the prosecution service) had handled matters of terrorism. However it appeared to the legislator that there was a need to go further. The international nature of terrorism and the existence in Paris of police departments which were very active in this field required that a competence be set up in Paris and that the magistrates in charge of terrorist cases should be specialists.

The principles governing this centralization have been defined by an implementing circular letter which provided that Paris should take on:

> terrorist cases involving foreign organizations, as well as terrorist cases attributable to groups acting or liable to act anywhere on the national territory. On the other hand, except in specific cases, it is not essential automatically to bring to Paris those terrorist cases which are purely local or regional in nature and which are unconnected with any national or foreign network'.[28]

The result of all this is that the competence of Paris is not exclusive. Whenever a terrorist case occurs in a judicial district other than Paris, the investigation has, of course, to be carried out under local police responsibility, provided that they notify the regional section of the judicial police and the 'Parquet', which in turn reports to the 'procureur général' who informs the 'Chancellerie' (the administrative services of the Ministry of Justice).

Thus either the Parisian and the provincial magistrates will come to an agreement on whether the case should be transferred or left where it is, or, if the Parisian prosecution's opinion differs from that of the local service, the 'Chancellerie' will arbitrate.

Difficulties, which we will not go into,[29] may occur if the appointed magistrate considers himself incompetent, or if parties question his competence. In all cases, the Court of Cassation is the arbiter.

In Paris, M. Jean-Louis Bruguière is responsible for terrorist cases. This magistrate made himself known to the general public in connection with the attack on the UTA DC-10. He did not hesitate to implicate Libya by issuing four international warrants of arrest for Libyan representatives in October 1991, and by circulating two search orders against two other Libyan officials.[30] In April 1989 the late Judge Boulouque, in charge of the case concerning terrorist attacks in Paris in 1986, had already issued seven arrest warrants against Lebanese citizens who were presumed to be members of Hezbollah, a pro-Iranian Shiite organization.

ii Changes in the procedure for questioning suspects

The complexity of the cases and the often international nature of terrorist incidents led the legislator to increase the duration of detention in police custody to four days (Art. 706–23 Code of Criminal Procedure). The extension is decided by a 'magistrat du siège' (a judge sitting in court), either the President of the court in the case of a full investigation, or the 'juge d'instruction' (examining magistrate) in the case of an inquiry.

It does not appear that this extension is in conflict with the requirements laid down by the European Convention, Article 5 paragraph 3 of which provides that 'everyone arrested or detained . . . shall be brought promptly before a judge or other officer authorized by law to exercise judicial power'.[31]

On the other hand, the validity of the rule according to which the second extension is decided by a judge and not by a prosecuting magistrate has been questioned. It is true that, as far as drugs are concerned, it is the 'procureur de la République' (State prosecutor) who decides all extensions to the duration of detention in police custody. The legislator of 1986 decided upon the 'magistrat du siège' (judge sitting in court), possibly in order to conform to the Schiesser judgment of the European Court of Human Rights on 4 December 1979, which held that in order to be competent as regards detention on remand, the magistrate must offer 'guarantees befitting the judicial power conferred on him by law, the first of such guarantees being independence of the executive and of the parties'.[32] The legislator of 1986 feared that in terrorist cases of a political nature, the 'magistrat du Parquet' (prosecuting magistrate) might appear to be dependent on the executive, since he is subordinate to the Ministry of Justice.

Another rule exceptional to the common law is that property searches, entry to an individual's home and seizure of exhibits may take place during an investigation into non-flagrant offences ('enquête préliminaire') without the need to obtain the consent of the occupant. This is an important exception to the principle of the non-coercive nature of the investigations into non-flagrant offences. It is justified by the need to act speedily in order to obtain information before the opening of an inquiry ('ouverture d'une information') and by the fact that the terrorists' determination excludes by definition any possibility of obtaining their consent. In this case, the judicial police officer must be given permission by the President of the court or the judge nominated by him.

The new Penal Code significantly increases penalties: from three years to life imprisonment (Arts 421–3 and 421–4).

At the international level

Here, one can make the distinction between a defensive and a positive response.

Defensive response

First the examining magistrate may use international letters rogatory. These are treated as a mandate given to foreign authorities. They are embodied in a written document comprising a statement of the facts, the established charges and the investigating measures required.[33] The only bloc reserve to the implementation of these letters rogatory lies in treaty law, and mainly refers to the potential breach of sovereignty, security or public order of the country in which the implementation is to take place. The rules of transmission of these letters rogatory require that the act itself has to be forwarded to the Ministry of Foreign Affairs which refers the matter to the foreign authorities. This process often takes a long time, hence the resort to other means.

Interpol (OIPC: 'Organisation Internationale de Police Criminelle', International Organization of Criminal Police) is based in Lyons and consists of more than 150 members representing the countries. Since 1985 this organization has had an anti-terrorist data file and computerized network. It receives a copy of all international letters rogatory, so its central Bureau can keep foreign authorities informed and assist in implementing letters rogatory.[34]

Bilateral cooperation with our neighbours has been set up. Four agreements have been signed: with Italy (1986), Germany (1987), Spain (1987) and the United Kingdom (1989). They deal with the exchange of civil servants and the nomination of liaison officers.

The Trevi conference In a broader sense, cooperation against terrorism among the Twelve has been developed by the Trevi conference. This cooperation also deals with the fight against serious crime and training agents to combat these threats. The conference is chaired successively by each country, which also acts as host.[35]

The Schengen Accord (signed on 14 June 1986 by France, Germany and the Benelux countries) provides in the short term for a strengthening of the cooperation between the customs and police authorities, especially as regards the fight against crime (Art. 9),[36] whereas the Paris Charter for a New Europe, dated 21 November 1990, refers to the need to eliminate terrorism 'at the bilateral level as well as through multilateral cooperation'.[37]

The Copenhagen Meeting The final document of the Copenhagen Meeting held between 5 June and 29 June 1990, itself confirmed by the Paris Charter, includes a number of provisions expressing the beginnings of a criminal legal space. This document urges States to adhere to international conventions. It also includes an undertaking by the States to protect the democratic order against terrorist acts, and this undertaking was further defined in the Paris Charter.

In this respect, one must not forget the idea, launched by President Mitterrand in August 1982, of the establishment of a Community Court in charge of judging terrorists guilty of murder.[38] This suggestion was bound to amaze everybody, since it represented a partial renunciation of sovereignty. This is why M. Badinter proposed to the Ministers of Justice of EC Member States the creation of a European penal court which would specifically not seek to undermine national sovereignty in so far as it would have been called upon to judge only those cases extending beyond the specific competence of individual Member States.

This suggestion, if it were to succeed, would constitute an unquestionable progress of the law.[39]

The Maastricht Treaty The Treaty on European Union, dated 7 February 1992, includes in Title VI provisions on cooperation in the field of Justice and Home Affairs.

Article K 1 provides:

For the purposes of achieving the objectives of the Union, in particular the free movement of persons, and without prejudice to the powers of the European Community, Member States shall regard the following areas as matters of common interest:

1. asylum policy;

2. rules governing the crossing by persons of the external borders of the Member States and the exercise of controls thereon;

3. immigration policy and policy regarding nationals of third countries:
(a) conditions of entry and movement by nationals of third countries to the territory of Member States;
(b) conditions of residence by nationals of third countries on the territory of member-States, including family reunion and access to employment;

(c) combating unauthorised immigration, residence and work by nationals of third countries on the territory of Member States;

4. combating drug addiction insofar as this is not covered by 7 to 9;

5. combating fraud on an international scale insofar as this is not covered by 7 to 9;

6. judicial cooperation in civil matters;

7. judicial cooperation in criminal matters;

8. customs cooperation;

9. police cooperation for the purposes of preventing and combating terrorism, unlawful drug trafficking and other serious forms of international crime, including if necessary certain aspects of customs cooperation, in connection with the organization of a Union-wide system for exchanging information within a European Police Office (Europol).

Anticipating ratification of the Treaty, Europol was set up in Strasbourg on 4 September 1992. At first, it will be limited to the exchange of information relating to drug trafficking. In the eyes of the Home Affairs Minister, Paul Quilès, EUROPOL is in this way 'the embryo of a European police force'.[40]

Positive response

This second form of response consists in taking the political message into account. This does not mean a recognition of the legitimacy of the terrorists' cause, but an integration of the terrorist act into an identifiable political context. This obviously excludes terrorist acts such as those perpetrated by the Red Brigades and the like or separatist movements, but may well be applied for what is the heart of present terrorism (Palestine, Arab terrorism, Ireland).

This positive response imposes on the victim State a change in its behaviour, in particular the resort to procedures such as negotiation and mediation. On this subject, we would recall the secret negotiations with the FLNC, the bargaining with 'Action Directe' and the normalization of relations with Iran.[41]

The strengthening of international solidarity is going to help this type of response tremendously. The collapse of the Soviet bloc and the triumph of the democracies has isolated those countries which are accomplices of terrorism. The defeat of Iraq in the Gulf War speeded up this process. Held aloof from the civilized nations, the States which sustained terrorism are disintegrating one after the other. Syria, ally of the Americans during the Gulf War, and Libya, forced to submit to judicial investigations, have demonstrated a radical evolution. It is comforting and significant to notice that about forty States, gathered in Geneva in November 1991, adopted a draft declaration on 'the protection of all persons against forced disappearances'. This text, which must be submitted to the General Assembly of the United Nations, proclaims that systematic practising of such disappearances is comparable to a crime against mankind.

This initiative was taken up by the Security Council which voted on 21 January 1992 a resolution *'urgently'* enjoining Gaddhafi's regime to collaborate *'immediately'* in the investigations of both air attacks (Lockerbie and Ténéré) with which it appeared to be associated. To our knowledge, this is the first time that the Security Council has taken such an initiative. It is obviously an advance in international law which deserves to be emphasized. For their part, the United States and the United Kingdom issued charges which have led to the trial of two Libyans charged with involvement in the Lockerbie bombing and who will have to answer before the United States or Scottish Courts.[42]

Then in February 1992, we learned through the newspapers that Colonel Gaddhafi was prepared to hand over both men in the first instance to the Islamic Conference Organization or to the African Development Bank, and thence to the Arab League for them to be tried – provided that the United States and the United Kingdom produced evidence.[43] In the end, Libya has decided to submit its dispute to the International Court of Justice at The Hague, and is purporting to leave it to the Court to decide.[44]

This concession constitutes an encouraging step forward even if the outcome of the trial appears uncertain.[45] Faced by prevarications of Colonel Gaddhafi, the Security Council has recently passed another resolution condemning Libya.[46]

The suppression of the act of terrorism

The specificity of the system provided for by the new French law appears both in the composition of the court and in its capacity to pass sentence.

The composition of the court

According to an old French custom, authors of crimes are judged by a court which includes ordinary citizens. However, having acts of terrorism judged by an ordinary 'Cour d'Assises' proves to be difficult to implement, in view of the possibility that the jurors may apply to be excused jury service. One will remember that in 1962 jurors from Nîmes were frightened by phone threats from the Organisation Armée Secrète (OAS) and refused to take their place on the jury. This is why the 1986 law provided that the Cour d'Assises would be constituted only of professional judges (Art. 706–25 Code of Criminal Procedure). A further law on 30 December 1986 made this text immediately enforceable, after a Cour d'Assises earlier that month had been unable to produce a verdict, several of its jurors having failed to appear. Such a flagrant infringement of the principle that a more severe provision of penal law should never be made retroactively clearly represents a deplorable deterioration in quality of law.

Sentencing

Wielding carrot and stick in turn, the 1986 law alternates between severity and leniency.

Severity

This is expressed by the requirement that the judge deliver an order denying access to specified places ('interdiction de séjour') for a period of time between two and ten years. This provision aims to cut the offender off from his usual environment in order to reduce the risk of recidivism. The new Penal Code makes provision for more severe sentences (Art. 421–3).[47]

Leniency

Following the example of some foreign legislations (e.g. Italy), the 1986 law organizes an exemption and a reduction of the sentence.

Exemption from sentence is not new in French law.[48] But the 1986 law adds two new cases to Article 463–1 Penal Code.
     According to the first paragraph of this article,

> if a person has attempted to commit, as an author or as an accomplice, one of the offences listed in the eleventh paragraph of article 44 [of the Penal Code, i.e. the offences listed in Art. 706–16 of the Code of Criminal Procedure], and such person is party to an individual or a collective undertaking whose intention is seriously to disturb the public order by intimidation or terror, then that person shall be exempt from sentence if he has prevented an offence from being committed, by warning the administr0ative or judiciary authority, and if he identifies, as required, the other guilty parties.

In support of this text, the implementing circular gives the following example: a group of terrorists decides to explode a bomb in a public place; but an accomplice, who provided the explosive, then changes his mind, warns the police and gives information which allows the other members of the group to be identified.
     According to the second paragraph of the same article,

> if a person has committed as an author or as an accomplice one of the offences listed in the eleventh paragraph of article 44 [same observation as above], and such person is party to an individual or collective

undertaking whose intention is seriously to disturb the public order by intimidation or terror, then that person shall be exempt from sentence if he has prevented the offence from causing death or permanent disability, by warning the administrative or judiciary authority, and if he identifies, as required, the other guilty parties.

Here, the legislator's indulgence goes further, since the offence has been committed, so the repentant's action can only enable its consequences to be limited. (Compare this with Art. 62, para. 1 Penal Code, making it a crime to fail to prevent an offence from being committed when it is still possible to limit its consequences.) Here again the circular gives a simple example: some terrorists take somebody hostage and decide to subject this person to conditions of detention which endanger his life. Afterwards, one of the authors of the abduction warns the police, who free the hostage safe and sound, and then gives indications which lead to the arrest of the other members of the group.

Regardless of the moral dimension, one can debate how justifiable these new provisions are, given the very wide opportunities for judges to interpret them individually.[49]

However, the experience of Italy and the United Kingdom suggests that the system of repentance practised abroad has generally proved to be satisfactory.[50]

Reduction in sentence based on considerations of criminal policy come to the aid of someone who commits an offence but then tries to reduce or eliminate its consequences. The sentence is reduced by half, and, if the law provides for life imprisonment, the reduction brings the sentence down to twenty years.

The same applies in the preliminary draft of the Penal Code (Art. 422–3).

It has to be added that the mechanism of indemnification of the victims of acts of terrorism, instituted by Art. 9 of the law of 9 September 1986, fills a gap in a system which would have remained otherwise far too inhuman.[51]

Enforcement of the sentence

It is up to the penitentiary authority to maintain order in the establishment of which it is in charge. The Code of Criminal Procedure provides a range of measures for this purpose.[52]

Particular rules had been set up for particularly dangerous prisoners, who were put in top-security wings or establishments. But these rules were abolished in 1982.[53]

CONCLUSION

French criminal law does not emerge unscathed from its confrontation with the ordeal of terrorism. Over the past years, under the influence of terrorist violence, a few rules which make exception to common law have been shed and new rules have appeared which lead to some forms of terrorism being treated in the same way as acts of war.[54]

One may regret that the fight against terrorism has led many European States to establish specific legislation which has sometimes been censured by the Court of Justice or the Commission. Penitentiary authorities have at their disposal an arsenal of coercive measures against terrorists which has not failed to attract the vigilance of the Commission and the Court of Justice. In the Klass case, the Court declared that

> being aware of the danger ... of undermining, or even destroying democracy on the grounds of defending it, [the Court] affirms that the Contracting States may not, in the name of the struggle against espionage and terrorism, adopt whatever measures they deem appropriate.[55]

For its part, the United Kingdom was condemned for inhuman and degrading treatment in the use of certain techniques in interrogation on some members of the IRA.[56] On the other hand, in the Baader-Meinhof case, the Commission deemed that exceptional measures were justified in the case in point (particularly strict isolation, virtual suppression of contacts with the outside, continuous lighting, forbidding the visit of lawyers and so on).[57]

The difficult balance between respect for human rights and the requirements of public order is underlined by the Maastricht Treaty which, within the framework of the provisions regarding cooperation in the fields of justice and home affairs, brings reserves: in the form of Article K2.

Article K2

> 1) The matters referred to in article K1 shall be dealt with in compliance with the European Convention for the Protection of Human Rights and Fundamental Freedoms of November 4th, 1950 and the Convention relating to the Status of Refugees of July 28th, 1951 and having regard to the protection afforded by Member States to persons persecuted on political grounds.

> 2) This title shall not affect the exercise of the responsibilities incumbent upon Member States with regard to the maintenance of law and order and the safeguarding of internal security.

Finally, difficulties of a political nature may arise. First, it may happen that certain police investigations or requests for extradition are blocked for reasons of State. It has to be recalled that France, in 1981, established an exaggerated doctrine of the right of asylum, which brought fierce criticism from its neighbours and led to a drastic reorientation of its policy in 1982.[58] More recently, on the subject of Arab terrorism, the French Minister of Foreign Affairs considered that there was a need 'for the page to be turned'.[59] A great deal of progress remains to be made in order to set up a European judicial dimension in criminal affairs.

NOTES

1 J. Servier, 'Le terrorisme' in *Que sais-je?* (Presses Universitaires de France, 1979) p. 124. See also G. Bouthoul, 'Le terrorisme', *Etudes polémologiques* 8 (April 1973) 37; G. Levasseur and G. Guillaume, 'Terrorisme international', cours Institut Hautes Etudes Internationales (1977); C. Bassiouni, 'Perspectives en matière de terrorisme' in *Mélanges Bouzat* (Pédone, 1980) p. 471; W. Laqueur, *Le terrorisme* (PUF, 1977).
2 M. Wieviorka, 'Mouvements terroristes et action anti-terroristes: l'expérience française', Les cahiers de la sécurité intérieure 1990–95; J. Borricand, 'L'extradition des terroristes', *Revue de science criminelle et de droit pénal comparé* (1980) 661; 'Actualité et perspectives du droit extraditionnel français', *Jurisclasseurs périodiques* I (1983) 3102.
3 See also the 1949 Geneva Convention relative to the Protection of Civilian Persons in Time of War (Art. 33).
4 E. David, 'Le terrorisme en droit international', in *Brussels Colloquium* (Université de Bruxelles, 1974); A. Cooper, 'The terrorist and the victim: victimology', in *International Journal* I (2) (1976) 229.
5 Y. Rodriguez, 'Le complexe de Procuste ou la convention européenne pour la répression du terrorisme', *Revue de science criminelle et de droit pénal comparé* (1979) 471.
6 P. Mertens, 'L'introuvable acte de terrorisme', in *Brussels Colloquium* (Université de Bruxelles, 1973), 'Réflexions sur la définition et la répression du terrorisme'; see also David, *op. cit.* note 4.
7 David, *ibid.* p. 11.
8 Laqueur, *op. cit.* note 1.
9 Speech at the Assemblée Nationale (the lower house), *JO* (French Official Journal) 8 Aug. 1986, p. 4125 and at the Sénat (the upper house), *JO* 8 Aug. 1986, p. 3795.
10 *Ibid.*
11 J. Pradel, 'Les infractions de terrorisme', in S. Dalloz, *Chronicle* (1987) 39(10).
12 Martin Schleyer.
13 Aldo Moro.
14 Court of Appeal of Paris, 4 Dec. 1967, JCP (1968) II.15387: bank hold-up carried out in order to serve a political cause. However, the indicting chamber (part of the Court of Appeal) refused to put forward an opinion in favour of extradition.
15 E.g. the Salman Rushdie affair.
16 David, *op. cit.* note 6, p. 110. See also Art. 22 of the Regulations annexed to The Hague Fourth Convention of 1907, which specifies that 'the belligerents do not have an illimited right as regards the choice of means to harm the enemy', quoted by M. Glaser, *Droit international pénal conventionnel*, 2 vols, 1970–8, vol. 2 (1978), p. 68, note 56.
17 Pradel, *op. cit.* note 11.

18 B. Bouloc, 'Le terrorisme' in *Problèmes actuels de science criminelle* (Presses de l'Université d'Aix-Marseille III, 1989), p. 65; R. Vouin and Rassat, *Précis de droit pénal spécial* (6th edn) Dalloz (ed.) (1988) p. 35.

19 Court of Cassation (crim. section) 20 Dec. 1985, Bull. 407, and 25 Nov. 1986, Bull. 233.

20 Bouloc, *op. cit.* note 18, p. 68; Court of Cassation (crim. section) 6 Feb. 1975, Touvier case, D. 1975–186, Chapar report, note by Coste-Floret.

The new Penal Code comprises two provisions, one regarding genocide, the other relative to crimes against mankind (Arts. 211–1, 211–2).

21 J.B. Herzog, 'Contribution à l'étude du crime contre l'humanité', *Revue internationale de droit pénal* (1945) 155.

22 We will not itemize here the preventive measures that have been developed in various places (searchings in airports etc) or at certain times (e.g. the Vigipirate plan during the Gulf War).

23 See 'Terrorisme: réponses de la société et de l'Etat; le F.L.N.C.', *Journées de l'Institut de Criminologie de Paris* XVI (June 1988).

24 *Le Monde*, 2 November 1989.

25 R. Merle and A. Vitu, *Traité de procédure pénale* (6th edn), 79 (art. 122 CPP); R. Koering-Joulin and H. Labayle, 'Dix ans après... De la signature (1977) à la ratification (1987) de la Convention européenne pour la répression du terrorisme', *Jurisclasseurs périodiques* (1988) I 3349.

26 *Le Figaro*, 31 Jan. 1992; *Le Monde*, 1 Feb. 1992.

27 M. Danti-Juan, 'Le terrorisme, la sûreté de l'Etat et le principe d'égalité', in *Quelques aspects actuels des sciences criminelles* (Presses Universitaires de France, 1990).

28 Circular letter, p. 10.

29 Cf. J. P. Marguenaud, 'La qualification pénale d'actes de terrorisme', *Revue de science criminelle et de droit pénal comparé* (1990) 1.

30 *Le Figaro*, 28 Nov., 29 Nov., 11 Dec. 1991.

31 Pradel, *op. cit.* note 11, (17).

32 Sér. A, vol. 34, pp. 11–14.

33 G. Boulouque, 'Les commissions rogatoires internationales en matière de terrorisme', *Revue Internationale de Police Technique* (Sept.–Oct. 1990).

34 B. Babovic, 'Terrorisme international et Interpol', *Revue de science criminelle et de droit pénal comparé* (1989) 261; Ch. Joubert and H. Bevers, 'La police et l'Europe', *Revue de science criminelle et de droit pénal comparé* (1992) 707.

35 The Bern Club, created in 1971, forms another structure whose aim is to coordinate the fight against terrorism in some European countries and in the USA. The Vienna Club, set up in 1979, strives towards the same goal.

36 *JO* 5 Aug. 1986; see also the Villepin Report, Senate 167, session 91/92; *JO* 12 Dec. 1991.

37 Cited by R. de Gouttes, 'Vers un espace judiciare pénal pan-européen', in S. Dalloz (ed.), *Chronicle* (1991) 31: 154.

38 *Le Monde*, 19 Aug. 1982.

39 See J. Borricand, 'Actualités et perspectives du droit extraditionnel français', *Jurisclasseurs périodiques* (1983) 3102.

40 *Le Monde*, 6–7 Sept. 1992.

41 S. Mekboul, 'Les incidences du terrorisme sur la vie politique', Llm dissertation, Université d'Aix-Marseille III, 1987.

42 *Le Figaro*, 18 Feb. 1992.

43 *Ibid.*

44 *Le Monde*, 5 March 1992; *Le Figaro*, 26 March 1992.

45 *Le Figaro*, 24 Feb. 1992: 'We are confronted with State terrorism, asserts

Colonel Gadhafi'. For its part, Switzerland is going to extradite Sarhadi, member of the Iranian secret police, involved in the murder of Chapour Bakhtiar on 6 Aug. 1991. 'This is a success for judge Bruguière', *Le Figaro*, 25 Feb. 1992.

46 *Le Figaro*, 1 Apr. 1992; *Le Monde*, 2 Apr. 1992.

47 The maximum prison sentence incurred for the offences mentioned in paras 1, 2 and 3 of Art. 421–1 is increased as follows when these offences constitute acts of terrorism:

1 The sentence is increased to life imprisonment if the offence is punishable by thirty years imprisonment;

2 The sentence is increased to thirty years imprisonment if the offence is punishable by twenty years imprisonment;

3 The sentence is increased to thirty years imprisonment if the offence is punishable by fifteen years imprisonment;

4 The sentence is increased to fifteen years imprisonment if the offence is punishable by ten years imprisonment;

5 The sentence is increased to ten years imprisonment if the offence is punishable by seven years imprisonment;

6 The sentence is increased to seven years imprisonment if the offence is punishable by five years imprisonment;

7 The sentence is doubled in length, if the offence is punishable by three years imprisonment at most.

The first two paragraphs of article 132–23 relating to the period of safety are applicable to crimes, as well as to offences punishable by ten years imprisonment, listed in the present article.

For its part, Art. 421–4 provides that: the act of terrorism defined there in is punished by fifteen years imprisonment and by a fine of 1,500,000 FF.

When this act has led to the death of one or more persons, it is punished by life imprisonment and by a fine of 5,000,000 FF.

The first two paragraphs of Art. 132–23 relating to the period of safety are applicable to the crime listed in the present article.

48 Art. 101 Penal Code, breach of State security; Art. 138 Penal Code, counterfeiting of coins; Art. 268 Penal Code, criminal conspiracy, etc.

49 B. Bouloc, 'La tradition française relativement au statut des repentis', *Revue de science criminelle et de droit pénal comparé* (1986) 771.

50 Pradel, *op. cit.* note 11, (21).

51 Cf. European Convention relating to the Indemnification of Victims of Violent Offences, dated 24 Nov. 1983, entered into force on 1 June 1990.

52 B. Bouloc, 'Pénologie' in S. Dalloz (ed.) (1991) *Chronicle* 207.

53 C. Charmes, 'Enquête sur les quartiers de sécurité renforcée', 18 *Promovere* (1979) 35.

54 Bulletins Défense Armée Nation (2nd term, 1986) No. 42; R. Ottenhof, 'Le droit pénal français à l'épreuve du terrorisme', *Issue de science criminelle et de droit pénal comparé* (1987) 607; F. Haut, 'Vers l'an 2000: la menace terroriste dans un monde éclaté' *Senate* 20 Nov. 1991.

55 *Klass and others*, judgment of 6 Sept. 1978 (Sec. A, vol. 28).

56 *Ireland v United Kingdom*, judgment of 18 Jan. 1978. (Sec. A, vol. 25).

57 *Baader and others* v FRG, Com. Dec. 30 May 1975 (DR 2, p. 58).

58 Ministerial note, 10 Nov. 1982; J. Borricand, 'Actualités et perspectives du droit extraditionnel français', *Jurisclasseurs périodiques* I (1983) 3102.

59 *Le Monde*, 18 Nov. 1992.

9   Terrorism and extradition: a British perspective

Leonard Leigh

INTRODUCTORY

Terrorism has posed problems both of extradition to Britain and extradition from Britain. With regard to the former difficulties have arisen in connection with extradition from Ireland and extradition from the United States. Until 1987, when the Dail passed legislation to abridge the political offence exception to extradition, extradition from Ireland was inhibited.[1] Particularly in relation to Ireland, British responses to refusals to extradite have sometimes been petulant and ill-informed.[2] As we shall see, Irish courts themselves did not find it easy to develop or apply a satisfactory doctrine of political offences. The same comment is true of American and British courts and of British legislators.[3] This is hardly surprising: the political offence doctrine is deeply rooted in the Western liberal tradition.[4] It has as a correlative the value of preserving the right of political asylum in the United Kingdom.[5] It must, however, co-exist with a tradition which places considerable emphasis on public order.

On the other hand, the United Kingdom was not perceived as a country from which it was easy to secure extradition. Although the 'political offence' exception was truncated in 1978, difficult procedural hurdles confronted States requesting extradition, and particularly States with a civilian tradition who were often not well-acquainted with the niceties of the *prima facie* case requirement. A Home Office Working Paper noted:

> The United Kingdom is widely regarded as one of the most difficult countries from which to secure extradition. There is a notable rate of failure of applications made to the United Kingdom for extradition, and this deters states on many occasions from even making a request.[6]

It is certainly true that few requests for extradition are made in any given year.[7]

A further problem concerned the fact that there are many countries with which the United Kingdom has no standing extradition arrangements – some with deplorable human rights records, and some with acceptable records.[8] In such cases a fugitive could not be surrendered to the foreign state.[9] Furthermore, a fugitive, once admitted, cannot be deported as an alternative to extradition, but must be allowed to remain until such time as he so misconducts himself that his deportation can be said to be for the public good.[10]

All this had to be seen not only in the context of terrorist crime but also in the context of transnational crime generally. In relation to terrorism, the Home Office noted an increasing threat to ordinary individuals who might become victims of explosions, of aircraft hijacking, and of kidnapping. In relation to crime generally there was felt to be an ever-more pressing need to ensure that criminals should not escape justice by crossing national boundaries. These problems had also to be seen in the context of States which, although disposed to cooperate in the fight against crime, were not always ready either to extend their own jurisdictions, or to suffer gladly claims by others to extend jurisdiction. EEC initiatives to establish Community-wide legislation in matters of terrorism were met with the assertion that criminal law was a vital reserved part of national sovereignty and that therefore although other methods of cooperation were desirable, extradition retained a primary importance.[11]

These matters made it imperative that States – particularly the United Kingdom which has now faced two decades of terrorist violence – should act. Such action could plainly best be taken bilaterally, or within the context of a particular grouping of States essentially allied in outlook and interest. There are no universally accepted international standards dealing with these matters. The notion of the 'political offence' will not necessarily attract the same definition in all States, and not all States will be prepared to abandon their traditional approach to such matters. Indeed, States which are not signatories to or which have not implemented the 1977 European Convention on Terrorism, or the 1988 Maritime Law Convention, are free to consider that terrorist offences committed with a political motivation are indeed political offences in relation to the United Kingdom, and the converse also applies.[12] In this chapter I deal first with reforms to British law in relation to extradition, and then discuss some of the problems which have arisen concerning extradition from Ireland and the United States. Very few requests for extradition of terrorist offenders come from other jurisdictions.[13]

THE 'POLITICAL OFFENCE' BAR IN RELATION TO WESTERN EUROPE

The UK response to extradition in relation to terrorist offences has taken two forms. The first, by no means restricted to terrorism, is the recent reform of extradition law in order to bring UK practice into line with the speedy procedures envisaged by the European Convention on Extradition of 13 December 1957. The Extradition Act 1989 thus institutes speedier procedures in extradition matters, notably by removing the requirement that the requesting state prove a *prima facie* case against the fugitive before a magistrate, thus easing relations with our nearest European neighbours.[14] The second, which enables the United Kingdom to implement the European Convention on the Suppression of Terrorism, done at Strasbourg, 27 January 1977, is, for the purposes of extradition to States Parties to the Convention, to remove certain offences from the category of political offences, so enabling persons to be extradited for them – whatever may have been the underlying motivation for their commission.[15]

The Act represents a response by the United Kingdom to its problems and to those of other European States which share common democratic values and a commitment to human rights. It was recognized as a radical step when it was passed, and the government of the day was anxious not to endanger genuine political refugees. Obviously it also represents an unwillingness to admit that in the context of States sharing democratic values, acts of gross violence can be tolerated under the rubric of political motivation.[16] In this respect the Act precisely reflects the values which underly the Convention and it follows the scheme of the Convention itself. For the purposes of extradition to other States the political offence bar subsists unless it has been limited by bilateral treaty – as has been done in relation to the United States.

The statute approaches the problem of terrorism by providing in section 24(1) that no offence to which section 1 of the Suppression of Terrorism Act 1978 applies shall be regarded as an offence of a political character, and by subsection (2) that no proceedings in respect of an offence to which that section applies shall be regarded as a criminal matter of a political character or as criminal proceedings of a political character. These latter could include the taking of evidence in proceedings. This regime is then applied in respect of countries designated by the Secretary of State as parties to the European Convention on the Suppression of Terrorism,[17] or to a country in relation to which the Secretary of State has made an order under section 5 of the Suppression of Terrorism Act 1978, applying that section. Currently, only the United States falls within the latter limb of the provision.[18]

The principle of exclusion thus adopted corresponds to that employed in the Terrorism Convention. Neither, wisely, seeks to define terrorism.[19] Most definitions found in the literature are flawed.[20] By not venturing a definition, it becomes unnecessary to inquire into questions of political motivation, or to inquire into whether crimes correspond to any standard of rationality in terms of terrorist purposes.[21] Article 2 of the Convention capitulates matters which are not to be regarded as political, whatever their motivation.[22] So too does the Suppression of Terrorism Act 1978, to which the Extradition Act 1989 refers. Britain has taken advantage of Article 2 of the Convention to extend the list of offences which are not to be regarded as political beyond the obligatory list in Article 1 to all those matters which are comprehended in Article 2.

The Suppression of Terrorism Act 1978 (as amended[23]) comprehends the serious traditional offences against the person – and conspiracies to commit them – including torture, murder, solicitation to commit murder, manslaughter, rape, kidnapping, abduction, false imprisonment, assault occasioning actual bodily harm, or causing injury and wilful fire-raising. It includes abduction and hostage-taking. Genocide is deemed by section 23 of the Extradition Act 1989 not to bear a political character. In respect of abduction and hostage-taking it should be noted that the Taking of Hostages Act 1982, which adds hostage-taking to the list, does not apply only to taking hostages in order to put pressure on governments, but applies also where the intention is to put pressure on international organizations or persons – which latter could presumably include corporate bodies within both the public and private sectors.[24] This certainly seems apt to meet the problem of IRA gangsters who abduct businessmen in order to extract ransom from their companies.

The list further comprehends explosives offences in relation to person or property, firearms offences of possession, the use of a firearm or imitation firearm in order to resist arrest, and damaging property intending to endanger life or being reckless as to such endangerment. Offences under the Nuclear Material (Offences) Act 1983 are also included.

In relation to aircraft, offences under the Hijacking Act 1971 are also included, and offences under Part 1 of the Aviation Security Act 1982 other than offences of having dangerous articles in possession (s. 4) or obstructing a constable seeking to prohibit a suspected person from travelling on an aircraft (s. 7). Also included are certain offences under section 1 of the Aviation and Maritime Security Act 1990.[25] These are offences of endangering safety at aerodromes serving civil aviation by means of devices, substances or weapons, and acts of violence which are likely to cause death or serious personal injury, or endanger the safe operation of aircraft. The Act makes hijacking ships extraditable.[26] It also provides that offences of hijacking ships, destroying platforms, ships or fixed installations or endangering their safety or doing acts likely to impede safe navigation are deemed not to be political offences.[27]

The fact that these offences are deemed not to be political for the purposes of extradition does not mean that a person's political views are of no relevance for extradition purposes. A detainee can resist extradition by proving that a request is made with a view not to punishing him for what he has done, but rather to punishing him for his political opinions (or race, religion or nationality).[28] One supposes that such an opinion could be that terrorism is a desirable means of attaining a political end. This type of provision is regarded as a necessary protection for politically motivated fugitives. Some scholars would argue that it is not sufficient simply because it implies a delicate evaluation of the requesting State's criminal justice system.[29]

It should also be noted that extradition, even within the Western European community, can be resisted on the political offence bar. These are offences which do not fall under section 24 of the Extradition Act 1989. Seditious speech would continue to be protected by the political offence principle unless, indeed, it took the form of an immediate exhortation to violence. The emphasis of both the Convention and the statute is upon deeds. The political offence bar is considered in connection with extradition generally, but its applicability even as between Western European States should be noted here.

Thirdly, the burden of proving that the offender's return is sought in order to punish him for his political opinions lies upon him, and such a plea is unlikely to succeed given that the machinery in question applies as between the United Kingdom and its European partners or with States in whom Britain has sufficient confidence to make an order designating the State as one to which the political offence provisions apply. The same point – that the machinery operates as between States which Britain regards as functioning democracies sharing the same value system – enables Britain not to become embroiled in debate concerning the merits of persons and organizations which employ violence for political purposes.

EXTRADITION GENERALLY AND POLITICAL OFFENCES

With the exception of the United States, considered below, the political offence bar to extradition remains fully effective. It will thus apply to proceedings by all States with which we have general extradition arrangements. It is perhaps worth noting that by section 22 of the Extradition Act 1989, such arrangements may be extended to States with which we have otherwise no such arrangements, in respect of offences created to implement a range of international conventions relating to the protection of civil aviation, to hostages, to the protection of nuclear material and to the prohibition of torture. The effect is to place the United Kingdom under a *prima facie* obligation to extradite a fugitive to a requesting State notwithstanding that otherwise the matter would have to be specially considered under *ad hoc* provisions. The political offence bar applies fully in relation to such requests. It is however the case that many of these requests would, as between Western European countries, be deemed not to be political and that in any event extradition for them may be requested by any State party to the relevant Conventions.[30] This obviously erodes the protection which a politically motivated fugitive might otherwise have had. Such a person will have to show either that his extradition is sought for ulterior purposes or that the system of criminal justice of the requesting State is such that no fugitive should be returned to it.[31] Indeed, in the latter case, the European Convention on Human Rights would seem to impose an obligation not to extradite a fugitive to such a State.[32] It is noteworthy that the Home Secretary has ruled against extradition, in particular against certain unspecified African States.[33]

As between Western European states and the United States, the political offence bar will apply to offences which are not excepted from its ambit under section 24 of the Extradition Act 1989. With respect to other States it will apply generally. The bar refers only to the politically motivated offence itself, and not to offences 'connected with' such an offence unless provision is explicitly made for it do so – as it is, for example, under Article 4 of the Anglo-Spanish Extradition treaty of 1986.[34] The effect is that a fugitive cannot resist his extradition from the United Kingdom on the ground that the offence charged against him was connected with a political offence. The United Kingdom may, however, not be able to secure the return of a fugitive from a country which does not permit extradition for a crime connected with a politically motivated offence. The Republic of Ireland, as will be seen, is such a State.

Few requests for extradition are brought before the English courts, and fewer still are resisted on the ground that the offence was political. There is, accordingly, no great bulk of caselaw on the topic and such no satisfactory definition of 'political offence' is disclosed. It has been doubted whether it is feasible to venture such a definition.[35] One principle is clear: a fugitive cannot raise the bar where he was not at odds politically with the State on whose territory the crime was committed. Thus a fugitive who attempted while in New York to murder the Vice-Premier of Taiwan, could not resist extradition to the United States on the ground that the crime was political.[36]

European decisions on political offences deal with questions of motivation, proportionality, and the relationship between the objective and the means selected for its realization. Some courts insist that the offence must be such as adversely to affect the political organization or rights of the State.[37] Some of these themes appear, not always explicitly, in the English cases as well.

We may start with the question of motivation. In order to resist extradition the offence must have been politically motivated, but whilst this is a necessary condition it is not a sufficient one.[38] What precisely the motivation must be remains obscure however. It is well known that originally the test was put in terms of an offence committed in the course of acting in a political matter, or of a political rising, or in the course of a dispute between two parties in a State as to which is to have the government in its hands. The offence must, it was said, be incidental to and form part of political disturbances.[39] This two-party model immediately excluded anarchists whose acts were not directed towards any particular government.[40]

Under the stimulus of the Cold War, the courts departed from the two-party model in the case of *Kolczynski*.[41] There, Polish seamen who jumped ship, wounding a ships' officer in the process, successfully avoided extradition, the court concluding that the historic definition was inadequate to modern circumstances and that the fugitives might resist extradition by showing that they acted to forestall prosecution for offences which were regarded as political by Polish law. It is clear that the definition was changed to accommodate fugitives from States where the monolithic power of the state was such that no political movement aimed at seizing power in the state would be possible.

The issue was further addressed in the *Schtraks* case, which remains the leading modern authority.[42] There it is said that an offence may be evidently political or, while not overtly political, may be so considered by reference to the context in which the offence occurred. The underlying idea was expressed thus by Viscount Radcliffe: first, the offender must be politically motivated; second, there need not necessarily be found any disturbance of the character of an uprising or other struggle for State power, but third, the applicant must be at odds with the State applying for his extradition on some issue connected with the political control or government of the country. Lord Reid stressed that while the offence need not disturb the political order, there must be some element of direct pressure on the State. Lord Hodson stressed that there must be in some sense a struggle between the fugitive and the State, and in some states, where politics and justice are inextricably mixed, special considerations may have to be taken into account. Their lordships concluded that while a given case might raise a political issue, it would not necessarily follow that the offence was committed as a demonstration against any policy of the requesting state.

Cases decided since *Schtraks* have not led to any closer definition. It has, for example, been said that an offence is of a political character where the accused behaved politically in such a way as to make it attractive to those in power that he should be rendered silent or inactive, and further that an offence may be political where it is committed in order to escape from a political ordering which the fugitive regards as intolerable.[43] It has also been suggested that the test is whether the fugitive committed the offence in connection with some issue connected with government or control of the country but, further, that not every offence committed in relation to a disputed governmental policy is a political offence.[44] This is evidently vague and unhelpful. The fundamental proposition is, apparently, that the conflict urged must refer to a relationship of political conflict between the offender and the government of the State within whose territory the offence was committed.[45]

A second criterion insisted upon by British courts is that the offence be not remote from the political object. The relevant mental element must involve some less immediate object which the accused sought to achieve by doing the physical act, but how remote that object may be cannot be determined in the abstract. Lord Diplock thus states:

> If the accused had robbed a bank in order to obtain funds to support a political party, the object would in my view, clearly be too remote to constitute a political offence. But if the accused had killed a dictator in

the hope of changing the government of the country, his object would be sufficiently immediate to justify the epithet 'political' . . . 'Political', as descriptive of an object to be achieved must . . . be confined to the object of overthrowing or changing the government of a state or inducing it to change its policy or escaping from its territory the better to do so.[46]

It may parenthetically be noted that this formula would not cover an offence committed in order to escape from a totalitarian regime by a person who did not propose thereafter to engage in political activities in relation to that State.[47]

English courts have, historically, not relied on proportionality to defeat a political offence argument. In *In re Castioni* where the applicant shot one Rossi in the course of an uprising, Hawkins J remarked that the deed, though against all reason, was nonetheless done during the course of a political uprising so that the applicant could resist extradition. In *Tzu-Tsai Chin v Governor of Pentonville Prison* none of their Lordships concluded that the political offence bar either cannot be raised where the crime alleged is murder or cannot be raised where the murder is disproportionate to the end to be achieved. This has not always been well understood.[48]

Faced with international terrorism and the difficulty of defining 'political offence' sufficiently narrowly to be tolerable, it is not surprising that States sought to restrict the ambit within which the defence could operate. The political offence bar will hardly operate against the United Kingdom in practice since almost all requests for extradition are made to Western European States or to the United States, with some few requests made to Commonwealth countries. The converse is also true.[49] Western Europe and the United States are jurisdictions in which, for almost all serious offences of violence, the political offence bar has been jettisoned save for the proposition that a State may not secure the extradition of a person who can show that the State has an ulterior purpose in mind. Second, there is a presumption of good faith in extradition arrangements to which courts routinely give effect.[50] Third, it is the fugitive who must make out a case either that the offence was political or that his return is sought for ulterior purposes. Whatever the precise burden of proof may be, it will not be easy for the fugitive to make out.[51] Three further points deserve mention. The United Kingdom, like other States, is not obliged to grant entry to a fugitive and will wish to regulate carefully the granting of asylum. It may parenthetically be noted that if the United Kingdom excludes a person from the country under terrorism legislation, France, Germany, Canada, Italy and the United States have undertaken not to admit the person to their countries. This is another element in the international control of terrorist movement.[52] Second, while statutory authority is required in order to extradite a fugitive, it is submitted that the Crown has full power under the prerogative to accept custody of a fugitive surrendered to it, at its request, by a foreign State.[53] Third, many of the modern conventions provide for extended and sometimes near universal jurisdiction.[54] This will facilitate action by a State which does not extradite its own nationals.[55]

EXTRADITION FROM IRELAND

Until the coming into force of the Irish Extradition (European Convention on the Suppression of Terrorism) Act 1987, extradition from Ireland was often fraught with problems. Irish courts necessarily applied a political offence bar, and under the relevant legislation this extended to offences connected with a political offence. Between 1969 and 1981 thirty-four requests for extradition emanating from the Royal Ulster Constabulary were refused on political grounds.[56] At the same time, cross-border co-operation between the police services was generally good. Furthermore, the Irish authorities were prepared to try terrorists under reciprocal jurisdiction legislation, although proof was not always easy to make out in the Republic since witnesses and evidence were often in the North.[57] Nonetheless, the Irish Government's failure to implement the European Convention on the Suppression of Terrorism was a constant irritant to Anglo-Irish relations.[58]

The situation improved considerably after the signing of the Anglo-Irish Agreement of 1985.[59] That agreement provided, *inter alia*, that there was to be an Anglo-Irish conference and that that conference was to be concerned with policy aspects of extradition and extra-territorial jurisdiction as between the Republic and Northern Ireland. The Irish Government stated its intention to adhere as soon as possible to the European Convention on the Suppression of Terrorism. Shortly thereafter technical problems concerning extradition from Ireland were taken under review under the auspices of an inter-governmental conference.[60] Legislation to implement the terrorism convention was passed by the Dail in 1987, and since then extradition matters have been kept under review by the inter-governmental conference.[61]

The structure of Irish law in relation to extradition is not fundamentally different to that of English law. If the offence imputed to the fugitive is in relation to the United Kingdom, and if it falls within the ambit of the Irish legislation of 1987, the fugitive will not be able to rely on the political offence bar. If it falls outwith the statute the fugitive will be entitled to argue the political offence bar. Irish caselaw in these matters is distinctive if no less confused than that enunciated by the English courts. For the purposes of this chapter, Irish law as it relates to other states may be ignored.

Those offences to which the 1987 Act applies are not to be regarded either as political offences or as offences connected with a political offence, and no proceedings outside Ireland in relation to such offences shall be regarded as criminal matters of a political character.[62] The Act specifies in section 3(3) the offences to which it applies. The drafting is somewhat complicated, but the Act clearly applies to a range of offences in connection with the seizure of aircraft; with endangering the safety of aircraft; to offences against the life, physical integrity or liberty of an internationally protected person; to kidnapping, hostage-taking and false imprisonment; to offences involving the use of an explosive or automatic firearm if such use endangers persons; and to an offence of attempting any of the foregoing offences.

More broadly, the court or a minister may conclude that any serious offence involving an act of violence against the life, physical integrity or liberty of a person, or involving an act against property if the act created a collective danger for persons, is *not* to be regarded as a political offence.[63] The section applies to an offence of which a person is accused or has been convicted outside Ireland. In reaching a decision whether or not to treat the offence as political, the court or minister must take into account particular features of aggravation including whether it created a collective danger to others, or affected persons foreign to the motives behind it, or that cruel or vicious means were used in the commission of the offence.

This mode of drafting, though far removed from that employed in the United Kingdom, is permissible under the terrorism convention. The Irish Act contains some offences which are *per se* terrorist and others which may be treated as not political according to normative considerations. The normative considerations are those specified in Article 13 of the convention, and this approach has attracted academic support on the footing that it permits assessment by the requested State of the facts and the context in which they occurred.[64]

Ireland, in common with other European States applies the rule: *aut dedere, aut judicare.* It has thus passed counterpart legislation to that which applies in the United Kingdom, enabling its courts to take jurisdiction over terrorist acts committed in Northern Ireland.[65] It has, furthermore, extended its jurisdiction over those offences which the statute specifies are not political *per se*, where these are committed outside Irish territory, whether the perpetrator be an Irish citizen or not.[66]

Most serious offences are thus covered by the legislation. They are either not political *per se*, or the cloak of 'political offence' may be removed from them. Some offences remain troublesome. Prison breach (e.g. in Ulster) may still be considered political.[67] So too may simple possession of automatic weapons, or false imprisonment which is not deemed to be serious.[68] In these cases the political offence bar may well be argued. Furthermore, Irish courts and the Attorney-General will certainly deal with the question whether the fugitive, if surrendered, will be fairly dealt with or will receive a fair trial in the requesting State. This was the reason for refusing to return Fr Ryan in a case which received much publicity in England. The Irish authorities took the view that as a result of the publicity, Fr Ryan may not have received a fair trial. British reaction was to treat this as a gratuitous slur on the integrity of the English criminal justice system – yet it must be remembered that the English procedure of contempt of court is justified precisely on the basis that undue publicity may prejudice a fair trial.[69]

The leading cases concerning possible maltreatment of surrendered prisoners arise out of proceedings to return persons who, having been convicted of certain offences in Northern Ireland, broke out of prison and sought refuge in the south.[70] There was compelling evidence before the court that, at the time of the prison breach, there had been gross maltreatment of prisoners in the Maze prison in Belfast, and that while compensation was being paid to prisoners with proven injuries, no criminal or disciplinary proceedings had been brought against those responsible. On this ground alone, extradition was refused, the Irish Supreme Court holding that it had to enforce constitutional guarantees that the accused would be humanely dealt with. This, in itself, seems defensible. It is for the Irish courts, in accordance with the Irish constitution, to determine whether the requesting State has shown that it can guarantee the bodily integrity of those incarcerated in its prisons. It is not for such a court to question the validity of a criminal conviction in the courts of a foreign State, and the Irish courts specifically declined to do so.[71] In England, a judgment concerning the integrity of another State's system of criminal justice, and specifically the integrity of its prison system, will be left to the executive which may well prove more accommodating to the requesting State than courts would be. This is not a matter about which one can pontificate. It is appropriate to point out that the Irish courts have not, in any event, simply assumed that fugitives will be ill-treated. The court's remarks were made in the specific context of the Maze prison escape and its aftermath. In the later case of *Sloan* v *Culligan* the court gave effect to evidence that matters had very much improved in the Maze prison since the earlier decision.

The problem of political offences, as the phrase is understood in domestic Irish law, causes the most difficulty. For the future, the problem only arises in respect of offences which are not specified in the legislation as not benefiting from the political offence exception either *per se* or by reference to normative criteria. For example, the Irish court quite rightly found that the 1987 legislation implementing the European Convention did not apply to cases involving offences of prison breach and of possession of explosives and firearms, as distinct from their use.[72] As in Britain, these cases will fall outside the most serious offence category. The list can be extended if the Irish and British Governments have a will to do so.

The definition of political offence has varied over time. At present, the Irish courts hold that offences are not political where they are directed towards the unconstitutional subversion of the Irish Constitution. The political offence bar cannot be made out where the object of the offence, wherever committed, is subversion of the Irish constitutional order.[73] For a time, this test was applied to the subversion of foreign States. Recently, the test has been restricted to offences directed at the Irish constitution.[74]

In relation to such activities it applies in full measure.[75] Irish courts consider that membership of the IRA neither disqualifies an individual from raising the political offence bar nor, conversely, does it establish that any offence which such a person may commit is political. While some objects of the IRA are subversive of the constitutional order of the Republic, and so disentitle the fugitive to raise the political offence bar in respect to a request from a foreign State, the question must be whether the particular activity for which the applicant's extradition is sought can legitimately be construed as subverting the constitution and usurping or attempting to usurp the functions of government under the Constitution. This principle does not have an unlimited ambit. In *Sloan v Culligan*, Lynch J for the court states:

> The fact that the policy or activities followed by persons acting outside the jurisdiction of the State is opposed to or contrary to the policy adopted by the government of Ireland in relation to the unity of the country is not, in my view, sufficient to equate it to a policy to overthrow this State or to subvert the constitution of this State.[76]

In the result, considerable latitude is left for invocation of the political offence bar. It must, however, be remembered that principles of proportionality are incorporated in the new legislation. Serious offences against the person are likely to be excluded from the rubric of political offences because of their gravity. *Sloan v Culligan* again illustrates the point. The kidnapping and false imprisonment of one Kennedy was held to be serious, though it lasted for only three hours, because during that time the IRA who imprisoned him were deciding whether he should be let free, punished or murdered on suspicion of being an informer. Nothing in the court's judgment suggests that it is likely to view such offences with indulgence.

In the result, if an offence is political, extradition is only possible on the basis of the appropriate statute which reflects a convention – the terms of which are generally satisfactory but which, in relation to the possession of arms and explosives, would in British eyes be too narrow.[77]

It is submitted, with respect, that the existing state of Irish law, and the practice of the Irish Government need occasion no alarm. Professor Michael Zander concludes:

> The effect of the decision [*Finucane v McMahon*] is that the IRA do qualify for the political offence exception to extradition provided that they choose their target and their weapons with care. If the violence used is regarded by the judges as legitimate in a war or quasi war situation, IRA terrorists should now be able to avoid extradition.[78]

This seems to be an extravagant conclusion. First, the Irish courts are constitutionally bound to enforce human rights. It behoves Britain not to criticize, but to ensure that reasonable criticisms of its conduct are met. In *Sloan v Culligan* Irish courts noted that this had been done in respect of prison conditions. Second, courts may uphold the concept of 'political offence' without regarding the cause as legitimate. Third, classical liberal reasoning would suggest that those who commit such offences should not be extradited, though there has always been a tendency to impose limits on the violence employed.[79] Finally, most terrorist offences now, both by Irish and British statutes, fall outwith the concept of 'political offences', so that those persons who commit them may be extradited. There is no reason to conclude that Irish courts will not extradite persons under the 1987 Act provided that they conclude that such persons will be fairly treated after surrender.

Extradition from the United States

There is a voluminous American caselaw and literature on extradition for political offences, much of which is concerned with alleged IRA fugitives. What follows is merely a summary of the position before account is taken of the United States–United Kingdom Supplementary Treaty of 1986.[80] First, US courts will not, in general, adjudicate upon the fairness of procedures adopted in foreign States, or adjudicate upon the justice of convictions pronounced in such States. Extradition will follow a simple assurance of a fair and impartial trial abroad, 'not an assurance that all of the procedural safeguards of an American trial will be available'.[81] Indeed, US courts have criticized the holding in *Soering* as going too far in limiting extradition based upon probable conditions in the requesting country.[82] The emphasis should favour extradition. Third (a consideration unlikely to affect Britain or other States signatory to the European Convention on Human Rights), the United States generally will not enter into extradition arrangements with States in whose criminal justice systems they lack confidence. This is to some extent qualified by the necessity, in order to suppress terrorism, to enter into treaties with some countries whose criminal justice systems are antithetical to those of the United States.

Finally, the United States recognizes the 'political offence' exception to extradition. It is generally agreed that a satisfactory definition of 'political offence' is difficult to formulate. An offence is certainly deemed political where there is a violent political disturbance in the requesting country and the act charged was incidental to this disturbance. It is not clear, in classifying offences as political or not, what weight is to be given to motivation, nor whether account is to be taken of whether the acts performed were acts of international terrorism, or political acts of mass destruction. The judgments in the most celebrated of the IRA extradition cases from the United States, *Quinn* v *Robinson*, reveal great confusion on these matters.[83] Some offences committed by the individuals belonging to the IRA or other terrorist groups fall within the exception, others outside it, and the criteria for inclusion or exclusion were indefinite to an unacceptable degree.

Faced with a growing problem of terrorism and politically motivated violence, the United Kingdom and the United States entered into a supplementary extradition treaty in 1986. Both countries took and still take the view that gross violence is not an acceptable or even tolerable means of political activity in a basically just democratic State. As the Rt Hon. Leon Brittan, then Home Secretary put it:

> Both governments believe that the present political offence exception to extradition, as it applies to violent offences, is not suitable to extradition arrangements between two democratic countries sharing the same high regard for the fundamental principles of justice and operating similarly independent judicial systems.[84]

While the resulting treaty has been criticized from an American perspective, it has also been strongly supported – on the grounds that the treaty applies between two democratic countries; affects crimes of violence only; and attracts a trial which respects due process guarantees.[85]

The scheme of the supplementary treaty is to exclude certain offences from the ambit of the political offence exemption. These are offences against conventions dealing with: the safety of aircraft; of internationally protected persons; of hostage-taking; and very serious offences against the person such as murder, manslaughter, malicious wounding, kidnapping, abduction, false imprisonment, unlawful detention and hostage-taking. The list also includes offences relating to explosives where an explosion likely to endanger life or property is caused or where explosives are made with such a purpose. Similarly, firearms offences including possession are included, provided that there is an intent to use them so as to endanger life. Property damage endangering life is also included. It will be seen that three principles underly inclusion in the treaty. These are first, that there is an intent to take life or cause bodily injury; second, endangerment to life or bodily integrity; third, that where bodily harm is in issue, that that harm be serious. Offences which involve lesser harms, or which are not crimes of violence, may still fall within the political offence bar. The treaty is thus circumscribed in such a way as to protect rights of dissent and asylum. It represents a necessary accommodation to an increasingly violent world.

CONCLUSIONS

In common with her European partners, the United Kingdom has taken large steps to remove terrorism from the protections afforded by an inherited body of doctrine inspired by liberal ideals. We have had to choose between two polar alternatives. The first, which applied for over a century (though we should note that Art. 3.3 of the European Convention on Extradition already excluded the taking or attempted taking of the life of a Head of State or his family from the category of political offences), apparently treated the motivation as all-important. The second treats motivation as unimportant: to the crimes capitulated the political offence bar cannot be set up. The former caused great problems where the struggle did not correspond to a struggle for power as between contending factions within a State – in effect the common Western model. It is still capable of causing problems in respect of requisitions by States falling outside the ambit of those party to the Terrorism Convention or designated under the Extradition Act 1989. The latter is only appropriate in the case of shared values – and then at the price of ignoring possible State action by our partners which we might think unacceptable. We are committed to the proposition that where we and our partners are concerned, democratic means exist to bring arguments for change into debate. It follows that in the context of a basically just State, offences of violence are intolerable, however necessary a dissident group may believe them to be. If this be arbitrary, then so be it. The State must take itself at its own estimation and those of its neighbours. In my submission it is worse, in the context of crimes of violence, to give free rein to communalism, or to try to distinguish between different communal and sectarian claims.

The breadth of the UK provisions is particularly marked when one recalls that the United Kingdom permits the extradition of its own nationals.[86] Article 6 of the Terrorism Convention requires a State Party to the Convention either to permit extradition on request, or where it does not do so, to take such measures as may be necessary to establish its jurisdiction over the offence. In fact, UK law not only permits a wide measure of extradition but, over certain offences takes jurisdiction on the nationality principle, and even (as respects aircraft hijacking), the universal principle. These matters, and the question of mutual assistance generally in Articles 7 and 8 of the Treaty, are for other contributors to this work.

It should also be noted that improved extradition procedures are but one means of addressing the problem of terrorism. In recent years the UK Government has introduced legislation conferring jurisdiction on British courts on bases far wider than territoriality, and most recently, in the Criminal Justice (International Cooperation) Act 1989, has authorized investigations in the United Kingdom into serious arrestable offences arising abroad. This, while again not restricted to terrorism, has obvious potential in that connection, and is consistent with Article 8.1 of the Terrorism Convention. The primary mode of cooperation between States, however, remains extradition.

ACKNOWLEDGEMENT

I am grateful to the London School of Economics and Political Science for providing me with a research assistant, and to Miss Sharmishta Chakrabarti LlB for the exemplary way in which she acted as such.

NOTES

1 Extradition (European Convention on the Suppression of Terrorism) Act 1987 (No. 1 of 1987).

2 See e.g. the comments of the Prime Minister a propos the case of Fr. Patrick Ryan where the Attorney-General of Ireland refused extradition on the basis that he might, by reason of prejudicial publicity, not receive a fair trial in Britain (1988) 143 HC Deb. (VI Ser.) cols 767–8. Irish sensitivities in these matters were not then well understood.

3 See e.g. the exchange between Mr Peter Archer QC and Tom King at (1985) 98 HC Deb. (VI Ser.) col. 1072.

4 On this see C. van den Wyngaert, 'The political offence exception to extradition: how to plug the terrorists' loophole without departing from fundamental human rights' 19 *Israel Year Book of Human Rights* (1989) 297; L.C. Green, 'Terrorism, the extradition of terrorists and the political offence defence' 31 *German Year Book of International Law* 337 (1988).

5 *Zacharia* v *Republic of Cyprus* [1963] AC 634.

6 *Extradition*, Cmnd. 9421 (1985–6) para. 1(3).

7 See e.g. tables reproduced at (1983) 51 HC Deb. (VI Ser.) cols 127–8*w*.

8 For a contemporary list see (1984) 68 HC Deb. (VI Ser.) col. 451*w*, but note that there is now a treaty with Spain.

9 As Lord Simon of Glaisdale (*diss.*) points out in *Tzu Tsai Chin* v *Governor of Pentonville Prison* [1973] AC 931 at 955, extradition requires the authority of a treaty and a statute.

10 These matters were adumbrated in the case of Fiore, an Italian national against whom Italy could not make out a *prima facie* case as was then required: see (1985) 83 HC Deb. (VI Ser.) col. 665; and vol. 153, col. 257*w*.

11 See (1988) 142 HC Deb. (VI Ser.) col. 669. On EEC coordination, see (1986) 97 HC Deb. (VI Ser.) col. 211*w*.

12 Cf. A. Cassese, 'The international community's "legal" response to terrorism' 38 *International and Comparative Law Quarterly* (1989) 589; Van den Wyngaert, *op. cit.* note 4.

13 For comment see (1988) 143 HC Deb. (VI Ser.) col. 641. For statistics of extradition requests by the UK in terrorist matters see (1989) 147 HC Deb. (VI Ser.) col. 505*w*.

14 (1987) 486 HL Deb. at col. 1271 per the Earl of Caithness.

15 At present all Western European countries save Malta adhere to the Convention: (1986) 100 HC Deb. (VI Ser.) col. 147*w*.

16 See remarks of Dr Shirley Summerskill at (1978) 948 HC Deb. (V Ser.) cols 1576*ff*.

17 E.g. France, see Extradition (Suppression of Terrorism) Order, (SI 1978/1106).

18 Suppression of Terrorism Act 1978 (Application of Provisions) (United States of America) Order 1986 (SI 1986/2146 (Sch. 1)).

19 Indeed, the British statute which does define terrorism, the Prevention of Terrorism (Temporary Provisions) Act 1989 simply provides that it consists of the use of violence for political ends, and includes any violence for the purpose of putting the public or any section of the public in fear.

20 See e.g. that of C. Blakesley, 'Terrorism, law and our constitutional order', 60 (1989) *University of Colorado Law Review* (UCLR) 471; K. Skubiszewski, 'Definition of terrorism', 19 *Israel YBHR* (1989) 39; J.F. Murphy, 'Defining international terrorism: a way out of the quagmire', 19 *Israel YBHR* 13 concludes, in my submission rightly, that a satisfactory definition is almost impossible to formulate.

21 P. Wilkinson, *Terrorism and the Liberal State* (2nd edn) (Macmillan, 1986), pp. 51–2.

22 Cf. O. Lagodny, 'The European Convention on the Suppression of Terrorism'; 60 UCLR (1989) 583.

23 This statute has been several times amended and the reader should beware of consulting it in its original form.

24 Taking of Hostages Act 1982 s. 1(1)(b).

25 Aviation and Maritime Security Act 1990, Sch. 3, para. 6, adding offences to the Suppression of Terrorism Act 1978.

26 *Ibid.*, ss 9 and 49.

27 *Ibid.*, Sch. 2, para. 6.

28 Extradition Act 1989, s. 3 and see European Convention on the Suppression of Terrorism, Art. 5.

29 Van den Wyngaert, *op. cit.* note 4.

30 Extradition Act 1989, s. 22.

31 The UK has always stated that it will respect the status of genuine political refugees: see e.g. (1978) 948 HC Deb. (V Ser.) col. 1576, (1986) 106 HC Deb. (VI Ser.) col. 367.

32 *Soering v United Kingdom*, ECHR, Ser. A, No. 161 (1989) and see generally C. Van den Wyngaert, 'Applying the European Convention on Human Rights to extradition: opening Pandora's Box' 39 *International and Comparative Law Quarterly* (1990) 757.

33 See (1986) 106 HC Deb. (VI Ser.) col. 371.

34 Extradition Treaty between the Government of the United Kingdom of Great Britain and Northern Ireland and the Government of the Kingdom of Spain, 1985–6, Cmnd. 9615.

35 *R. v. Governor of Pentonville Prison, ex p. Budlong* [1980] 1 All ER 701 at 712j.

36 *Tzu-Tsai Chin v Governor of Pentonville Prison* [1973] AC 931.

37 Green, *op. cit.* note 4.

38 *Tzu-Tsai Chin v Governor of Pentonville Prison*.

39 *In re Castioni* [1891] 1 QB 149.

40 *In re Meunier* [1894] 2 QB 415.

41 *Re Kolczynski* [1955] 1 QB 540.

42 *Schtraks v Government of Israel and Others* [1964] AC 556.

43 *In re Extradition Act 1870; ex p. Treasury Solicitor* [1969] 1 WLR 12.

44 *R v Governor of Pentonville Prison, ex p. Budlong*.

45 *Tzu-Chai Chin v Governor of Pentonville Prison*.

46 *Tzu-Tsai Chin v Governor of Pentonville Prison* at 945B-C; see also *R v Governor of Winson Green Prison, ex p. Littlejohn* [1975] 1 WLR 893.

47 *Cf Re Kolczynski* (though it is improbable that their Lordships meant to cast doubt upon the authority of that case).

48 See e.g. the misapprehensions voiced by Sir Michael Havers (later Lord Chancellor) in (1978) 948 HC Deb. (V Ser.) at col. 1584: 'We must not confuse the liberal approach which gave political asylum to those who held intellectual views that disagreed with their country's ideologies with those who seek, by murder and atrocity, to force Governments to act against their will'.

49 See tables at (1983) 51 HC Deb. (VI Ser.) cols 127–8w, and figures given at (1989) 147 HC Deb. (VI Ser.) col. 505w.

50 *Zachariah v Government of Cyprus* [1963] AC 634.

51 The test appears to be one of a degree of likelihood rather than a balance of probabilities: see *Fernandez v Government of Singapore* [1971] 2 All ER 691. See also on burden of proof, *R v Governor of Pentonville Prison, ex p. Teja*

[1971] 2 All ER 11; *R* v *Brixton Prison Governor, ex p. Keane* [1970] 3 All ER 741.

52 See (1986) 97 HC Deb. (VI Ser.) col. 307*w*.

53 On this see the persuasive authority of the High Court of Australia in *Barton* v *Commonwealth of Australia*, 48 ALJR (1974) 161.

54 In English law some crimes committed by British nationals abroad have long been subject to the jurisdiction of English courts: see Offences Against the Person Act 1861, s. 9 as to murder and manslaughter, and generally *Blackstone's Criminal Practice 1996* paras D.1.64–D.1.73.

55 E.g. the Anglo-Spanish treaty (1985–6) Cmnd. 9615, Art. 7(2); United Kingdom–Italy Extradition Treaty Italy No. 1 (1986) Cmnd. 9807, Art. 4. The obligation is to submit the case to the proper prosecuting authority for consideration.

56 See (1981) 9 HC Deb. (VI Ser.) col. 45*w*.

57 In praise of efforts in the Republic, see e.g. (1982) 22 HC Deb. (VI Ser.) col. 607; (1988) 132 HC Deb. (VI Ser.) cols 21 *ff*; (1987) 114 HC Deb. (VI Ser.) col. 440; (1988) 130 HC Deb. (VI Ser.) col. 495. These are but representative extracts.

58 See in particular the debate at (1982) 28 HC Deb. (VI Ser.) cols 1481 *ff*.

59 *Agreement between the Government of the United Kingdom of Great Britain and Northern Ireland and the Government of the Republic of Ireland* (1985) Cmnd. 9657.

60 See (1986) 106 HC Deb. (VI Ser.) col. 483*w*.

61 See (1989) 151 HC Deb. (VI Ser.) col. 388*w*.

62 Extradition (European Convention on the Suppression of Terrorism) Act 1987, s. 3(1)(a) and (b).

63 *Ibid.*, s. 4.

64 Van den Wyngaert, *op. cit.* note 4.

65 Criminal Law (Jurisdiction) Act, 1976 (Ireland).

66 Extradition (European Convention on the Suppression of Terrorism) Act 1987 (No. 1), s. 5.

67 *Finucane* v *McMahon et al.* [1990] 1 IR 165.

68 This follows from the statute, but *cf. Sloan* v *Culligan* [1991] ILRM 641.

69 On British reactions, see comments of Sir P. Mayhew, Attorney-General, at (1989) 144 HC Deb. (VI Ser.) 481*w*; and remarks of the Prime Minister at (1988) 143 HC Deb. (VI Ser.) cols 767–8. On contempt of court see L.H. Leigh, 'Le royaume-uni' in M. Delmas-Marty (ed.) *Raisonner la raison d'état* (PUF, 1989).

70 *Finucane* v *McMahon et al.*; *Clarke* v *McMahon* [1990] 1 IR 228; *Carson* v *McMahon* [1990] 1 IR 239.

71 *Clarke* v *McMahon*.

72 *Finucane* v *McMahon*.

73 *McGlinchey* v *Wren* [1982] IR 154.

74 *Finucane* v *McMahon*; *Sloane* v *Culligan*.

75 *Sloan* v *Culligan*, cited in G. Gilbert, 'Political offence in Irish law', 41 *International and Comparative Law Quarterly* (1992) 66 at 80.

76 *Ibid.* [1991] ILRM 641.

77 See the Extradition (European Convention on the Suppression of Terrorism) Act 1987.

78 M. Zander, 'Extradition of terrorists from Ireland: a major judicial setback', 140 *New Law Journal* (1990) 474.

79 But see *per* Lord Diplock in *Cheng* v *Governor of Pentonville Prison* [1973] AC 931.

80 I have relied upon K. Wellington, 'Extradition: a fair and effective weapon in the war against terrorism', 51 *Ohio State Law Journal* (1990) 1447.
81 *Ibid.* at 1452.
82 *Ibid.* at 1454 citing *United States* v *Ahmed* 726 F. Supp. at 414.
83 783 F. 2d. 776 (9th Cir., 1986).
84 (1985) 81 HC Deb. (VI Ser.) cols 285–286*w*; see also (1986) 106 HC Deb. (VI Ser.) cols 3676 *ff.*
85 *Cf.* S. Lubet, 'International criminal law and the "Ice-Nine" error: a discourse on the fallacy of universal solutions' 28 *Virginia Journal of International Law* (1987–8) 963; for criticism see C. Blakesley 'Terrorism, law and the constitutional order', *University of Colorado Law Review* (1989) 471. In my submission, Prof. Lubet has the better of the argument, but it is unnecessary to enter upon a purely American debate.
86 For a general discussion see P. Richard, 'Droit de l'extradition et terrorisme: risques d'une pratique incertaine', 34 *Annuaire français de droit international* (1988) 652.

10 Terrorism and extradition: a French perspective

Henri Labayle

It is commonplace today to emphasize the relationship between extradition and terrorism, for extradition has become an everyday fact, making people accustomed to regard its use as virtually natural in the fight against terrorism. However, when selecting a subject for this round table, it became clear that one cannot discuss international cooperation in this field without an overall assessment of the characteristic feature of States' response to terrorism – their tendency to use extradition.

It is not my intention here – I have done it elsewhere and on other occasions – to stress the extent to which States have deliberately placed their response to terrorism in a legal setting. Here it is enough to grasp that within this set of essentially legal responses, one cooperation technique stands out very clearly – extradition (so much so as almost to eclipse all the others) – and that it serves a genuine political plan. This will be the major theme of this chapter. However, it is worth mentioning beforehand some key features of the relationship between extradition and terrorism.

In the first place, extradition is part of international cooperation in suppressing crime; it has a long history whose successive stages cast light on the contemporary suppression of terrorism. It is worth mentioning that extradition was originally a means adopted by sovereigns for handing over to each other violent protesters (according to Cherif Bassiouni, the first extradition treaty dates back to ancient Egyptian civilization, about 1230 BC) and that such was the agreement which our own monarchs, Philippe le Bel and Edward III, came to in 1303. Extradition was by its nature a political tool, not an instrument of criminal law, for its aim was to repress political crime. It was not until the eighteenth century that common law crime came to be affected by its use. At the same time, as a result of what one might call 'political romanticism', there evolved the contrary tendency – to be indulgent towards so-called political crime; from the nineteenth century onwards, a person would no longer be handed over for such offences, and this laid the foundations of the system we all know, and which has caused problems with regard to terrorism. All things considered, the history of the use of extradition invites us to exercise some caution now, if only because of these changes over the course of time.

The second point to emphasize is that this history is clearly characterized by a progressive and highly instructive invasion of the law. There was no trace of the law in the favours which princes paid one another by handing over trouble-makers, but it did progressively creep into the matter as extradition became more and more legalized from the nineteenth century onwards. International courtesy was thus converted into international obligations, defined by a considerable network of bilateral extradition treaties; reciprocal trust was clearly a factor in building solidarity here, just as lack of it also explains a certain reluctance to enter into multilateral conventions. International law on its own could not fulfil the need for codification in such a sensitive field, and the second high-point of the invasion by the law was its organizing the whole area by means of domestic law and enactment of national legislation at the beginning of this century. These extradition laws were essential for public liberties, and coupled with the bilateral conventions just mentioned, led to the conclusion of the major multilateral extradition conventions that we know today, many of which came into being after World War Two. It is evident that the increase in international trade, which organized crime could not ignore, and also the progressive opening of frontiers, particularly in Europe, accentuated the logic of 'rediscovering' the use of extradition in the fight against crime. Terrorism illustrates this logic perfectly, both in general and specific terms.

Nevertheless, this standardization of extradition law has not led to true standardization with respect to this matter, in which municipal law coexists with international law, criminal law with the law of public liberties, and administrative practices with judicial procedures. Such standardization reflects the need of States to fight together against crime, and in particular against that crime which is protected by international frontiers. No wonder that terrorism is considered so important.

Extradition is, therefore, the most classical expression of a form of international repressive cooperation made necessary by the application of the rules governing international jurisdiction. In so doing, public international law demands utmost attention with regard to the diplomatic dimension of extradition. Diplomacy allows the requesting State to ask the requested State to exercise its jurisdiction in order to apprehend the offender and hand him over to the requesting State, in a sovereign manner but on the basis of a freely agreed obligation. By agreeing to comply, the requested State demonstrates its solidarity without any disturbance of its own public order, and in most cases, without having to find any legal fault with the presence on its territory of the person being sought after. The importance of the impact of extradition in the context of terrorism requires no further emphasis here.

All things considered therefore, the matter of extradition is characterized on the one hand by the increasingly important role of the law, and on the other hand by the renewal of interest aroused by its use over the past decade. If we apply these considerations (the importance of the law and the generalization of the process) to the fight against terrorism, we can see that the use of extradition in response to terrorism was both logical and to be expected. On the other hand, nobody could have foreseen that it would settle at the very heart of the machinery designed to repress terrorism, and that extradition law would come to serve as a test-bed and model for all law relative to the fight against terrorism.

One explanation may be offered: if extradition is a technique, an instrument which has actually facilitated the repression of terrorism because it has made penal punishment possible, is this not because its use is the expression of political will?

EXTRADITION: THE PREFERRED TECHNIQUE IN THE FIGHT AGAINST TERRORISM

The use of extradition has become so widespread today, in law as well as in public opinion, that this observation seems obvious. However, such generalization or preference for this technique of international repressive cooperation has been accompanied by the near abandonment of the other solutions regarded as necessary in response to terrorist violence.

International repressive cooperation

It is an understatement to say that extradition appears to be the focal point of today's campaign against international terrorism, whereas there was no hint of it only twenty years ago. In 1991, at the very moment when France had just handed over its second Spanish Basque terrorist, who still remembered the controversy surrounding the first extradition to Madrid in 1985? The preference for extradition reflects a summary but implacable logic. Since international frontiers were the major obstacle to the repression of terrorism, abolishing them was actually the most logical way of bringing the offenders to justice. This is technically what distinguishes extradition from the other processes of removing foreigners, such as expulsion and deportation, which are put into operation unilaterally.

Extradition is really a bilateral or multilateral commitment to cooperate in the repression of a specific offence, to help to appease public order which has been disturbed in a foreign land. For this is what is to be noted with respect to extradition: there must be enough solidarity to convince a State, which is by definition foreign to the offence, its motives and its targets, actively to participate in the punishment of the terrorist.

The fight against terrorism was obviously very quickly challenged by this fundamental difficulty in an international society whose heterogeneous nature prevented the establishment of such minimal links of solidarity, without even coming to confront the technical difficulties due to differences between the criminal systems thus juxtaposed. The fact that the offender presented no danger for the country receiving him strengthened this indifference.

For this reason, the first conventions criminalizing international terrorism were very cautiously drafted, being unable to assert this solidarity in repressive mutual aid. Thus the first major anti-terrorist convention, the Tokyo Convention, concerning aircraft hijacking, took the lowest profile, by limiting itself to making extradition possible.

In this way, the great majority of conventions, yielding to the temptation to make simple lists, merely assert the '*extraditability*' (if I may coin the phrase) of the offences mentioned. Article 8 of both the Hague Convention and the Montreal Convention regarding aerial terrorism; Article 10 of the New York Convention concerning the protection of diplomatic services; its counterpart on the taking of hostages (Art. 8); Article 11 of the Vienna Nuclear Convention; Article 11 of the Rome Convention on maritime navigation, all merely include in the list of offences justifying extradition the ones with which they are concerned. As of right, therefore, these offences become extraditable within the terms of extradition agreements already concluded or yet to come.

To say that such a system is unsound is an understatement. One frequent criticism of these conventions is that they attach little importance to an in-depth analysis of the criminal phenomenon. Moreover, it has to be stressed here that they are of little use, even from a technical point of view. First, because a valid and viable extradition agreement is in practice still required for somebody to be extradited – the anti-terrorist convention being in a sense 'added' to the existing agreements. (Hence for example the maintenance of the previous rules concerning political offences or asylum.) Second, and more importantly, because these texts do not automatically provide the equivalent of an extradition treaty, despite attempts to that effect, in particular at The Hague. Because of the opposition of the Anglo-Saxon systems which require the existence of a treaty in order to extradite, the conventions repressing terrorism merely offer States a 'possibility', not an obligation, to be regarded as sufficient legal basis for extradition.

Such caution called for a palliative. This was the renewal of interest in standard agreements on extradition which, as everybody knows, form the common law on extradition. Now, this renewed attention to texts that were often rather outdated actually accentuated imperfections of the law as regards the fight against terrorism in particular, and sometimes it exacerbated differences in the resulting legal protection for the individual. The wave of extradition requests made to France in the 1970s illustrates perfectly how paradoxical it was to refuse to some what was granted to others, for almost identical offences.

The result was the unexpected promotion of multilateral conventions on extradition, notably the European Convention of 1957 which replaced the tangle of bilateral agreements in Europe.

This success had important consequences. Though one cannot state at exactly which psychological moment it occurred, extradition suddenly became the preferred technique for international cooperation against terrorism. Accordingly, the last wave of international texts relating to terrorism – the 1977 Convention on the Suppression of Terrorism – is entirely dedicated to extradition. Admittedly, its authors delight in emphasizing that it is not 'an extradition agreement as such', but the fact remains that 'for the needs of extradition' it progresses from being an interpretative text to a normative one, since all its provisions have to be taken into account. Modifying, supplementing, qualifying the offence of terrorism, the Convention on the Suppression of Terrorism lies at the heart of international law on extradition, of which it is a component.

All things considered then, the generalization of the use of extradition as a method of fighting terrorism has truly resulted in a radical development in international criminal law. Preferring remodelling to innovation, this has led to the exclusion of the alternative options.

Other possible techniques

Extradition, even when well established, was capable of occupying various positions within the anti-terrorist armoury. Either one could consider the handover of the offender as essentially a palliative measure – in which case it would become necessary above all to organize judicial repression at the scene of arrest – or else it could contribute to a new solution – the establishment of a European jurisdiction – or it might be a priority in itself – which is how it finally turned out.

The first alternative, with which the name of Grotius has long been associated, is well known: in accordance with the rule '*aut dedere, aut punire*', the offender is either handed over or he is prosecuted. Let us confine ourselves to a few thoughts about the option of interest to us, that is the handing over of a wanted person.

First observation: only a lax use of Latin could have led to the belief that punishment would be the result of the *aut punire* option. In reality, it is at its best an obligation to judge the offender, and at its least an obligation to prosecute him, that is to institute criminal proceedings. As has applied for a long time in criminal affairs (repression of the counterfeiting of money) or in some regards to terrorism itself (1937), this desire to make prosecution automatic has come to inspire the entire conventional machinery relating to terrorism: Article 7 of The Hague, Montreal and New York (1973) Conventions, Article 8 of the 1979 text, and Article 10 of the Rome and Vienna Conventions all adopt it. It is therefore necessary and sufficient to bring criminal proceedings in order to fulfil the obligations assumed there. In this context, extradition features as the solution proposed to a State which considers it inappropriate to bring the terrorist before its own courts. Furthermore – and this argument must be emphasized – that obligation makes an indirect but significant contribution to the law concerning extradition. States must necessarily include in their criminal law the elements required to bring proceedings. Hence the emergence of a real 'internal law on terrorism' which greatly facilitates the use of extradition: one of the major obstacles, the rule of double incrimination, is removed, which was far from being obvious considering the characteristics of the offence.

Second observation: the original sense of alternative (hand-over or prosecution) no longer exists today because a hierarchy has progressively been established between these options. As long as there was a true choice, extradition was *de facto* optional since the State fulfilled its obligation by prosecuting the offender. In point of fact, practicalities and indeed the law of the 1977 Convention demonstrate that the priority given to extradition has modified the system. *'Primo dedere, secundo punire'* is therefore the appropriate rule from now on. From being optional, extradition has become compulsory, and prosecution is now a secondary obligation to which a State can subscribe in default of fulfilling its main obligation; the Strasbourg text allows for this once the State in question has established a reserve on the matter.

The fight against terrorism enunciated a very different ambition under the title 'European judicial area' without managing to achieve it, and this subject will have to be reconsidered later, as extradition was its main technical device. France was its main instigator under two successive Presidents, and their failure has confirmed the function of extradition.

The origins of the scheme, in the mid-1970s, stemmed from a French refusal to implement two fundamental texts relating to terrorism: the European Convention on Extradition of 1957 (known as 'the Paris Convention') and the Convention on the Suppression of Terrorism (even though it had been sponsored by a French Minister of Justice . . .). In the light of the wave of terrorism in the mid-1970s, European States felt obliged to give due consideration to the successive French proposals. Valéry Giscard d'Estaing wished in this way to establish, and then to strengthen criminal law links between the Member States of the Community – a new Convention on extradition being the first step in this plan, to be followed by the development of judicial cooperation, the transfer of proceedings, and the transmission of prisoners. But the first step was blocked, leading to the failure of the whole plan.

France had indeed agreed to sign the 'Dublin Agreement' only in exchange for a general commitment from its partners in favour of this project. Now, after two years of negotiation on a draft convention on co-operation in criminal affairs, the Conference of the Ministers of Justice which should have signed it on 19 June 1980 ended without any agreement on the text. This stalemate, which was attributable – so it seems – to the Netherlands who wished to stick with the pre-existing agreements, was only temporary. In 1982 François Mitterrand revived it, once again with a proposal to improve extradition mechanisms between the Member States of the Community (not specifically identifying terrorism, but guaranteeing human rights) and above all with a new departure in the case of refusal to extradite. Rejecting the *aut punire* option, referral to a European criminal court would then have become compulsory; this could have offered some interesting developments in international criminal law, even if the idea itself was hardly original, the League of Nations having already debated it in 1937. Again, the opposition of The Netherlands, and also of the United Kingdom and Belgium, brought the French Republic to reconsider its attitude to the existing system and the appropriateness of finally implementing it.

This change in position, as is well known, was undertaken in a far-reaching and striking fashion. The change in French criminal legislation with respect to capital punishment provided a general justification for the French ratification of the European Convention on Extradition, which entered into force in France on 11 May 1986. Abolishing the previous bilateral relationships with other Member States of the Community by unifying them (itself a good thing), this step also allows extradition links to be set up with the other members of the Council of Europe. French practice concerning extradition having markedly changed since 1984, one can say that this *volte-face* had become inevitable. More specifically, it can be attributed as much to the wave of terrorism in 1986 as to the new political balance of power, and besides to the innocuousness of the Strasbourg and Dublin texts, the first practical implementation of which is after all still being awaited.

All things considered, the use of old techniques within the framework of equally old conventions seeks to characterize the fight against terrorism. Having become a priority, because it was made virtually compulsory, and giving rise to new developments in order to refine its application, extradition is indeed the preferred instrument in the fight against terrorism. One may suggest that the new texts presented for signature on the implementation of the *non bis in idem* rule (1987) or the 1989 San Sebastian agreement on the simplification and modernization of extradition requests are just the beginning of a very fruitful process.

It is from this perspective that the implementing Convention of Schengen should be construed, both as a complementary instrument and as a substitute. The Convention of Schengen is complementary, as Article 59 expressly asserts with regard both to the European Convention on Extradition and to Chapter 1 of the Benelux Treaty, though it does not reject the possible adoption of wider bilateral agreements. Furthermore, Article 64 refines the whole body of European law on extradition, since a notification made according to the 'Schengen system' is equivalent to a request for arrest under the former system: Article 95 in particular offers some technical improvements which will probably be discussed in another chapter. Substitution, on the other hand, is expressed in the links between the different instruments on extradition outlined in the Schengen text.

Thus, Article 60 provides a legal basis for extradition between the contracting parties, even if one of them is not party to the European Convention on Extradition, which is true of Belgium for example. Hence there is a supplementary impact, one more notch in the extraditionary 'ratchet': by virtue of Article 61 of the Schengen Convention, the French Republic has been led to remove a reservation lodged on the occasion of its ratification of the European Convention on Extradition relating to the extradition limit.

It is apparent that extradition law has undergone profound adjustments and technical improvements, to a large extent in response to terrorism. More in-depth examination shows that the prime motivation was the political benefit derived by States.

EXTRADITION: A POLITICAL INSTRUMENT IN THE FIGHT AGAINST TERRORISM

If one drew up statistics on international cooperation in the matter of extradition of terrorists, the figures would probably be ridiculously low. It thus appears difficult to demonstrate the benefits derived by States in terms of efficiency. On the other hand, the political debate raised by the possible extradition of this or that terrorist has, in a quite unexpected way, both facilitated a political response to aggression, and having aroused that, consolidated the development of a genuine European public order in this field.

A political response to aggression

One may be surprised by the fact that extradition as such could be a political means of response to terrorist aggression, because like most legal techniques, the mechanism of extradition is in itself deprived of any political significance. Apart from the will to cooperate in the repression of a given offence, it conveys no ideological message. Whilst in regard to terrorism, one may weigh up the real results of cooperation on extradition (in particular with regard to the Middle East), it is nevertheless clear that the debate opened as to the appropriateness of extradition in cases of terrorism was used as a starting-point for creating a genuine repressive dimension, both internally and internationally. By making terrorism a commonplace offence equivalent to common law crime, extradition has deprived it of any support in public opinion and has accelerated the legal reaction which today regards terrorist activity as entirely without legal justification.

However, things got off to a bad start in the 1970s, from a general as well as a specific point of view. We noticed before that, if extradition was initially conceived in order to apprehend violent protesters against established political power, later on an exactly opposite trend prevailed, starting in the last century and faithfully reflected in all the conventions on extradition: the offender who is driven by political considerations cannot be extradited.

Obviously, the international cooperation for the repression of terrorism immediately and directly came up against this important obstacle. Apart from a technical question – the 'extraditability' of the terrorist – it has to be emphasized that the real question was the possibility that there might be clauses justifying terrorism.

Classical extradition law expresses the prohibition elliptically: extradition is not granted when the requested party considers that the incriminated offence is political or closely related to a political offence. Once the rule has been stated, it still has to receive concrete expression and there the difficulties start, which are described in a profusion of literature. Basically, a political offence or an offence committed for political motives is the main reason justifying the refusal of a requested State to hand over an offender found on its territory. It is up to that State to assess the facts for which another State demands justice – which is obviously a source of international tension owing to the suspicion cast on the requesting State which is recognized as being particularly vulnerable to acts of violence. It should be noted on the other hand that in internal law the notion of political offence has little importance – no criminal system being indulgent enough to allow itself to be contested by force of arms.

When applied to terrorism, the notion of political crime could only impede the repression of crime. In so far as extradition was a favoured anti-terrorist technique, and as the recognition of a political offence forbids this extradition on the basis of international conventions as well as internal legislation, the obstacle could well be final and wreck the whole structure.

Because of its physical characteristics, terrorism can indeed be related very easily to one or another of the conceptions of political crime. Whether it be political crime by nature or by motive, the murder of civil guards in the Basque Country or policemen in Northern Ireland well illustrates this point, because of the highly focused nature of the offence. Even when the victim of the murder attempt is not subject to any political identification, the authors' motives (to destabilize the nation) lead to the same result. To distinguish between two notions, terrorism and political crime, which were well known for their lack of precision, was thus quite a feat.

With great caution, the first generation of texts requiring the extradition of terrorists, in cases of air hijacking or the protection of diplomatic services (in short the generation of texts with universal impact), avoided tackling the heart of the matter. On the contrary, while emphasizing the 'objective gravity' of the incriminated offences in order to attempt to systematize their prosecution, these texts paradoxically evoke the possibility of excuses such as exercise of the right of self-determination, domination and foreign occupation (in the 1973 text), or they reconfirm (in both 1973 and 1979) the possibility of asylum being granted, or else (in 1979) insert references to humanitarian law which indirectly make the terrorist equivalent to a guerrilla in a national war of liberation. Therefore, the essential tasks fell to the judge. Regarding Ireland or Israel, courts in the United States, as well as in the United Kingdom or in France, refined their perception of terrorism to such an extent that they artificially excluded it from the category of political violence. The written law helped the judge in this direction, thanks in particular to what is called the 'Belgian clause' which has denied reality by establishing that the murder of a Head of State is a common law crime. The murder of Sadi Carnot, of Paul Doumer or of the King of Yugoslavia and Louis Barthou is evidence of the ostracism established in the conventional law and particularly in the European Convention on Extradition, Article 3(3). If one also cites the possibility to extradite for 'anarchistic' or 'barbarous' attempts of murder committed during civil war, in accordance with the law in France of 10 March 1927, one can see that the way was already marked out.

Confronted by requests for extradition, judges were to follow this path even before the second generation of texts took into account this evolution. In the courts, it has proved impossible to strike the balance between an objective and a subjective conception of political violence, in view of the very different situations existing in the Middle East, Western Europe or South America. It appeared more realistic and politically profitable to adopt a global and objective approach. Disregarding the given circumstances and systematically advancing the criterion of the 'seriousness' of means used, the judge has thus denied the terrorist the benefit of refusal of extradition. Such benefit is not equivalent to a total exemption, thanks to the implementation of the rules of universal competence, but it is a real snub for the requesting State which is confronted with it. This was not acceptable in the long run for States facing a common threat, and a change of position, even an acrobatic one, was inevitable. The French example illustrates this perfectly, whereby the French Republic overcame accusations of indulgence towards terrorism (Basque in particular) at the expense of a total political and doctrinal U-turn. Without going back over the detail, it should nevertheless be noted how much the Council of Ministers communiqué of 10 November 1982 owed both to the national judge and to the Convention on the Suppression of Terrorism (which France was refusing to ratify at that time), when it affirmed that in matters relating to terrorism:

> the political nature of the offence will not be considered when, in a State respectful of freedoms and fundamental rights, criminal acts have been committed of such a nature that the alleged political aim could not justify the employment of unacceptable means.

The 1977 Convention, at last ratified by France, will use these principles as its main line of argument. From this point of view, it appears as a modification of the European Convention on Extradition. By virtue of Article 1 of the 1977 text, it is no longer possible to invoke the political character of terrorism on the basis of Article 3 of the 1957 text, or of other texts included in its field of action which are silent on this point, without any need even to cite the French law of 1927. An additional exclusion clause against political violence has thus been added: that relating to terrorist violence. Two arguments need to be considered.

On the one hand, the question that has to be asked today concerns the survival of the notion of political crime, particularly with general regard to the upheavals on the European continent. As the Consultative Assembly of the Council of Europe asserted in 1979, 'violence for political purposes is not justified in a democratic society which has in its possession legal instruments allowing change, progress and development by political persuasion'. By 'evacuating' violence from the category of political crime, this argument allows an even more fundamental need to be satisfied.

The disqualification of terrorism as an acceptable means of political action is indeed the major benefit derived by States and this must be stressed. Confronted by the 'gravity' and the 'odious' nature of terrorism emphasized by the judicial decisions, the political authorities were thrown into disarray for a while by terrorist aggression, but yet managed to use the law on extradition to their benefit by distorting it. How could one find any sympathy for the terrorist cause when internal public opinion is convinced that terrorist action is unacceptable, since the 'romanticism' of the notion has disappeared? In this way likening violent and residual internal anti-establishment movements to 'hard' terrorism allows them to be marginalized, whatever the other risks may be, in particular that of convincing them that they are what they are not.

This psychological success is surely incomparable in terms of usefulness to States to the few minor surrenders of persons that may occur in the form of extraditions. Thus it is clear that the reality of terrorism for political purposes may have been denied and that this is the main use of extradition, relayed by internal law. It is not, however, its only use.

Towards the development of European public order

The use of extradition in the matter of terrorism has not only disqualified terrorism by making it commonplace; it has also enabled the strengthening of links between States which until then were too different, or too indifferent, to cooperate.

The principle of reciprocity is, historically, one of the first bases of international law on extradition, and without this reciprocity handover would often not be possible. It therefore implies a minimum common basis between the criminal systems thus brought into contact, and requires their respective cooperation. One of the unknown aspects of the fight against terrorism has been the contribution of extradition to developing this 'common denominator', this similarity of values without which the handover of persons could neither be contemplated nor undertaken.

First of all, technical constraints had to be satisfied so that the use of extradition in terrorism cases would be possible. The first of them, the principle of double incrimination, thus led the States concerned to question the content of their criminal law and its appropriateness for the fight against terrorism. Here again, some qualifications (e.g. 'belonging to an armed gang', 'association of criminals') in Spain or Germany might have given rise to confusion and caused difficulties of implementation. Then, the law of imitation allowed them to check that, if a terrorist could be extradited, this was indeed both because terrorism is punishable and because it is identically perceived as regards its gravity. In the same way, the rule *non bis in idem*, or the thresholds of gravity required, inevitably led the criminal systems concerned to converge in order for the required repression to materialize. Here again, the implementing Convention of the Schengen Agreement perfectly fulfils the function, as regards extradition, precisely with respect to these questions, through Articles 54 to 58 as far as the *non bis in idem* rule is concerned, and Chapter 4 as regards other questions, including the simplification of procedures of transmission of requests. All of which testifies to the ever-developing integration and reconciliation between repressive systems.

Political necessities above all allow one to make an outline sketch of a real system of European public order. The fear of political persecution, also known as the French clause, dominates the law on extradition every bit as much as the problem of political crime. Both explicitly – through the different Conventions on asylum of which the Geneva Convention is the most important – and implicitly – through all the Conventions on extradition (Article 3 of the 1957 Convention; Article 5 of the 1977 Convention) – or through internal legislation (Article 5 of the 1977 law), any person 'persecuted because of his race, religion, nationality, membership of a given social group or political opinions' may refuse to go back to his home country. In that case, expulsion or extradition to countries where there could be real danger becomes impossible. If one adds both the protections offered by the Convention on Torture or the European Convention of Human Rights, and the jurisprudence of the Court in the *Soering* case, one has a very substantial legal edifice, further enriched by the prohibition against requesting extradition for political purposes.

In a superficial way, we can sum up as follows: extradition is possible only between 'commendable' States, that is towards countries in which the minimum standards of a state of law are respected. The argument may seem to be banal, but it is nevertheless essential. First of all, it allows one to put into perspective the chances of implementation of the great universal conventions on the suppression of terrorism: even if all or most States adhere to these conventions, there are countries to which democratic States will not extradite, not for reasons of opportunity, but for legal reasons. Then new light is thrown on regional cooperation, particularly between European States. As far as punishment (death sentence) and penal conditions (the risk of torture) are concerned, for a State to have its request answered requires it to respect minimum rules, either laid down by texts or developed dynamically by the jurisprudence of the European Court of Justice of the Human Rights. Ankara or Madrid have appreciated this well, even if some of their 'democratic guarantees' may sometimes have left others in doubt.

As with political offence, asylum is less and less liable to be invoked in cases of terrorism, especially in the context of a homogeneous society such as the growing understanding among European States. Except for certain individual cases, as in France fifteen years ago, and because the use of terrorist techniques is hardly likely to attract the support of democratic regimes, the grant of asylum to a terrorist is improbable today, at least explicitly, and this will be increasingly true. Article 1 F-b of the Geneva Convention declares that committing a common law crime debars a person from refugee status, and this notion has been accepted by the Council of State. But one need only stress that the problem is usually solved in a tacit way and often with the agreement of the victim State besides – proof if any is needed of the predominance of politics over law in this matter. Consequently, the famous debates of an almost theological nature on the question of asylum with regard to terrorism could well come to an end of their own accord, for lack of subject-matter.

For this is how I must conclude: despite a few sensational affairs, statistics in the matter of extradition clearly demonstrate, for France at least, that the renewal of interest in the process of extradition in terrorist cases has not been reflected in a growing volume of such extraditions. On the other hand, the content of the law and the increasing concern for fundamental rights testify that States did not make concessions to extremism when confronted by terrorist aggression. Qualitatively they reacted both by developing solidarity (reflected clearly in Schengen) and by protecting liberties. Without doubt, this can largely be accounted for by the careful consideration paid to extradition in the context of terrorism, and the greatest possible satisfaction for a lawyer is to have contributed towards it.

Part IV
The limits of State action

11 International action against State terrorism

Yves Daudet

The evolution of international society during the twentieth century saw remarkable progress in international law, a refinement of its rules and the development of mechanisms of international collaboration.

The appearance of state terrorism casts a shadow on this picture, evidenced by violations of fundamental and perfectly established rules of international law (such as the status of diplomats). The solutions invoked by international law have proved both awkward and inadequate. Just as democratic States are internally almost defenceless against totalitarianism, terrorism and violence, precisely because they will respect law and individual rights and freedoms, so international society is not well protected from international terrorism as its actions are, perforce, limited by the precepts of international law.

This situation inevitably leads to tit for tat reprisals, as victim States take the law into their own hands, in violation of their obligations to apply international law in all circumstances – notwithstanding its inherent shortcomings. In effect, some of these States have argued that odious acts of State terrorism constitute a fundamental breach of international law, which in turn exonerate them from abiding by its rules, conceived to govern relationships between civilized nations committed to the same standards of conduct. By a sort of vicious circle all parties then find themselves in breach of international law.

The extent and gravity of international terrorism imputable to some States require the international community to adopt powerful legal devices suited to both preventive and repressive needs. However, international cooperation in this field is largely inadequate and the existing mechanism needs strengthening.

States will first demand the extradition of the terrorists themselves – the simplest though by no means the most effective formula. This action against terrorists is clearly insufficient and must be completed by actions against terrorism itself, attacking the roots of the problem by tracing back to the entity which sustains and animates the terrorists. Nowadays, this entity will often turn out to be a sovereign State, which in turn raises the difficult issue of State status and privilege.

State terrorism is of particular seriousness as it constitutes a fundamental breach of international law. It takes different forms – from direct action to mere tolerance on one's territory of individuals preparing illicit acts. Such tolerance is in itself likely to make a State internationally responsible, according to ordinary rules of liability, for having breached its obligation to monitor acts which take place on its territory or which are launched from it. More specifically in relation to terrorism, the General Assembly's declaration on friendly relations (2625 (XXV)) states:

> Each State has a duty not to organise or encourage acts of civil war and terrorism on another State's territory or to tolerate on its own territory activities organised with a view to perpetrating such acts.

International cooperation in the fight against terrorism is further weakened by the feeble legal arsenal in this domain, not so much in terms of quantity (indeed, there might be too many texts touching on this issue), but rather in terms of quality. This lack of imagination on the part of law-makers has been denounced by Henri Labayle:

> The elaboration of rules dealing specifically with international terrorism is devoid of particular research, and of any determination to enrich legal concepts and techniques. This poverty of thought contrasts with the imagination exhibited by terrorists and has serious consequences. Leaving the issue to be dealt with by national legislation creates the risk of growing contradictions and takes away any interest in ratifying international rules of law.[1]

In addition to this lack of creativity, opportunities to develop international law in this field have been missed. Terrorism might conceivably have been included in the framework of discussions of the International Law Commission on international crimes leading to increased State responsibility. However until now the position of the International Court of Justice (ICJ) on the issue has been otherwise. In the case of the American diplomats in Teheran, the Court declined to take the opportunity to develop this notion of international crime – a failure which various authors have not failed to regret.[2]

Clearly, the lack of assertiveness demonstrated by institutions and the difficulties associated with the implementation of efficient preventive and repressive measures have driven individual States to fill the void with methods of their own, whose legality remains doubtful. However one would be hard pressed to find an argument likely to satisfy national public opinion that a State injured by terrorism should not react unilaterally even when international law and institutions are unable to offer any effective aid.

It seems evident that the means necessary to strike back against international terrorism are only partially and imperfectly provided by existing principles of international law, and that further improvement depends on strengthening international collaboration.

THE INADEQUACY OF PRINCIPLES OF INTERNATIONAL LAW

Terrorism is, by nature, different from any other known form of threat to security. As a result, the existing international framework of laws and institutions is not well adapted to deal with it. States have to operate under difficult circumstances which often are not the same as those presupposed by the definition of a lawful action under international law.

The usual body of norms which define legitimate self-defence in the case of aggression is ill-adapted to handle terrorist action. But in default of any other coercive means under modern international law, States will incorrectly invoke self-defence. Gradually departing thereafter from the dictates of international law, they will resort to intervention, until with retaliation and armed counter-measures they reach a breaking point which seems almost inevitable in the light of the existing judicial arsenal.

Legitimate self-defence

The issue of whether anti-terrorist air strikes fall within the definition of self-defence was first raised in relation to air attacks carried out in 1986 by Israel against Palestinian targets in Lebanon, by South Africa against Botswana, Zambia and Zimbabwe and by the United States against Libya.[3] It was crucial for their authors to get them so classified as they could not otherwise be legal under international law. In effect, air strikes constitute a violation of section 2(4) of the UN Charter.[4] However, a look at recent practice shows that section 51 is loosely interpreted, in a way that considerably departs from the letter and spirit of the Charter.

It must first be established whether terrorist actions are 'armed aggression' within the meaning of section 51 of UN Charter which defines legitimate self-defence. Israel and South Africa, following their traditional extensive conception of self-defence[5] answer in the affirmative. However, such a free interpretation is not acknowledged by the international community. Moreover, other attempts at expanding the grounds to resort to self-defence have failed. Such was the case with the United Kingdom's 1964 proposition, as elaborated in 1966 by a group of Western States within the UN Committee on Friendly Relations, which stated that:

> The right for States to adopt adequate measures, according to international law, to defend themselves individually or collectively against different forms of intervention is a fundamental element of the natural right to self-defence.

This proposition met with opposition from the group of socialist States and the group of 77 which considered that it 'dangerously departed from the Charter and generally accepted international law'. The proposition was finally withdrawn.[6]

But the strict regime of section 51 supposes that the action be both necessary and proportional in its scope. It strictly aims at counter-attacks, excluding thereby all measures of a preventive nature (although some authors have rightly pointed out the unrealistic character of this last requirement in face of a nuclear threat; one cannot reasonably expect a State to remain idle while waiting for a nuclear attack, for it will not be in a position to retaliate once the enemy attack is launched).[7] On various occasions, Israel has argued the legitimate character of preventive measures on grounds of self-defence – as was the case in 1975 when it raided Palestinian camps in Lebanon on the pretext that this was the only way of preventing sabotage attacks. Following the event, the Americans vetoed a Security Council resolution condemning Israel because the text of the resolution did not also condemn terrorist actions imputable to the Palestinians. None the less, the Israeli attitude was much condemned during the debate in the Security Council and it soon became apparent that the American veto was not to be interpreted as an endorsement of the Israeli position. Similarly, it was demonstrated that the 1985 raid on Tunis, presented as a reprisal for an assault on three Israeli tourists in Larnarca by a Palestinian commando, had, in fact, evidently been planned before that.[8]

With respect to the requirements of necessity and proportionality, Israel maintained that the mere existence of the PLO constituted a permanent threat which called for retaliation, independently of the occurrence of any specific facts which may be used as a legitimizing factor. Hence, necessity becomes permanent and in the absence of precise facts there is no way to test for proportionality. In all cases, Israel invokes 'indirect aggression' which consists in a State sponsoring or even only shielding terrorists and which therefore justifies an act of self-defence against the 'aggressor' State. This view was condemned in the United Nations by socialist States, Third World countries and even Western States.[9]

Moreover, self-defence also comprises the idea of a prompt retaliation on the part of the victim State (or from a group, in the case of collective action). The act of retaliation is only justified by the urgency of adopting immediate measures to prevent the worsening of a situation until the Security Council is in a position to play its role, putting the situation in the hands of the United Nations with which lies the ultimate responsibility for maintaining peace. This is the scheme envisaged by Article 51 of the Charter which allows for State action 'until the Security Council has taken the necessary measures'.[10]

Finally, while invoking self-defence, neither Israel nor South Africa have respected the procedure intended by the terms of Article 51 which requires States to keep the Security Council informed of their actions. In practice, the Security Council did examine the situation but on different grounds – complaints by the States whose territorial sovereignty had been infringed by the raids.

In the case of Israel, which feels its very existence to be in danger, the State contends that it is impossible to distinguish and isolate the elements of what is allegedly a permanent, diffuse and ever-changing attack. Consequently, the act of self-defence is seen as a necessity at virtually every instant and any of its manifestations is possible in order to counter the threat to State integrity. From that point of departure all sorts of legal constructions can be deployed but they have little to do with the equilibrium originally intended by authors of the Charter.

The 1986 American raid against Libya after the bombing of a disco in West Berlin which killed one American soldier and wounded many others, took place in a different political context. The Americans also labelled the raid an act of self-defence, but complied with the formal requirements of section 51 in that they informed the Security Council of the actions they had taken against Libya. In essence however, the required elements of necessity and proportionality were just as absent as in the cases mentioned above. Here again, the interpretation lent to section 51 was biased, as there was no manifest link between the bombing and the air raid, in the absence of any formal proof of Libyan responsibility. Moreover, the interpretation of section 51 was also biased because of the preventive nature of the American operation, justified by information obtained by the United States, according to which other actions were in the making. On 14 April 1986, President Reagan addressed the nation and talked of 'preventive action designed not only to reduce the means at Colonel Gaddhafi's disposal to export terror, but also to provide him with the opportunity and the reasons to change his criminal behaviour'.[11] But, as was previously seen, a strict interpretation of section 51 only allows for a counter-strike to an aggression which has already taken place, not preventive strikes. However, the doubts cast on the lawfulness of such operations should not obscure their underlying cause which is the criminal terrorist action, particularly loathsome when perpetrated by a State benefiting from the protection associated with sovereignty. The perverse effect of terrorism is clearly seen in the way that it leads States to resort themselves to breaches of international law, in the absence of any adequate legal means of defence. An analysis of the possibilities offered by the international institutional framework leads to similar conclusions.

Intervention

With respect to intervention as an answer to State terrorism, two problems are raised. First, can some types of intervention be considered lawful under international law? Second, can the liability of a State resorting to intervention be lessened depending on the circumstances and the conditions under which such intervention takes place, without drifting towards facile invocations of self-protection and a far-reaching notion of authorized recourse to force?

Lawful intervention

In the case of the Corfu Channel, the International Court of Justice firmly recalled that the alleged right of intervention 'cannot, whatever the present defects in international organization, find a place in international law.'[12] Taking into account what has been said earlier regarding the shortage of international rules and collaboration for the fight against terrorism, this indication from the International Court of Justice is highly relevant. The position of international law is plain. Even in the presence of very serious actions such as hostage-taking, the rule of non-intervention is paramount, and the condemnation of the International Court of Justice in the case of the Corfu Channel remains the current situation.

Moreover, section 14 of the United Nations Convention of 17 December 1979 on hostage-taking, prescribes that 'nothing in the present Convention can be interpreted as justifying the violation of territorial integrity or political independence of a State in contravention with the Charter'.

To the unequivocal dictate of the Court in the case of the Corfu Channel must be added the cautious decision of 27 June 1986 (Nicaragua/United States[13]), as well as the view expressed by the ICJ in the decision of 24 May 1980 in the case of the American diplomatic personnel in Teheran.[14] In this case, the Court expressed sympathy in light of the extreme gravity of taking diplomats hostage and talked about the 'understandable frustration felt by the American government', but insisted above all:

> the Court cannot fail to express its concern in regard to the United States' incursion into Japan. . . . The Court therefore feels bound to observe that an operation undertaken in those circumstances, from whatever motive, is of a kind calculated to undermine respect for the judicial process in international relations.[15]

The Court however, did not consider the lawfulness of the action, on the grounds that this was not an issue which the Court was required to decide.[16] The position of international law, in the final analysis, is remarkably consistent in condemning intervention, regardless of the nature of the actions which might provoke it and of the feeling of frustration which can result from the obligation to refrain from using violence. Respect of the law and action in conformity with the principles must prevail over any other behaviour.

The view is different for intervention based on grounds of humanity, despite all the uncertainties attached to such notion. Such intervention is not expressly allowed, nor is it sufficiently condemned, to give rise to an *opinio juris* that clearly affirms its lawfulness.[17] One can say without doubt that it is tolerated. But in order to apply it in cases of State reprisals against terrorism a legitimate basis for this type of intervention, distinct from the rules of classic international law, remains to be found.

On this issue, we have witnessed in recent years the growth of modernistic notions referring to 'humanitarian reasons broadly conceived'[18] in addition to the principles of protection of nationals or humanitarian intervention *stricto sensu*. Human rights issues are accordingly often invoked to justify a form of intervention broader in scope than the traditional notion of humanitarian intervention, but still within the meaning of assistance to people. Recourse to the notion of human rights also allows intervention not to be too closely linked to the victims' nationality, thus increasing the possibilities of widening the principles of Article 2(4) of the Charter. However, the issue of nationality still plays an important role in the decision to intervene at all – as was the case with the Israeli intervention in Entebbe, prompted by the fact that many passengers on the hijacked Air France flight were Israeli nationals.

The circumstances of the intervention

Can the liability of the intervening State be attenuated under certain circumstances? For example, the Israeli intervention in Entebbe took place because the authorities in Uganda were not in a position to put an end to the illegal situation occasioned by the hijack. Israel substituted itself for Uganda, whose territorial sovereignty was thus violated. In these circumstances, the intervening State is usually exonerated, or at least its responsibility diminished, on the grounds of the incapacity of the victim State. The legal basis for this solution was established in the case of the Corfu Channel, in which the Court, while finding that Albanian sovereignty had been violated, none the less observed that Albania's complete failure to exercise its sovereign powers created 'attenuating circumstances for the United Kingdom government'.[19]

It should be recognized that in cases akin to the Entebbe affair, it is weak and developing countries which are likely to fall victim to some other State's intervention, as they do not generally have the means of action to oppose terrorism. As for the intervening powers, they will articulate a justification stressing the gravity of the terrorist act and the unacceptable and compelling character of the situation in order to vindicate their own breach of international law, which will be portrayed as relatively minor in comparison to the act of terrorism.

Hence, repeated breaches of international law become banal and any protest threat is likely to be portrayed as an endorsement of terrorism, which in the end imperils the core principles of international law.

The drift toward armed counter-strikes

In modern international law, the use of force by States is outlawed, unless it is a legitimate case of self-defence. The United Nations has the monopoly of collective action. Armed counter-measures are therefore excluded.

Admittedly, there is a long and varied list of possible unarmed actions, but their success in opposing State terrorism is doubtful. It should also be said that the objective of the victim State is less to exert pressure on the sponsoring State than to apply restraining force on the terrorism itself. The behaviour displayed by the United States during the *Achille Lauro* episode is quite exemplary.[20] The case appeared closed once Egypt had negotiated the release of the hostages in exchange for the free passage of the Palestinian terrorists. But once the world discovered the cruel assassination of a paraplegic American passenger, the American and Italian governments resolved not to let this odious crime pass unpunished. So the US Airforce intercepted the Egyptian aircraft with the terrorists on board, whilst it was in international air space. This show of force was clearly animated by a desire to repress terrorist activity, and though one can understand the political and moral imperatives to do so, it remained an illegal action.

The US government sought to justify its conduct on the basis of an American law which provides for a procedure against terrorists when an American citizen has been killed. Obviously, this explanation does not in any way render legal the interception of a foreign aircraft in international air space, which has led one author to observe: 'the way America proceeded on this occasion derives from terrorist methods which they themselves firmly condemn'.[21] On this issue, the United States later clarified its position, indicating that they are opposed to hijackings 'except when there are clear and solid proofs that the wanted terrorists are aboard'.[22] The same argument is made in a Report on 6 March 1986 in which the United States recommended 'judicious use of military force'[23] to fight terrorism.

The American raid against Tripoli also shows how the use of defensive measures leads to illegal action. As Serge Regourd has aptly stated:

> The American argument starts from what is common, to counter-measures and to self-defence and then passes surreptitiously from one to the other, invoking the one to legitimise what the use of the other does not permit.[24]

The question is then, whether certain measures that do not constitute self-defence within the meaning of section 51 of the Charter could be included in the broader notion of counter-measures. Counter-measures are free from procedural and time constraints. They encapsulate the notion of sanction, which R. Ago stressed in his Eighth Report before the United Nations International Law Commission on State responsibility.[25] It must be recalled however, that counter-measures cannot be armed. The arbitration on 9 December 1978 (France/United States), on the interpretation of the Franco-American Accord on International Transportation, positively stated that counter-measures can only be resorted to 'subject to the general rules of international law on armed constraints'.[26] The Americans protested that they had tried everything and that the use of armed forced remains 'a last resort'.[27] In truth, this recourse of last resort is rather unconvincing. Rather, the illegal use of force appears to have been the act of a government exasperated by the terrorist attack and determined to strike a blow which was demanded by public opinion. In the *Achille Lauro* incident, one can only wonder if American Jews would have understood that their government stayed idle, leaving the killers of a member of their community to walk free?

Turning our attention to economic counter-measures, they have also been used to retaliate against terrorism. As an example, the United States have frozen Iranian commercial and financial assets on their territory, and so did the EEC in May 1980 until the release of the American diplomats in Teheran. Within some limitations, the legality of such measures is accepted. Leaving aside the ongoing issue of whether economic sanctions are just another form of the use of coercion in international relations,[28] it will suffice to recall the unanimous doctrine based on the ruling on armed retaliation in the famous case of the Naulilaa incident:[29] sanctions must be in response to an internationally illegal act, they must be directed at the actual author of the violation and they must follow the requirement of proportionality. We could add today, that the measure must not contradict a norm of *jus cogens*.[30]

THE NECESSITY OF INTERNATIONAL COLLABORATION

Designed as governing rules between members of the international community, the principles of international law are designed for States which show respect for ethical considerations in their general behaviour even if they are prone to break them occasionally when under pressure. It can therefore be seen that the same principles cannot easily solve problems arising from the behaviour of States which have consciously rejected these common ethics to becomes 'terrorist States'. Only intensified international collaboration can provide adequate means to cope with this phenomenon. This increased collaboration can take place at the level of existing institutions or through new organs such as an international penal jurisdiction.

Collaboration within existing institutions

As international terrorism undermines peace and security, the United Nations are the proper forum for organizing collaboration against this threat. Consequently, the world context, and in particular the uncertainties associated with the Cold War, have cast a decisive influence over the options open to the Security Council – the ultimate responsible body for maintaining international peace and security.

The case of the American hostages in Iran provides a typical illustration. The defects of the UN were clearly shown by the reaction of the EC Member States, Canada and Japan toward Iran. None of these State's domestic law was infringed by the events so they could only base their action on UN sanction powers.[31] However, as happened throughout the Brezhenev era, the Soviet veto effectively blocked the work of the Security Council. This led EC ministers to:

> request their national parliaments to adopt sanctions against Iran immediately, if necessary, in accordance with the Security Council resolution on Iran, dated January 13, 1980 (which has been subject to a veto) and in accordance with rules of international law.[32]

P.M. Dupuy writes:

> that everything happened as though the United States and the European Community Member States considered the Soviet veto as an incidental set-back to the mere formal expression of the resolution, leaving its substantive content intact. The condemning States thus portrayed themselves as the diligent substitute executors of a community whose will had been thwarted by a Great Power.[33]

Therefore, as was said earlier, the conduct adopted by these States should not be analysed as a reaction to a breach of a subjective norm, but rather as the defence of an international public order, whose safeguard is of interest to the international community. The International Court of Justice itself insisted on this point in stressing the fundamental character of norms 'whose safeguard is essential for the security and the well-being of today's complex international community'.[34] To this effect, P.M. Dupuy points out the similarity of the terms used by the Court and the International Law Commission with respect to international crime.[35]

Whereas the international community strongly objects to terrorism and shows its concern to repress it (and international crime aims at arriving at State penal responsibility), we can only be amazed at the extraordinary weakness of international institutions in the 1980s and their powerlessness to put into place a rigorous body of rules.

However, the changes in political conditions arising from the end of Great Power bipolarism are clearly shown in the attitude of the Security Council in respect of the Lockerbie incident of 21 December 1988, when 270 people were killed, of whom eleven were inhabitants of the village. On 14 November 1991, the United States and the United Kingdom announced that they had issued international warrants against two members of the Libyan intelligence service, and furthermore, the United States emphasized that it was inconceivable that Libya was not connected with the bombing.[36] In spite of Anglo-American threats of retaliation, Libya refused to deliver the suspects contending that it could not extradite its nationals.

It is likely that had this event taken place during the Cold War, it would have been next to impossible to organize international collaboration and the incident would no doubt have received a similar treatment to that of the American hostages in Iran. By contrast, in 1992 the Security Council was able, on 21 January, to adopt resolution 731 requesting Libya to comply fully and immediately with Anglo-American claims, so as to offer its contribution to eliminate international terrorism. Admittedly, the above resolution, which was not based on Chapter VII of the Charter, was never obeyed and Libya maintained its refusal to extradite the alleged perpetrators of the bombing.

On 3 March Libya filed a motion with the ICJ based on the Montreal Convention of 23 September 1971 on the repression of illicit acts directed against civil aviation. Libya maintained that there were no extradition treaties between her and the United States or the United Kingdom, and that her own legislation forbids the extradition of nationals. This situation naturally did not impede the prosecution of the accused before Libyan tribunals, according to the principle of *aut dedere aut judicare*. Libya thus stressed that she was acting in compliance with the Montreal Convention. On the same day, it filed with the Court an application for conservatory measures, to preserve its right under the Montreal Convention against any armed action by the United States. Some saw Libya's move simply as an attempt to escape condemnation by the Security Council.[37] Resolution 748, voted on 3 March 1992 (three days after Court proceedings were terminated), commanded Libya to abide by the terms of resolution 731 and decided on a military and air embargo to take effect from 15 April if she still refused to extradite the suspects.[38]

This resolution, based on Chapter VII of the Charter, was legally binding on Libya. The ICJ reminded the Member States that section 25 of the Charter creates an obligation to apply Security Council decisions. It affirmed the supremacy of this obligation over any other derived from the Charter and considered that at present, the rights alleged by Libya are not open to protection by conservatory measures. In the end, the Court rejected Libya's claims, based on the circumstances of the case as heard.[39]

Given the circumstances, one can hardly see how Libya could have taken advantage of the judgment it sought from the Court. The majority of the bench, as well as individual and dissenting opinions, offered a range of reasoning. Judge Bedjaoui, dissenting, expressed the subtle opinion that the Court could have exercised its discretion in granting the remedy (either that desired by Libya or even better, that which the Court found most appropriate), while ruling that resolution 748 had a nullifying effect on this remedy.

Above all, notwithstanding doubts inspired by Libya's propensity to play with international law according to the interests of the moment, and the existing possibility that Libya will not comply with it when her interests are not best served, the whole affair shows how the post-Cold War political climate allowed greatly increased collaboration among members of the Security Council (with the exception of China which abstained throughout) and led to the adoption of resolution 748. The situation contrasts with the difficulties surrounding the proposed resolution of 13 January 1980, dealing with the hostages in Iran. Resolution 748 is a clear expression of will to deal with a concrete situation with realism rather than legal arguments. Libya's arguments were perceived as a mere attempt to escape liability. Resolution 748, carefully drafted to undermine Libya's scheme must not however amount to an obstacle to the correct use of the judicial function.[40] The risk of conflict between the Court and the Security Council in what are termed the 'grey zones' by Judge Bedjaoui was raised in the individual and dissenting opinions of the judges. With respect to this issue, the Court, dealing at this point with the order for conservatory measures, clearly states that at this stage it did not have to decide upon the legal effect of resolution 748.[41] The substantive question remains to be decided later.[42] One can imagine (and hope) that the Court will seize that opportunity to decide on the legality of the Security Council's resolution and to exercise a control over its actions. Scrutiny by the Court is welcome as it would prevent the political organs from stepping outside the provisions of the Charter.[43] Whatever solution the Court retains in this respect, it will at least ensure that international collaboration is based on a sound legal footing.

Recourse to an international penal jurisdiction

A second form of international collaboration dealing with international terrorism would be the creation of an international penal jurisdiction, competent to hear and decide cases of terrorism. During its 42nd session on 1990, the International Law Commission adopted, on the basis of Part 2 of the Report by Mr Doudou Thiam, a section including international terrorism in the proposed code of crimes against the peace and security of humanity. State-sponsored terrorism is qualified as a crime against peace. It is supposed that the jurisdiction of a new penal tribunal would extend to crimes specified in the code, including in particular, terrorist actions.

We know how difficult and risky the creation of this jurisdiction is in the sense that 'the stake is not merely the creation of a new international institution with specific powers. It challenges the very foundations of international law, being as it is a system for coexistence and competition among sovereign States'.[44] An international tribunal called upon to judge acts of terrorism would inevitably have to scrutinize the involvement of States which sponsor these acts, and as such would take the form of 'a genuine supranational organ'.[45]

A comparison can be made between State sponsorship of terrorism and war crimes committed in Yugoslavia, although the latter constitute a category of their own. As far as such crimes are concerned, the Security Council's resolution 808, adopted unanimously on 22 February 1993, provides some foresight into the legal and practical difficulties which may come to be associated with the functioning of an international tribunal to judge these crimes. Notwithstanding the inherent shortcomings of such a tribunal, the fact remains that its creation due to exemplary collaboration within the Security Council, opens the door to a similar development with respect to terrorism.

CONCLUSION

The legal consequences of the fight against terrorism are of fundamental importance. The indignation which terrorism produces, the cowardly methods to which it resorts, outside the most basic rules of the game in a fair fight, and the pressure which it exercises on public opinion, all effect international law in a most pernicious way. As neither international law nor the existing institutions can react effectively, States are left to fend for themselves. They sometimes resort to measures which, if not in themselves contrary to law, have an influence on the State's international obligations.[46] At other times, they disregard certain procedural requirements in the application of a rule; sometimes they even resort to illegal means. The seriousness of terrorism itself and the serious breaches of obligations by terrorist States not only affect the legality of authorized counter-actions but also encourage resort to actions inadmissible in law.

In order that they conform to international law many of these counter-actions should be taken to the UN; this would guarantee their legality and provide a hope of their being effective. For a long time, the integrity of international law and its institutions was brought into question by the paralysis of the Security Council which left States to substitute themselves for the competent body.[47] It remains to be seen if the end of the Cold War has changed this situation. Obviously terrorist activities linked to the East–West conflict will disappear only to be replaced by others. One can assume that now that the Security Council is no longer paralysed by the veto, it will presumably be able to take the necessary measures – though naturally all will depend on the circumstances of each situation.

Some authors have shown imagination in proposing to 'consider, in extreme cases, legalising the use of force, if a number of strict conditions are met'.[48] Such a position should only be envisaged as an ultimate recourse (precisely the argument defended by the US Government), to redress a violation of the most fundamental norms of international law (e.g., the seizure of diplomats). Finally, such intervention should be limited in scope, in accordance with the requirement of proportionality.

Perhaps by interpreting the prohibition of the use of force moderately and with realism, such a scheme could well serve its purpose. However if one takes terrorism to be just one more manifestation of what is commonly referred to as 'the crisis of the Nation State', then the solution will not be found in a simple tinkering with the existing rules of law.

NOTES

1 H. Labayle, 'Droit international et lutte contre le terrorisme', 32 *Annuaire français de droit international* (1986) 114.
2 P. Weil, 'Vers une normativité relative en droit international', *Revue générale de droit international public* (1982) 47.
3 S. Regourd, 'Raids anti-terroristes et non-intervention', 32 *Annuaire français de droit international* (1986) 79.
4 M. Virally, 'Art. 2 § 4' in J.-P. Cot and A. Pellet (eds), *La Charte des Nations Unies* (Economica, 1985) 113.
5 A. Cassese, 'Art. 51', in Cot and Pellet, *ibid.*, pp. 769 *et seq.*
6 *Ibid.*, p. 781.
7 This is the position of M. McDougal, 'The Soviet-Cuban quarantine and self defense', 57 *American Journal of International Law* (1963), 600.
8 On all these questions, see Regourd, *op. cit.* note 3, 85.
9 Cassese, *op. cit.* note 5, p. 779.
10 Even though the Gulf War has given rise to extensive conceptions of self-defence aiming at providing a legal basis for the Security Council resolution 678 of 24 Nov. 1990. See R. Zacklin, 'Les Nations Unies et la crise du Golfe' in B. Stern (ed), *Les aspects juridiques de la crise et de la guerre du golfe* (Montchrestien, 1992).
11 Cited by Regourd, *op. cit.* note 3, 90.
12 ICJ Report 1949, p. 35.
13 ICJ Report 1986, p. 14.
14 ICJ Report 1980, p. 3.
15 *Ibid.*, p. 43.
16 *Ibid.*, p. 43.
17 P. Daillier and A. Pellet, *Droit international public* (LGDJ, 1987) para. 581.
18 D. Simon and L.A. Sicilianos, 'La "contre-violence" unilatérale, pratiques étatiques et droit international' *Annuaire français de droit international* (1986) 57.
19 ICJ Report (1949) p. 35.
20 J.P. Pancracio, 'L'affaire de l'Achille Lauro et le droit international' 31 *Annuaire français de droit international* (1985), 221 and following.
21 *Ibid.*, 323.
22 This clarification was presented by the US representative to the Security Council during the debate on a similar issue, the hijacking of a Libyan aircraft which was supposedly carrying terrorists.
23 *Ibid.*
24 Regourd, *op. cit.* note 3, 96.
25 *Yearbook of the International Law Commission* (1980) Vol. I, p. 7, para. 9.
26 *1978 Reports of International Arbital Awards*, Vol. XVIII, p. 417.
27 Message of President Reagan, cited by Regourd, *op. cit.* note 3, 96.
28 D. Carreau, *Droit international* (3rd edn) (Pédone, 1991) p. 1337.
29 *1928 Reports of International Arbitral Awards*, Vol. II, p. 1025.
30 Daillier and Pellet, *op. cit.* note 17, 585.
31 Regourd, *op. cit.* note 3, 100.
32 ONU Chr. Mens. 1980/3, p. 878, cited by P.M. Dupuy. 'Observations sur la pratique récente des sanctions de l'illicite', *Revue générale de droit international public* (1983) 505 and following.
33 Dupuy, *ibid.*, 519.
34 'Aff. relative au personnel diplomatique et consulaire à Téhéran,' ICJ Rec. 24 May (1980) 43, 92.
35 Dupuy, *op. cit.* note 30, 32, p. 536.

36 Ch. Rousseau, 'Chronique des faits internationaux' *Revue générale de droit international public* (1992) 382.
37 W. Michael Reisman, 'Notes and comments. The constitutional crisis in the United Nations', 87 *American Journal of International Law* (1) (1993), 86.
38 The sanctions were put into effect on 16 Apr. 1992. Their effect is, however, quite limited. A year later, on 8 Apr. 1993, the Security Council renewed the embargo on arms sales and flight connections. However, the only effective measure would be an embargo on petrol. In spite of pressure exercised by the victims' families on the American authorities, this has never been invoked. Indeed, as the French newspaper *Le Monde* has stated (10 Apr. 1993): 'Libya's national revenue is almost entirely made up of the tens of billions of dollars it receives each year for its petrol. Although the correct treatment seems quite simple, there is little chance it will ever see the light of day. Aside from the United States, the industrialised States have too much to lose from a petrol embargo against Libya. An embargo risks provoking a price increase at a time when European countries are facing economic slowdown and unemployment effecting millions of workers, and are badly in need of cheap supplies.'
39 Case related to the question of interpretation and application of the Montreal Convention of 1971, resulting from the Lockerbie incident. Application for conservatory measures. Order of 14 Apr., ICJ Rec. (1992) 10 and following.
40 On this issue, one can only appreciate the disingenuous comment made by Judge Bedjaoui in his dissenting opinion, where the fundamental issues are described as follows: 'Unless one supposes that resolution 748 (1992) has as its object, or effect, not to withdraw a right from an Applicant State, but to prevent the exercise, by the Court itself, of the judicial function with which it has been invested by the Charter, in which case one might be led to ponder seriously over the lawfulness of that resolution, even at this stage of provisional measures. It would, indeed, be manifestly incompatible with the Charter for an organ of the United Nations to prevent the Court from accomplishing its mission, or for it actually to place the Court in a state of subordination which would be contrary to the principle of separation and independence of the judicial from the executive power, within the United Nations.' (ICJ Report 1992, p. 156, n. 1)
41 Ord of 14 April *ICJ* Report 1992 126 para 43.
42 See comment of Judge G. Guillaume in Y. Daudet (ed.) *Rencontres internationales de l'IEP d'Aix-en-Provence, actualités des conflits internationaux* (Pedone, 1993) p. 112.
43 Mohammed Bedjaoui, 'Du contrôle de la légalité des actes du Conseil de sécurité', in *Mélanges en l'honneur de François Rigaux* (Bruylant, 1993) pp. 11–52.
44 M. Bennouna, 'La création d'une juridiction pénale internationale et la souveraineté de l'État' *Annuaire français de droit international* (1990) 100.
45 *Ibid.* 304.
46 The US exhibited such behaviour when, following the *Achille Lauro* incident, they voted in Dec. 1987 for the Anti-terrorist Act, which provided for the closing down of the PLO offices in the US (s. 1003). This situation raised the issue of the compatibility of the Act with the 1947 Headquarters Agreement, submitted to the Federal Court of the South district of New York, whose judgment led to the respect by the US of their international obligation under the Accord. See W. Michael Reisman, 'An international farce: the sad case of the PLO mission', *Yale Journal of International Law* 14(2), 412 and following, which clearly explains the role and positions of the institutions which debated and heard the case: the US Congress, the Attorney-General, the Federal Court of the district of New York, 29/6/1988, ICJ, Opinion of 26/4/1988. On this

opinion see J.D. Sicault, 'L'avis rendu par la CIJ le 26 avril 1988 dans l'affaire de l'applicabilité de l'obligation d'arbitrage en vertu de la section 21 de l'accord du 26 juin 1947 relatif au Siège de l'Organisation des Nations Unies et l'affaire de la mission d'observation de l'OLP auprès des Nations Unies', *Revue générale de droit international public* (1988), 881 and following see also, on the question as a whole, E. Zoller, 'Securité nationale et diplomatic multilaterale – l'expérience des Etats-Unis comme l'Etat hôte de l'O.N.U.' *Annuaire français de droit international* (1988) 109 and following; and B. Stern, 'L'affaire du buerau de l'O.L.P. devant les juridictions internes et internationales' *Annuaire français de droit international* (1988) 165 and following.

47 Dupuy, *op. cit.* note 32.
48 Carreau, *op cit.* note 28, p. 1320.

12 The jurisprudence of the European Commission and Court of Human Rights with regard to terrorism

Patrice Jean

The uninformed reader, who is primarily and legitimately worried about his or her security, will undoubtedly be insufficiently reassured by this brief glimpse of jurisprudence. The European Commission and Court of Human Rights have not been attributed the task of punishing, let alone preventing, terrorism. The principal countries which support international terrorism[1] are not High Contracting Parties to the 4 November 1950 Convention, and therefore cannot be condemned by its authorities. The procedure which it sets out is very open as to the individual applicant,[2] but limited as to the State which can be held liable.[3] Libya cannot be brought before this jurisdiction.[4] It is the Security Council of the UN which demanded that Iraq cease supporting terrorist activities.[5] The European Court of Human Rights is not a criminal court, let alone a State security court. Its competence is limited by the principle of subsidiarity.

The judgments of the European Court of Human Rights do, however, have authority. They are obligatory in law,[6] respected in fact, and without doubt comprise the best international human rights law jurisprudence in the world.

The gravity of the challenge is equal to the prestige of the institution. Terrorism, whatever its justifications, is one of the most formidable enemies of our democracies.[7] Since terrorism conspicuously violates fundamental rights, it would be surprising if the Commission and Court had not been confronted with it on at least a few occasions, even given the limited scope of the Convention. Several cases have indeed surpassed both the resources and the reason of State, so to speak.

Before proceeding further, an acceptable, if not indisputable, definition of terrorism is necessary in order to delimit the scope of the discussion. The question is neither new nor settled. The notion '. . . is unclear for both jurists and political scientists. No satisfactory definition of terrorism has been given, either by international or by internal law'.[8] The concept is 'legally doubtful',[9] and the internal/external distinction hardly clarifies the situation.[10] It is therefore tempting to evade the necessity of making any generalizations at all by acknowledging that '. . . there is not one but several terrorisms'.[11]

The abundance of the doctrine,[12] prompted by the gravity and complexity of the phenomenon, contrasts with the quasi-impossibility of agreeing on any operational criteria. It is true that the three constituent elements of terrorism which are the most often invoked, almost always in association with each other, are very difficult to systematize.

The first element of terrorism, etymologically and tautologically, is the terror that it induces. The individual's fear of being physically harmed is admittedly not limited to the dangers of terrorism, but the extreme uncertainty as to the time, place and victims of a terrorist attack can provoke a degree of anxiety among a population which other forms of armed conflict do not necessarily bring about. Faced with the 'language of terror',[13] the rule of law can become 'the rule of fear'.[14] None the less, this psychological element is essentially subjective and difficult to measure. One can therefore only presume – without at this initial stage unduly limiting our scope of investigation – whether a given threat provokes collective fear or not.

The second element, violence, is closely linked to the first.[15] Very diverse as to their form,[16] these acts of violence have in common the effect of intimidation: this effect depends on the severity, both objective and subjective, of the acts committed. In general, a threat which is not followed by action becomes less credible with time. This does not mean that cases in which a threat is not carried through but is dissuasive enough to lead to the desired result should be excluded *a priori*.

The third element is the political aim, 'objective linked to "power" . . . as understood according to its widest meaning and in its many diverse forms'.[17] This element usually allows us to distinguish terrorists from regular criminals. Although this distinction is not always easy to make,[18] omitting this intentional criterion in order to widen our field of investigation, although safer methodologically, would certainly surpass the scope of our modest aspirations. In order to limit the scope of investigation, we must therefore read the European Convention on the Suppression of Terrorism[19] between the lines, and limit the depoliticization of terrorism which it sets out to the context of extradition.[20] The simple definition provided by the Prevention of Terrorism Act remains very useful: '. . . every use of violence with political ends, including every use of violence with the objective of frightening the public or a certain segment of the public'.[21]

We can ask whether other elements should be considered in the definition of terrorism. Several countries, inspired by resolution (74) 3 of the Committee of Ministers,[22] made reservations to the Strasbourg Convention of 27 January 1977 which attach a particular stigma to acts which,[23] '. . . affect innocent persons foreign to the motives behind them'.[24] The underlying distinction is analogous to that made between armed forces and civilians in international humanitarian law.[25] This traditional and fundamental distinction is also consecrated by humanitarian law as concerns internal conflicts.[26] Given the variety of persons potentially concerned, the distinction is sometimes difficult to apply.[27] In cases of doubt, it appears preferable to exclude only those attacks made against persons who are participating directly in the anti-terrorist struggle;[28] that is to say, for example, that an attack against employees working for the security forces in Northern Ireland would not be considered, *a priori*, an act of war.[29] As for the criterion of the disproportion between small means and big results, it is hardly useful.

The topic, thus defined, remains vast. It touches on numerous rights and numerous articles of the European Convention on Human Rights. But the jurisprudence of the Commission and Court does not appear, at least at first glance, equal to the magnitude of the danger. Not only is the jurisprudence scarce, but it also appears to favour the terrorists. The majority of the individual applications in this matter come from the terrorists – when and if they are captured. Their complaints against the police, prison and judicial authorities are often accepted and sometimes successful.

If the imbalance between the protection afforded criminals and that afforded society is quantitatively real, it is, however, partially misleading. The State, after all, is meant to generally be the defendant in the jurisdictional system of the Convention; and those whom the State sets out to oppose, the applicants. It is as if after a war, the loser had a right of action against the winner. A more in-depth reading of the jurisprudence, however, reveals the other side of the coin: the Convention acknowledges that the State has *substantial legal means of prevention and suppression*. As for the fate of the *victims and their successors*, the scarcity of their applications – certainly at least partially due to the fact that they are ultimately allies of the State and therefore do not wish to drag it before the courts – reveals that they are not sufficiently taken into account.

The *protection* of the fundamental rights *of the terrorists* who are arrested is necessary, for without it they have won. Allowing governments to indulge in excessive counter-violence is a trap. Avoiding this trap reinforces, in the long run, the free society. Can we torture the person who has planted a bomb in order to defuse it in time? The answer – most often negative – to this question illustrates, admittedly in a simplistic manner, as much the quality as the fragility of the European democracy.

THE PROTECTION AGAINST TERRORISM

This chapter is not interested or concerned with making a value judgment of terrorism,[30] but with briefly describing the application of the European Convention on Human Rights to the difficult circumstances engendered by terrorism. In practice, the protection of civilian populations sometimes requires the reinforcement of State powers.

The rights of the State

For many the interrelation of terrorism and human rights is limited to the question of derogations.[31] Even if the topic appears wider to us, the issue of derogations is undoubtedly essential.

The right to derogate

Expressly set out by Article 15 of the Convention,[32] this right is not arbitrary. The possibility of suspending the exercise of most of the protected rights is, however, a major concession to sovereignty: 'If there is a domain where the jurisdictional or political control is the most delicate, it is certainly that of exceptional circumstances'.[33] The State thus has at its disposal, as long as it respects the conditions of Article 15, a wide variety of means which are contrary to public liberties and yet legal.

The meaning of Article 15

The jurisprudence of the institutions of the Convention is made up of only five cases with respect to derogation, of which only two are principally concerned with terrorism.[34] These cases do allow us, however, along with references to several others and to the doctrine, to better grasp the spirit and the letter of Article 15.

The derogation clause, originally an amendment of the United Kingdom,[35] must be seen in the light of '... the analogous institutions in the internal legal systems of the contracting states, of which it is the extension in the system of the Convention. . . . '[36] The objective is comparable: the temporary and partial suspension of the rule of law in order to enable it to survive. These safety mechanisms can none the less be very diverse in nature. The cases of *Lawless*[37] and *Ireland v The United Kingdom*[38] enable us to distinguish, for example, between escape clauses, the French theory of 'circonstances exceptionnelles',[39] and mechanisms such as that set out by Article 16 of the French Constitution.[40] The principle of the restrictive interpretation of limitations to fundamental rights is difficult to apply to the two latter mechanisms;[41] whereas, notably in the case of *Ireland v The United Kingdom*,[42] the Commission specifies that the formal and substantive requirements set out by Article 15 can not be derogated from. This means that the general wording ' ... measures derogating from its obligations under this Convention . . . ' is limited in its scope; certain provisions, and notably Article 15 itself, are inviolable.

The International Law Commission Draft Articles On the Liability of States for Internationally Illicit Acts exclude liability in 'situations of necessity',[43] a concept which is close to that set out by Article 15. The Court, in the cases of *Lawless* and *Ireland v The United Kingdom*, reasoned in two steps: first, declaring the illegality of certain anti-terrorist measures, and, second, excluding the finding of illegality by applying the derogation clause.[44] The Court has thus consecrated the right of the State to act deliberately, when necessary and not disproportional, in a way which suspends the application of fundamental rights.

Article 15 has also been elucidated, paradoxically, by a case (dealing with anti-terrorist measures) in which the derogation was not invoked. In order to justify State interferences which were apparently excessive, the Commission relied, in the case of *McVeigh and Others*, on the fact that organized terrorism had become a '. . . feature of modern life [which] democratic governments must cope with . . .'[45] This analysis alters, albeit indirectly, the restrictive interpretation of Article 15.

Conditions with respect to substance

'In time of war . . .'

That is to say a full-blown 'public emergency threatening the life of the nation'. In the *Lawless* case, one of the commissioners wanted to limit this category to major conflicts exclusively, in which '. . . the military operations represented a real danger to the existence of the State'.[46] In particular, the term 'war', used by itself (as opposed to civil war) usually applies to an international conflict of a magnitude which terrorist activities do not attain.

'. . . or other public emergency threatening the life of the nation . . .'

Three cases can be cited with respect to this category, of which two concern our topic.[47]

G.R. Lawless applied to the Commission, claiming a violation of the Convention resulting from his being detained without charge or trial during approximately five months in 1957. Suspected of terrorist activism, he had been arrested pursuant to the Offences Against the State (Amendment) Act of 1940 which granted exceptional powers to the Ministers of State of the Republic of Ireland. The Government claimed the armed acts of the IRA had resulted in an 'emergency threatening the life of the nation'.[48] The Commission, and then the Court, agreed that a state of public emergency justifying the use of Article 15 did exist, based on three essential reasons;

- First, the IRA, a militarily structured clandestine organization, represented at that time '. . . a serious threat to the democratic principles and institutions within the Irish state'.[49]
- Second, if the violence itself was not of a sufficient magnitude[50] to satisfy the condition of a '. . . public emergency threatening the life of the nation . . .', '. . . the steady and alarming increase in terrorist activities from the autumn of 1956 and throughout the first half of 1957 . . .'[51] had to be taken into account.

- Third, international law imposed on the Republic of Ireland the obligation of not allowing its territory to become the starting-point of armed actions aimed at another State, namely the United Kingdom.

This third argument appears to be juridically convincing, but does not discharge the requirement of demonstrating that the threat to the life of the nation, as defined by Article 15, exists in the country that wishes to avail itself of the derogation, in this case the Republic of Ireland. Unless one is to argue that British Ulster is part of the Republic of Ireland, most of the acts of the IRA concerned not its territory, but that of its neighbour. We could be led to think that:

> ... the situation which the institutions of the Convention qualified as being a public emergency were in fact merely potential or latent ... a preoccupation to avoid the development of an irreversible situation ... a justification which, by relegating the imminence of the threat to a consideration of secondary importance, enables the supposedly exceptional derogation to be abused ... an approach based most likely on political motives ... to avoid, at least in the first case, exercising too strict a control which might arouse the mistrust of the contracting states ... not to exercising too strict a control which might arouse the mistrust of the contracting States ... not to condemn a Government which traditionally respected human rights and was trying to cope with a particularly difficult situation[52].

The resulting definition remains flexible.[53]

In the case of *Ireland* v *The United Kingdom*, Ireland is no longer the accuser but the accused. Both paradoxically and logically, the existence of an emergency justifying the use of the Article 15 derogation was evident to the point of not even being debated: the applicant government did not deny that the United Kingdom was confronted in Northern Ireland with a crisis of an exceptional seriousness, with an organized and terribly effective terrorism, and with a situation close to civil war. The security forces were often overwhelmed, the population divided, the number of victims elevated, the institutions shaken. The Court easily accepted the Article 15 argument.[54]

Conditions with respect to form

Article 15, paragraph 3 requires that the Council of Europe be notified of all measures taken pursuant to the derogation and of the reasons therefore, and the jurisprudence sets out a maximum delay for this notification.[55] The extent of this obligation to inform can be interpreted in several ways. The Commission considers it to be of '... crucial importance'.[56] The Court raises *proprio motu* the question of whether this duty to notify has been fulfilled.[57] But it does not seem that every minor violation of this duty will invalidate the derogation – a situation that would undoubtedly lead to the communication of false information and generally of bad faith.[58]

First, the Secretary-General of the Council of Europe must be notified of the texts of the measures taken. The Commission does not attach much importance to the listing by the Government of the provisions of the Convention which it intends to derogate from.[59] It is obviously preferable that the notice of derogation be the most complete possible.[60]

Second, the reasons for the measures must be indicated. In the cases which concern us, however, several basic arguments have sufficed, as if the struggle against terrorism were sufficiently explicit in and of itself.[61]

Third, the Commission has, despite the silence of the text, requested that notification occur '. . . without delay'.[62] Twelve days, in the *Lawless* case, was not held to be excessive.

The measures

The measures taken, must be limited to the 'extent strictly required by the exigencies of the situation' (Art. 15, para. 1). The general principle of proportionality is stringently set out. But it can only be applied *in concreto* by comparing the means with the ends. The institutions of the Convention thus eschew all dogmatism, and recognize that the government confronted with a major threat is usually in a better position than them to make the appropriate choices. In *Ireland* v *The United Kingdom*, the applicant government put forward the appealing argument that the non-necessary nature of the United Kingdom's derogating measures was demonstrated, *a posteriori*, by their ineffectiveness. The Court rejected this argument and granted the defendant a large margin of appreciation, basing its decision on the subsidiary nature of the mechanism created by the Convention.[63] The State therefore has the right to make a mistake. Any judgement of the measures taken must be based upon a reasonable forecast of their success at the time they were decided upon, more than upon their actual effectiveness as ascertained after the fact. This judgement will only be negative '. . . in extreme cases in which there was clearly no link between the facts of the public emergency in question and the measures chosen to cope with it. . . .'[64]

The restrictions to fundamental freedoms imposable by the State (see below) are therefore variable in degree. The measures taken, however, remain circumscribed at a minimum, in a democratic society, by the separation of powers.[65] The best protection against abuses by the executive is judicial control;[66] otherwise, parliamentary or even administrative control are necessary.[67]

The issue of the potentially discriminatory nature of these measures is distinct from that of their proportionality. Article 14 of the Convention[68] adds a requirement of non-discrimination to the conditions of Article 15.[69] In the case of *Ireland* v *The United Kingdom*, Ireland criticized the United

Kingdom for having arrested many more IRA terrorists than it had Protestant terrorists. The Commission and the Court, however, implicitly admitted that a State can be justified, in such circumstances, in favouring the struggle against one threat rather than another.[70]

It should be noted that, as concerns Article 17[71] taken together with Article 15, terrorism appears to be treated more favourably by the jurisprudence than is Communism. After the Commission had held that the objectives of the West German Communist Party were incompatible with the Convention and particularly with Article 17,[72] the Court later limited the scope of this Article:

> ... this provision, which is negative in scope, could not, however, deprive G.R. Lawless – who did not rely on the Convention in order to justify or perform acts contrary to the rights and freedoms recognised in the Convention – of the fundamental rights guaranteed in Articles 5 and 6.[73]

The impact of the applicants' ability to invoke Articles 5 and 6 is none the less limited by the fact that the State can derogate from these Articles.[74]

The second condition with respect to the substance of the State's derogating measures is, as set out at Article 15, paragraph 1, that they must not be '... inconsistent with its other obligations under international law'. Other international instruments could therefore provide complementary human rights protection through the application of Article 15. The Commission found, however, in the case of *Ireland* v *The United Kingdom*, that the Article 3 common to all four Geneva Conventions of 12 August 1949 was '... not directly applicable here ...'[75] In any case, the Court did not find that any measure taken by the Government in this case – or in that of *Lawless* – was contrary to its international law obligations outside of the Convention.

In conclusion, it should also be noted that the right to derogate is obviously not an obligation. A State can choose not to avail itself of its right, and may indeed often consider in good faith that its measures are consistent with the Convention and therefore do not require the use of Article 15. In such a case, Article 15 and the safety mechanism of derogation it provides are not applicable.[76]

The right to restrict

The right of a government to restrict in certain cases the extent of individual protection is not set out in the Convention; our use of the expression 'right to restrict' is unusual. It is true that the Convention is, thankfully, primarily concerned with human rights and the duties of governments. These governments do, none the less, generally enjoy considerable freedom in their ability to constrain the autonomy of individuals with a more or less dense web of obligations. The fundamental difference between derogations and restrictions appears simple;[77] whereas the prior actually suspend the enjoyment of the right concerned, the latter comprise of interferences which merely make the enjoyment of the right more onerous... but not impossible; they are restricted, but still exist. This ability of governments to restrict without actually suspending rights is provided for by the Convention at paragraph 2 of certain of its articles,[78] but can also be generalized.

Such restrictive measures must satisfy three cumulative conditions: they must be provided for by law, have a legitimate objective, and be necessary in a democratic society. The second and third conditions must also respect a criterion of proportionality. In their struggle against terrorism, the governments have attempted to satisfy these conditions in their drafting of restrictive or public order clauses.

Article 8 of the Convention protects the right to private and family life, to home and to correspondence.[79] In the *McVeigh* case, the United Kingdom did not invoke Article 15, and the Commission did not (although once again in the context of Northern Ireland) discuss whether it had been respected.[80] The three plaintiffs, suspected of belonging to the IRA, had been detained for forty-five hours. Basing itself on Article 8, the Commission admitted that certain measures may have interfered with the right to respect for private life.[81] The Commission immediately justified these measures however, as they had been taken in accordance with the law, and were necessary in a democratic society for the prevention of crime.[82] The subsequent 'retention of records of the applicants' examination', that is to say of their files including their fingerprints and photographs, was the subject of more expansive discussion, due to the desire to adapt the jurisprudence to the seriousness of the circumstances. In contrast to a previous case,[83]

> ... no criminal proceedings were brought against the applicants and, furthermore, it is not established that there was any 'reasonable suspicion' against them in relation to any specific offence. ... However, the Commission accepts that the specific purpose of retaining the records in question is the prevention of terrorism. ... Bearing in mind also the serious threat to public safety posed by organised terrorism in the United Kingdom, the Commission considers that the retention for the time being of records ... can properly be considered necessary in the interests of public safety and for the prevention of crime.[84]

McFeeley and Others[85] were all prisoners condemned for 'terrorist-type'[86] infractions to the Law of 1978 on the state of emergency in Northern Ireland. Based on Article 8, several of the prisoners complained of extraordinary body-searches; the Commission found that they did constitute interferences with the right to respect for private life, but were justified on the facts of the case.[87] The reasoning is similar with respect to the prohibition on contact with other prisoners: if, '... this element in the concept of privacy extends to the sphere of imprisonment',[88] the prohibition is here allowed as a disciplinary punishment, necessary to maintain order, just as is the restriction of family visits to one per month.[89]

The exceptionally dangerous nature of the Baader-Meinhof Group explains in large part the rigorous conditions of its detention and the Commission's tolerance of these conditions.[90] A. Baader had previously been freed from custody by force of arms; a policeman was fatally wounded during the arrest of W. Grundmann; U. Meinhof was carrying, at the time of her arrest, a home-made bomb and a document dealing with the seizure of hostages in order to free accomplices ... 'The circumstances described show that the applicants are particularly dangerous and ... indicate the necessity for guarding against attempts by the applicants to break out of prison'.[91] The restrictions to the prisoners' Article 8 rights were therefore authorized, especially as the rules regarding contacts, visits and correspondence were gradually relaxed.

Along the same lines, the Commission held that the application of a German national complaining about the interception of one of his letters in which he commended a recent terrorist act was manifestly ill-founded: '... the interference was necessary to maintain the order in prison and perhaps even for the prevention of crime'.[92]

The case of *Klass and Others* is famous not only because it managed to come before the Court, but also because it allowed, at least as concerned the facts of that case, a system of secret telephone and mail surveillance which is characteristic of 'police states'.[93] The applicants' claim that they were victims was allowed, despite the understandable difficulty of proving that they had ever actually been under surveillance.[94] The essential claims of the applicants were, however, rejected. Article 8 was not held to have been violated:

> ... the Court ... cannot but take judicial notice of ... the development of terrorism in Europe in the last few years. Democratic societies nowadays find themselves threatened ... the State must be able ... to undertake the secret surveillance of subversive elements operating within its jurisdiction. ... the existence of some legislation granting powers of secret surveillance over the mail, post and telecommunications is, under exceptional circumstances, necessary ... .[95]

The power of the State to record telephone conversations has been held to be compatible with the Convention, even as concerns the tapping of journalists who had imprudently – although not unethically – communicated with a law firm suspected of supporting terrorism. The reasoning of the Commission in this case[96] can be summarized as follows:

> ... the fact that the authorities charged with the telephone tapping generally did not fully respect the directives given to them[97] – however regrettable this may be – does not by itself constitute a violation of the

Convention. . ... the measures in question have not been shown to have in any way restricted or negatively affected the applicants in the carrying out of their professional activities. It cannot therefore be found that they were out of proportion in relation to the legitimated aims pursued.[98]

Article 9 of the Convention has rarely surfaced in this matter. The struggle against terrorism has been carried out without interfering with the freedom of thought, conscience and religion. The Commission has none the less had to specify that this provision does not imply the right to a preferential status as political prisoner, thus rejecting the contentions of *McFeeley and Others* that the obligation of wearing a prison uniform and doing prison work was an interference with their freedom of conscience.[99]

Article 10 (freedom of expression) was not violated either in that case. The Commission held, first, that '. . . where interference is alleged in the communication of information or ideas by correspondence, Article 8 is the lex specialis rather than Article 10'.[100] Second, the Commission accepted the argument that the restriction of access to mass means of communication was justified as a punishment for difficult prisoners.[101] Similar reasoning can be found in the *Baader-Meinhof* case.[102]

Article 11 (freedom of peaceful assembly, of association), like the two preceding articles, is not fundamentally related to the matter of terrorism and is rarely discussed in the jurisprudence of the Commission or the Court. We therefore limit ourselves to pointing out briefly that the applicants in *McFeeley and Others* were unable to obtain from this provision a right to the company of other prisoners.[103]

Articles 3, 5 and 6 of the Convention[104] do not contain general public order clauses (second paragraphs). The State can, however, impose some restrictions – *lato sensu* – on these very important individual rights.

Article 3 has been invoked by several prisoners who were subjected to exceptional detention arrangements because of their 'dangerous character'. The case of *G. Ensslin, A. Baader & J. Raspe v The FRG*[105] becomes even more dramatic and, cynically speaking, revealing, when the fact that the decision of the Commission came out after the death in prison of the applicants is taken into account.[106] They had been condemned to a life sentence on 28 April 1977, and had, since their arrest in 1972, been subjected to almost absolute social if not sensoral isolation. Their physical and psychological state was poor. The Commission none the less sanctioned the

exceptional detention arrangements . . . convinced that in this particular case there were pressing reasons for subjecting the applicants to arrangements more directly based on security measures. . ... The special arrangements imposed on them were therefore not in the nature of inhuman or degrading treatment.[107]

The case of *G. Kröcher & C. Möller* v *Switzerland* goes in the same direction.[108] The two Germans, arrested in 1977 at the border between France and Switzerland,[109] were subjected to exceptional detention arrangements, and notably to an extended degree of isolation, and confined to a special security area.[110] The Commission, although '. . . seriously concerned . . .' by some considerations,[111] estimated that the minimum level of severity necessary to constitute a breach of Article 3 had not been reached.[112]

Article 5 has been discussed by several cases dealing with the question of terrorism. Among these cases, which concede considerable powers to the State,[113] one is particularly interesting. The case of *L. Ferrari-Bravo* v *Italy*[114] followed from the 2 May 1978 assassination of Aldo Moro by the 'Red Brigades'. The applicant, a university professor suspected of having helped to found and direct a terrorist organization, was arrested and held in detention on remand for more than four years.[115] Basing himself on Article 5, paragraph 1, the applicant complained of an absence of reasonable grounds for suspecting him.[116] The Commission, however, stressed that it is not necessary that, '. . . the reality and nature of the offences charged have been proved. . . .'[117] Two essential considerations, based on the facts of the case but which can perhaps be generalized, emerge from the reasoning of the Commission with respect to Article 5, paragraph 3.[118] First, '. . . both the investigating judge and later the Assize Court encountered exceptional difficulties, owing to the nature of the proceedings, the structures of the various subversive organizations and the many forms which their strategies took (acts of terrorism, ideological support and liaison)'.[119] Second, '. . . the danger of the accused's absconding is inherent in the very nature of the offences charged against him, which form part of an overall plan to provoke civil war and armed insurrection against the authority of the State'.[120] The Commission concludes that, given the seriousness of the accusations and of the potential resulting sentence, and given the nature of these accusations, the sacrifice inflicted on the applicant was not unreasonable.[121]

The applicants' successors in the case of *G. Ensslin, A. Baader & J. Raspe*[122] were unable to convince the Commission that the deceased's trial had been unfair within the meaning of Article 6.[123] Although the Commission had previously admitted that the media could influence a trial,[124] it observed, '. . . that the press and even the authorities responsible for crime policy, cannot be expected to refrain from all statements, not about the guilt of the accused persons but about their dangerous character. . . . '[125] With respect to Article 6, paragraph 3(b) and (c),[126] the Commission admits that 'Refusal to accept, or the exclusion of, a defence is a more difficult question. . . .'[127] Several defence lawyers having been excluded, the Commission pointed out that the right to defence counsel of one's own choosing is limited by the State's right to regulate the appearance of barristers before the courts. Moreover, Article 6(3) does not guarantee the right of the accused to be present in person: 'In order to determine, in the case in point, whether the continuation of the trial when the accused were absent (though not excluded) may have infringed the right secured by Article 6(1), account must however be taken of the particular circumstances of the case. . . .'[128] The Commission has therefore admitted that the allowable degree of State discretion with respect to the right to a fair trial also varies in proportion to the seriousness of the terrorist threat.

The limited protection of victims' rights

The jurisprudence dealing with this question is dismaying but explainable. It is dismaying because there are so few cases in comparison to the seriousness of the injuries, and among these cases, almost no applications have been successful. It is explainable because, in its struggle against terrorism, the State usually does too much rather than not enough, and the victims or their successors are usually allied to the objectives of the State. The result being that those who perhaps most deserve the protection of the Convention have, until now, benefited very little from it.

The concept of victim can be understood in a very large sense. An extensive interpretation could lead us to include the family of the imprisoned or deceased terrorists. We will concentrate, however, on the more common interpretation of the term, which encompasses those persons who suffered from the violence generated by the terrorists, and not from the neutralizing of the terrorists by the State.

The rights at issue

One might think that the Convention has considerable potential in this matter.[129] The jurisprudence, however, has only elaborated on the right to life, and, to a limited extent, the right to the respect for family life.

The right to life

The right to life of Article 2 is one of the rights and freedoms of the Convention which have not yet been discussed by the Court.[130] Paradoxically, as concerns the Convention, judicial effectiveness is inversely proportional to the seriousness of the injury. This right to life is, after all, the right of rights, the only one whose breach is irreversible. Moreover, the violation of the right to life due to a terrorist act is particularly unjust because of the 'innocence', by definition, of the victims.

The direct victims can, of course, if they survive, bring an action before the institutions of the Convention against the State which insufficiently protected or compensated them. But it could be argued that this was not really an Article 2 case, since life was not eliminated but merely threatened? Protecting the right only in cases of actual death would be tragically inadequate; and Article 3,[131] which could undoubtedly cover cases of injured survivors, has not been interpreted in this way.[132]

Most of the cases relevant to this question were initiated by indirect victims, who were intimately related to the actual victims and had sufficient interest to have a right of action. The requisite conditions to have such a right of action have been, in large part, elaborated by cases dealing specifically with our topic of inquiry.

The case of *Mrs W. v The United Kingdom*[133] was initiated by a resident of Northern Ireland whose husband and brother were killed, undoubtedly by the IRA.[134] The Commission held that Mrs W. was not acting as the representative of a direct victim, but as the next-of-kin affected by the death of her brother who was single, as a victim in her own right within the meaning of Article 25.[135] The Commission finds that '. . . the applicant's complaint, concerning the killing of her husband by terrorists, raises the question of State responsibility for the protection of the right to life . . . ,'[136] but declares the complaint inadmissible.[137]

The daughter (and later the husband) of the applicant in the case of *Mrs H. v The United Kingdom & Ireland*[138] was killed by three neighbours, who were terrorists. The Commission admitted that all domestic remedies had been exhausted, but refused the contention that she was the victim of a continuing situation. The delay of six months (Art. 26) was therefore calculated as of the date of the death, and, on the facts, Mrs H.'s application was too late.

The right of a potential victim to bring an action, although admitted with respect to other rights (see, e.g., the case of *Klass and Others* in which the claimed phone tapping was not proved), has never been recognized with respect to the right to life.[139] In the case of *X v The United Kingdom*,[140] the applicant was a Turk detained in London awaiting extradition back to Turkey. X claimed that '. . . his life is endangered by the terrorist activities of the party of the Turk Hal Kurtukis Ordusu'.[141] The Commission did not consider it necessary to:

> . . . take into account an alleged danger arising, not from public authorities, but from autonomous groups, for the applicant has not provided evidence to substantiate his claims . . . there has been a lack of frankness in his various accounts and he remained in Turkey for a long time after the terrorist activities of which he complains were underway.[142]

The right to the respect of family life

This right, which can be invoked by indirect, and even direct,[143] victims, is usually discussed in the context of applications brought by family members of prisoners who are suspected or condemned of terrorism. Article 8 cannot, of course, be used to free criminals in order to protect harmonious conjugal relations. The Commission has held,[144] however, that the close surveillance of the visit of a prisoner's wife and children, and notably the monitoring of their conversations, can constitute an interference with their right to the respect of private and family life. On the facts of that case, though:

> ... the applicant's husband['s] ... conviction was connected with the activities of the IRA. Exceptional security risks may clearly be involved in the detention of persons connected with such terrorist organisations and in the circumstances the Commission concludes that ... the measures applied in relation to visits to the applicant's husband were necessary ...[145]

The positive obligations of the State

Although the Convention consists essentially of civil and political rights, the effective protection of these rights can sometimes require action in the economic and social spheres. In the case of *Mrs W.* v *The United Kingdom*, discussed above, the Commission envisages an extension of the rights set out by the Convention into the sphere of public order and security. The applicant claimed that the United Kingdom did not provide an adequate and commensurate response to the terrorist campaign,[146] and:

> ... that Article 2, first sentence ... requires the United Kingdom, in the emergency situation prevailing in Northern Ireland, to protect the right to life not only by criminal prosecution of offenders but also by such preventive control, through deployment of its armed forces, as appears necessary to protect persons who are considered to be exposed to the threat of terrorist attack.[147]

Although it admits that '... Article 2 ... may ... indeed give rise to positive obligations on the part of the State',[148] the Commission declares the application inadmissible on the facts of the case as the obligation of the State cannot extend so far as to make it responsible for preventing all possibilities of violence.

If we include in the positive obligations of the State that of preventing the negative effects of its anti-terrorist measures, we can evoke the cases of indirect victims who have lost close family members because of an accident resulting from the State's repression campaign – situations which are more promising as far as damages are concerned.[149]

THE PROTECTION OF TERRORISTS

One result of the remarkable system created by the authors of the Convention, which they undoubtedly did not intend, is that it is better suited to the protection of terrorists than of society in general and its victims. The State cannot use the mechanisms set out by the Convention to bring its formidable enemies before justice, whereas the reverse is typical. In most cases, the judges are confronted with a claim that the State violated the Convention through the use of excessive prevention and repression measures. To be sure, we have seen that the appearances can be misleading, as the Commission and Court often concede a large degree of discretion to the national authorities in their anti-terrorist struggle.

Several cases have none the less defined a minimum humanitarian level which must be respected. This minimum level, guaranteed judicially, is particularly important as States are often tempted, given the circumstances, to suspend fundamental rights and freedoms altogether. We will, in our discussion, follow the order of the articles in the Convention, without however aspiring to an exhaustive survey of the topic.

The prohibition of torture and of inhuman or degrading treatment

The importance of Article 3 for the average prisoner is obvious.[150] The protection of Article 3 is essential for the terrorist or suspected terrorist, as he or she is particularly susceptible to treatment aimed at extorting information in the supposed interest of society. However, '... as a rule of *jus cogens*, the prohibition set out by Article 3 is absolute.... '[151] Article 15 prohibits any derogation from Article 3 even in the case of war, let alone of terrorism. Moreover, Article 3 itself does not provide for any restriction.

Ireland v *The United Kingdom* is the leading case in this matter. It was the first and is still the only judgment of the Court with respect to allegations of terrorism.[152] The United Kingdom was condemned for its use of five techniques of sensory disorientation and deprivation,[153] qualified as inhuman and degrading treatment, but not as torture:

> ... the five techniques, as applied in combination ... although their object was the extraction of confessions, the naming of others and/or information and although they were used systematically, they did not occasion suffering of the particular intensity and cruelty implied by the word torture as so understood.[154]

The distinction between 'torture' and 'inhuman treatment' therefore seems to be, '... more one of degree than of nature. ... Torture is an inhuman treatment which is particularly offensive',[155] and which causes '... very serious and cruel suffering'.[156] This subtle distinction based on intensity is further qualified by taking into account the circumstances:

> ... the greater the threat to the democratic social order, the higher the threshold for the application of Article 3. Thus, when the victims are dangerous terrorists whose detention requires draconian safety measures which, *prima facie*, would be inconsistent with Article 3.[157]

None the less, a very important limit has, after some debate, been established: the Commission sees Article 3 as prohibiting the torture in order to save human lives of the terrorist who has planted a bomb.[158] The Commission does not, however, prohibit national administrative and judicial authorities from considering that the culprits of the condemnable torture had commendable objectives which could constitute attenuating circumstances.[159]

The judgment in the case of *Tomasi v France*[160] reaffirms and extends the precedent. The applicant complained of a particularly traumatizing two days spent in police custody in the context of the anti-terrorist campaign in Corsica.[161] The Court, with respect to, '... the large number of blows ... and their intensity',[162] establishes a presumption that the bodily injuries observed by doctors were caused by the alleged mistreatment. According to the Commission, these injuries '... constituted outward signs of the use of physical force on an individual deprived of his liberty and therefore in a state of inferiority'.[163] Article 3 is therefore an effective screen against such excesses by security forces. 'The requirements of the investigation and the undeniable difficulties inherent in the fight against crime, particularly with respect to terrorism, cannot result in limits being placed on the protection to be afforded in respect of the physical integrity of individuals'.[164] The qualification of the actions in this case as 'inhuman and degrading treatment',[165] does not appear to exclude the use of the more extreme term 'torture' in more serious cases.[166]

The treatment of prisoners in the context of an interrogation can violate Article 3. Prison employees are, admittedly, conceded a large degree of discretion with respect to their choice of means of supervision and discipline, especially concerning dangerous prisoners. But even dangerous prisoners have the right not to be subjected to unbearable living conditions.

The minimum standards for the treatment of prisoners are clearly set out in the Commission's Decision in the case of *G. Ensslin, A. Baader & J. Raspe v the FRG*:[167]

> Complete sensory isolation coupled with complete social isolation can no doubt ultimately destroy the personality; thus it constitutes a form of inhuman treatment which cannot be justified by the requirements of security, the prohibition on torture and inhuman treatment contained in Article 3 ... being absolute in character.[168]

The German terrorists in the case of *G. Kröcher & C. Möller v Switzerland*[169] were subjected to severe prison conditions. It is true that Switzerland, confronted for the first time with such criminals, feared, among other risks, the possibility of their prisoners dying (committing suicide?) as G. Ensslin, A. Baader and J. Raspe had recently done in a German jail. Although they were later relaxed, the prison conditions imposed on the terrorists during the first month resulted in '... almost total isolation'.[170] In particular, they were allowed almost no contacts with the outside and none between themselves; they had no access to television, newspapers or tobacco; their windows were walled up; they were subjected to constant artificial lighting; G. Kröcher was under permanent closed-circuit television surveillance . . . and visits from lawyers were forbidden.[171] As has been discussed, the Commission did not, in this case, conclude that Article 3 had been violated. The fact that the Swiss authorities had substantially relaxed the special conditions to which the prisoners were subjected was, however, an important, and perhaps decisive, element informing the Commission's opinion.[172] Echoing the view it had expressed in its *G. Ensslin, A. Baader, & J. Raspe* Decision, the Commission states that subjecting prisoners to sensory and social isolation over a period of several months raises problems with respect to Article 3.[173]

The Right to Liberty and Security of the Person[174]

The protection against arbitrary arrest and detention provided by the long Article 5 has several facets.

Paragraph 1, which sets out six cases of justified detention, has not as yet been very useful to terrorists. M. Guzzardi,[175] who was debatably a terrorist, did not initially invoke this provision. The Commission, which raised the issue *proprio motu*, and later the Court, considered that the strictly enforced restriction of residence to the Island of Asinara was a deprivation of liberty unjustified by paragraph 1(e). If this provision justifies the imprisonment of vagabonds, '. . . it does not necessarily follow that it implicitly justifies the imprisonment of more dangerous persons'.[176] This case thereby reaffirms the strict interpretation of paragraph 1 as comprising an exhaustive list of justifications (see *Engel* judgment of 8 June 1976).

In the case of *B. Fox, M. Campbell & S. Hartley* v *The United Kingdom*,[177] the applicants had been arrested and detained as suspected terrorists pursuant to the Northern Ireland (Emergency Provisions) Act 1978, but without any precise reasons. The Commission and Court concluded that the arrest constituted a breach of paragraph 1(c) (requirement of '. . . reasonable suspicion . . .') as this requirement consists of an objective test which is not satisfied by the mere subjective appreciation of the arresting policeman.[178]

Article 5, paragraph 3 limits the time that a suspect can be held in custody, by according him or her the right to be 'promptly' brought before a judge or authorized officer. The case of Brogan and Others v *The United Kingdom*[179] resembles the preceding case somewhat. In the context of the Nothern Ireland derogating legislation, four British subjects were held in custody over several days. These facts brought the Commission and the Court to interpret the words 'promptly' and '*aussitôt*', both of which are equally authentic, '. . . in a way that reconciles them as far as possible and is most appropriate in order to realise the aim and achieve the object of the treaty'.[180] According to the Court's interpretation of these terms:'

> ... even the shortest of the four periods of detention, namely the four days and six hours ... falls outside the strict constraints as to time permitted by the first part of Article 5 paragraph 3. To ... justify so lengthy a period of detention ... would be an unacceptably wide interpretation of the word 'promptly' ... would entail consequences impairing the very essence of the right protected. ... The undoubted fact that the arrest and detention of the applicants were inspired by the legitimate aim of protecting the community as a whole from terrorism is not on its own sufficient to ensure compliance with the specific requirements of Article 5 paragraph 3.[181]

Thus, even during exceptional periods of public emergency, detainees can only be held in police custody for a relatively brief time without appearance before a judge or judicial officer.

With respect to the right to a trial within a reasonable time (Art. 5(3), continuation), the five years and seven months of *F. Tomasi*'s detention on remand[182] – from his arrest to his acquittal – led the Court to declare that '... the French courts did not act with the necessary promptness'.[183] The seriousness of the acts of which the detainee is accused[184] cannot indefinitely justify the deprivation of liberty combined with the absence of a trial. The duration of the detention is the fundamental issue: '... there was a risk of prejudice to public order at the beginning, but it must have disappeared after a certain time ...'[185], '... there was, from the outset, a genuine risk that pressure might be brought to bear on the witnesses. It gradually diminished ....'.[186] 'In conclusion, some of the reasons for dismissing Mr Tomasi's applications were both relevant and sufficient, but with the passing of time they became much less so. ... '[187]

A violation of Article 5, paragraph 4 was not excluded by the Commission in *A. Ruga v Italy*.[188] The applicant, who had been arrested and charged during an operation against the Mafia, was invoking his right to '... take proceedings by which the lawfulness of his detention shall be decided speedily by a court. ... ' (Art. 5(4)) The Commission held that the applicant's complaint that he had been isolated in a cell as of the moment of his arrest to the point of being unable to exercise this right was not manifestly ill-founded. Moreover, the Commission considered that the appeal's being dismissed by the Italian District Court fourteen days after it was introduced 'gave rise to problems' with respect to the requirement of a 'speedy' decision.

The breach of Article 5, paragraph 3 in the case of *Brogan and Others* led the Court to recognize the four applicants' right to compensation based on paragraph 5.[189] The Court came to the same conclusion in the context of paragraph 1 of Article 5 in the case of *B. Fox, M. Campbell & S. Hartley v The United Kingdom*.

The right to a fair trial

The first Spanish case[190] is perhaps the most interesting terrorism case concerning Article 6 of the Convention. It is also dramatic, both because of the conditions surrounding the death of the victim and because of the doubts concerning the guilt of the applicants. The facts and the procedural history of the case can be summarized briefly.

A group of men assailed a 77-year-old Catalonian businessman in the home of his family and tied a bomb to his chest, declaring that they would only defuse it if they received a large ransom within twenty-five days. They released him, but the bomb exploded that very night. Several weeks later, four people were arrested, one of whom was recognized by witnesses. As members of the terrorist organization E. PO. CA. (Catalonian Popular Army), the four were charged, notably, with having committed an act of terrorism as well as with murder. The *Audiencia Nacional* (the competent court in the matter), however, applied an amnesty law to them, and they were liberated ... and never reappeared before the courts. The Supreme Tribunal overturned this decision, and the investigation resumed, leading to other arrests. One detainee, who was held incommunicado pursuant to the applicable anti-terrorist legislation, designated the applicants as being pro-independence activists and claimed that two of them (Barberà and Mesegué) were responsible for the murder. He later withdrew his statements after having consulted with a lawyer, and did not, in any case, testify at the trial of the applicants because, his sentence having run concurrently with the time spent in police custody, he was released and never reappeared. The applicants themselves confessed and later withdrew their confessions.

The Commission and the Court declared that there had been a string of violations of Article 6, paragraph 1.[191]

The presiding judge of the *Audiencia Nacional* had to be replaced the day of the hearing (because a brother-in-law had been taken ill), as well as another judge; neither the applicants nor their lawyers had been notified. The new presiding judge was, apparently, hardly familiar with the complex 1,600-page file ... and had to rule within three days. The hearing opened on the morning of 12 January and closed that same evening. The accused had been made to travel the 600 km to Madrid the night before. Only one of the witnesses called by the prosecution testified, and did not recognize any of the accused. The file prepared by the investigating judge was not read during the hearing (it is true with the agreement of the defence) – not even the parts regarding the central elements of proof put forward by the prosecution. The European Court pointed out that the confessions '... [which] were moreover obtained during a long period of custody in which they were held incommunicado ... give rise to reservations. ...'[192] The central investigating judge had not even attempted to question the 'informer', who, once released, was never really searched for by the police.

Finally:

> the Court also notes that the central investigating judge in 108 Madrid never heard evidence from the defendants in person – even after the temporary transfer of one of them to the capital – despite the obvious contradictions in their successive statements . . . he proceeded by way of letters rogatory. . . .

It is therefore not in the least surprising that:

> . . . the Court concludes that the proceedings in question, taken as a whole, did not satisfy the requirements of a fair and public hearing. Consequently, there was a violation of Article 6, paragraph 1.[193]

The notion of a 'reasonable time' within which an accused has the right to a hearing (set out in the same paragraph of Article 6), is usually understood in opposition to an excessively long time. That being said, the preceding case highlights the potential risk in the opposite direction, that is, the risk of over-expeditious judgments, particularly in terrorist cases. In the case of *R. Kofler* v *Italy*,[194] the Commission declared admissible the complaint of an Italian who had been arrested in October 1966, and not conclusively judged until a decision of the Court of Cassation in December 1977. He had been accused, before being acquitted on this count,[195] of having blown up a barracks, with victims, in the name of the South Tyrol patriots. The barracks contained munitions and it was uncertain whether the explosion had been criminal or accidental. The Commission recited in detail the absurd history of an expert opinion ordered by the Court of Appeal in October 1971 and completed in June 1975. It should be pointed out that the panel of experts, after having been laboriously convened, partially reconstructed the barracks in order to destroy it again, which raised numerous problems with respect to the authorization for and supply of explosives.[196]

The applicant in the *Tomasi* case also complained of a violation of Article 6, paragraph 1. In that case, the examination of the applicant's grievance against persons unknown, lodged together with an application to join the proceedings as a civil party, was completed after . . . five years and ten months.[197] The Court found that the applicant's comportment had hardly contributed to delaying the proceedings and that the case was not particularly complex. Since, 'responsibility for the delays found lies essentially with the judicial authorities',[198] the Court concluded that there had been a violation of Article 6, paragraph 1.

The right to a defence set out at Article 6, paragraph 3(b) and (c) underlies the admissibility of the application of a Catholic priest who was condemned for his involvement with the IRA in the case of *P. Fell* v *The United Kingdom*.[199] The Commission in that case, combining Articles 6 and 8, concluded that the limited severity of the acts of which the applicant was accused did not necessarily justify his being prohibited from communicating in private with a lawyer.

The right to a minimum level of outside contacts and correspondence

This wording is not in the Convention. Article 8 speaks of everyone's right to '... respect for his private and family life, his home and his correspondence'. The requirements inherent in the detention of arrested terrorists (or suspected terrorists), however, generally render the principles of Article 8 void of all substance. The right to correspondence with the outside remains: its protection is fundamental, in particular, as concerns the prisoner's right to contact with defence counsel (combination with Art. 6 discussed above).

Contacts with one's family are in principle possible even for dangerous criminals, except during certain high-risk periods when isolation is tolerated by the jurisprudence. The time immediately following arrest is a crucial moment in the deprivation of liberty. The Commission, in the case of *McVeigh & Others*, considered that refusing a suspect who has just been apprehended the right to contact his wife or common-law wife constituted a violation of Article 8. The defendant government had submitted the strong argument that:

> ... if a terrorist suspect is allowed immediately to intimate the fact of his arrest to outsiders, there is or may be a risk that accomplices will be alerted and may escape, destroy or remove evidence, or commit offences.[200]

The Commission accepted this argument only on condition that the facts of the case indicated that a particular danger existed:

> Whilst the Government have referred in general terms to the nature of the risks which may arise from allowing such notification, there is no evidence before the Commission to suggest that there were specific reasons why in the present case the wives of the two applicants could not be notified of their whereabouts.[201]

In such cases, the right of the detainee to notify others of his situation is particularly worthy of consideration since it also affects the right of his family to obtain such information.

The freedom of expression

It is understandable that States oppose themselves to the justification of terrorism. Moreover, the censor of activists is certainly less reprehensible than the torture of detainees. The last judgment we will discuss is nevertheless a borderline case. *Castells* v *Spain*[202] dealt with a sympathizer rather than an actual terrorist, but should be briefly discussed as it is revealing. Mr Miguel Castells, a lawyer, was at the relevant time an elected senator representing a party which advocated Basque independence. In 1979 he had published an article decrying the outrageous impunity of anti-terrorist groups supported by the Government which were, according to the article, guilty of numerous murders: '... fascist associations ... [carrying out] the ruthless hunting down of Basque terrorists and their physical elimination.'[203] The author set out a long list of victims, requesting on several occasions that those responsible be identified and brought before justice. The Court observed that he '... recounted facts of great interest to the public opinion. ... '[204] Beyond the system of the Convention itself, these facts evoke the idea of a hard core within the freedom of expression, relative to the denunciation of violations of the right to life which, if true, would be blatantly contrary to Article 2 at least. Moreover, the applicant's status as an opposition member of parliament led to a '... call for the closest scrutiny on the part of the Court',[205] especially since 'the limits of permissible criticism are wider with regard to the Government than in relation to a private citizen, or even a politician'.[206]

The State's alternatives in its anti-terrorist campaign obviously do not include murder. It is therefore desirable that the State not be allowed to censor information relating to such acts.

Many facets of this topic, and several articles of the Convention,[207] have not been discussed. The issue of the specificity of the jurisprudential treatment of terrorism, taken up by this chapter, has not been resolved. The greater severity observed does not seem to indicate that the litigation in question is different by nature. Other studies could confirm or dispute this hypothesis, especially in the analogous domain of drug trafficking.

In any case, it is certain that the quality of the Commission and Court's search for a difficult balance between the protection of society and of those who oppose it has enriched the law. Confronted with a global challenge, the European Court of Human Rights has provided some answers, preserving its fundamental principles and building for the future.

NOTES

1 The report on terrorism published annually by the US State Department lists these countries. The list published 30 Apr. 1991 included North Korea, Iraq, Iran, Libya and Syria.
2 Art. 25 of the Convention does not require that the applicant be of any specific nationality ('... any person ...').
3 '... violation by one of the High Contracting Parties ...'
4 This State is generally considered a hotbed of international terrorism. The author wishes to point out however, that its responsibility in the bombings of the Pan Am (1988) and UTA (1989) flights has not to this day been indisputably established, despite corroborating presumptions and resolution 731 of the UN Security Council.
5 Res. 687, para.32:

> Requires Iraq to inform the Security Council that it will not commit or support any act of international terrorism or allow any organization directed towards commission of such acts to operate within its territory and to

condemn unequivocally and renounce all acts, methods and practices of terrorism.

6 See, notably, Art. 53 of the Convention.

7 '... terrorism menaces the constitutional order and democratic stability of the State ...' (Parliamentary Assembly of the Council of Europe, Recommendation 852 'on terrorism in Europe', 31 Jan. 1979, para. 4) (unofficial translation from the French text).

8 G. Soulier, 'Lutte contre le terrorisme et droits de l'homme, de la Convention à la Cour européenne des droits de l'homme'. *Revue de science criminelle et de droit pénal comparé* (1987), 663 (trans. from the French text).

9 In the preamble of projet de loi n.155 (French National Assembly 1985–86, law of 9 Sept. 1986) (unofficial trans. from the French text)

10 'Things appear more complex if one envisages what can be called, for lack of a better term, internal terrorism, as opposed to external terrorism ...' (Soulier, *op. cit.* note 8, 664) (trans. from the French text).

11 R. Ottenhof, 'Le droit pénal français à l'épreuve du terrorisme'. *Revue de science criminelle et de droit pénal comparé* (1987), 612 (trans. from the French text).

12 'That which is striking at first glance with respect to the elaboration of a definition of "terrorism" is the overabundance of doctrine ...' (J. Eigner, 'Les aspects juridiques de la répression du terrorisme en Europe', dissertation (Strasbourg, 1985), p. 8). '... the analysis of the phenomenon, distorted by the absence of a global approach to terrorism. There are few forms of criminal behaviour which have brought about so many studies. These have, however, most often been single discipline studies devoted to a particular form of terrorism, and have not resulted in a veritable synthesis of the matter' (Ottenhof, *op. cit.* note 11, 608) (both trans. from the French texts).

13 Ottenhof, *op. cit.* note 11, 607 (trans. from the French text).

14 'L'Etat de droit' and 'l'Etat de peur' in the original French text. J.M. Varaut, 'L'Etat de droit contre l'Etat de peur, terrorisme et démocratie', Conference of the Confédération Syndicale des Avocats, Montpellier, May 1986, cited by Ottenhof, *op. cit.* note 11, 608.

15 R.A. Friedlander, *Terror Violence, Aspects of Social Control* (Oceanar Publications: New York, 1983) cited by Ottenhof, *op. cit.* note 11, 612.

16 E.g. conventions on aircraft hijacking (The Hague 6 Dec. 1970; Montreal 23 Sept. 1971), hostage-taking (18 Dec. 1979).

17 Ch. Bassiouni, 'Perspectives en matière de terrorisme', in *Mélanges Bouzat* (Pédone: Paris, 1980), p. 471 (trans. from the French text).

18 Terrorists sometimes hope to gain both political and pecuniary satisfaction from their acts.

19 Strasbourg Convention, 27 Jan. 1977, which is in fact rarely applied to questions of extradition, as they are usually settled by bilateral conventions.

20 Art.1(1) of this Convention:

> For the purposes of extradition between Contracting States, none of the following offences shall be regarded as a political offence or as an offence connected with a political offence or as an offence inspired by political motives: . . .

This depoliticization, given the political motives of terrorism, is theoretically questionable. It is true, perhaps regrettably in these cases, that our criminal law traditions make it difficult to punish more severely criminals who are considered less responsible.

21 Originally, the Prevention of Terrorism (Temporary Provisions) Act 1974 (in

force 29 Nov. 1974), renewed every six months, then every year (as of 1976), until becoming a permanent law (trans. from a French translation).

22 Resolution on International Terrorism of 24 Jan. 1974; reservations made, notably, by Belgium, Italy, Norway and Switzerland.

23 As well as to acts which '. . . create a collective danger to human life, liberty or safety;' or when 'cruel or vicious means are used in the commission of these acts' (para.1).

24 Resolution (74) 3, para. 1.

25 We know that the Fourth Geneva Convention of 12 Aug. 1949 is devoted to the treatment of civilians in times of war, and Art. 48 of Prot. 1 (10 June 1977) specifies, '. . . the Parties to the conflict [international armies] must at all times distinguish between civil populations and armed forces' (unofficial trans. from the French text).

26 Prot. 2 (10 June 1977) does include a Title IV specific to civilian populations, although it does not set out the obligation of distinguishing between armed forces and civilians as regards non-international armies.

27 Even if, '. . . in unclear cases, the person in question shall be considered a civilian' (Art. 50(1) of Prot. 1) (unofficial trans. from the French text).

28 Even excluding attacks against military personnel stationed in their barracks or occupied with other tasks is debatable.

29 The attack of 17 Jan. 1982 killed seven Protestant employees. Such a case illustrates the juridical importance of the civilian/armed forces distinction, in particular that of Art. 13(2) of Prot. 2 (internal conflicts): 'Are prohibited all acts or threats of violence whose main objective is to spread terror among the civilian population' (unofficial trans. from the French text).

30 As is, e.g., that of I. Shamir, in order to justify Jewish terrorism at the time of the creation of Israel (*Le Monde*, 6 Sept. 1991), or the reverse, on behalf of the PLO.

31 Thus Soulier, *op. cit.* note 8, divides his analysis between legitimated and inadmissible derogations ('dérogations légitimées et dérogations inadmissibles').

32 Art. 15(1):

> In time of war or other public emergency threatening the life of the nation any High Contracting Party may take measures derogating from its obligations under this Convention to the extent strictly required by the exigencies of the situation, provided that such measures are not inconsistent with its other obligations under international law.

33 R. Ergec, *Les droits de l'homme à l'épreuve des circonstances exceptionnelles, étude sur l'article 15 de la Convention européenne des droits de l'homme*, (Bruylant, 1987), p. 4 (trans. from the French text).

34 *Greece v the UK* ((A Series) Vol. 3) the first Cyprus case, which ended in 1959 with a political settlement; *Lawless (Yearbook of the European Convention on Human Rights*, 1969, vol. 12, pp. 29–119), first case before the Court, and first case with respect to terrorism in its judgment of 1 Jan. 1961, the Court allowed the use of Art. 15; *The Greek Case* (v Denmark, Sweden, Norway and The Netherlands) ((A Series) Vol. 25), in which the colonel's regime was disavowed by the Commission, which found in its Report of 5 Nov. 1969 that Art. 15 had been violated; *Ireland v. The UK (Yearbook of the European Convention on Human Rights*, 1985, vol. 28, p. 150), second IRA terrorism case: here again the Court held in its 18 Jan. 1978 judgment that the recourse to Art. 15 was justified . . . but condemned the UK based on Art. 3; *The Turkish Case* (v France, Denmark, Norway, The Netherlands and Sweden),

ended with a friendly settlement in 1985, after the Commission had declared the petitions receivable on 6 Dec. 1983: the validity of the derogation never examined since, for inter-State applications, the Commission is not competent with respect to the merits of the case at the admissibility phase of the procedure; the case is none the less interesting to the extent that the state of emergency declared by the Turkish military in 1980 followed a dramatic wave of terrorism: an average of 25 dead per day in early 1980.

35   In order to avoid uncontrollable derogations; the justification offered by M. Merle was:

> ... to enable the authorities to deal with the methods of groups which, protected by the network of democratic freedoms, might attempt to seize power in order to overthrow the order based on the principle of political freedom. The spectre of totalitarian regimes was a constant preoccupation during the negotiations in Strasbourg, ('La Convention européenne des droits de l'homme et des libertés fondamentales' *Revue du droit public et de la science politique* (1951), 714) (trans. from the French text).

More specifically, the amendment was aimed at avoiding the suspension of a treaty because of war.

36   Ergec, *op. cit.* note 33, p.101 (trans. from the French text).

37   See note 45.

38   See note 45.

39   Which allows the executive to exercise, exceptionally, legislative and judicial powers.

40   Of which the particularity is that the President is the sole judge of the measures he takes in the legislative domain.

41   This is evident as regards Art. 16; as for the rules of exception developed by the French jurisprudence, they are not necessarily doomed to a restrictive interpretation (see, e.g., Conseil d'Etat 6 Aug. 1915, Delmotte).

42   Comm. Rep. of 25 Jan. 1976 (B Series), Vol. 23–1, p.92.

43   Art. 33. Unofficial translation of 'l'état de nécessité' in the French text.

44   *Lawless* judgment (on the merits), 1 Jul. 1961 (A series), Vol. 3, paras 15, 48. *Ireland* v *The UK* judgment, 18 Jan. 1978 (A series), Vol. 25, paras 200, 224. As to the characterization of Art. 15 as a clause of necessity, see Ergec, *op. cit.* note 33, pp.45 ff.

45   ... the Commission ... will confine itself to considering whether the measures taken against the applicants breached their rights under Articles 5, 8 or 10.... Nonetheless, in examining that question the Commission must still take into account the general context of the case. ... It is well established in the case-law of the Court that the Convention must be interpreted and applied in the light of present day conditions. . .. The existence of organised terrorism is a feature of modern day life whose emergence since the Convention was drafted cannot be ignored. . .. It faces democratic governments with a problem of serious organised crime which they must cope with in order to preserve the fundamental rights of their citizens. (Case of *McVeigh and others*, Comm. Rep. 18 Mar. 1981, Decision and Reports, Vol. 25, p. 34, paras 156–7).

46   Commissioner Süsterhenn, in Comm. Rep. 19 Dec. 1959 (B Series), Vol. 4, p. 94, whose opinion was very much in the minority (unofficial trans. from the French text).

47   The *Greek Case* will not be examined here as it does not concern terrorism as much as a political and public order crisis.

48   The IRA, dedicated to opposing the maintenance of the British Government

in Northern Ireland, has existed since the creation of the Irish State in 1921. In early 1957, the violence spread to the Republic of Ireland, who is the defendant in this case.

49 Comm. Rep. 19 Dec. 1959 (B Series), Vol. 1, p. 87 (unofficial trans. from the French text).

50 Mostly isolated acts of violence were at issue, but they were potentially dangerous for the future (theft of munitions), and effective (intimidation of witnesses).

51 The Court pointed to, in particular, the seriousness of an ambush of 3 Jul. 1957, shortly before the historically important date of 12 July, on which day demonstrations were planned (judgment of 1 Jul. 1961, supra note 44, p. 56, para. 29).

52 Ergec, *op. cit.* note 33, p. 157, distinguishes the good faith of Ireland from the '. . . total absence of good faith of the derogating state which was characteristic of the *Greek Case*' (trans. from the French text).

53 . . . in the general context of Article 15 on the Convention, the natural and customary meaning of the words 'other public emergency threatening the life of the nation' is sufficiently clear; whereas they refer to an exceptional situation of crisis or emergency which affects the whole population and constitutes a threat to the organised life of the community of which the State is composed . . .
(*Lawless* judgment, supra note 44, p. 56, para. 28).

54 'held, unanimously, that there existed at the time in Northern Ireland a public emergency threatening the life of the nation, within the meaning of Article 15, para.1' (judgment, supra note 44, p. 95).

55 Art. 15:

Any High Contracting Party availing itself of this right of derogation shall keep theSecretary-General of the Council of Europe fully informed of the measures which it has taken and the reasons therefore. It shall also inform the Secretary-General of the Council of Europe when such measures have ceased to operate and the provisions of the Convention are again being fully executed.

56 *Lawless*, Comm. Rep. 19 Dec. 1959, supra note 49, p. 7 (unofficial trans. from the French text).

57 *Ireland* v *The UK* judgment, supra note 44, para. 223.

58 See in particular the declaration of Sir H. Waldock before the Court in the *Lawless* case. (Comm. Rep. supra note 49, p. 389.)

59 Art. 15, para. 3 '. . . does, not require a Government to indicate expressly the Articles of the Convention from which it is derogating' (Comm. Rep. 25 Jan 1976, *op. cit.* note 42, p. 96) (unofficial trans. from the French text).

60 E.g., the French notice derogating from the Convention in New Caledonia of 7 Feb. 1985 (Council of Europe, doc. DH(85)1, *Yearbook 28*, pp.13–14).

61 In the *Lawless* case, the notice of the Irish Government did not contain much in the way of reasons; in particular, it did not explain why the measures it could have taken without derogating were insufficient to defeat the terrorist threat. (Comm. Rep., supra note 49, pp. 57, 73; judgment, supra note 44, p. 62, para. 47). In comparison, the Commission, in the *Greek Case*, which was not really concerned with terrorism, was not satisfied with the partial information provided by the Greek Government (Comm. Rep. 5 Nov. 1969, Vol. 1–1, para. 81).

62 Comm. Rep., supra note 49, p.73.

63 It is certainly not the Court's function to substitute for the British

Government's assessment of what might be the most prudent or most expedient policy to combat terrorism. The Court must do no more than review the lawfulness, under the Convention, of the measures adopted by the Government from 9 August 1971 onwards. For this purpose the Court must arrive at its decision in the light, not of a purely retrospective examination of the efficacy of those measures, but of the conditions and circumstances reigning when they were originally taken and subsequently applied. Adopting, as it must, this approach, the Court accepts that the limits of the margin of appreciation left to the Contracting States by Art. 15 para. 1 were not over-stepped by the United Kingdom when it formed the opinion that extrajudicial deprivation of liberty was necessary from August 1971 to March 1975. (judgment of 18 Jan. 1978, supra note 44, p.82. para 214)

64   Ergec, *op. cit.* note 34, p.190, citing the Commission's Report in the case of *Ireland* v *The UK*, supra note 42, p.119 (trans. from the French text).

65   This minimum requirement set out by the jurisprudence explains, *a posteriori*, France's reservation to Art. 15 para. 1. which allows the President to assume all powers in a time of crisis: '. . . with respect to the interpretation and application of Article 16 of the Constitution of the [French] Republic, the terms "to the extent strictly required by the exigencies of the situation," do not limit the power of the President of the Republic to take "the measures required by the circumstances"' (unofficial trans. from the French text). On this reservation, see V. Coussirat-Coustère, *La réserve française à l'article 15 de la Convention européenne des droits de l'homme* (Clunet, 1975).

66   'The rule of law implies . . . an effective control which should normally be assured by the judiciary, at least in the last resort, judicial control offering the best guarantees of independence, impartiality and a proper procedure' (*Klass* judgment 9 Sept. 1978, infra note 79, pp. 25–6, para.55).

67   See *Lawless* judgment, supra note 44, p.58, para.37 and *Ireland* v *The UK* judgment, supra note 44, p.83, paras 217 ff. In the *Lawless* case, as in *Ireland* v *The UK*, the persons subject to administrative detention could contest the decision to detain them. The Commission pointed out, in particular, that in addition to the constant supervision by Parliament of the enforcement of the Offences against the State (Amendment) Act of 1940, any detainee could refer his case to the Detention Commission provided for by the Act (before which G.R. Lawless had appeared), and the opinions of this Commission were binding upon the Government (Comm. Rep. 19 Dec. 1959, supra note 49, pp. 122 ff.).

68   Art. 14: 'The enjoyment of the rights and freedoms set forth in this Convention shall be secured without discrimination on any ground such as sex, race, colour, language, religion, political or other opinion, national or social origin, association with a national minority, property, birth or other status'.

69   According to the Commission, the fact that a State measure is proportional and therefore satisfies the Art. 15 requirement, '. . . does not exclude the possibility that derogatory powers may have been exercised in a discriminatory manner such that there was a violation of Art. 5 combined with Art. 14' (Comm. Rep., supra note 42, p. 203) (unofficial trans. from the French text).

70   According to the Court, the extrajudicial detention measures could, '. . . reasonably have been considered strictly required for the protection of public security and . . . in the context of Article 15, their intrinsic necessity, once recognised, could not be affected by the restriction of their field of application' (judgment, supra note 44, p. 81, para. 213).

71   Art. 17: 'Nothing in this Convention may be interpreted as implying for any State, group or person any right to engage in any activity or perform any act

aimed at the destruction of any of the rights and freedoms set forth herein or at their limitation to a greater extent than is provided for in the Convention'.

72 *German CP* v *FRG*, Comm. Decision 20 Jul. 1957, *Yearbook I*, p. 225.

73 Judgment of 1 Jul. 1961, *Yearbook IV*, p.432.

74 Arts. 5 and 6 are not among the rights set out at Art.15(2) which can not be derogated from.

75 Comm. Rep., supra note 42, p. 379.

76 Opinion of the principal delegate of the Commission, M. Sperduti, with respect to an Italian Order-in-Council of 15 Dec. 1979 which derogated from Art. 5 without there having been a derogation notice. Cited by Ergec, *op. cit.* note 34, p. 314.

77 The distinction is not always this clear, e.g., the excellent work of J. Velu and R. Ergec elaborates a further distinction between 'particular restrictions' on the one hand, and 'general restrictions', which include derogations, on the other; the prior result from '. . . clauses which authorise restrictions for various reasons which have to do with public order as understood according to its widest meaning' (J. Velu and R. Ergec, *La Convention européene des droits de l'homme* (Bruylant, 1990), p.147) (trans. from the French text).

78 Arts. 8, 9, 10, 11, para. 2; Fourth Protocol, Art. 2, paras. 3,4; Seventh Protocol, Art. 1, para. 2 (other types of restrictions are provided for in Arts. 16 and 18).

79 Art.8(2):

> There shall be no interference by a public authority with the exercise of this right except such as is in accordance with the law and is necessary in a democratic society in the interests of national security, public safety or the economic well-being of the country, for the prevention of disorder or crime, for the protection of health or morals, or for the protection of the rights and freedoms of others.

80 *McVeigh and Others* v *The UK*, Comm. Rep. 18 Mar. 1981, Decisions and Reports, Vol. 25, pp.15 ff.

81 The Commission did not specify which measures exactly, among: questioning, searching, finger-printing and photography.

82 The measures were set out in The Prevention of Terrorism (Temporary Provisions) Act 1976 and the Prevention of Terrorism (Supplemental Temporary Provisions) Order 1976 (Report, note 80, p.49, para. 224).

83 *X* v *FRG*, Decisions and Reports, Vol. 9, p.53.

84 Report, supra note 80, p. 51, para. 230.

85 Comm. Decision 15 May 1980, Decisions and Reports, Vol. 20, pp.44 ff.

86 Decision, supra note 85, p.47.

87 '. . . justified as being in accordance with the law (i.e. the prison rules) and "necessary in a democratic society for the prevention of disorder or crime" within the meaning of Article 8, paragraph 2' (p.90, para.81).

88 Decision, supra note 85, p.91, para.82.

89 *Ibid.*, pp.91–92, para.84.

90 *Baader and Others* v *FRG*, Comm. Dec. 30 May 1975, Decisions and Reports, Vol. 2, pp.58 ff.

91 *Ibid.*, p.62.

92 *X* v *Switzerland*, Comm. Decision 9 May 1977, Decisions and Reports, Vol. 9, pp.206 ff. X, who had been detained in Switzerland (where his correspondence was subsequently intercepted), was detained in the FRG at the moment of the filing of his application.

93 *Klass* judgment 6 Sept. 1978 (A Series), n. 28, p.21, para.42.

94 Such surveillance is obviously difficult to prove; the German lawyers for the

applicants therefore chose to challenge the legislative and constitutional amendments of 1968.

95 Judgment, supra note 93, p.23, para. 48. It should be noted that the Court also justifies these measures by the necessity of combating espionage.

96 *ABC and D* v *The FRG*, Comm. Decision 13 Dec. 1979, Decisions and Reports, Vol. 18, pp.176 ff.

97 The Commission points out that, '. . . all telephone calls arriving at G's law firm were automatically recorded on sound carriers and no erasures had been effected. . .. This practice was clearly in contradiction with the directives given by the investigating judge . . .' (p. 180).

98 *Ibid.*, pp.180–81.

99 Comm. Decision, supra note 85, p.77, para. 30.

100 *Ibid.*, p.44.

101 The petitioners were complaining about having no access to television, radio or newspapers and about the withdrawal of religious literature (p.96, para. 105).

102 Comm. Decision 30 May 1975, supra note 90, p.62.

103 Comm. Decision 15 May 1980, supra note 85, p.98, para.115.

104 Art.3: 'Prohibition of Torture and of Other Inhuman or Degrading Treatment or Punishment'. Art.5: 'Right to Liberty and to Security of the Person.' Art.6: 'Right to a Fair Trial' (titles used by V. Berger in *Jurisprudence de la Cour européenne des droits de l'homme* (3rd edn) (Sirey, 1991), pp. 7, 25, 83 (trans. from the French text).

105 Comm. Decision 8 Jun. 1978, Decisions and Reports, Vol. 14, pp.64 ff.

106 They died on 18 Oct. 1977. The applications were maintained on the roll of cases, according to the wishes of the applicants' successors, in the names of the deceased and of their successors. It should be noted that the circumstances of the applicants' deaths being a point of contention, two representatives of the Commission went to Stuttgart-Stammheim prison to obtain information (19, 20 Oct. 1977). The Government's contention that they had committed suicide could not be demonstrated conclusively.

107 *Ibid.*, pp.109, 111, paras. 5, 10.

108 Comm. Rep. 16 Dec. 1982, Decisions and Reports, Vol. 34, pp.24 ff.

109 They were arrested on 20 Dec. 1977. Gabrielle Kröcher was suspected of having taken part in the events of Vienna during the OPEC Conference of 1976.

110 For more details, see the facts set out by the Report.

111 Comm. Rep. supra note 108, p.57, para.75.

112 *Ibid.*

113 E.g., *X & Y* v *Sweden*, Comm. Decision 7 Oct. 1976, Decisions and Reports, Vol.7, pp.123 ff.; *X* v *Austria*, Comm. Decision 18 May 1977, Decisions and Reports, Vol.9, pp.210 ff.; *G* v *FRG*, Comm. Decision 6 Jul. 1983, D.R.25, pp.5 ff.; *S* v *FRG*, Comm. Decision 16 Dec. 1983, Decisions and Reports, Vol. 35, pp.213 ff.

114 Comm. Decision 14 Mar. 1984, Decisions and Reports, Vol.37, pp.15 ff.

115 From April 1979 to July 1983.

116 Art. 5, para.1 (c):

> Para.1: . . . No one shall be deprived of his liberty save in the following cases and in accordance with a procedure prescribed by law; . . . (c) the lawful arrest or detention of a person effected for the purpose of bringing him before the competent legal authority on reasonable suspicion of having committed an offence or when it is reasonably considered necessary to prevent his committing an offence or fleeing after having done so.

The applicant claimed that the accusations were based solely on his own written and oral declarations.

117 Comm. Decision, supra note 114, p.37, para.3.

118 Art. 5, para.3: 'Everyone arrested or detained in accordance with the provisions of paragraph 1(c) of this Article shall be brought promptly before a judge or other officer authorized by law to exercise judicial power and shall be entitled to trial within a reasonable time or to release pending trial' (first sentence).

119 Comm. Decision, supra note 114, p.39, para.17.

120 *Ibid.*, para.14. In the case at hand, the danger was very real. Prof. M. Negri (represented in front of the Commission by his brother G. Ferrari-Bravo), was liberated in July 1983 after his election to the Chamber of Deputies; a warrant for his arrest was reissued after the termination of his immunity as Deputy . . . and he absconded in September 1983.

121 *Ibid.* For a decision that went the other way, see the *Tomasi* judgment, infra note 160.

122 Comm. Decision 8 Jul. 1978, supra note 105.

123 Art. 6 (beginning of para.1): '... everyone is entitled to a fair and public hearing within a reasonable time by an independent and impartial tribunal established by law'.

124 Comm. Decisions n.1476/62 v *Austria* (Coll. 11, p.31), and n.3444/67 v *Norway* (*Yearbook 13*, p. 302).

125 Comm. Decision, supra note 105, p.112, para.15.

126 Art. 6, para.3:

Everyone charged with a criminal offence has the following minimum rights:
. . .
(b): to have adequate time and facilities for the preparation of his defence;
(c): to defend himself in person or through legal assistance of his own choosing or, if he has not sufficient means to pay for legal assistance, to be given it free when the interests of justice so require;

127 Comm. Decision, supra note 105, p. 114, para. 20.

128 *Ibid.*, p.115, para. 22.

129 Articles other than Art. 2 which could be relevant: Art. 3 (torture, inhuman or degrading treatment); Art. 5 (provides for the possibility of restricting the liberty of the person); Art. 6 (fair trial, with respect to the 'trial' of hostages); Art. 7 (same reasoning as for Art. 6); Art. 8 (see infra, note 143); Art.14 (non-discrimination); Prot.1, Art.1 (the enjoyment of possessions); Prot.4, Art.2 (free movement of persons); Prot.6 (prohibition of the death penalty).

130 Berger, *op. cit.* note 104, p.390.
Art. 2(1): 'Everyone's right to life shall be protected by law. No one shall be deprived of his life intentionally save in the execution of a sentence of a court following his conviction of a crime for which this penalty is provided by law'.
Art. 2(2): 'Deprivation of life shall not be regarded as inflicted in contravention of this Article when it results from the use of force which is no more than absolutely necessary: (a) in defence of any person from unlawful violence; (b) in order to effect a lawful arrest or to prevent the escape of a person lawfully detained; (c) in action lawfully taken for the purpose of quelling a riot or insurrection'.

131 Art. 3: 'No one shall be subjected to torture or to inhuman or degrading treatment or punishment'.

132 '... the Commission's previous jurisprudence that the extradition of someone to a particular country may in exceptional circumstances raise an issue under Article 3. ... In most of the relevant previous cases ... the threat of ill-treatment came from receiving State authorities not private individuals or factions ...' (Comm. Decision, infra note 140, p. 52).

133 Comm. Decision 28 Feb. 1983, Decisions and Reports, Vol.32, pp.190 ff.
134 The husband's murder was claimed by the Provisional IRA (p.192, para.4).
135 Comm. Rep., supra note 133, p.199, para.8.
136 *Ibid.*, p.198, para.4. The question is less clearly framed as concerns the brother (p.199).
137 The husband having been killed in the Republic of Ireland, the Commission held that it was incompetent *ratione loci* with respect to his murder (p.199, para.5).
138 Comm. Decision 7 Mar. 1985, Decisions and Reports, Vol.42, pp.53 ff.
139 As far as we know.
140 Comm. Decision 6 Mar. 1980, Decisions and Reports, Vol.29, pp.48 ff.
141 *Ibid.*, p.51.
142 *Ibid.*, pp.54–5.
143 E.g. by persons who have suffered physical or psychological interference susceptible of seriously afflicting or shattering their family life. It should be noted that Art. 8 also protects the respect of the home, and Art. 1 of Prot. 1 protects the enjoyment of possessions.
144 *X* v *The UK*, Comm. Decision 3 May 1978, Decisions and Reports, Vol.14, pp.246 ff.
145 *Ibid.*, p.248.
146 Comm. Decision, supra note 133, p.197.
147 *Ibid.*, pp. 199–200, para. 11.
148 *Ibid.*, p.200, para.12.
149 E.g. Comm. Rep. 2 Oct. 1984 in the case of *O. Farrel* v *the UK*, Decisions and Reports, Vol.38, pp.44 ff., cited by M. de Salvia, 'Il terrorismo e la Convenzione europea del diritti dell'uomo', *Rivista internazionale dei diritti dell'uomo* (1989), p.24. The applicant, whose application was declared admissible, was complaining about the circumstances of her husband's death, who was killed by a patrol which, according to the Government, mistakenly thought that he was going to commit a terrorist attack against a bank. The case ended in a friendly settlement, with compensation.
150 The prohibition of Art.3 underlies all of the Standard Minimum Rules for the Treatment of Prisoners (resolution 73(5) of the Committee of Ministers of the Council of Europe, 19 Jan. 1973); Committee of Ministers Recommendation n.R(82)17 regarding the 'custody and treatment of dangerous prisoners'; Parliamentary Assembly Recommendation 971, (1983) 'on the protection of detainees from cruel, inhuman or degrading treatment or punishment'; and especially the 'European Convention for the Prevention of Torture and Inhuman or Degrading Treatment or Punishment', 26 Nov. 1987 (EC Doc.H.(87)4), which sets out an unprecedented protective machinery which is preventive and non-judicial, based on visits upon mere notification.
151 Ergec, *op. cit.* note 33, p.249 (trans. from the French text).
152 In the case of *J. Soering* v *The UK* (judgment of 7 Jul. 1989 (A Series), Vol.161), the Court's ruling (overturning the opinion of the Commission) that the threshold of Art.3 had been surpassed (by what is known as the 'death row' syndrome in the US) did not really constitute a case of torture (the element of intention, in particular, was debatable). In the case of *Tomasi* v *France*, infra note 160, torture was not alleged.
153 The five techniques applied in combination for hours at a stretch consisted of: being placed upright against a wall; hooded; subjected to noise (whistling); sleep deprivation; partial deprivation of solid and liquid sustenance (judgment, supra note 44, paras 96–104, 106–7, 167).
154 *Ibid.*, p.67, para. 167.

155 Ergec, *op. cit.* note 33, p.251 (trans. from the French text).
156 *Ireland* v *The UK* judgment, supra note 44, p.66, para. 167.
157 Ergec, *op. cit.* note 33, p.254 (trans. from the French text).
158 Comm. Rep. 25 Jan. 1975, supra note 42, p.387; see, however, the separate opinion of Fitzmaurice, (judgment, supra note 44, p.129).
159 *Ibid.*, p.387. Attenuating circumstances, not accepted practice.
160 Judgment of 27 Aug. 1992 (A series), Vol.241.
161 *Ibid.* esp. paras 52ff.
162 *Ibid.*, p.42, para.115.
163 *Ibid.*, p.41, p.113.
164 *Ibid.*, p.42, para.115.
165 *Ibid.*
166 See the concurring opinion of De Meyer J. at 47:
    Any use of physical force in respect of an individual deprived of his liberty which is not made strictly necessary as a result of his own conduct . . . must . . . be regarded as a breach of the right guaranteed under Article 3. . .. At the most the severity of the treatment is relevant in determining, where appropriate, whether there has been torture.
167 Although they were, according to the Commission, respected in that case. See supra note 105.
168 Comm. Decision 8 Jul. 1978, supra note 105, pp.109–10, para.5.
169 Comm. Decision 9 Jul. 1981, Decisions and Reports, Vol.34, pp.24ff., and Rep. 16 Dec. 1982, supra note 108.
170 Comm. Rep., supra note 108, p.52, para.58.
171 For a more complete description of the isolation measures, see Comm. Decision, supra note 169, pp.40ff.
172 Comm. Rep., supra note 108, p.57, para.76.
173 Comm. Decision 9 Jul. 1981, supra note 169, p.50, para.6.
174 Or simply the right to security, the 'advanced protection of all freedoms' (*protection avancée de toutes les libertés*), an expression elaborated notably by J. Rivero in 'Les libertés publiques', *Thémis* II (1977), 21. We use the wording of the Convention.
175 *M. Guzzardi* v *Italy*, Comm. Rep. 7 Dec. 1978; judgment of 6 Nov. 1980. See Berger, *op. cit.* note 104, pp.30ff. The case concerned a kidnapping and ransom in the context of the Mafia.
176 Berger *op. cit.* note 105, p. 32.
177 Applications Nos 12244/86, 12245/86, 12383/86; Comm. Rep. 4 May 1989 (21.062–06.2); court judgment 30 Sept. 1990 (A Series), Vol. 182.
178 'The only relevant question to be answered is whether the constable in his own mind suspected the person concerned and whether this was an honest opinion. The Commission cannot find that this subjective test is sufficient to satisfy the requirements of Article 5, paragraph 1(c) . . .' (Comm. Rep., supra note 177, p. 11).
179 Comm. Rep. 14 May 1987 (13.113–06.2); Court judgment 29 Nov. 1988 (A Series), Vol. 145.
180 Judgment, supra note 179, p. 32, para. 59.
181 *Ibid.*, pp. 33–4, para. 62.
182 From 23 Mar. 1983 to 22 Oct. 1988. Acquitted by the Cour d'Assises of Gironde (judgment of 27 Aug. 1992, supra note 161, p. 34, para. 83).
183 Judgment, supra note 160., p. 39, para. 102.
184 '. . . the attack against the Foreign Legion rest centre was a premeditated act of terrorism, responsibility for which was claimed by a clandestine organisation which advocated armed struggle'. (judgment, supra note 160, p. 36, para. 91).

185 *Ibid.*, p. 36, para. 91.
186 *Ibid.*, p. 37, para. 95.
187 *Ibid.*, pp. 37–8, para. 99. The Court therefore found that there was a clear violation of Art. 5(3).
188 Comm. Rep. 10 Mar. 1988, Decisions and Reports, Vol. 55, pp. 69 ff. (includes the Decision of 7 May 1987 as to the admissibility of the application).
189 Art. 5(5): 'Everyone who has been the victim of arrest or detention in contravention of this Article shall have an enforceable right to compensation'.
190 *Barberà, Messegué & Jabardo,* judgment of 6 Dec. 1988 (A Series), Vol. 146.
191 Art. 6(1): '. . . everyone is entitled to a fair and public hearing within a reasonable time by an independent and impartial tribunal established by law' (first sentence).
192 Judgment, supra note 190, p. 37, para. 87.
193 *Ibid.*, pp. 3–8, paras 87, 89.
194 Comm. Decision 8 Jul. 1981, Decisions and Reports, Vol. 25, pp. 157 ff.
195 For lack of proof, in March 1969, but the Milan Court of Assizes sentenced him nonetheless to two years and four months of prison on a count of political conspiracy.
196 Judgment, supra note 194, pp. 162–3, para. 18.
197 . . . and several days: from 29 Mar. 1983 to 6 Feb. 1989 (judgment, supra note 160, p.43, para.124).
198 Judgment, supra note 160, p.44, para.125. The Court pointed out in particular that the Bastia public prosecutor took more than a year and a half to ask the Court of Cassation to designate an investigating authority, and the Bordeaux investigating judge heard Mr Tomasi only once . . .
199 Comm. Decision 19 Mar. 1981, D.R. 23, pp.102 ff.
200 Comm. Rep., supra note 79, p.53, para.238.
201 *Ibid.*, para.239.
202 Judgment of 23 Mar. 1992 (A Series), Vol.236.
203 Art. reproduced in *ibid.*, p.11, para.7.
204 *Ibid.*, p.23, para.45.
205 *Ibid.*, para.42.
206 *Ibid.*, para.46.
207 In particular Arts 7, 13 and 14 which were mentioned in passing at most.

13 The rights of victims and liability of the State

Thierry S. Renoux and André Roux

Over the last few years, there has been an increased tendency towards 'socialization of risks', and the law has established specific regimes of indemnification for damages sustained by certain categories of victims who are deemed particularly worthy of interest.[1] This tendency is particularly apparent wherever the principle of 'national solidarity' has been put into operation, even though such a notion is hardly free from uncertainty, still less ambiguities.[2]

Thus, indemnification is more and more frequently dissociated from liability. It has been accepted for a long time that indemnification can operate without clear liability needing to be established,[3] but more recently the legislator has been moved to create new systems of indemnification, independent of any separate liability actions that may be brought against the authors of the damage.[4]

The establishment of these independent systems of indemnification is obviously explained by the extreme difficulty that victims in certain cases can experience in bringing into play the usual mechanisms of private law or administrative liability law, whereas the losses that they sustain – above all physical ones – are particularly serious.

The system of indemnification of victims of acts of terrorism has been presented, in some respects, as a model in comparison to foreign ones. To a large extent the French legislator has extended its benefit to all victims of criminal offences (law 90–589 of 6 July 1990, modifying the Code of Criminal Procedure and the Code of Insurance as regards victims of criminal offences).[5]

In view of recent legislative developments and comparative law in general, it therefore seems appropriate briefly to review the whole subject of the rights of victims of terrorist acts, before considering the special features of the system of compensation or indemnification which applies to them.

For a long time, the victims remained the 'forgotten ones of terrorism'. The attention of the mass-media is much more focused on the authors of terrorist acts than on the actual victims, and the emotion that these acts provoke at the time is very quickly forgotten.

Lawyers, for their part, were originally inclined to concentrate above all on the suppression of terrorism, especially international terrorism.[6] Later on, criminologists began to establish a science of 'victimology' and to consider the position of victims in general, by studying the relationships established between them and the authors of offences.[7]

The increasing number of terrorist attacks and thus of victims, either abroad[8] or on home territory[9] over the last twenty years or so has led the victims and their relatives to form organizations to assert their rights.[10]

The question does indeed arise as to what real 'right to compensation' the victims or their heirs can enjoy for the physical losses, and indeed the often very grave psychological problems, which result from such attacks.

Recently, 'the public indemnification of victims of terrorist attacks'[11] has been recognized as a necessity, as the private law rules governing compensation appear ineffective or at least inadequate. It is difficult, not to say impossible, to obtain compensation from the author of the attack, even if he is identified and arrested. As for the insurance companies, they have for a long time excluded terrorist attacks from their risks covered. In the last few years some indemnity has been offered at the cost of a punitive rise in premiums (about 40 per cent for properties in high-risk locations), but personal injuries are in general hardly covered. The State had therefore to intervene in order to establish an appropriate system of compensation.

The legal systems of the major European countries offer different answers to the question of indemnification of victims. For its part, France has chosen a system which is relatively generous to them. But it has to be stressed that the implementation of this special system gives rise to certain difficulties in connection both with the actual definition of the act of terrorism and with the extreme diversity of victims' personal circumstances, all of which tend to complicate the consideration of specific individuals' rights.

It is possible[12] to identify objective and subjective elements, which characterize the act of terrorism. From an objective point of view, it is first of all an act of exceptional violence, a particularly odious crime (bombing, taking of hostages . . .) as is stressed by international conventions against terrorism which mention particularly serious acts, cruel and treacherous methods, common danger, etc.[13]

The terrorist act may thus be defined objectively by reference to a list of offences in criminal law, as is done by the law of 9 September 1986 on the fight against terrorism and breaches of State security (Art. 706–16 of the Code of Criminal Procedure),[14] which mentions offences of violence against the person (e.g. wilful homicide, violence resulting in mutilation), attacks against property which cause a public danger (e.g. damage to public buildings committed by means of explosives), abductions, hostage-taking and illegal confinement of persons.

But the act of terrorism is also characterized by subjective elements pertaining to the final goal sought by its authors and to the motives which drive them.

The act of terrorism is premeditated. It presupposes an organization from which chance seems to be excluded. The law of 9 September 1986 provides in confirmation that offences are of a terrorist nature when 'they are linked to an individual or collective undertaking whose intention is to seriously disturb the public order by intimidation or terror'. The act of terrorism also appears as the vehicle of an ideology in that it serves a cause, and that it is part of a global strategy intended to generate a psychosis in the population, a reflex of great fear, by intimidation or terror with the sole purpose of seeing the triumph of the cause it espouses.

As far as the victims and the compensation for damage are concerned, the question of the definition of the act of terrorism is raised only if a specific regime of indemnification is applied to them, as is the case in France. Alternatively, one can disregard the motives of the act and evade the delicate question of its definition, by providing a mechanism of public indemnification which applies to any victims of acts of violence without distinction.

Failing these, one would have to consider whether any right to compensation exists which victims of terrorist acts can claim against the State, and by what technical means it can be brought into operation.

One can conceive of a system allowing for State liability in the matter to be invoked, but it must be emphasized that such a system appears difficult to implement, owing in particular to the need to demonstrate a causal link between the damage to be indemnified and the action (or inaction) of the State. This is why more and more States have moved towards setting up a guarantee system, which is more likely to provide complete compensation for the damage sustained.

LIMITS OF THE LIABILITY SYSTEM

Can the State be held responsible for the damage resulting from acts of terrorism committed on the national territory or abroad against its own nationals, and must it then compensate entirely for such damage?

To confine ourselves to the example of the French system, the mechanisms of liability law give victims only limited chances of obtaining compensation.

It is true that the State may answer favourably their submission for an out-of-court settlement and may agree to indemnify them partially without this constituting an official admission of liability.[15]

In the field of litigation, however, the success of the liability action brought against the State presupposes, according to the principles governing administrative liability law, that the cause of the prejudicial fact is not a cause extraneous to the State's activity. Now, as far as terrorist attacks are concerned, establishing a link of causality is made extremely delicate for several reasons: the attack is planned and organized in the utmost secrecy, and it is carried out in ill-defined circumstances; the judge's assessment is made all the more complex in that the perpetration of an attack gives rise to a combination of different administrative activities, all capable of causing a damage or of increasing the main damage. Does the loss sustained originate in the measures taken by the police in the field which proved to be insufficient? Or on the contrary, is it the result of the legal preventive orders enacted by the government which proved to be tardy or inadequate? Or again, have inadequacies of the rescue services increased the damage? One immediately notices the difficulty which victims come up against, whether they choose to bring their action by arguing a fault committed by the government or if they ask for compensation by claiming liability without the government having been at fault.

As a first category, the State may be required to indemnify the victims if it is established that the damage originates in a fault attributable to it.

It may well be a fault resulting from a dereliction of duty by the police services, from a breakdown in their operations, or from inadequacies in the preventative or protective regulations.

Still it has to be stressed that the administrative judge considers that as far as terrorist attacks are concerned, government action (whether this involves legislation or the activities of police forces in the field) encounters specific difficulties, and will therefore accept State liability only in cases of gross negligence.[16]

In concrete terms, the administrative judge may find for serious negligence on the part of the police services or a total lack of preventative measures, in so far as the act of terrorism was not absolutely unpredictable with regard to its time and place, and the authorities had failed to take notice[17] of information suggesting the possibility of a terrorist attack.[18]

The judge certainly has quite considerable freedom in assessing the gravity of the fault, but in reality it is not so much the requirement for there to have been gross negligence as the proof itself of any fault that makes it difficult for the State to be held responsible.

Is it then possible to envisage that the government be held responsible even without it having committed a fault?

Referring to the established grounds for liability such as this, one would have to determine whether the victim of a terrorist attack might be considered to be undertaking a public duty which should be indemnified, or to have suffered damage resulting from a risk linked to activities of the State which should be compensated as such.

In the present state of caselaw, it appears clear that the Council of State has refused to indemnify the victims of terrorist attack on the grounds of unfair imposition of public duties:

in the absence of legislative provisions to this express effect, the State cannot be held responsible, on the grounds of citizens' rights to equal treatment, for acts of terrorism which take place on French territory.[19]

This caselaw can easily be explained:

While it is not doubted that the victims of acts of terrorism bear a burden and have obviously sustained a specific and abnormal damage, it seems difficult to link this burden to the activity of a public community and to consider that the victims have been exposed to the risk of terrorist attack in the public interest, without making a gross confusion between 'public duties' and 'social duties'. In order for the liability of the State to be brought into question, one would have to admit that some victims have been more exposed to risks of terrorist attacks than the rest of the population, and in a way 'sacrificed' to the reason of State in order to enable other human lives to be saved. If this scenario may unfortunately be envisaged (e.g. in the case of hostage-taking), it must be admitted that it is not the normal situation in terrorist cases.

As for being held liable without fault on the ground of risk, this also seems rather uncertain. At the very most, the State may have its liability called into question if one of its agents, by virtue of his office, is in a situation which involves exceptional risks to his person as well as to his property.[20]

Likewise, by virtue of the theory of voluntary assistance to the public service,[21] a person who has helped the police forces in combating terrorism can be indemnified for damages, without needing to prove that these are special or exceptional, provided that they result from his or her act of assistance.

Lastly, the legislation providing State compensation for damage caused by crowds or assemblies of people (laws of 7 Jan. 1983 and 9 Jan. 1986) seems for its part hardly suited to the compensation of damage sustained by the victims of acts of terrorism, even if the Court of Cassation[22] admitted the principle of public indemnification for damage caused by terrorist attacks against property, using explosives or incendiary devices.[23]

In fact, even if the first two conditions for applying this specific regime of liability raise no difficulty (crimes and offences committed against persons or property, acts committed by open force or by violence), the third is in most cases lacking, since the damage must also be the result of crimes and offences committed by 'armed or unarmed crowds or assemblies'. Even if the jurisprudence considers that a small group of people, even only two people, may constitute a crowd or assembly[24] (which is the case of a terrorist commando), the existence, on the scene and at the time of the event, of a gathering even constituted by a group of a few people, has nevertheless to be proved (a simple claim being insufficient). The attack must therefore have been committed conspicuously, which is generally not the case with terrorist actions.[25]

In sum, State liability does not always turn out to offer practicable grounds for litigation by the victims of acts of terrorism, and it can lead to no compensation being won.[26]

It is precisely in order to make up for the deficiencies or inadequacies of the system of liability, that a guarantee system has been established which is much more favourable to the victims.

THE ESTABLISHMENT OF A GUARANTEE SYSTEM

In a system such as this, the victim does not have to bring into play the State's liability, provided that certain legal conditions are fulfilled. On a simple request from the victim, the State is obliged to provide compensation. In other words, the question is to guarantee, socially and in advance, the indemnification of the victim.

The systems of guarantee are based on the principle of solidarity, referred to in a certain number of international texts relating to the indemnification of the victims of acts of violence.[27]

The setting up of such systems has become the norm over recent years in most European States which have been victims of internal or international terrorism. The solutions are, however, far from being homogeneous. Several options are conceivable. Thus, the system of guarantee may be addressed directly and specifically to victims of acts of terrorism, or such persons may be absorbed in the wider circle of victims of 'acts of violence' whatever their nature. Furthermore, systems of guarantee may protect all victims whatever their nationality, or the citizens of the State in which the act is committed, or citizens of those foreign States which have established reciprocal agreements.

First of all, the victims of acts of terrorism may be entitled to a regime of compensation provided for the victims of violent offences.

The act of terrorism is here considered from the point of view of criminal law. This approach offers the advantage of not linking indemnification of the victims to the aim of the act and of dealing with victims on an equal basis. The situation of the victims of acts of terrorism is thus assimilated to that of the victims of violent offences whose authors remain unknown or who are incapable of paying damages.

It is a mechanism of this nature which was applied before 1986 to victims of acts of terrorism in France. The law of 3 January 1977, modified several times, did indeed provide indemnification to various persons injured or killed during bombing or attacks by unknown or insolvent agents.

However, despite the improvements made to it,[28] the system of indemnification, if it was appropriate for providing comparatively satisfactory succour to victims of common law offences, seemed on the contrary totally inadequate for the indemnification of often very serious bodily and material damage sustained by the victims of acts of terrorism. Indemnification, indeed, proved to be incidental and partial. The victims could appeal to committees of indemnification only when they were totally unable to obtain compensation for damages on their own account. For that, they had to wait for the result of the action brought before the criminal judge, and for the author of the act to be declared insolvent or for the case to be closed with a formal declaration that the authors could not be identified. Despite the possible grant of provisional funds, the victims of terrorist attacks had to wait months, even years, for the final settlement of their compensation. Moreover, these being in the form of lump-sum payments, they often fell far short of covering all the damage suffered.[29]

This system of indemnification, which does not attribute any liability at all to the State, but which is, in fact, more of a form of assistance for destitute victims, is very widely used abroad.[30] In many countries, indeed, damage resulting from criminal offences (including acts of terrorism, which are sometimes subject to special criminal prosecution, as in Germany or Great Britain) are indemnified by a lump-sum payment from a special committee.

Thus, in Belgium, the law of 1 August 1985 (s. 2, Art. 28ff.) provides for aid from the State to the victims of intentional acts of violence. This aid, granted by a committee, is financed by a special fund into which are paid contributions from persons sentenced to criminal punishments or penalties. Here again this is a supplementary, lump-sum aid which can be granted to foreign nationals, subject to reciprocity.

Likewise, in The Netherlands, the victim of an offence aggravated by violence may lodge a request for compensation with the indemnification fund for violent acts, set up by the law of 26 May 1975. Compensation is granted only in cases of bodily harm, and there is an upper limit on it.

In Sweden, law 413 of 1978 on damage caused by criminal acts allows for public indemnification of human damage and, in certain cases, material loss.

In Germany, the law of 7 January 1985 on indemnification of victims of terrorist attacks provides for the granting of compensation, borne by the Länder and the Federal State, in aid of the victims of a 'premeditated and illegal attack' (including foreigners, subject to reciprocity).

A comparable system also exists in the United Kingdom[31], United States[32] and Japan.[33]

Some countries that have been confronted with the development of terrorist attacks, whether it is internal terrorism (ETA in Spain, Red Brigades in Italy) or international terrorism (as in France) have established systems to indemnify the victims of such acts which take into account the specificity of their situation.

In France, under pressure from the associations of victims of terrorist attacks, taken up by various parliamentary initiatives, the law on the fight against terrorism and breaches of State security was first adopted on

9 September 1986.[34] This mechanism, reinforced by the law of 6 July 1990,[35] combines insurance and aid.

Thus, as far as material losses are concerned, it falls to the insurance companies to provide indemnity for them, whether the victims are individuals or legal entities. To this effect, Article 9 of the 1986 law provides that 'property insurance policies cannot refuse cover for damage resulting from acts of terrorism or bombing committed on the national territory' – any conflicting clause being held to be void.

This compulsory material-damage cover by private insurance companies constitutes a noteworthy development from the previous provision, adopted in 1983. At that time, only risks of fire or explosion caused by terrorist attack were taken into account; these had to be covered, but at special rates and by pollicitation (i.e. provisionally, from the moment that the client had made a specific request).

Physical damage – and this is the main contribution of the 1986 law – is now indemnified by the Guarantee Fund, a legal entity financed by a levy on property insurance contracts.[36]

This law has been given a very broad sphere of application. It concerns all victims of acts of terrorism, French or foreign, whether or not they are in any way insured, and whether the terrorist act occurs on national territory or abroad (in this last case, only the French victims can be indemnified).

The definition of the act of terrorism is also very extensive and results from one of the offences or circumstances listed in Article 706–16 of the Code of Criminal Procedure,[37] and Article L 126–1 of the Code of Insurance, when they are 'linked to an individual or a collective undertaking whose intention is seriously to disturb the public order by intimidation or terror'. This definition enables not only terrorist attacks, but also hostage-taking to be taken into account. Thus, the Guarantee Fund was used to indemnify French nationals detained in Iraq during the Gulf War,[38] which means that 'State terrorism' itself is not excluded by the 1986 law.

All victims of terrorist acts committed on the national territory, and also French victims of such acts committed abroad, have ten years to bring an action against the Fund (Art. L 126–1 and Art. L 422–3 of the Code of Insurance). As soon as an act of terrorism occurs, the *Procureur de la République* (Chief Prosecutor) or the relevant diplomatic or consular authority must inform the Guarantee Fund without delay of the circumstances of the event and the identity of the victims. In addition, any person who considers himself to have been a victim of an act of terrorism may appeal directly to the Fund. The Fund may itself open a case and is responsible for assisting victims in drawing up the paperwork for their claim for compensation.[39]

The compensation procedure is, in principle, quick. Indeed, the Guarantee Fund is obliged, within a month from the request for indemnification, to pay a provisional amount to the victim or his heirs, who still retain the right to appeal to the *juge des référés* (judge in summary proceedings) on this ground.

The final offer of indemnification must be made within three months following proof of damage, and if it is accepted by the victim, it becomes a settlement between the latter and the Guarantee Fund (Art. R 422–8 of the Code of Insurance).[40] Failing this, any sums of money unpaid will automatically earn interest at the official rate increased by half for the first two months and at twice the official rate thereafter.

Compensation for damages resulting from attacks against the person is comprehensive, so account is taken of benefits or indemnifications already received, or due to be received, on the same account. The compensation can be reduced or refused if the victim has been at fault, but the Fund's assessment of damages is not binding on the victim, as he or she retains the right to bring an action to establish the correct amount of compensation. So far, however, there has been only one appeal to the courts against an amicable settlement.

The damages to be indemnified are also defined in a very broad way. They include, in particular; medical expenses; temporary or permanent disability; occupational damage; the cost of a home help; harm to existence (serious disruption of living conditions); *pretium doloris* – aesthetic damage or damage to quality of life; material losses linked to an attack against the person; and the form of post-traumatic syndrome which particularly affects victims of terrorism.[41]

The law of 23 January 1990 has moreover extended to victims of acts of terrorism the benefit of the provisions of the code of military disablement pensions and of civilian war victims (this brings a pension and associated benefits with regard to health, employment and social security, plus the other rights offered to members of the National Office of War Veterans and War Victims).

The system of indemnification established in 1986 constituted for the victims of acts of terrorism a very distinct advance in comparison with the one concerning the victims of common law offences.[42] As the condition of the latter had to be improved as well, the law of 6 July 1990 allows a total compensation package to be granted to them also. (Until then, an upper limit of 400,000 FF had applied, even with permanent 100 per cent disablement and the necessity for a third person's help.) The 1990 law also removes the restrictive conditions of the earlier 1977 law which required a serious disruption in living conditions, and stipulated that compensation would only be subsidiary.

However, contrary to the original intent of the Government bill, this law does not achieve the complete unification of the two indemnification regimes (that of victims of acts of terrorism and that of victims of other offences) except as regards the payment office – the Guarantee Fund which had been created in 1986 became in 1990 'the Fund for victims of acts of terrorism and of other offences'.

Consequently, when acts of terrorism are involved, the assessment of damages is the direct responsibility of the Guarantee Fund itself, as we have already seen, but as regards other offences there is a commission[43] (with civil jurisdiction, subject to the *tribunal de grande instance*) which determines what indemnification is then paid by the Fund.[44]

However that may be, the regime for indemnification of victims of terrorist acts has played a trail-blazing role, and by acting as a point of reference, has led to a marked improvement in compensation for all victims of crime, though by the same token losing its uniqueness.

The principle of special treatment is more or less followed in other European countries. Thus in Spain, the organic law 9–84 of 26 December 1984 on measures against activities of armed groups and terrorist rebellion contains a Chapter IV which provides indemnification by the State for physical harm sustained as a result of or at the time of terrorist incidents, according to a scale determined by decree.[45] The Ministry of the Interior is in charge of examining claims and the compensation granted can be drawn in addition to any other indemnification.

In Italy, law number 466 of 13 August 1980 institutes for its part 'special allowances for civil servants and citizens who are victims of duty or of acts of terrorism', and these are also available to foreigners.[46] The allowances, which are subject to an upper limit, are paid to the victims only in case of at least 80 per cent permanent incapacity, or to the relatives of the victims in case of death. This is a system which is closer to assistance than to insurance.

In fact, the evolution of the legislation on the indemnification of the victims of acts of terrorism is a perfect example of the development of what has been called the 'socialization of risks', since we have moves – especially in France – towards the implementation of a general 'social guarantee' for the benefit of victims.

NOTES

1 Concerning this tendency, see J.M. Pontier, 'Le législateur, l'assureur et la victime' *Revue français de droit administratif* (1986) 2(1), 98ff, and Th. S. Renoux, 'Un nouveau cas de garantie sociale' *Revue française de droit administratif* (1987), 3(6), 911ff.

2 See J.M. Pontier, 'De la solidarité nationale' *Revue de droit public* (1983), 99(4), 899ff.

3 E.g. legislation regarding war damage, laws of 31 Mar. and 24 June 1919; and damage resulting from natural disasters; see J.M. Pontier, *Les calamités publiques* (Berger-Levrault, 1980).

4 See J.M. Pontier, 'Sida, de la responsabilité à la garantie sociale' *Revue française de droit administratif* (1992), 537.

5 *JO* (French Official Journal) 11 July 1990.

6 See Donnedieu de Vabres, 'La répression du terrorisme' *Revue de droit international et de législation comparée* (1938), 37; M. Glaser, 'Le terrorisme international et ses divers aspects' *Revue de droit pénal et de criminologie* (1947–48), 786.

7 See L. Szabo, 'La victimologie et la politique criminelle' *Revue internationale de criminologie et de politique pénale* (1981), 343; M. Delmas-Marty, 'Des victimes, repères pour une approche comparative' *Revue de science criminelle* (1984), 207; F. Lombard, 'Des différents systèmes d'indemnisation des victimes d'actes de violence' *Revue de science criminelle* (1984), 277.

8 According to the 'Assessment of International Terrorism' adopted by the NATO Assembly on 24 Mar. 1987, 5,175 attacks were recorded in the world between 1973 and 1983, killing 3,689 people and injuring 7,791 others. Since 1980 the number of fatal attacks is said to have increased on average by 20 per cent per annum, with Europe alone suffering about half of these. A report of the American State Department dated 16 Jan. 1987 indicates 1985 as the record year for international terrorism (800 dead and 1,200 injured).

9 Statistics established in 1987 by the NGO Associations to Aid the Victims of Bombing, give 145 dead and 1,000 injured for the last ten years. Terrorist activity reached a peak in France in 1986 (10 bombings, including the rue de Rennes incident which killed seven people and injured fifty-one), but on 19 Sept. 1989 the mid-flight explosion above the Ténéré of a UTA DC10 travelling from Brazzaville to Paris killed 170 passengers.

10 Creation of the associations 'S.O.S. Attentats', 'Solidarité Attentats' and of the 'Institut National d'Aide aux Victimes et de Médiation'.

11 To quote the title of the book by Th. S. Renoux on this question (Economica-PUAM, 1988).

12 Renoux, *op. cit.* note 1, p. 19 ff.

13 See resolution 74–3 on international terrorism adopted by the Committee of Ministers of the Council of Europe, from which originates the European Convention on the Suppression of Terrorism, signed on 27 Jan. 1977 and ratified by France (law 87–542 of 16 July 1987).

14 *JO*, 10 Sept. 1986.

15 Thus, in 1985, 10 million FF were granted in allowances to the victims of various bombings (rue de Copernic, the 'Le Capitole' train) on application for out-of-court settlements.

16 Conseil d'Etat, 10 Feb. 1982, *Air Inter, Rec. Tables*, pp. 696, 744, 763. The Council of State dismissed the claim of Air Inter for State compensation following destruction of a Caravelle by bombing at the airport of Bastia-Poretta, on the grounds that the Prefect was not guilty of gross negligence for having refrained from taking any police measures.

17 See Conseil d'Etat, 17 June 1959, *Delle Victor, Rec. Tables* p. 336.

18 Conseil d'Etat, 11 May 1984, *Société Anonyme Alta et Chemt-Vincent* (unrep.).

19 Conseil d'Etat, 28 May 1984, *Société française de production, Rec.* p.728., S. Dalloz, *Informations rapides* (1986, I.R.), p. 22, observations by F. Moderne and P. Bon; Conseil d'Etat, 29 Apr. 1987, *Yener et Erez*, submissions by C. Vigouroux, *Revue française de droit administratif* (1987), 4, p. 636f. This case concerned the Turkish ambassador to France and his chauffeur, who were victims of a terrorist attack in Oct. 1985.

20 Conseil d'Etat, 19 Oct. 1962, *Sieur Perruche, Rec.* p. 555; Conseil d'Etat, 16 Oct. 1970, *Epoux Martin, Rec.* p. 593; Conseil d'Etat, 6 Nov. 1968, *Benajam, Humbert, Morichère, Ronchaud, Rec.* p. 545.

21 For this theory see Conseil d'Etat, 21 June 1895 *Comes* judgment, Recueil Sirey 1897 (III), 33.

22 Since the law of 9 Jan. 1986, this kind of litigation is a matter for the administrative courts.

23 See, in particular, Court of Cassation (civil chamber), 24 June 1982, *Bulletin*

des arrêts de la Cour de Cassation (Chambre civile). II, no. 97 p. 70, and the decisions mentioned by Renoux, *op.cit.* note 1, pp. 108 and 109.

24 See, in particular, Court of Cassation (criminal chamber), 11 Jan. 1984, *Juris-classeurs périodiques* 1984, IV, 87; Court of Cassation (civil chamber), 4 Feb. 1985, unpublished.

25 See Court of Cassation (civil chamber), 28 Nov. 1984, *Ville de Paris c. Compagnie d'Assurance 'La Concorde', Bulletin des arrêts de la Cour de Cassation (Chambre civile),* II, no. 177, p. 124. In this case, concerning a series of bombings committed against head offices of the magazine *France-URSS,* Aeroflot, and the Tass news agency, the Court of Cassation held that only if the bombing were manifestly committed by a demonstration or a group of demonstrators would the legislation be applicable. See also Tribunal des Conflits, 24 June 1985, 'Préfet, comm. de la République du Val de Marne c. T.G.I. de Créteil et Mme Carme', *Revue du droit public* (1986), 928: the concerted nature of an action does not of itself prove the existence of a crowd or an assembly in the meaning of the law.

26 E.g., the case of a seriously burnt victim of the attack on the concourse of Orly Airport on 15 July 1983 (see Tribunal des Conflits 24 June 1985, *op.cit.* note 25). The State finally came to offer compensation for this bombing.

27 Cf. resolution of the General Assembly of the UN (40th Session) stating the basic principles of justice relating to the victims of crime and to the victims of misuse of power (res. 40/34 of 29 Nov. 1985):

> point 12: 'when it is not possible to obtain complete indemnification from the offender or other sources, the States must endeavour to provide financial compensation to the victims themselves and to their relatives';
> point 14: 'the victims must receive the material, medical, psychological and social assistance which they need through State, voluntary, community and local organisms';
> point 15: 'the victims must be informed of the existence of health services, social services and other forms of assistance which may be useful to them and they must have easy access to these'.

The idea of solidarity can also be found in the European Convention on the Compensation of Victims of Violent Offences (1983):

> Whereas for reasons of equity and social solidarity, it is necessary to be concerned for the situation of the victims of violent intentional offences who have suffered attacks against their life and their health . . .
> Whereas it is necessary to introduce and develop regimes of compensation for these victims by the State on whose territory such offences were committed, especially where the author of the offence is unknown and with no resources.

In the Convention, the principle of solidarity is used in a broad sense: it is intended to provide compensation not only for the nationals of the State on whose territory the act was committed, but also for:

- the nationals of States party to the Convention;
- the nationals of all Member States of the Council of Europe permanently resident in the country where the offence was committed.

28 Laws of 2 Feb. 1981, 8 July 1983 and 3 Dec. 1985.
29 See Renoux, *op. cit.* note 1, p. 145.
30 See Lombard, *op. cit.* note 7.
31 Indemnification by the Criminal Injuries Compensation Board.

32 See in particular Victims of Crime Act, 1984, title XIV: victim compensation and assistance.

33 'Crime Victims Benefit Payment Law', law no. 36 of 1 May 1980 and Cabinet for Crime Victims Benefit Payment Law, law no. 287 of 4 Nov. 1980.

34 *JO*, 16 Sept. 1986, p. 10956.

35 Law 90–589 of 6 Jul. 1990 modifying the Code of Criminal Procedure and the Code of Insurance, on Victims of Offences, *JO* 11 Jul. 1990, p. 8179.

36 See Decree 86–1111 of 15 Oct. 1986 on the indemnification of victims of acts of terrorism (*JO* 16 Oct. 1986, p. 2469). This fund is chaired by a member of the Council of State or the Court of cassation and is composed of six members representing insurance companies; three personalities who have shown concern for victims of acts of terrorism in France and abroad; and three members of the National Council of Insurance chosen to represent insured persons. See V.F. Quérol, 'Le financement du fonds de garantie', *Revue française de droit administratif* (1988), 106.

37 Wilful homicide, use of torture or cruelty, violence resulting in unintentional death or permanent disability, illegal arrests or detention of persons, threats, crime committed at the same time as another crime, criminal conspiracy, theft or extortion of money, destruction of property by explosives or fire, the hijacking of aircraft, ships or any other means of public transport, derailing a train or causing a collision, possessing or carrying weapons or explosives without authorization, making, possessing or transferring biological weapons or toxin-based weapons.

38 Payments between 10,000 and 30,000 FF. See, in particular, F. de Bouchony, 'La colère des ex-otages français de l'Irak', *Le Monde*, 18 Dec. 1990.

39 'L'indemnisation des victimes de la violence, Journées d'études et d'information'; Paris, 15 Dec. 1990, Ministère de l'Economie, des Finances et du Budget et Ministère de la Justice, Dossier Bilan, Imprimerie Nationale (1991), p. 104f.

40 The victim retains the possibility to renounce the settlement within fifteen days of its conclusion. If the draft settlement concerns a minor or an adult in the care of a guardian, it must be submitted to the judge supervising guardianships or to the board of guardians.

41 This last item of compensation addresses the persistent psychological effects of terrorist acts, as identified by a national epidemiological survey carried out in 1987 on 254 persons who had been involved in terrorist attacks. The specific post-traumatic syndrome can be defined as a lasting condition marked by a repetition syndrome (nightmares, flash-back memories), regressive introspection (phobias, regressions . . .) and a range of symptoms and psychosomatic disorders (irritability, feelings of guilt, problems with sleep and concentration). The frequency observed among seriously injured victims is higher than that noted among US Vietnam veterans. See *op. cit.* note 39, p. 146f.

42 So much so that an unscrupulous victim could be tempted to construct a terrorist dimension to the act which had caused him damage; thus the casualty of a traffic accident occurring at the same time as the attack at la Défense in Sept. 1986 attempted to secure indemnification from the Guarantee Fund.

43 Commission for Indemnification of Victims of Criminal Offences. Its decisions, which are immediately enforceable, cannot be contested or directly appealed. The only possibility is a referral to the Court of Cassation, within two months of notification of the Committee's decision.

44 Initially, the Government bill (law of 6 July 1990) provided for a 'judiciarization' of the procedure of indemnification of the victims of acts of terrorism, which would have abolished the immediate referral to the Guarantee Fund, and

probably slowed down the procedure. It would also have undermined many of the victims' rights, such as jurisdiction at two levels, the inclusion of various medical expenses, and taking post-traumatic syndrome into account (see above). Parliament, sensitive to the arguments put forward by the Association 'S.O.S. Attentats', therefore modified the Government bill and maintained a double procedure which takes into account the specificity of the victims of acts of terrorism (see *op. cit.* note 39, p. 157.)

45 See Royal Decree 336/1986 of 26 Jan. 1986.
46 Law no. 720 of 4 Dec. 1981.

Annexes

1   International treaties*

CONTENTS

* Unless otherwise indicated, both the UK and France are parties to all the treaties.

(Tokyo Convention)

CONVENTION
ON OFFENCES AND CERTAIN OTHER ACTS COMMITTED ON BOARD AIRCRAFT

THE STATES Parties to this Convention
HAVE AGREED as follows:

Chapter I–Scope of the Convention

ARTICLE 1

1. This Convention shall apply in respect of:
(*a*) offences against penal law;
(*b*) acts which, whether or not they are offences, may or do jeopardize the safety of the aircraft or of persons or property therein or which jeopardize good order and discipline on board.

2. Except as provided in Chapter III, this Convention shall apply in respect of offences committed or acts done by a person on board any aircraft registered in a Contracting State, while that aircraft is in flight or on the surface of the high seas or of any other area outside the territory of any State.

3. For the purposes of this Convention, an aircraft is considered to be in flight from the moment when power is applied for the purpose of take-off until the moment when the landing run ends.

4. This Convention shall not apply to aircraft used in military, customs or police services.

ARTICLE 2

Without prejudice to the provisions of Article 4 and except when the safety of the aircraft or of persons or property on board so requires, no provision of this Convention shall be interpreted as authorizing or requiring any action in respect of offences against penal laws of a political nature or those based on racial or religious discrimination.

Chapter II–Jurisdiction

ARTICLE 3

1. The State of registration of the aircraft is competent to exercise jurisdiction over offences and acts committed on board.

2. Each Contracting State shall take such measures as may be necessary to establish its jurisdiction as the State of registration over offences committed on board aircraft registered in such State.

3. This Convention does not exclude any criminal jurisdiction exercised in accordance with national law.

ARTICLE 4

A Contracting State which is not the State of registration may not interfere with an aircraft in flight in order to exercise its criminal jurisdiction over an offence committed on board except in the following cases:

(*a*) the offence has effect on the territory of such State;

(*b*) the offence has been committed by or against a national or permanent resident of such State;

(*c*) the offence is against the security of such State;

(*d*) the offence consists of a breach of any rules or regulations relating to the flight or manoeuvre of aircraft in force in such State;

(*e*) the exercise of jurisdiction is necessary to ensure the observance of any obligation of such State under a multilateral international agreement.

Chapter III–Powers of the aircraft commander

ARTICLE 5

1.   The provisions of this Chapter shall not apply to offences and acts committed or about to be committed by a person on board an aircraft in flight in the airspace of the State of registration or over the high seas or any other area outside the territory of any State unless the last point of take-off or the next point of intended landing is situated in a State other than that of registration, or the aircraft subsequently flies in the airspace of a State other than that of registration with such person still on board.

2.   Notwithstanding the provisions of Article 1, paragraph 3, an aircraft shall for the purposes of this Chapter, be considered to be in flight at any time from the moment when all its external doors are closed following embarkation until the moment when any such door is opened for disembarkation. In the case of a forced landing, the provisions of this Chapter shall continue to apply with respect to offences and acts committed on board until competent authorities of a State take over the responsibility for the aircraft and for the persons and property on board.

ARTICLE 6

1.   The aircraft commander may, when he has reasonable grounds to believe that a person has committed, or is about to commit, on board the aircraft, an offence or act contemplated in Article 1, paragraph 1, impose upon such person reasonable measures including restraint which are necessary:

(*a*) to protect the safety of the aircraft, or of persons or property therein; or

(*b*) to maintain good order and discipline on board; or

(*c*) to enable him to deliver such person to competent authorities or to disembark him in accordance with the provisions of this Chapter.

2.   The aircraft commander may require or authorize the assistance of other crew members and may request or authorize, but not require, the assistance of passengers to restrain any person whom he is entitled to restrain. Any crew member or passenger may also take reasonable preventive measures without such authorization when he has reasonable grounds to believe that such action is immediately necessary to protect the safety of the aircraft, or of persons or property therein.

ARTICLE 7

1.   Measures of restraint imposed upon a person in accordance with Article 6 shall not be continued beyond any point at which the aircraft lands unless:

(*a*)   such point is in the territory of a non-Contracting State and its authorities refuse to permit disembarkation of that person or those measures have been imposed in accordance with Article 6 paragraph 1(*c*) in order to enable his delivery to competent authorities;

(*b*)   the aircraft makes a forced landing and the aircraft commander is unable to deliver that person to competent authorities; or

(*c*)   that person agrees to onward carriage under restraint.

2.   The aircraft commander shall as soon as practicable, and if possible before landing in the territory of a State with a person on board who has been placed under restraint in accordance with the provisions of Article 6, notify the authorities of such State of the fact that a person on board is under restraint and of the reasons for such restraint.

ARTICLE 8

1.   The aircraft commander may, in so far as it is necessary for the purpose of subparagraph (*a*) or (*b*) of paragraph 1 of Article 6, disembark in the territory of any State in which the aircraft lands any person who he has reasonable grounds to believe has committed, or is about to commit, on board the aircraft an act contemplated in Article 1, paragraph 1(*b*).

2.   The aircraft commander shall report to the authorities of the State in which he disembarks any person pursuant to this Article, the fact of, and the reasons for, such disembarkation.

ARTICLE 9

1.   The aircraft commander may deliver to the competent authorities of any Contracting State in the territory of which the aircraft lands any person who he has reasonable grounds to believe has committed on board the aircraft an act which, in his opinion, is a serious offence according to the penal law of the State of registration of the aircraft.

2.   The aircraft commander shall as soon as practicable and if possible before landing in the territory of a Contracting State with a person on board whom the aircraft commander intends to deliver in accordance with

the preceding paragraph, notify the authorities of such State of his intention to deliver such person and the reasons therefor.

3. The aircraft commander shall furnish the authorities to whom any suspected offender is delivered in accordance with the provisions of this Article with evidence and information which, under the law of the State of registration of the aircraft, are lawfully in his possession.

ARTICLE 10

For actions taken in accordance with this Convention, neither the aircraft commander, any other member of the crew, any passenger, the owner or operator of the aircraft, nor the person on whose behalf the flight was performed shall be held responsible in any proceeding on account of the treatment undergone by the person against whom the actions were taken.

Chapter IV–Unlawful Seizure of Aircraft

ARTICLE 11

1. When a person on board has unlawfully committed by force or threat thereof an act of interference, seizure, or other wrongful exercise of control of an aircraft in flight or when such an act is about to be committed, Contracting States shall take all appropriate measures to restore control of the aircraft to its lawful commander or to preserve his control of the aircraft.

2. In the cases contemplated in the preceding paragraph, the Contracting State in which the aircraft lands shall permit its passengers and crew to continue their journey as soon as practicable, and shall return the aircraft and its cargo to the persons lawfully entitled to possession.

Chapter V–Powers and Duties of States

ARTICLE 12

Any Contracting State shall allow the commander of an aircraft registered in another Contracting State to disembark any person pursuant to Article 8, paragraph 1.

ARTICLE 13

1. Any Contracting State shall take delivery of any person whom the aircraft commander delivers pursuant to Article 9, paragraph 1.

2. Upon being satisfied that the circumstances so warrant, any Contracting State shall take custody or other measures to ensure the presence of any person suspected of an act contemplated in Article 11, paragraph 1, and of any person of whom it has taken delivery. The custody and other measures shall be as provided in the law of that State but may only be continued for such time as is reasonably necessary to enable any criminal or extradition proceedings to be instituted.

3. Any person in custody pursuant to the previous paragraph shall be assisted in communicating immediately with the nearest appropriate representative of the State of which he is a national.

4. Any Contracting State, to which a person is delivered pursuant to Article 9, paragraph 1, or in whose territory an aircraft lands following the commission of an act contemplated in Article 11, paragraph 1, shall immediately make a preliminary enquiry into the facts.

5. When a State, pursuant to this Article, has taken a person into custody, it shall immediately notify the State of registration of the aircraft and the State of nationality of the detained person and, if it considers it advisable, any other interested State of the fact that such person is in custody and of the circumstances which warrant his detention. The State which makes the preliminary enquiry contemplated in paragraph 4 of this Article shall promptly report its findings to the said States and shall indicate whether it intends to exercise jurisdiction.

ARTICLE 14

1. When any person has been disembarked in accordance with Article 8, paragraph 1, or delivered in accordance with Article 9, paragraph 1, or has disembarked after committing an act contemplated in Article 11, paragraph 1, and when such person cannot or does not desire to continue his journey and the State of landing refuses to admit him, that State may, if the person in question is not a national or permanent resident of that State, return him to the territory of the State of which he is a national or permanent resident or to the territory of the State in which he began his journey by air.

2. Neither disembarkation, nor delivery, nor the taking of custody or other measures contemplated in Article 13, paragraph 2, nor return of the person concerned, shall be considered as admission to the territory of the Contracting State concerned for the purpose of its law relating to entry or admission of persons and nothing in this Convention shall affect the law of a Contracting State relating to the expulsion of persons from its territory.

ARTICLE 15

1. Without prejudice to Article 14, any person who has been disembarked in accordance with Article 8, paragraph 1, or delivered in accordance with Article 9, paragraph 1, or has disembarked after committing an act contemplated in Article 11, paragraph 1, and who desires to continue his journey shall be at liberty as soon as practicable to proceed to any destination of his choice unless his presence is required by the law of the State of landing for the purpose of extradition or criminal proceedings.

2. Without prejudice to its law as to entry and admission to, and extradition and expulsion from its territory, a Contracting State in whose territory a person has been disembarked in accordance with Article 8,

paragraph 1, or delivered in accordance with Article 9, paragraph 1, or has disembarked and is suspected of having committed an act contemplated in Article 11, paragraph 1, shall accord to such person treatment which is no less favourable for his protection and security than that accorded to nationals of such Contracting State in like circumstances.

Chapter VI–Other Provisions

ARTICLE 16

1. Offences committed on aircraft registered in a Contracting State shall be treated, for the purpose of extradition, as if they had been committed not only in the place in which they have occurred but also in the territory of the State of registration of the aircraft.

2. Without prejudice to the provisions of the preceding paragraph, nothing in this Convention shall be deemed to create an obligation to grant extradition.

ARTICLE 17

In taking any measures for investigation or arrest or otherwise exercising jurisdiction in connection with any offence committed on board an aircraft the Contracting States shall pay due regard to the safety and other interests of air navigation and shall so act as to avoid unnecessary delay of the aircraft, passengers, crew or cargo.

ARTICLE 18

If Contracting States establish joint air transport operating organizations or international operating agencies, which operate aircraft not registered in any one State those States shall, according to the circumstances of the case, designate the State among them which, for the purposes of this Convention, shall be considered as the State of registration and shall give notice thereof to the International Civil Aviation Organization which shall communicate the notice to all States Parties to this Convention.

. . .

ARTICLE 23

1. Any Contracting State may denounce this Convention by notification addressed to the International Civil Aviation Organization.

2. Denunciation shall take effect six months after the date of receipt by the International Civil Aviation Organization of the notification of denunciation.

List of parties

AFGHANISTAN 15 Apr 77; ANTIGUA 19 Jul 85; ARGENTINA 23 Jul 71; AUSTRALIA 22 Jun 70; AUSTRIA 7 Feb 74; BAHAMAS 15 May 75;

BAHRAIN 9 Feb 84; BANGLADESH 25 Jul 78; BARBADOS 4 Apr 72; BELGIUM 6 Aug 70; BHUTAN 25 Jan 89; BOLIVIA 6 Jul 79; BOTSWANA 16 Jan 79; BRAZIL 14 Jan 70; BRUNEI 23 May 86; BULGARIA 28 Sep 89; BURUNDI 14 Jul 71; BYELORUSSIAN SSR 3 Feb 88; CAMEROON 24 Mar 88; CANADA 7 Nov 69; CAPE VERDE 4 Oct 89; CENTRAL AFRICAN REPUBLIC 11 Jun 91; CHAD 30 Jun 70; CHILE 24 Jan 74; CHINA 14 Nov 78; COLOMBIA 6 Jul 73; COMOROS 23 May 91; CONGO 13 Nov 78; COSTA RICA 24 Oct 72; CROATIA 8 Oct 91; CYPRUS 31 May 72; CZECH REBUBLIC 1 Jan 93; DENMARK 17 Jan 67; DJIBOUTI 10 Jun 92; DOMINICAN REP 3 Dec 70; ECUADOR 3 Dec 69; EGYPT 12 Feb 75; EL SALVADOR 13 Feb 80; EQUATORIAL GUINEA 27 Feb 91; ESTONIA 31 Dec 93; ETHIOPIA 27 Mar 79; FIJI 18 Jan 72; FINLAND 2 Apr 71; FRANCE 11 Sep 70; GABON 14 Jan 70; GAMBIA 4 Jan 79; GFR 16 Dec 69; GHANA 2 Jan 74; GREECE 31 May 71; GRENADA 28 Aug 78; GUATEMALA 17 Nov 70; GUYANA 20 Dec 72; HAITI 26 Apr 84; HONDURAS 8 Apr 87; HUNGARY 3 Dec 70; ICELAND 16 Mar 70; INDIA 22 Jul 75; INDONESIA 7 Sep 76; IRAN 28 Jun 76; IRAQ 15 May 74; IRELAND 14 Nov 75; ISRAEL 19 Sep 69; ITALY 18 Oct 68; IVORY COAST 3 Jun 70; JAMAICA 16 Sep 83; JAPAN 26 May 70; JORDAN 3 May 73; KENYA 22 Jun 70; KOREA (NORTH) 9 May 83; KOREA (SOUTH) 19 Feb 71; KUWAIT 27 Nov 79; LAOS 23 Oct 72; LEBANON 11 Jun 74; LESOTHO 28 Apr 72; LIBYA 21 Jun 72; LUXEMBOURG 21 Sep 72; MADAGASCAR 2 Dec 69; MALAWI 28 Dec 72; MALAYSIA 5 Mar 85; MALDIVES 28 Sep 87; MALI 31 May 71; MALTA 28 Jul 91; MARSHALL ISLANDS 15 May 89; MAURITANIA 30 Jun 77; MAURITIUS 5 Apr 83; MEXICO 18 Mar 69; MONACO 2 Jun 83; MONGOLIA 24 Jul 90; MOROCCO 21 Oct 75; NAURU 17 May 84; NEPAL 15 Jan 79; NETHERLANDS 14 Nov 69; NEW ZEALAND 12 Feb 74; NICARAGUA 24 Aug 73; NIGER 27 Jun 69; NIGERIA 7 Apr 70; NORWAY 17 Jan 67; OMAN 9 Feb 77; PAKISTAN 11 Sep 73; PANAMA 16 Nov 70; PAPUA 5 Nov 75; PARAGUAY 9 Aug 71; PERU 12 May 78; PHILIPPINES 26 Nov 65; POLAND 19 Mar 71; PORTUGAL 25 Nov 64; QATAR 6 Aug 81; ROMANIA 15 Feb 74; RWANDA 17 May 71; ST LUCIA 31 Oct 83; ST VINCENT 18 Nov 91; SAUDI ARABIA 21 Nov 69; SENEGAL 9 Mar 72; SEYCHELLES 4 Jan 79; SIERRA LEONE 9 Nov 70; SINGAPORE 1 Mar 71; SLOVENIA 25 Jun 91; SOLOMON IS 23 Mar 82 suc; SOUTH AFRICA 26 May 72; SPAIN 1 Oct 69; SRI LANKA 30 May 78; SURINAME 10 Sep 79 suc; SWEDEN 17 Jan 67; SWITZERLAND 21 Dec 70; SYRIA 31 Jul 80; TANZANIA 12 Aug 83; THAILAND 6 Mar 72; TOGO 26 Jul 71; TRINIDAD 9 Feb 72; TUNISIA 25 Feb 75; TURKEY 17 Dec 75; UGANDA 25 Jun 82; UKRAINIAN SSR 29 Feb 88; UAE 16 Apr 81; UK 29 Nov 68; US 5 Sep 69; USSR 3 Feb 88; UPPER VOLTA 6 Jun 69; URUGUAY 26 Jan 77; VANUATU 31 Jan 89; VENEZUELA

4 Feb 83; VIETNAM 10 Oct 79; YEMEN 26 Sep 86; YUGOSLAVIA 12 Feb 71; ZAIRE 20 Jul 77; ZAMBIA 14 Sep 71; ZIMBABWE 8 Mar 89.

Reservations and declarations

In a communication accompanying their instrument of ratification the Government of the United Kingdom declared:

'The Government of the United Kingdom of Great Britain and Northern Ireland do not regard as valid the reservation made by Iraq in respect of paragraph (1)(*b*) of Article 1 of the said Convention.'

(Hague Convention)

CONVENTION FOR THE SUPPRESSION
OF UNLAWFUL SEIZURE OF AIRCRAFT

PREAMBLE

THE STATES PARTIES TO THIS CONVENTION

HAVE AGREED AS FOLLOWS:

ARTICLE 1

Any person who on board an aircraft in flight:

(*a*) unlawfully, by force or threat thereof, or by any other form of intimidation, seizes, or exercises control of, that aircraft, or attempts to perform any such act, or

(*b*) is an accomplice of a person who performs or attempts to perform any such act

commits an offence (hereinafter referred to as 'the offence').

ARTICLE 2

Each Contracting State undertakes to make the offence punishable by severe penalties.

ARTICLE 3

1. For the purposes of this Convention, an aircraft is considered to be in flight at any time from the moment when all its external doors are closed following embarkation until the moment when any such door is opened for disembarkation. In the case of a forced landing, the flight shall be deemed to continue until the competent authorities take over the responsibility for the aircraft and for persons and property on board.

2. This Convention shall not apply to aircraft used in military, customs or police services.

3. This Convention shall apply only if the place of take-off or the place of actual landing of the aircraft on board which the offence is committed is situated outside the territory of the State of registration of that aircraft; it shall be immaterial whether the aircraft is engaged in an international or domestic flight.

4. In the cases mentioned in Article 5, this Convention shall not apply if the place of take-off and the place of actual landing of the aircraft on board which the offence is committed are situated within the territory of the same State where that State is one of those referred to in that Article.

5. Notwithstanding paragraphs 3 and 4 of this Article, Articles 6, 7, 8 and 10 shall apply whatever the place of take-off or the place of actual landing of the aircraft, if the offender or the alleged offender is found in the territory of a State other than the State of registration of that aircraft.

ARTICLE 4

1. Each Contracting State shall take such measures as may be necessary to establish its jurisdiction over the offence and any other act of violence against passengers or crew committed by the alleged offender in connection with the offence, in the following cases:

(*a*) when the offence is committed on board an aircraft registered in that State;

(*b*) when the aircraft on board which the offence is committed lands in its territory with the alleged offender still on board;

(*c*) when the offence is committed on board an aircraft leased without crew to a lessee who has his principal place of business or, if the lessee has no such place of business, his permanent residence, in that State.

2. Each Contracting State shall likewise take such measures as may be necessary to establish its jurisdiction over the offence in the case where the alleged offender is present in its territory and it does not extradite him pursuant to Article 8 to any of the States mentioned in paragraph 1 of this Article.

3. This Convention does not exclude any criminal jurisdiction exercised in accordance with national law.

ARTICLE 5

The Contracting States which establish joint air transport operating organizations or international operating agencies, which operate aircraft which are subject to joint or international registration shall, by appropriate means, designate for each aircraft the State among them which shall exercise the jurisdiction and have the attributes of the State of registration for the purpose of this Convention and shall give notice thereof to the International Civil Aviation Organization which shall communicate the notice to all States Parties to this Convention.

ARTICLE 6

1. Upon being satisfied that the circumstances so warrant, any Contracting State in the territory of which the offender or the alleged offender is present, shall take him into custody or take other measures to ensure his presence. The custody and other measures shall be as provided in the law of that State but may only be continued for such time as is necessary to enable any criminal or extradition proceedings to be instituted.

2. Such State shall immediately make a preliminary enquiry into the facts.

3. Any person in custody pursuant to paragraph 1 of this Article shall be assisted in communicating immediately with the nearest appropriate representative of the State of which he is a national.

4. When a State, pursuant to this Article, has taken a person into

custody, it shall immediately notify the State of registration of the aircraft, the State mentioned in Article 4, paragraph 1 (*c*), the State of nationality of the detained person and, if it considers it advisable, any other interested States of the fact that such person is in custody and of the circumstances which warrant his detention. The State which makes the preliminary enquiry contemplated in paragraph 2 of this Article shall promptly report its findings to the said States and shall indicate whether it intends to exercise jurisdiction.

ARTICLE 7

The Contracting State in the territory of which the alleged offender is found shall, if it does not extradite him, be obliged, without exception whatsoever and whether or not the offence was committed in its territory, to submit the case to its competent authorities for the purpose of prosecution. Those authorities shall take their decision in the same manner as in the case of any ordinary offence of a serious nature under the law of that State.

ARTICLE 8

1. The offence shall be deemed to be included as an extraditable offence in any extradition treaty existing between Contracting States. Contracting States undertake to include the offence as an extraditable offence in every extradition treaty to be concluded between them.

2. If a Contracting State which makes extradition conditional on the existence of a treaty receives a request for extradition from another Contracting State with which it has no extradition treaty, it may at its option consider this Convention as the legal basis for extradition in respect of the offence. Extradition shall be subject to the other conditions provided by the law of the requested State.

3. Contracting States which do not make extradition conditional on the existence of a treaty shall recognize the offence as an extraditable offence between themselves subject to the conditions provided by the law of the requested State.

4. The offence shall be treated, for the purpose of extradition between Contracting States, as if it had been committed not only in the place in which it occurred but also in the territories of the States required to establish their jurisdiction in accordance with Article 4, paragraph 1.

ARTICLE 9

1. When any of the acts mentioned in Article 1 (*a*) has occurred or is about to occur, Contracting States shall take all appropriate measures to restore control of the aircraft to its lawful commander or to preserve his control of the aircraft.

2. In the cases contemplated by the preceding paragraph, any Contracting State in which the aircraft or its passengers or crew are present

shall facilitate the continuation of the journey of the passengers and crew as soon as practicable, and shall without delay return the aircraft and its cargo to the persons lawfully entitled to possession.

ARTICLE 10

1. Contracting States shall afford one another the greatest measure of assistance in connection with criminal proceedings brought in respect of the offence and other acts mentioned in Article 4. The law of the State requested shall apply in all cases.

2. The provisions of paragraph 1 of this Article shall not affect obligations under any other treaty, bilateral or multilateral, which governs or will govern, in whole or in part, mutual assistance in criminal matters.

ARTICLE 11

Each Contracting State shall in accordance with its national law report to the Council of the International Civil Aviation Organization as promptly as possible any relevant information in its possession concerning:

(*a*) the circumstances of the offence;
(*b*) the action taken pursuant to Article 9;
(*c*) the measures taken in relation to the offender or the alleged offender, and, in particular, the results of any extradition proceedings or other legal proceedings.

. . .

ARTICLE 14

1. Any Contracting State may denounce this Convention by written notification to the Depositary Governments.

2. Denunciation shall take effect six months following the date on which notification is received by the Depositary Governments.

List of parties

AFGHANISTAN 29 Aug 79; ANTIGUA 22 Jul 85; ARGENTINA 11 Sep 72, 20 Sep 72, 21 Sep 71; AUSTRALIA 9 Nov 72; AUSTRIA 11 Feb 74; BAHAMAS 11 Aug 76, 13 Aug 76, 30 Aug 76; BAHRAIN 20 Feb 84; BANGLADESH 28 Jun 78; BARBADOS 2 Apr 73; BELGIUM 24 Aug 73; BENIN 13 Mar 72; BHUTAN 28 Dec 88; BOLIVIA 18 Jul 79; BOTSWANA 28 Dec 78; BRAZIL 14 Jan 72; BRUNEI 16 Apr 86, 13 May 86; BULGARIA 19 May 71, 26 May 71, 23 Feb 72; BURKINA FASO 19 Oct 87; BYELORUSSIAN SSR 30 Dec 71; CAMEROON 14 Apr 88; CANADA 19 Jun 72, 20 Jun 72, 23 Jun 72; CAPE VERDE 20 Oct 77; CENTRAL AFRICAN REPUBLIC 1 Jul 91; CHAD 12 Jul 72; 17 Aug 72; CHILE 2 Feb 72; CHINA 10 Sep 80; COLOMBIA 3 Jul 73; CONGO 24 Nov 89; COSTA RICA 9 Jul 71; CYPRUS 6 Jun 72, 3 Jun 72, 5 Jul 72; CZECHOSLOVAKIA 6 Apr 72; DENMARK 17 Oct 72; DJIBOUTI 24

Nov 92; DOMINICAN REP 22 Jun 78; ECUADOR 14 Jun 71; EGYPT 28 Feb 75; EL SALVADOR 17 Jan 73; EQUATORIAL GUINEA 3 Jan 91; ESTONIA 22 Dec 93; ETHIOPIA 26 Mar 79, 9 Apr 79, 20 Apr 79; FIJI 27 Jul 72, 14 Aug 72, 29 Aug 72; FINLAND 15 Dec 71; FRANCE 18 Sep 72; GABON 14 Jul 71; GAMBIA 28 Nov 78; GDR. 3 Jun 71; GFR 11 Oct 74; GHANA 12 Dec 73; GREECE 20 Sep 73; GRENADA 10 Aug 78; GUATEMALA 16 May 79; GUINEA 2 May 84; GUINEA-BISSAU 20 Aug 76; GUYANA 21 Dec 72; HAITI 9 May 84; HONDURAS 13 Apr 87; HUNGARY 13 Aug 71; ICELAND 29 Jun 73; INDIA 12 Nov 82; INDONESIA 27 Aug 76; IRAN 25 Jan 72, 2 Feb 72; IRAQ 30 Dec 71, 4 Jan 72; IRELAND 24 Nov 75; ISRAEL 16 Aug 71; ITALY 19 Feb 74; IVORY COAST 9 Jan 73; JAMAICA 16 Sep 83; JAPAN 19 Apr 71; JORDAN 16 Nov 71, 18 Nov 71, 1 Dec 71; KENYA 11 Jan 77; KOREA (SOUTH) 18 Jan 73; KOREA (NORTH) 28 Apr 83; KUWAIT 25 May 79, 29 May 79, 6 Jun 79; LAOS 6 Apr 89; LEBANON 10 Aug 73, 5 Jun 74; LESOTHO 27 Jul 78; LIBERIA 1 Feb 82; LIBYA 4 Oct 78; LUXEMBOURG 22 Nov 78; MADAGASCAR 18 Nov 86; MALAWI 21 Dec 72; MALAYSIA 4 May 85; MALDIVES 1 Sep 87; MALI 17 Aug 71, 29 Sep 71; MALTA 14 Jun 91; MARSHALL ISLANDS 31 May 89; MAURITANIA 1 Nov 78; MAURITIUS 25 Apr 83; MEXICO 19 Jul 72; MONACO 3 Jun 83; MONGOLIA 8 Oct 71; MOROCCO 24 Oct 75; NAURU 17 May 84; NEPAL 10 Jan 79, 11 Jan 79, 22 Feb 79; NETHERLANDS 27 Aug 73; NEW ZEALAND 12 Feb 74; NICARAGUA 6 Nov 73; NIGER 15 Oct 71; NIGERIA 3 Jul 73, 9 Jul 73, 20 Jul 73; NORWAY 23 Aug 71; OMAN 2 Feb 77; PAKISTAN 29 Nov 73; PANAMA 10 Mar 72; PAPUA 11 Dec 75, 15 Dec 75, 17 Jan 76; PARAGUAY 4 Feb 72; PERU 28 Apr 78, 12 Jul 78, 8 Aug 78; PHILIPPINES 26 Mar 73; POLAND 21 Mar 72; PORTUGAL 27 Nov 72; QATAR 26 Aug 81; ROMANIA 10 Jul 72; RWANDA 3 Nov 87; ST LUCIA 8 Nov 83; ST VINCENT 29 Nov 91; SAUDI ARABIA 14 Jun 74; SENEGAL 3 Feb 78; SEYCHELLES 29 Dec 78; SIERRA LEONE 13 Nov 74; SINGAPORE 12 Apr 78; SLOVENIA 27 May 92; SOUTH AFRICA 30 May 72; SPAIN 30 Oct 72; SRI LANKA 30 May 78, 2 Jun 78, 29 Jun 78; SUDAN 18 Jan 79; SURINAME 27 Oct 78; SWEDEN 7 Jul 71; SWITZERLAND 14 Sep 71; SYRIA 10 Jul 80; TANZANIA 9 Aug 83; THAILAND 16 May 78; TOGO 9 Feb 79; TONGA 21 Feb 77; TRINIDAD 31 Jan 72; TUNISIA 16 Nov 81, 2 Dec 81, 14 Jan 82; TURKEY 17 Apr 73; UGANDA 27 Mar 72; UKRAINIAN SSR 21 Feb 72; UAE 14 Apr 81; UK 22 Dec 71; USSR 24 Sep 71; US 14 Sep 71, 21 Sep 71, 23 Sep 71; URUGUAY 12 Jan 77; VANUATU 22 Feb 89; VENEZUELA 7 Jul 83; VIETNAM 17 Sep 79; YEMEN 29 Sep 86, 30 Sep 86, 11 Aug 87; YUGOSLAVIA 2 Oct 72; ZAIRE 6 Jul 77; ZAMBIA 3 Mar 87; ZIMBABWE 6 Feb 89.

(Montreal Convention)

CONVENTION FOR THE SUPPRESSION OF UNLAWFUL ACTS AGAINST THE SAFETY OF CIVIL AVIATION

THE STATES PARTIES TO THIS CONVENTION

. . .

HAVE AGREED AS FOLLOWS:

ARTICLE 1

1. Any person commits an offence if he unlawfully and intentionally:
   (*a*) performs an act of violence against a person on board an aircraft in flight if that act is likely to endanger the safety of that aircraft; or
   (*b*) destroys an aircraft in service or causes damage to such an aircraft which renders it incapable of flight or which is likely to endanger its safety in flight; or
   (*c*) places or causes to be placed on an aircraft in service, by any means whatsoever, a device or substance which is likely to destroy that aircraft, or to cause damage to it which renders it incapable of flight, or to cause damage to it which is likely to endanger its safety in flight; or
   (*d*) destroys or damages air navigation facilities or interferes with their operation, if any such act is likely to endanger the safety of aircraft in flight; or
   (*e*) communicates information which he knows to be false, thereby endangering the safety of an aircraft in flight.

2. Any person also commits an offence if he:
   (*a*) attempts to commit any of the offences mentioned in paragraph 1 of this Article; or
   (*b*) is an accomplice of a person who commits or attempts to commit any such offence.

ARTICLE 2

For the purposes of this Convention:
(*a*) an aircraft is considered to be in flight at any time from the moment when all its external doors are closed following embarkation until the moment when any such door is opened for disembarkation; in the case of a forced landing, the flight shall be deemed to continue until the competent authorities take over the responsibility for the aircraft and for persons and property on board;
(*b*) an aircraft is considered to be in service from the beginning of the preflight preparation of the aircraft by ground personnel or by the crew for a specific flight until twenty-four hours after any landing;

the period of service shall, in any event, extend for the entire period during which the aircraft is in flight as defined in paragraph (*a*) of this Article.

ARTICLE 3

Each Contracting State undertakes to make the offences mentioned in Article 1 punishable by severe penalties.

ARTICLE 4

1. This Convention shall not apply to aircraft used in military, customs or police services.

2. In the cases contemplated in subparagraphs (*a*), (*b*), (*c*) and (*e*) of paragraph 1 of Article 1, this Convention shall apply, irrespective of whether the aircraft is engaged in an international or domestic flight, only if:
   (*a*) the place of take-off or landing, actual or intended, of the aircraft is situated outside the territory of the State of registration of that aircraft; or
   (*b*) the offence is committed in the territory of a State other than the State of registration of the aircraft.

3. Notwithstanding paragraph 2 of this Article, in the cases contemplated in subparagraphs (*a*), (*b*), (*c*) and (*e*) of paragraph 1 of Article 1, this Convention shall also apply if the offender or the alleged offender is found in the territory of a State other than the State of registration of the aircraft.

4. With respect to the States mentioned in Article 9 and in the cases mentioned in subparagraphs (*a*), (*b*), (*c*) and (*e*) of paragraph 1 of Article 1, this Convention shall not apply if the places referred to in subparagraph (*a*) of paragraph 2 of this Article are situated within the territory of the same State where that State is one of those referred to in Article 9, unless the offence is committed or the offender or alleged offender is found in the territory of a State other than that State.

5. In the cases contemplated in subparagraph (*d*) of paragraph 1 of Article 1, this Convention shall apply only if the air navigation facilities are used in international air navigation.

6. The provisions of paragraphs 2, 3, 4 and 5 of this Article shall also apply in the cases contemplated in paragraph 2 of Article 1.

ARTICLE 5

1. Each Contracting State shall take such measures as may be necessary to establish its jurisdiction over the offences in the following cases:
   (*a*) when the offence is committed in the territory of that State;
   (*b*) when the offence is committed against or on board an aircraft registered in that state;
   (*c*) when the aircraft on board which the offence is committed lands in its territory with the alleged offender still on board;

(*d*) when the offence is committed against or on board an aircraft leased without crew to a lessee who has his principal place of business or, if the lessee has no such place of business, his permanent residence, in that State.

2.   Each Contracting State shall likewise take such measures as may be necessary to establish its jurisdiction over the offences mentioned in Article 1, paragraph 1 (*a*), (*b*) and (*c*), and in Article 1, paragraph 2, in so far as that paragraph relates to those offences, in the case where the alleged offender is present in its territory and it does not extradite him pursuant to Article 8 to any of the States mentioned in paragraph 1 of this Article.

3.   This Convention does not exclude any criminal jurisdiction exercised in accordance with national law.

ARTICLE 6

1.   Upon being satisfied that the circumstances so warrant, any Contracting State in the territory of which the offender or the alleged offender is present, shall take him into custody or take other measures to ensure his presence. The custody and other measures shall be as provided in the law of that State but may only be continued for such time as is necessary to enable any criminal or extradition proceedings to be instituted.

2.   Such State shall immediately make a preliminary enquiry into the facts.

3.   Any person in custody pursuant to paragraph 1 of this Article shall be assisted in communicating immediately with the nearest appropriate representative of the State of which he is a national.

4.   When a State, pursuant to this Article, has taken a person into custody, it shall immediately notify the States mentioned in Article 5, paragraph 1, the State of nationality of the detained person and, if it considers it advisable, any other interested States of the fact that such person is in custody and of the circumstances which warrant his detention. The State which makes the preliminary enquiry contemplated in paragraph 2 of this Article shall promptly report its findings to the said States and shall indicate whether it intends to exercise jurisdiction.

ARTICLE 7

The Contracting State in the territory of which the alleged offender is found shall, if it does not extradite him, be obliged, without exception whatsoever and whether or not the offence was committed in its territory, to submit the case to its competent authorities for the purpose of prosecution. Those authorities shall take their decision in the same manner as in the case of any ordinary offence of a serious nature under the law of that State.

ARTICLE 8

1.   The offences shall be deemed to be included as extraditable offences in any extradition treaty existing between Contracting States. Contracting

States undertake to include the offences as extraditable offences in every extradition treaty to be concluded between them.

2. If a Contracting State which makes extradition conditional on the existence of a treaty receives a request for extradition from another Contracting State with which it has no extradition treaty, it may at its option consider this Convention as the legal basis for extradition in respect of the offences. Extradition shall be subject to the other conditions provided by the law of the requested State.

3. Contracting States which do not make extradition conditional on the existence of a treaty shall recognize the offences as extraditable offences between themselves subject to the conditions provided by the law of the requested State.

4. Each of the offences shall be treated, for the purpose of extradition between Contracting States, as if it had been committed not only in the place in which it occurred but also in the territories of the States required to establish their jurisdiction in accordance with Article 5, paragraph 1 (*b*), (*c*) and (*d*).

ARTICLE 9

The Contracting States which establish joint air transport operating organizations or international operating agencies, which operate aircraft which are subject to joint or international registration shall, by appropriate means, designate for each aircraft the State among them which shall exercise the jurisdiction and have the attributes of the State of registration for the purpose of this Convention and shall give notice thereof to the International Civil Aviation Organization which shall communicate the notice to all States Parties to this Convention.

ARTICLE 10

1. Contracting States shall, in accordance with international and national law, endeavour to take all practicable measures for the purpose of preventing the offences mentioned in Article 1.

2. When, due to the commission of one of the offences mentioned in Article 1, a flight has been delayed or interrupted, any Contracting State in whose territory the aircraft or passengers or crew are present shall facilitate the continuation of the journey of the passengers and crew as soon as practicable, and shall without delay return the aircraft and its cargo to the persons lawfully entitled to possession.

ARTICLE 11

1. Contracting States shall afford one another the greatest measure of assistance in connection with criminal proceedings brought in respect of the offences. The law of the State requested shall apply in all cases.

2. The provisions of paragraph 1 of this Article shall not affect obliga-

tions under any other treaty, bilateral or multilateral, which governs or will govern, in whole or in part, mutual assistance in criminal matters.

ARTICLE 12

Any Contracting State having reason to believe that one of the offences mentioned in Article 1 will be committed shall, in accordance with its national law, furnish any relevant information in its possession to those States which it believes would be the States mentioned in Article 5, paragraph 1.

ARTICLE 13

Each Contracting State shall in accordance with its national law report to the Council of the International Civil Aviation Organization as promptly as possible any relevant information in its possession concerning:

(*a*) the circumstances of the offence;

(*b*) the action taken pursuant to Article 10, paragraph 2;

(*c*) the measures taken in relation to the offender or the alleged offender and, in particular, the results of any extradition proceedings or other legal proceedings.

. . .

ARTICLE 16

1. Any Contracting State may denounce this Convention by written notification to the Depositary Governments.

2. Denunciation shall take effect six months following the date on which notification is received by the Depositary Governments.

List of parties

ANTIGUA 22 Jul 85; ARGENTINA 26 Nov 73; AUSTRALIA 12 Jul 73; AUSTRIA 11 Feb 74; BAHAMAS 27 Dec 84; BAHRAIN 20 Feb 84; BANGLADESH 28 Jun 78; BARBADOS 6 Aug 76; BELGIUM 13 Aug 76; BHUTAN 28 Dec 88; BOLIVIA 18 Jul 79; BOTSWANA 28 Dec 78; BRAZIL 24 Jul 72; BRUNEI 16 Apr 86, 13 May 86; BULGARIA 22 Feb 73, 28 Mar 73, 20 Mar 74; BURKINA FASO 19 Oct 87; BYELORUSS-IAN SSR 31 Jan 73; CAMEROON 11 Jul 73; CANADA 19 Jun 72, 20 Jun 72, 23 Jul 72; CAPE VERDE 20 Oct 77; CHAD 12 Jul 72, 17 Aug 72; CENTRAL AFRICAN REPUBLIC 1 Jul 91; CHILE 28 Feb 74; CHINA 10 Sep 80; COLOMBIA 4 Dec 74; COMOROS 1 Aug 91; CONGO 19 Mar 87; COSTA RICA 21 Sep 73; CYPRUS 27 Jul 73, 30 Jul 73; 15 Aug 73; CZECHOSLOVAKIA 10 Aug 73; DENMARK 17 Jan 73; DJIBOUTI 24 Nov 92; DOMINICAN REP 28 Nov 73; ECUADOR 12 Jan 77; EGYPT 20 May 75; EL SALVADOR 25 Sep 79; EQUATORIAL GUINEA 3 Jan 91; ESTONIA 22 Dec 93; ETHIOPIA 26 Mar 79, 9 Apr 79, 20 Apr 79; FIJI 5 Mar 73, 18 Apr 73, 27 Apr 73; FINLAND 13 Jul 73; FRANCE 30 Jun 76;

GABON 29 Jun 76; GAMBIA 28 Nov 78; GDR 9 Jun 72; GFR 3 Feb 78; GHANA 12 Dec 73; GREECE 15 Jan 74; GRENADA 10 Aug 78; GUATEMALA 19 Oct 78; GUINEA 2 May 84; GUINEA-BISSAU 20 Aug 76; GUYANA 21 Dec 72; HAITI 9 May 84; HONDURAS 13 Apr 87; HUNGARY 27 Dec 72; ICELAND 29 Jun 73; INDIA 12 Nov 82; INDONESIA 27 Aug 76; IRAN 10 Jul 73; IRAQ 10 Sep 74; IRELAND 12 Oct 76; ISRAEL 30 Jun 72, 6 Jul 72, 10 Jul 72; ITALY 19 Feb 74; IVORY COAST 9 Jan 73; JAMAICA 16 Sep 83; JAPAN 12 Jun 74; JOR-DAN 13 Feb 73, 19 Feb 73, 25 Apr 73; KENYA 11 Jan 77; KOREA (NORTH) 13 Aug 80; KOREA (SOUTH) 2 Aug 73; KUWAIT 27 Nov 79; LAOS 6 Apr 89; LEBANON 23 Dec 77, 27 Dec 77; LESOTHO 27 Jul 78; LIBERIA 1 Feb 82; LIBYA 19 Feb 74; LUXEMBOURG 18 May 82; MADAGASCAR 18 Nov 86; MALAWI 21 Dec 72; MALAYSIA 4 May 85; MALDIVES 1 Sep 87; MALI 24 Aug 72; MALTA 14 Jun 91; MAR-SHALL ISLANDS 31 May 89; MAURITANIA 1 Nov 78; MAURITIUS 25 Apr 83; MEXICO 12 Sep 74; MONACO 3 Jun 83; MONGOLIA 5 Sep 72, 14 Sep 72, 20 Oct 72; MOROCCO 24 Oct 75; NAURU 17 May 84; NEPAL 10 Jan 79, 11 Jan 79, 22 Feb 79; NETHERLANDS 27 Aug 73; NEW ZEALAND 12 Feb 74; NICARAGUA 6 Nov 73; NIGER 1 Sep 72; NIGERIA 3 Jul 73, 9 Jul 73, 20 Jul 73; NORWAY 1 Aug 73; OMAN 2 Feb 77; PAKISTAN 16 Jan 74; 24 Jan 74; PANAMA 24 Apr 72; PAPUA 11 Dec 75, 15 Dec 75, 7 Jan 76; PARAGUAY 5 Mar 74; PERU 28 Apr 78, 12 Jul 78, 8 Aug 78; PHILIPPINES 26 Mar 73; POLAND 28 Jan 75; POR-TUGAL 15 Jan 73; QATAR 25 Aug 81; ROMANIA 15 Aug 75, 19 Aug 75; RWANDA 3 Nov 87; ST LUCIA 8 Nov 83; ST VINCENT 29 Nov 91; SAUDI ARABIA 14 Jun 74; SENEGAL 3 Feb 78; SEYCHELLES 29 Dec 78; SIERRA LEONE 20 Sep 79; SINGAPORE 12 Apr 78; SLOVENIA 27 May 92; SOLOMON IS 13 Apr 82, 3 May 82; SOUTH AFRICA 30 May 72; SPAIN 30 Oct 72; SRI LANKA 30 May 78, 2 Jun 78, 29 Jun 78; SUDAN 18 Jan 79; SURINAME 27 Oct 78; SWAZILAND 18 May 88; SWEDEN 10 Jul 73; SWITZERLAND 17 Jan 78; SYRIA 10 Jul 80; TAN-ZANIA 9 Aug 83; THAILAND 16 May 78; TOGO 9 Feb 79; TONGA 21 Feb 77; TRINIDAD 9 Feb 72; TUNISIA 16 Nov 81, 2 Dec 81, 14 Jan 82; TURKEY 23 Dec 75; UGANDA 19 Jul 82; UKRAINIAN SSR 26 Feb 73; UAE 14 Apr 81; UK 25 Oct 73; USSR 19 Feb 73; US 1 Nov 72; URUGUAY 12 Jan 77; VANUATU 6 Nov 89; VENEZUELA 21 Nov 83; VIETNAM 17 Sep 79; YEMEN 29 Sep 86, 30 Sep 86, 11 Aug 87; YUGOSLAVIA 2 Oct 72; ZAIRE 6 Jul 77; ZAMBIA 3 Mar 87; ZIM-BABWE 6 Feb 89.

Reservations and declarations

In a statement dated 8 October 1971 and communicated to all States rec-ognized by the United Kingdom, Her Majesty's Government recalled their view that if a regime is not recognized as the Government of a State, neither signature nor the deposit of any instrument by it, nor notification of any of those acts will bring about recognition of that regime by any other State.

PROTOCOL FOR THE SUPPRESSION OF UNLAWFUL ACTS OF VIOLENCE AT AIRPORTS SERVING INTERNATIONAL CIVIL AVIATION, SUPPLEMENTARY TO THE CONVENTION FOR THE SUPPRESSION OF UNLAWFUL ACTS AGAINST THE SAFETY OF CIVIL AVIATION, DONE AT MONTREAL ON 23 SEPTEMBER 1971

The States Parties to this Protocol

. . .

Have agreed as follows:

ARTICLE I

This Protocol supplements the Convention for the Suppression of Unlawful Acts against the Safety of Civil Aviation, done at Montreal on 23 September 1971 (hereinafter referred to as 'the Convention'), and, as between the Parties to this Protocol, the Convention and the Protocol shall be read and interpreted together as one single instrument.

ARTICLE II

1. In Article 1 of the Convention, the following shall be added as new paragraph 1 *bis*:

'1 *bis*. Any person commits an offence if he unlawfully and intentionally, using any device, substance or weapon:

(*a*) performs an act of violence against a person at an airport serving international civil aviation which causes or is likely to cause serious injury or death; or

(*b*) destroys or seriously damages the facilities of an airport serving international civil aviation or aircraft not in service located thereon or disrupts the services of the airport, if such an act endangers or is likely to endanger safety at that airport.'

2. In paragraph 2(a) of Article 1 of the Convention, the following words shall be inserted after the words 'paragraph 1':
'or paragraph 1 *bis*'.

ARTICLE III

In Article 5 of the Convention, the following shall be added as paragraph 2 *bis*:

'2 *bis*. Each Contracting State shall likewise take such measures as may be necessary to establish its jurisdiction over the offences mentioned in Article 1, paragraph 1 *bis*, and in Article 1, paragraph 2, in so far as that paragraph relates to those offences, in the case where the alleged offender is present in its territory and it does not extradite him pursuant to Article 8 to the State mentioned in paragraph 1(a) of this Article.'

List of parties

ARGENTINA 12 Feb 92; AUSTRALIA 23 Oct 90; AUSTRIA 28 Dec 89; BULGARIA 26 Mar 91; BYELORUSSIAN SSR 1 May 89; CANADA 2 Aug 93; CENTRAL AFRICAN REP 1 Jul 91; CHILE 15 Aug 89; CZECH REP 25 Mar 93 suc; DENMARK 23 Nov 89; ESTONIA 22 Dec 93; FIJI 21 Sep 92; FRANCE 6 Sep 89; GREECE 25 Apr 91; HUNGARY 7 Sep 88; ICELAND 9 May 90; IRAQ 31 Jan 90; IRELAND 26 Jul 91; ISRAEL 2 Apr 93; ITALY 13 Mar 90; JORDAN 18 Sep 92; KOREA (SOUTH) 27 Jun 90; KUWAIT 8 Mar 89; MALI 31 Oct 90; MALTA 14 Jun 91; MARSHALL IS 30 May 89; MAURITIUS 17 Aug 89; MEXICO 11 Oct 90; MONACO 22 Dec 93; NORWAY 29 May 90; OMAN 27 Nov 92; PERU 7 Jun 89; RUSSIA 31 Mar 89; ST LUCIA 11 Jun 90; ST VINCENT 25 Nov 91; SAUDI ARABIA 21 Feb 89; SLOVENIA 27 May 92 suc; SPAIN 8 May 91; SWEDEN 26 Jul 90; SWITZERLAND 9 Oct 90; TOGO 9 Feb 90; TURKEY 7 Jul 89; UAE 9 Mar 89; UK 15 Nov 90; YUGOSLAVIA 21 Dec 89. (GDR acc 31 Jan 89 and CZECHOSLOVAKIA 19 Mar 90, but see Supplement Additional Notes.)

INTERNATIONAL CONVENTION AGAINST THE TAKING OF HOSTAGES

The States Parties to this Convention,

. . .

Have agreed as follows:

ARTICLE 1

1. Any person who seizes or detains and threatens to kill, to injure or to continue to detain another person (hereinafter referred to as the 'hostage') in order to compel a third party, namely, a State, an international intergovernmental organization, a natural or juridical person, or a group of persons, to do or abstain from doing any act as an explicit or implicit condition for the release of the hostage commits the offence of taking of hostages ('hostage-taking') within the meaning of this Convention.

2. Any person who:

(*a*) attempts to commit an act of hostage-taking, or

(*b*) participates as an accomplice of anyone who commits or attempts to commit an act of hostage-taking

likewise commits an offence for the purposes of this Convention.

ARTICLE 2

Each State Party shall make the offences set forth in article 1 punishable by appropriate penalties which take into account the grave nature of those offences.

ARTICLE 3

1. The State Party in the territory of which the hostage is held by the offender shall take all measures it considers appropriate to ease the situation of the hostage, in particular, to secure his release and, after his release, to facilitate, when relevant, his departure.

2. If any object which the offender has obtained as a result of the taking of hostages comes into the custody of a State Party, that State Party shall return it as soon as possible to the hostage or the third party referred to in article 1, as the case may be, or to the appropriate authorities thereof.

ARTICLE 4

States Parties shall co-operate in the prevention of the offences set forth in article 1, particularly by:

(*a*) taking all practicable measures to prevent preparations in their respective territories for the commission of those offences within or outside their territories, including measures to prohibit in their territories illegal activities of persons, groups and organizations that encourage, instigate, organize or engage in the perpetration of acts of taking hostages;

(*b*) exchanging information and co-ordinating the taking of administrative and other measures as appropriate to prevent the commission of those offences.

ARTICLE 5

1. Each State Party shall take such measures as may be necessary to establish its jurisdiction over any of the offences set forth in article 1 which are committed:

(*a*) in its territory or on board a ship or aircraft registered in that State;

(*b*) by any of its nationals or, if that State considers it appropriate, by those stateless persons who have their habitual residence in its territory;

(*c*) in order to compel that State to do or abstain from doing any act; or

(*d*) with respect to a hostage who is a national of that State, if that State considers it appropriate.

2. Each State Party shall likewise take such measures as may be necessary to establish its jurisdiction over the offences set forth in article 1 in cases where the alleged offender is present in its territory and it does not extradite him to any of the States mentioned in paragraph 1 of this article.

3. This Convention does not exclude any criminal jurisdiction exercised in accordance with internal law.

ARTICLE 6

1. Upon being satisfied that the circumstances so warrant, any State Party in the territory of which the alleged offender is present shall, in accordance with its laws, take him into custody or take other measures to ensure his presence for such time as is necessary to enable any criminal or extradition proceedings to be instituted. That State Party shall immediately make a preliminary inquiry into the facts.

2. The custody or other measures referred to in paragraph 1 of this article shall be notified without delay directly or through the Secretary-General of the United Nations to:

(*a*) the State where the offence was committed;

(*b*) the State against which compulsion has been directed or attempted;

(*c*) the State of which the natural or juridicial person against whom compulsion has been directed or attempted is a national;

(*d*) the State of which the hostage is a national or in the territory of which he has his habitual residence;

(*e*) the State of which the alleged offender is a national or, if he is a stateless person, in the territory of which he has his habitual residence;

(*f*) the international intergovernmental organization against which compulsion has been directed or attempted;

(*g*) all other States concerned.

3. Any person regarding whom the measures referred to in paragraph

1 of this article are being taken shall be entitled:

(*a*) to communicate without delay with the nearest appropriate representative of the State of which he is a national or which is otherwise entitled to establish such communication or, if he is a stateless person, the State in the territory of which he has his habitual residence;

(*b*) to be visited by a representative of that State.

4. The rights referred to in paragraph 3 of this article shall be exercised in conformity with the laws and regulations of the State in the territory of which the alleged offender is present subject to the proviso, however, that the said laws and regulations must enable full effect to be given to the purposes for which the rights accorded under paragraph 3 of this article are intended.

5. The provisions of paragraphs 3 and 4 of this article shall be without prejudice to the right of any State Party having a claim to jurisdiction in accordance with paragraph 1(*b*) of article 5 to invite the International Committee of the Red Cross to communicate with and visit the alleged offender.

6. The State which makes the preliminary inquiry contemplated in paragraph 1 of this article shall promptly report its findings to the States or organization referred to in paragraph 2 of this article and indicate whether it intends to exercise jurisdiction.

ARTICLE 7

The State Party where the alleged offender is prosecuted shall in accordance with its laws communicate the final outcome of the proceedings to the Secretary-General of the United Nations, who shall transmit the information to the other States concerned and the international intergovernmental organizations concerned.

ARTICLE 8

1. The State Party in the territory of which the alleged offender is found shall, if it does not extradite him, be obliged, without exception whatsoever and whether or not the offence was committed in its territory, to submit the case to its competent authorities for the purpose of prosecution, through proceedings in accordance with the laws of that State. Those authorities shall take their decision in the same manner as in the case of any ordinary offence of a grave nature under the law of that State.

2. Any person regarding whom proceedings are being carried out in connexion with any of the offences set forth in article 1 shall be guaranteed fair treatment at all stages of the proceedings, including enjoyment of all the rights and guarantees provided by the law of the State in the territory of which he is present.

ARTICLE 9

1. A request for the extradition of an alleged offender, pursuant to this

Convention, shall not be granted if the requested State Party has substantial grounds for believing:

(*a*) that the request for extradition for an offence set forth in article 1 has been made for the purpose of prosecuting or punishing a person on account of his race, religion, nationality, ethnic origin or political opinion; or

(*b*) that the person's position may be prejudiced:

    (i) for any of the reasons mentioned in subparagraph (*a*) of this paragraph, or

    (ii) for the reason that communication with him by the appropriate authorities of the State entitled to exercise rights of protection cannot be effected.

2. With respect to the offences as defined in this Convention, the provisions of all extradition treaties and arrangements applicable between States Parties are modified as between States Parties to the extent that they are incompatible with this Convention.

ARTICLE 10

1. The offences set forth in article 1 shall be deemed to be included as extraditable offences in any extradition treaty existing between States Parties. States Parties undertake to include such offences as extraditable offences in every extradition treaty to be concluded between them.

2. If a State Party which makes extradition conditional on the existence of a treaty receives a request for extradition from another State Party with which it has no extradition treaty, the requested State may at its option consider this Convention as the legal basis for extradition in respect of the offences set forth in article 1. Extradition shall be subject to the other conditions provided by the law of the requested State.

List of parties

ANTIGUA AND BARBUDA 6 Aug 86; ARGENTINA 18 Sep 91; AUSTRALIA 21 May 90; AUSTRIA 22 Aug 86; BAHAMAS 4 Jun 81; BARBADOS 9 Mar 81; BELARUS 1 Jul 87; BHUTAN 31 Aug 81; BOSNIA 6 Mar 92; BRUNEI DARUSSALAM 18 Oct 88; BULGARIA 10 Mar 88; CAMEROON 9 Mar 88; CANADA 4 Dec 85; CHILE 12 Nov 81; CHINA 26 Jan 93; CÔTE D'IVOIRE 22 Aug 89; CYPRUS 13 Sep 91; CZECH REP 1 Jan 93; CZECHOSLOVAKIA 27 Jan 88; DENMARK 11 Aug 87; DOMINICA 9 Sep 86; ECUADOR 2 May 88; EGYPT 2 Oct 81; EL SALVADOR 12 Feb 81; FINLAND 14 Apr 83; GERMANY 15 Dec 80; GHANA 10 Nov 87; GREECE 18 Jun 87; GRENADA 10 Dec 90; GUATEMALA 11 Mar 83; HAITI 17 May 89; HONDURAS 1 Jun 81; HUNGARY 2 Sep 87; ICELAND 6 Jul 81; ITALY 20 Mar 86; IVORY COAST 22 Aug 89; JAPAN 8 Jun 87; JORDAN 19 Feb 86; KENYA 8 Dec 81; KUWAIT 6 Feb 89; LESOTHO 5 Nov 80; LUXEMBOURG 29 Apr 91; MALAWI 17 Mar 86; MALI 8 Feb 90; MAURITIUS 17 Oct 80;

MEXICO 28 Apr 87; MONGOLIA 9 Jun 92; NEPAL 9 Mar 90; NETHERLANDS 6 Dec 88; NEW ZEALAND 12 Nov 85; NORWAY 2 Jul 81; OMAN 22 Jul 88; PANAMA 19 Aug 82; PHILIPPINES 14 Oct 80; PORTUGAL 6 Jul 84; REPUBLIC OF KOREA 4 May 83; ROMANIA 17 May 90; RUSSIAN FEDERATION 11 Jun 87; SAINT KITTS AND NEVIS 17 Jan 91; SAUDI ARABIA 8 Jan 91; SENEGAL 10 Mar 87; SLOVAK REP 1 Jan 93; SLOVENIA 6 Jul 92; SPAIN 26 Mar 84; SUDAN 19 Jun 90; SURINAME 5 Nov 81; SWEDEN 15 Jan 81; SWITZERLAND 5 Mar 85; TRINIDAD AND TOBAGO 1 Apr 81; TOGO 25 Jul 86; TURKEY 15 Aug 89; UKRAINE 19 Jun 87; UNITED KINGDOM 22 Dec 82; UNITED STATES OF AMERICA 7 Dec 84; VENEZUELA 13 Dec 88; YUGOSLAVIA 19 Apr 85

CONVENTION ON THE PREVENTION AND PUNISHMENT OF CRIMES AGAINST INTERNATIONALLY PROTECTED PERSONS, INCLUDING DIPLOMATIC AGENTS

The States Parties to this Convention,

. . .

Have agreed as follows:

ARTICLE 1

For the purposes of this Convention:

1. 'internationally protected person' means:
   (*a*) a Head of State, including any member of a collegial body performing the functions of a Head of State under the constitution of the State concerned, a Head of Government or a Minister for Foreign Affairs, whenever any such person is in a foreign State, as well as members of his family who accompany him;
   (*b*) any representative or official of a State or any official or other agent of an international organization of an intergovernmental character who, at the time when and in the place where a crime against him, his official premises, his private accommodation or his means of transport is committed, is entitled pursuant to international law to special protection from any attack on his person, freedom or dignity, as well as members of his family forming part of his household;

2. 'alleged offender' means a person as to whom there is sufficient evidence to determine *prima facie* that he has committed or participated in one or more of the crimes set forth in article 2.

ARTICLE 2

1. The intentional commission of:
   (*a*) a murder, kidnapping or other attack upon the person or liberty of an internationally protected person;
   (*b*) a violent attack upon the official premises, the private accommodation or the means of transport of an internationally protected person likely to endanger his person or liberty;
   (*c*) a threat to commit any such attack;
   (*d*) an attempt to commit any such attack; and
   (*e*) an act constituting participation as an accomplice in any such attack shall be made by each State Party a crime under its internal law.

2. Each State Party shall make these crimes punishable by appropriate penalties which take into account their grave nature.

3. Paragraphs 1 and 2 of this article in no way derogate from the oblig-

ations of States Parties under international law to take all appropriate measures to prevent other attacks on the person, freedom or dignity of an internationally protected person.

ARTICLE 3

1.   Each State Party shall take such measures as may be necessary to establish its jurisdiction over the crimes set forth in article 2 in the following cases:

(*a*)   when the crime is committed in the territory of that State or on board a ship or aircraft registered in that State;

(*b*)   when the alleged offender is a national of that State;

(*c*)   when the crime is committed against an internationally protected person as defined in article 1 who enjoys his status as such by virtue of functions which he exercises on behalf of that State.

2.   Each State Party shall likewise take such measures as may be necessary to establish its jurisdiction over these crimes in cases where the alleged offender is present in its territory and it does not extradite him pursuant to article 8 to any of the States mentioned in paragraph 1 of this article.

3.   This Convention does not exclude any criminal jurisdiction exercised in accordance with internal law.

ARTICLE 4

States Parties shall co-operate in the prevention of the crimes set forth in article 2, particularly by:

(*a*)   taking all practicable measures to prevent preparations in their respective territories for the commission of those crimes within or outside their territories;

(*b*)   exchanging information and co-ordinating the taking of administrative and other measures as appropriate to prevent the commission of those crimes.

ARTICLE 5

1.   The State Party in which any of the crimes set forth in article 2 has been committed shall, if it has reason to believe that an alleged offender has fled from its territory, communicate to all other States concerned, directly or through the Secretary-General of the United Nations, all the pertinent facts regarding the crime committed and all available information regarding the identity of the alleged offender.

2.   Whenever any of the crimes set forth in article 2 has been committed against an internationally protected person, any State Party which has information concerning the victim and the circumstances of the crime shall endeavour to transmit it, under the conditions provided for in its internal law, fully and promptly to the State Party on whose behalf he was exercising his functions.

ARTICLE 6

1. Upon being satisfied that the circumstances so warrant, the State Party in whose territory the alleged offender is present shall take the appropriate measures under its internal law so as to ensure his presence for the purpose of prosecution or extradition. Such measures shall be notified without delay directly or through the Secretary-General of the United Nations to:

(*a*) the State where the crime was committed;

(*b*) the State or States of which the alleged offender is a national or, if he is a stateless person, in whose territory he permanently resides;

(*c*) the State or States of which the internationally protected person concerned is a national or on whose behalf he was exercising his functions;

(*d*) all other States concerned; and

(*e*) the international organization of which the internationally protected person concerned is an official or an agent.

2. Any person regarding whom the measures referred to in paragraph 1 of this article are being taken shall be entitled:

(*a*) to communicate without delay with the nearest appropriate representative of the State of which he is a national or which is otherwise entitled to protect his rights or, if he is a stateless person, which he requests and which is willing to protect his rights; and

(*b*) to be visited by a representative of that State.

ARTICLE 7

The State Party in whose territory the alleged offender is present shall, if it does not extradite him, submit, without exception whatsoever and without undue delay, the case to its competent authorities for the purpose of prosecution, through proceedings in accordance with the laws of that State.

ARTICLE 8

1. To the extent that the crimes set forth in article 2 are not listed as extraditable offences in any extradition treaty existing between States Parties, they shall be deemed to be included as such therein. States Parties undertake to include those crimes as extraditable offences in every future extradition treaty to be concluded between them.

2. If a State Party which makes extradition conditional on the existence of a treaty receives a request for extradition from another State Party with which it has no extradition treaty, it may, if it decides to extradite, consider this Convention as the legal basis for extradition in respect of those crimes. Extradition shall be subject to the procedural provisions and the other conditions of the law of the requested State.

3. States Parties which do not make extradition conditional on the existence of a treaty shall recognize those crimes as extraditable offences

between themselves subject to the procedural provisions and the other conditions of the law of the requested State.

4.   Each of the crimes shall be treated, for the purpose of extradition between States Parties, as if it had been committed not only in the place in which it occurred but also in the territories of the States required to establish their jurisdiction in accordance with paragraph 1 of article 3.

ARTICLE 9

Any person regarding whom proceedings are being carried out in connexion with any of the crimes set forth in article 2 shall be guaranteed fair treatment at all stages of the proceedings.

List of parties

ARGENTINA 18 Mar 82; AUSTRALIA 20 Jun 77; AUSTRIA 3 Aug 77; BAHAMAS 22 Jul 86; BARBADOS 26 Oct 79; BELARUS 5 Feb 76; BHUTAN 16 Jan 89; BULGARIA 18 Jul 74; BURUNDI 17 Dec 80; CAMEROON 8 Jun 92; CANADA 4 Aug 76; CHILE 21 Jan 77; CHINA 5 Aug 87; COSTA RICA 2 Nov 77; CROATIA 12 Oct 92; CYPRUS 24 Dec 75; CZECHOSLOVAKIA 30 Jun 75; DENMARK 1 Jul 75; DEMOCRATIC PEOPLE'S REPUBLIC OF KOREA 1 Dec 82; DOMINICAN REPUBLIC 8 Jul 77; ECUADOR 12 Mar 75; EGYPT 25 Jun 86; EL SALVADOR 8 Aug 80; ESTONIA 21 Oct 91; FINLAND 31 Oct 78; GABON 14 Oct 81; GERMANY 25 Jan 77; GHANA 25 Apr 75; GREECE 3 Jul 84; GUATEMALA 18 Jan 83; HAITI 25 Aug 80; HUNGARY 26 Mar 75; ICELAND 2 Aug 77; INDIA 11 Apr 78; IRAN (ISLAMIC REPUBLIC OF) 12 Jul 78; IRAQ 28 Feb 78; ISRAEL 31 Jul 80; ITALY 30 Aug 85; JAMAICA 21 Sep 78; JAPAN 8 Jun 87; JORDAN 18 Dec 84; KUWAIT 1 Mar 89; LATVIA 14 Apr 92; LIBERIA 30 Sep 75; MALAWI 14 Mar 77; MALDIVES 21 Aug 90; MEXICO 22 Apr 80; MONGOLIA 8 Aug 75; NEPAL 9 Mar 90; NETHERLANDS 6 Dec 88; NEW ZEALAND 12 Nov 85; NICARAGUA 10 Mar 75; NIGER 17 Jun 85; NORWAY 28 Apr 80; OMAN 22 Mar 88; PAKISTAN 29 Mar 76; PANAMA 17 Jun 80; PARAGUAY 24 Nov 75; PERU 25 Apr 78; PHILIPPINES 26 Nov 76; POLAND 14 Dec 82; REPUBLIC OF KOREA 25 May 83; ROMANIA 15 Aug 78; RUSSIAN FEDERATION 15 Jan 76; RWANDA 29 Nov 77; SEYCHELLES 29 May 80; SLOVENIA 6 Jul 92; SPAIN 8 Aug 85; SRI LANKA 27 Feb 91; SWEDEN 1 Jul 75; SWITZERLAND 5 Mar 85; SYRIAN ARAB REPUBLIC 25 Apr 88; TOGO 30 Dec 80; TRINIDAD AND TOBAGO 15 Jun 79; TUNISIA 21 Jan 77; TURKEY 11 Jun 81; UKRAINE 20 Jan 76; UNITED KINGDOM 2 May 79; UNITED STATES OF AMERICA 26 Oct 76; URUGUAY 13 Jun 78; YEMEN 9 Feb 87; YUGOSLAVIA 29 Dec 76; ZAIRE 25 Jul 77.

Declarations and reservations

2 May 1979

'The Government of the United Kingdom of Great Britain and Northern Ireland do not regard as valid the reservation made by Iraq in respect of paragraph (1) (b) of article 1 of the said Convention.'

15 January 1982

'The purpose of this Convention was to secure the world-wide repression of crimes against internationally protected persons, including diplomatic agents, and to deny the perpetrators of such crimes a safe haven. Accordingly the Government of the United Kingdom of Great Britain and Northern Ireland regard the reservation entered by the Government of Burundi as incompatible with the object and purpose of the Convention, and are unable to consider Burundi as having validly acceded to the Convention until such time as the reservation is withdrawn.'

CONVENTION FOR THE SUPPRESSION OF UNLAWFUL ACTS AGAINST THE SAFETY OF MARITIME NAVIGATION

The States Parties to this Convention,

. . .

Have agreed as follows:

ARTICLE 1

For the purposes of this Convention, 'ship' means a vessel of any type whatsoever not permanently attached to the sea-bed, including dynamically supported craft, submersibles, or any other floating craft.

ARTICLE 2

1. This Convention does not apply to:
(a) a warship; or
(b) a ship owned or operated by a State when being used as a naval auxiliary or for customs or police purposes; or
(c) a ship which has been withdrawn from navigation or laid up.

2. Nothing in this Convention affects the immunities of warships and other government ships operated for non-commercial purposes.

ARTICLE 3

1. Any person commits an offence if that person unlawfully and intentionally:
(a) seizes or exercises control over a ship by force or threat thereof or any other form of intimidation; or
(b) performs an act of violence against a person on board a ship if that act is likely to endanger the safe navigation of that ship; or
(c) destroys a ship or causes damage to a ship or to its cargo which is likely to endanger the safe navigation of that ship; or
(d) places or causes to be placed on a ship, by any means whatsoever, a device or substance which is likely to destroy that ship, or cause damage to that ship or its cargo which endangers or is likely to endanger the safe navigation of that ship; or
(e) destroys or seriously damages maritime navigational facilities or seriously interferes with their operation, if any such act is likely to endanger the safe navigation of a ship; or
(f) communicates information which he knows to be false, thereby endangering the safe navigation of a ship; or
(g) injures or kills any person, in connection with the commission or the attempted commission of any of the offences set forth in subparagraphs (a) to (f).

2. Any person also commits an offence if that person:
(a) attempts to commit any of the offences set forth in paragraph 1; or

(b) abets the commission of any of the offences set forth in paragraph 1 perpetrated by any person or is otherwise an accomplice of a person who commits such an offence; or

(c) threatens, with or without a condition, as is provided for under national law, aimed at compelling a physical or juridical person to do or refrain from doing any act, to commit any of the offences set forth in paragraph 1, subparagraphs (b), (c) and (e), if that threat is likely to endanger the safe navigation of the ship in question.

ARTICLE 4

1. This Convention applies if the ship is navigating or is scheduled to navigate into, through or from waters beyond the outer limit of the territorial sea of a single State, or the lateral limits of its territorial sea with adjacent States.

2. In cases where the Convention does not apply pursuant to paragraph 1, it nevertheless applies when the offender or the alleged offender is found in the territory of a State Party other than the State referred to in paragraph 1.

ARTICLE 5

Each State Party shall make the offences set forth in article 3 punishable by appropriate penalties which take into account the grave nature of those offences.

ARTICLE 6

1. Each State Party shall take such measures as may be necessary to establish its jurisdiction over the offences set forth in article 3 when the offence is committed:

(a) against or on board a ship flying the flag of the State at the time the offence is committed; or

(b) in the territory of that State, including its territorial sea; or

(c) by a national of that State.

2. A State Party may also establish its jurisdiction over any such offence when:

(a) it is committed by a stateless person whose habitual residence is in that State; or

(b) during its commission a national of that State is seized, threatened, injured or killed; or

(c) it is committed in an attempt to compel that State to do or abstain from doing any act.

3. Any State Party which has established jurisdiction mentioned in paragraph 2 shall notify the Secretary-General of the International Maritime Organization (hereinafter referred to as 'the Secretary-General'). If such State Party subsequently rescinds that jurisdiction, it shall notify the Secretary-General.

4. Each State Party shall take such measures as may be necessary to establish its jurisdiction over the offences set forth in article 3 in cases where the alleged offender is present in its territory and it does not extradite him to any of the States Parties which have established their jurisdiction in accordance with paragraphs 1 and 2 of this article.

5. This Convention does not exclude any criminal jurisdiction exercised in accordance with national law.

ARTICLE 7

1. Upon being satisfied that the circumstances so warrant, any State Party in the territory of which the offender or the alleged offender is present shall, in accordance with its law, take him into custody or take other measures to ensure his presence for such time as is necessary to enable any criminal or extradition proceedings to be instituted.

2. Such State shall immediately make a preliminary inquiry into the facts, in accordance with its own legislation.

3. Any person regarding whom the measures referred to in paragraph 1 are being taken shall be entitled to:
(a) communicate without delay with the nearest appropriate representative of the State of which he is a national or which is otherwise entitled to establish such communication or, if he is a stateless person, the State in the territory of which he has his habitual residence;
(b) be visited by a representative of that State.

4. The rights referred to in paragraph 3 shall be exercised in conformity with the laws and regulations of the State in the territory of which the offender or the alleged offender is present, subject to the proviso that the said laws and regulations must enable full effect to be given to the purposes for which the rights accorded under paragraph 3 are intended.

5. When a State Party, pursuant to this article, has taken a person into custody, it shall immediately notify the States which have established jurisdiction in accordance with article 6, paragraph 1 and, if it considers it advisable, any other interested States, of the fact that such person is in custody and of the circumstances which warrant his detention. The State which makes the preliminary inquiry contemplated in paragraph 2 of this article shall promptly report its findings to the said States and shall indicate whether it intends to exercise jurisdiction.

. . .

ARTICLE 10

1. The State Party in the territory of which the offender or the alleged offender is found shall, in cases to which article 6 applies, if it does not extradite him, be obliged, without exception whatsoever and whether or not the offence was committed in its territory, to submit the case without

delay to its competent authorities for the purpose of prosecution, through proceedings in accordance with the laws of that State. Those authorities shall take their decision in the same manner as in the case of any other offence of a grave nature under the law of that State.

2. Any person regarding whom proceedings are being carried out in connection with any of the offences set forth in article 3 shall be guaranteed fair treatment at all stages of the proceedings, including enjoyment of all the rights and guarantees provided for such proceedings by the law of the State in the territory of which he is present.

ARTICLE 11

1. The offences set forth in article 3 shall be deemed to be included as extraditable offences in any extradition treaty existing between any of the States Parties. States Parties undertake to include such offences as extraditable offences in every extradition treaty to be concluded between them.

2. If a State Party which makes extradition conditional on the existence of a treaty receives a request for extradition from another State Party with which it has no extradition treaty, the requested State Party may, at its option, consider this Convention as a legal basis for extradition in respect of the offences set forth in article 3. Extradition shall be subject to the other conditions provided by the law of the requested State Party.

3. States Parties which do not make extradition conditional on the existence of a treaty shall recognize the offences set forth in article 3 as extraditable offences between themselves, subject to the conditions provided by the law of the requested State.

4. If necessary, the offences set forth in article 3 shall be treated, for the purposes of extradition between States Parties, as if they had been committed not only in the place in which they occurred but also in a place within the jurisdiction of the State Party requesting extradition.

5. A State Party which receives more than one request for extradition from States which have established jurisdiction in accordance with article 7 and which decides not to prosecute shall, in selecting the State to which the offender or alleged offender is to be extradited, pay due regard to the interests and responsibilities of the State Party whose flag the ship was flying at the time of the commission of the offence.

6. In considering a request for the extradition of an alleged offender pursuant to this Convention, the requested State shall pay due regard to whether his rights as set forth in article 7, paragraph 3, can be effected in the requesting State.

7. With respect to the offences as defined in this Convention, the provisions of all extradition treaties and arrangements applicable between States Parties are modified as between States Parties to the extent that they are incompatible with this Convention.

List of parties

ARGENTINA 15 Nov 93; AUSTRALIA 20 May 93; AUSTRIA 1 Mar 92; BARBADOS 4 Aug 94; CANADA 16 Sep 93; CHILE 21 Jul 94; CHINA 1 Mar 92; DENMARK 23 Nov 95; EGYPT 8 Apr 93; FRANCE 1 Mar 92; GAMBIA 1 Mar 92; GERMANY 1 Mar 92; GREECE 9 Sep 93; HUNGARY 1 Mar 92; ITALY 1 Mar 92; LEBANON 16 Mar 95; LIBERIA 3 Jan 96; MARSHALL ISLANDS 27 Feb 95; MEXICO 11 Aug 94; NETHERLANDS 3 Jun 92; NORWAY 1 Mar 92; OMAN 1 Mar 92; POLAND 1 Mar 92; ROMANIA 31 Aug 93; SEYCHELLES 1 Mar 92; SPAIN 1 Mar 92; SWEDEN 1 Mar 92; SWITZERLAND 10 Jun 93; TRINIDAD AND TOBAGO 1 Mar 92; UKRAINE 20 Jul 94; UNITED KINGDOM 1 Mar 92; UNITED STATES 6 Mar 95

PROTOCOL FOR THE SUPPRESSION OF UNLAWFUL ACTS AGAINST THE SAFETY OF FIXED PLATFORMS LOCATED ON THE CONTINENTAL SHELF

The States Parties to this Protocol,

. . .

Have agreed as follows:

ARTICLE 1

1. The provisions of articles 5 and 7 and of articles 10 to 16 of the Convention for the Suppression of Unlawful Acts against the Safety of Maritime Navigation (hereinafter referred to as 'the Convention') shall also apply *mutatis mutandis* to the offences set forth in article 2 of this Protocol where such offences are committed on board or against fixed platforms located on the continental shelf.

2. In cases where this Protocol does not apply pursuant to paragraph 1, it nevertheless applies when the offender or the alleged offender is found in the territory of a State Party other than the State in whose internal waters or territorial sea the fixed platform is located.

3. For the purposes of this Protocol, 'fixed platform' means an artificial island, installation or structure permanently attached to the sea-bed for the purpose of exploration or exploitation of resources or for other economic purposes.

ARTICLE 2

1. Any person commits an offence if that person unlawfully and intentionally:
   (a) seizes or exercises control over a fixed platform by force or threat thereof or any other form of intimidation; or
   (b) performs an act of violence against a person on board a fixed platform if that act is likely to endanger its safety; or

(c) destroys a fixed platform or causes damage to it which is likely to endanger its safety; or

(d) places or causes to be placed on a fixed platform, by any means whatsoever, a device or substance which is likely to destroy that fixed platform or likely to endanger its safety; or

(e) injures or kills any person in connection with the commission or the attempted commission of any of the offences set forth in subparagraphs (a) to (d).

2. Any person also commits an offence if that person:

(a) attempts to commit any of the offences set forth in paragraph 1; or

(b) abets the commission of any such offences perpetrated by any person or is otherwise an accomplice of a person who commits such an offence; or

(c) threatens, with or without a condition, as is provided for under national law, aimed at compelling a physical or juridical person to do or refrain from doing any act, to commit any of the offences set forth in paragraph 1, subparagraphs (b) and (c), if that threat is likely to endanger the safety of the fixed platform.

ARTICLE 3

1. Each State Party shall take such measures as may be necessary to establish its jurisdiction over the offences set forth in article 2 when the offence is committed:

(a) against or on board a fixed platform while it is located on the continental shelf of that State; or

(b) by a national of that State.

2. A State Party may also establish its jurisdiction over any such offence when:

(a) it is committed by a stateless person whose habitual residence is in that State;

(b) during its commission a national of that State is seized, threatened, injured or killed; or

(c) it is committed in an attempt to compel that State to do or abstain from doing any act.

3. Any State Party which has established jurisdiction mentioned in paragraph 2 shall notify the Secretary-General of the International Maritime Organization (hereinafter referred to as 'the Secretary-General'). If such State Party subsequently rescinds that jurisdiction, it shall notify the Secretary-General.

4. Each State Party shall take such measures as may be necessary to establish its jurisdiction over the offences set forth in article 2 in cases where the alleged offender is present in its territory and it does not extradite him to any of the States Parties which have established their jurisdiction in accordance with paragraphs 1 and 2 of this article.

5.   This Protocol does not exclude any criminal jurisdiction exercised in accordance with national law.

ARTICLE 4

Nothing in this Protocol shall affect in any way the rules of international law pertaining to fixed platforms located on the continental shelf.

List of parties

AUSTRALIA 20 May 93; AUSTRIA 1 Mar 92; BARBADOS 4 Aug 94; CANADA 16 Sept 93; CHILE 21 Jul 94; CHINA 1 Mar 92; DENMARK 23 Nov 95; EGYPT 8 Apr 93; FRANCE 1 Mar 92; GERMANY 1 Mar 92; GREECE 9 Sep 93; HUNGARY 1 Mar 92; ITALY 1 Mar 92; LEBANON 16 Mar 95; LIBERIA 3 Jan 96; MARSHALL ISLANDS 14 Jan 96; MEXICO 11 Aug 94; NETHERLANDS 3 Jun 92; NORWAY 1 Mar 92; OMAN 1 Mar 92; POLAND 1 Mar 92; ROMANIA 31 Aug 93; SEYCHELLES 1 Mar 92; SPAIN 1 Mar 92; SWEDEN 1 Mar 92; SWITZERLAND 10 June 93; TRINIDAD AND TOBAGO 1 Mar 92; UKRAINE 20 July 94; UK 1 Mar 92; USA 6 Mar 95.

EUROPEAN CONVENTION ON THE SUPPRESSION OF TERRORISM

The member States of the Council of Europe, signatory hereto,

...

Have agreed as follows:

ARTICLE 1

For the purposes of extradition between Contracting States, none of the following offences shall be regarded as a political offence or as an offence connected with a political offence or as an offence inspired by political motives:

(*a*) an offence within the scope of the Convention for the Suppression of Unlawful Seizure of Aircraft, signed at The Hague on 16 December 1970;

(*b*) an offence within the scope of the Convention for the Suppression of Unlawful Acts against the Safety of Civil Aviation, signed at Montreal on 23 September 1971;

(*c*) a serious offence involving an attack against the life, physical integrity or liberty of internationally protected persons, including diplomatic agents;

(*d*) all offence involving kidnapping, the taking of a hostage or serious unlawful detention;

(*e*) an offence involving the use of a bomb, grenade, rocket, automatic firearm or letter or parcel bomb if this use endangers persons;

(*f*) an attempt to commit any of the foregoing offences or participation as an accomplice of a person who commits or attempts to commit such an offence.

ARTICLE 2

1. For the purposes of extradition between Contracting States, a Contracting State may decide not to regard as a political offence or as an offence connected with a political offence or as an offence inspired by political motives a serious offence involving an act of violence, other than one covered by Article 1, against the life, physical integrity or liberty of a person.

2. The same shall apply to a serious offence involving an act against property, other than one covered by Article 1, if the act created a collective danger for persons.

3. The same shall apply to an attempt to commit any of the foregoing offences or participation as an accomplice of a person who commits or attempts to commit such an offence.

ARTICLE 3

The provisions of all extradition treaties and arrangements applicable between Contracting States, including the European Convention on

Extradition, are modified as between Contracting States to the extent that they are incompatible with this Convention.

ARTICLE 4

For the purposes of this Convention and to the extent that any offence mentioned in Article 1 or 2 is not listed as an extraditable offence in any extradition convention or treaty existing between Contracting States, it shall be deemed to be included as such therein.

ARTICLE 5

Nothing in this Convention shall be interpreted as imposing an obligation to extradite if the requested State has substantial grounds for believing that the request for extradition for an offence mentioned in Article 1 or 2 has been made for the purpose of prosecuting or punishing a person on account of his race, religion, nationality or political opinion, or that that person's position may be prejudiced for any of these reasons.

ARTICLE 6

1.   Each Contracting State shall take such measures as may be necessary to establish its jurisdiction over an offence mentioned in Article 1 in the case where the suspected offender is present in its territory and it does not extradite him after receiving a request for extradition from a Contracting State whose jurisdiction is based on a rule of jurisdiction existing equally in the law of the requested State.

2.   This Convention does not exclude any criminal jurisdiction exercised in accordance with national law.

ARTICLE 7

A Contracting State in whose territory a person suspected to have committed an offence mentioned in Article 1 is found and which has received a request for extradition under the conditions mentioned in Article 6, paragraph 1, shall, if it does not extradite that person, submit the case, without exception whatsoever and without undue delay, to its competent authorities for the purpose of prosecution. Those authorities shall take their decision in the same manner as in the case of any offence of a serious nature under the law of that State.

. . .

ARTICLE 10

1.   Any dispute between Contracting States concerning the interpretation or application of this Convention, which has not been settled in the framework of Article 9, paragraph 2, shall, at the request of any Party to the dispute, be referred to arbitration. Each Party shall nominate an arbitrator and the two arbitrators shall nominate a referee. If any Party has not nominated its arbitrator within the three months following the request for arbitration, he shall be nominated at the request of the other Party by

the President of the European Court of Human Rights. If the latter should be a national of one of the Parties to the dispute, this duty shall be carried out by the Vice-President of the Court or, if the Vice-President is a national of one of the Parties to the dispute, by the most senior judge of the Court not being a national of one of the Parties to the dispute. The same procedure shall be observed if the arbitrators cannot agree on the choice of referee.

2.   The arbitration tribunal shall lay down its own procedure. Its decisions shall be taken by majority vote. Its award shall be final.

List of parties

AUSTRIA 11 Aug 77; BELGIUM 31 Oct 85; CYPRUS 26 Feb 79; CZECH REP 1 Jan 93; DENMARK 27 Jun 78; FINLAND 9 Feb 90; FRANCE 21 Sep 87; GFR 3 May 78; GREECE 4 Aug 88; ICELAND 11 Jul 80; IRELAND 21 Feb 89; ITALY 28 Feb 86; LIECHTENSTEIN 13 Jun 79; LUXEMBOURG 11 Sep 81; NETHERLANDS 18 Apr 85; NORWAY 10 Jan 80; PORTUGAL 14 Dec 81; SLOVAK REP 1 Jan 93; SPAIN 20 May 80; SWEDEN 15 Sep 77; SWITZERLAND 19 May 83; TURKEY 19 May 81; UK 24 Jul 78.

Reservations and declarations

On signing the Convention the Government of the French Republic made the following declaration:

In deciding to sign the European Convention on the Suppression of Terrorism today, the Government wished to demonstrate its solidarity with the other European countries in combating a danger which has created – and continues to create – a number of innocent victims and very properly arouses public feeling.

This signature is the logical consequence of the action we have been taking for several years and which has caused us on several occasions to strengthen our internal legislation and to ratify The Hague and Montreal Conventions on air terrorism.

It is self-evident that efficiency in this struggle must be reconciled with respect for the fundamental principles of our criminal law and of our Constitution, which states in its preamble that 'anyone persecuted on account of his action for the cause of liberty has the right to asylum on the territory of the Republic'.

It is also clear that such a high degree of solidarity as is provided for in the Council of Europe Convention can only apply between States sharing the same ideals of freedom and democracy.

France will therefore subject the application of the Convention to certain conditions. On ratification it will make the reservations necessary to ensure that the considerations I have just mentioned will be taken into account and that human rights will at no time be endangered.

There is a further point of very special importance to the Government: this is the success of the work of the Nine in the same field following the decisions of the European Council on 13 July 1976. We wish to avoid risks of conflict between the two texts and the Government therefore does not intend to ratify the Strasbourg Convention before the instrument which will be prepared by the Nine.

Furthermore, taking action against terrorism does not absolve us from tackling the political problem of the causes of terrorism. For in many respects the real struggle against terrorism is a struggle for a just peace which guarantees everyone's legitimate rights.

AGREEMENT CONCERNING THE APPLICATION OF THE EUROPEAN CONVENTION ON THE SUPPRESSION OF TERRORISM AMONG THE MEMBER STATES OF THE EUROPEAN COMMUNITIES

The Member States of the European Communities;

Concerned to strengthen judicial co-operation among these States in the fight against acts of violence;

While awaiting the ratification without reservations of the European Convention on the Suppression of Terrorism signed at Strasbourg on 27 January 1977, described below as 'the European Convention', by all the Member States of the European Communities, described below as 'the Member States';

Have agreed as follows:

ARTICLE 1

This Agreement shall apply in relations between two Member States of which one at least is not a Party to the European Convention or is a Party to that Convention, but with a reservation.

ARTICLE 2

1.   In the relations between two Member States which are Parties to the European Convention, but of which one at least has made a reservation to that Convention, the application of the said Convention shall be subject to the provisions of this Agreement.

2.   In the relations between two Member States of which one at least is not a Party to the European Convention, Articles 1 to 8 and 13 of that Convention shall apply subject to the provisions of this Agreement.

ARTICLE 3

1.   Each Member State which has made the reservation permitted under Article 13 of the European Convention shall declare whether, for the application of this Agreement, it intends to make use of this reservation.

2.   Each Member State which has signed the European Convention but has not ratified, accepted or approved it, shall declare whether, for the application of this Agreement, it intends to make the reservation permitted under Article 13 of that Convention.

3.   Each Member State which has not signed the European Convention may declare that it reserves the right to refuse extradition for an offence, an offence connected with a political offence or an offence inspired by political motives, on condition that it undertakes to submit the case without exception whatsoever and without undue delay, to its competent authorities for the purpose of prosecution. Those authorities shall take their decision in the same manner as in the case of any offence of a serious nature under the law of that State.

4. For the application of this Agreement, only the reservations provided for in paragraph 3 of this Article and in Article 13 of the European Convention are permitted. Any other reservation is without effect as between the Member States.

5. A Member State which has made a reservation may only claim the application of this Agreement by another State to the extent that the Agreement itself applies to the former State.

ARTICLE 4

1. The declarations provided for under Article 3 may be made by a Member State at the time of signature or when depositing its instrument of ratification, acceptance or approval.

2. Each Member State may at any time, wholly or partially, withdraw a reservation which it has made in pursuance of paragraphs 1, 2 or 3 of Article 3 by means of a declaration addressed to the Department of Foreign Affairs of Ireland. The declaration shall have effect on the day it is received.

3. The Department of Foreign Affairs of Ireland shall communicate these declarations to the other Member States.

. . .

ARTICLE 7

1. Each Member State may, at the time of signature or when depositing its instrument of ratification, acceptance or approval, specify the territory or territories to which this Agreement shall apply.

. . .

ARTICLE 8

This Agreement shall cease to have effect on the date when all the Member States become Parties without reservation to the European Convention.

List of parties

BELGIUM; FRANCE; ITALY; LUXEMBOURG; NETHERLANDS.

Reservations and declarations

In accordance with paragraph 2 of Article 3 and of paragraph 1 of Article 4 of the Agreement concerning the Application of the European Convention on the Suppression of Terrorism among the Member States of the European Communities, France declares that, for the application of this Agreement, it intends to make use of the reservation provided for by Article 13 of the European Convention on the Suppression of Terrorism of 27 January 1977.

(*Unofficial translation*)

Paris Convention

EUROPEAN CONVENTION ON EXTRADITION

The Governments signatory hereto, being Members of the Council of Europe,

Considering that the aim of the Council of Europe is to achieve a greater unity between its Members;

Considering that this purpose can be attained by the conclusion of agreements and by common action in legal matters;

Considering that the acceptance of uniform rules with regard to extradition is likely to assist this work of unification,

Have agreed as follows:

ARTICLE 1

OBLIGATION TO EXTRADITE

The Contracting Parties undertake to surrender to each other, subject to the provisions and conditions laid down in this Convention, all persons against whom the competent authorities of the requesting Party are proceeding for an offence or who are wanted by the said authorities for the carrying out of a sentence or detention order.

ARTICLE 1

EXTRADITABLE OFFENCES

1. Extradition shall be granted in respect of offences punishable under the laws of the requesting Party and of the requested Party by deprivation of liberty or under a detention order for a maximum period of at least one year or by a more severe penalty. Where a conviction and prison sentence have occurred or a detention order has been made in the territory of the requesting Party, the punishment awarded must have been for a period of at least four months.

2. If the request for extradition includes several separate offences each of which is punishable under the laws of the requesting Party and the requested Party by deprivation of liberty or under a detention order, but of which some do not fulfil the condition with regard to the amount of punishment which may be awarded, the requested Party shall also have the right to grant extradition for the latter offences.

3. Any Contracting Party whose law does not allow extradition for certain of the offences referred to in paragraph 1 of this Article may, in so far as it is concerned, exclude such offences from the application of this Convention.

4. Any Contracting Party which wishes to avail itself of the right provided for in paragraph 3 of this Article shall, at the time of the deposit

of its instrument of ratification or accession, transmit to the Secretary-General of the Council of Europe either a list of the offences for which extradition is allowed or a list of those for which it is excluded and shall at the same time indicate the legal provisions which allow or exclude extradition. The Secretary-General of the Council shall forward these lists to the other signatories.

5.   If extradition is subsequently excluded in respect of other offences by the law of a Contracting Party, that Party shall notify the Secretary-General. The Secretary-General shall inform the other signatories. Such notification shall not take effect until three months from the date of its receipt by the Secretary-General.

6.   Any Party which avails itself of the right provided for in paragraphs 4 or 5 of this Article may at any time apply this Convention to offences which have been excluded from it. It shall inform the Secretary-General of the Council of such changes, and the Secretary-General shall inform the other signatories.

7.   Any Party may apply reciprocity in respect of any offences excluded from the application of the Convention under this Article.

ARTICLE 3

POLITICAL OFFENCES

1.   Extradition shall not be granted if the offence in respect of which it is requested is regarded by the requested Party as a political offence or as an offence connected with a political offence.

2.   The same rule shall apply if the requested Party has substantial grounds for believing that a request for extradition for an ordinary criminal offence has been made for the purpose of prosecuting or punishing a person on account of his race, religion, nationality or political opinion, or that that person's position may be prejudiced for any of these reasons.

3.   The taking or attempted taking of the life of a Head of State or a member of his family shall not be deemed to be a political offence for the purposes of this Convention.

4.   This Article shall not affect any obligations which the Contracting Parties may have undertaken or may undertake under any other international convention of a multilateral character.

ARTICLE 4

MILITARY OFFENCES

Extradition for offences under military law which are not offences under ordinary criminal law is excluded from the application of this Convention.

ARTICLE 5

FISCAL OFFENCES

Extradition shall be granted, in accordance with the provisions of this Convention, for offences in connection with taxes, duties, customs and exchange only if the Contracting Parties have so decided in respect of any such offence or category of offences.

ARTICLE 6

EXTRADITION OF NATIONALS

1.

(*a*) A Contracting Party shall have the right to refuse extradition of its nationals.

(*b*) Each Contracting Party may, by a declaration made at the time of signature or of deposit of its instrument of ratification or accession, define as far as it is concerned the term 'nationals' within the meaning of this Convention.

(*c*) Nationality shall be determined as at the time of the decision concerning extradition. If, however, the person claimed is first recognised as a national of the requested Party during the period between the time of the decision and the time contemplated for the surrender, the requested Party may avail itself of the provision contained in sub-paragraph (*a*) of this Article.

2. If the requested Party does not extradite its national, it shall at the request of the requesting Party submit the case to its competent authorities in order that proceedings may be taken if they are considered appropriate. For this purpose, the files, information and exhibits relating to the offence shall be transmitted without charge by the means provided for in Article 12, paragraph 1. The requesting Party shall be informed of the result of its request.

ARTICLE 7

PLACE OF COMMISSION

1. The requested Party may refuse to extradite a person claimed for an offence which is regarded by its law as having been committed in whole or in part in its territory or in a place treated as its territory.

2. When the offence for which extradition is requested has been committed outside the territory of the requesting Party, extradition may only be refused if the law of the requested Party does not allow prosecution for the same category of offence when committed outside the latter Party's territory or does not allow extradition for the offence concerned.

ARTICLE 8

PENDING PROCEEDINGS FOR THE SAME OFFENCES

The requested Party may refuse to extradite the person claimed if the competent authorities of such Party are proceeding against him in respect of the offence or offences for which extradition is requested.

ARTICLE 9

'NON BIS IN IDEM'

Extradition shall not be granted if final judgment has been passed by the competent authorities of the requested Party upon the person claimed in respect of the offence or offences for which extradition is requested. Extradition may be refused if the competent authorities of the requested Party have decided either not to institute or to terminate proceedings in respect of the same offence or offences.

ARTICLE 10

LAPSE OF TIME

Extradition shall not be granted when the person claimed has, according to the law of either the requesting or the requested Party, become immune by reason of lapse of time from prosecution or punishment.

ARTICLE 11

CAPITAL PUNISHMENT

If the offence for which extradition is requested is punishable by death under the law of the requesting Party, and if in respect of such offence the death-penalty is not provided for by the law of the requested Party or is not normally carried out, extradition may be refused unless the requesting Party gives such assurance as the requested Party considers sufficient that the death-penalty will not be carried out.

ARTICLE 12

THE REQUEST AND SUPPORTING DOCUMENTS

1.   The request shall be in writing and shall be communicated through the diplomatic channel. Other means of communication may be arranged by direct agreement between two or more Parties.

2.   The request shall be supported by:

(*a*) the original or an authenticated copy of the conviction and sentence or detention order immediately enforceable or of the warrant of arrest or other order having the same effect and issued in accordance with the procedure laid down in the law of the requesting Party;

(*b*) a statement of the offences for which extradition is requested. The time and place of their commission, their legal descriptions and a reference to the relevant legal provisions shall be set out as accurately as possible; and

(*c*) a copy of the relevant enactments or, where this is not possible, a statement of the relevant law and as accurate a description as possible of the person claimed, together with any other information which will help to establish his identity and nationality.

ARTICLE 13

SUPPLEMENTARY INFORMATION

If the information communicated by the requesting Party is found to be insufficient to allow the requested Party to make a decision in pursuance of this Convention, the latter Party shall request the necessary supplementary information and may fix a time-limit for the receipt thereof.

ARTICLE 14

RULE OF SPECIALITY

1.   A person who has been extradited shall not be proceeded against, sentenced or detained with a view to the carrying out of a sentence or detention order for any offence committed prior to his surrender other than that for which he was extradited, nor shall he be for any other reason restricted in his personal freedom, except in the following cases:

(*a*) When the Party which surrendered him consents. A request for consent shall be submitted, accompanied by the documents mentioned in Article 12 and a legal record of any statement made by the extradited person in respect of the offence concerned. Consent shall be given when the offence for which it is requested is itself subject to extradition in accordance with the provisions of this Convention;

(*b*) when that person, having had an opportunity to leave the territory of the Party to which he has been surrendered, has not done so within 45 days of his final discharge, or has returned to that territory after leaving it.

2.   The requesting Party may, however, take any measures necessary to remove the person from its territory, or any measures necessary under its law, including proceedings by default, to prevent any legal effects of lapse of time.

3.   When the description of the offence charged is altered in the course of proceedings, the extradited person shall only be proceeded against or sentenced in so far as the offence under its new description is shown by its constituent elements to be an offence which would allow extradition.

ARTICLE 15

RE-EXTRADITION TO A THIRD STATE

Except as provided for in Article 14, paragraph 1 (*b*), the requesting Party shall not, without the consent of the requested Party, surrender to another Party or to a third State a person surrendered to the requesting Party and sought by the said other Party or third State in respect of offences committed before his surrender. The requested Party may request the production of the documents mentioned in Article 12, paragraph 2.

ARTICLE 16

PROVISIONAL ARREST

1.   In case of urgency the competent authorities of the requesting Party may request the provisional arrest of the person sought. The competent authorities of the requested Party shall decide the matter in accordance with its law.

2.   The request for provisional arrest shall state that one of the documents mentioned in Article 12, paragraph 2 (*a*), exists and that it is intended to send a request for extradition. It shall also state for what offence extradition will be requested and when and where such offence was committed and shall so far as possible give a description of the person sought.

3.   A request for provisional arrest shall be sent to the competent authorities of the requested Party either through the diplomatic channel or direct by post or telegraph or through the International Criminal Police Organisation (Interpol) or by any other means affording evidence in writing or accepted by the requested Party. The requesting authority shall be informed without delay of the result of its request.

4.   Provisional arrest may be terminated if, within a period of 18 days after arrest, the requested Party has not received the request for extradition and the documents mentioned in Article 12. It shall not, in any event, exceed 40 days from the date of such arrest. The possibility of provisional release at any time is not excluded, but the requested Party shall take any measures which it considers necessary to prevent the escape of the person sought.

5.   Release shall not prejudice re-arrest and extradition if a request for extradition is received subsequently.

ARTICLE 17

CONFLICTING REQUESTS

If extradition is requested concurrently by more than one State, either for the same offence or for different offences, the requested Party shall make its decision having regard to all the circumstances and especially the relative seriousness and place of commission of the offences, the respective dates of the requests, the nationality of the person claimed and the possibility of subsequent extradition to another State.

ARTICLE 18

SURRENDER OF THE PERSON TO BE EXTRADITED

1.   The requested Party shall inform the requesting Party by the means mentioned in Article 12, paragraph 1 of its decision with regard to the extradition.

2.   Reasons shall be given for any complete or partial rejection.

3. If the request is agreed to, the requesting Party shall be informed of the place and date of surrender and of the length of time for which the person claimed was detained with a view to surrender.

4. Subject to the provisions of paragraph 5 of this Article, if the person claimed has not been taken over on the appointed date, he may be released after the expiry of 15 days and shall in any case be released after the expiry of 30 days. The requested Party may refuse to extradite him for the same offence.

5. If circumstances beyond its control prevent a Party from surrendering or taking over the person to be extradited, it shall notify the other Party. The two Parties shall agree a new date for surrender and the provisions of paragraph 4 of this Article shall apply.

ARTICLE 19

POSTPONED OR CONDITIONAL SURRENDER

1. The requested Party may, after making its decision on the request for extradition, postpone the surrender of the person claimed in order that he may be proceeded against by that Party or, if he has already been convicted, in order that he may serve his sentence in the territory of that Party for an offence other than that for which extradition is requested.

2. The requested Party may, instead of postponing surrender, temporarily surrender the person claimed to the requesting Party in accordance with conditions to be determined by mutual agreement between the Parties.

ARTICLE 20

HANDING OVER OF PROPERTY

1. The requested Party shall, in so far as its law permits and at the request of the requesting Party, seize and hand over property:
   (*a*) which may be required as evidence or
   (*b*) which has been acquired as a result of the offence and which, at the time of the arrest, is found in the possession of the person claimed or is discovered subsequently.

2. The property mentioned in paragraph 1 of this Article shall be handed even if extradition, having been agreed to, cannot be carried out owing to the death or escape of the person claimed.

3. When the said property is liable to seizure or confiscation in the territory of the requested Party, the latter may, in connection with pending criminal proceedings, temporarily retain it or hand it over on condition that it is returned.

4. Any rights which the requested Party or third parties may have acquired in the said property shall be preserved. Where these rights exist, the property shall be returned without charge to the requested Party as soon as possible after the trial.

ARTICLE 21

TRANSIT

1. Transit through the territory of one of the Contracting Parties shall be granted on submission of a request by the means mentioned in Article 12, paragraph 1, provided that the offence concerned is not considered by the Party requested to grant transit as an offence of a political or purely military character having regard to Articles 3 and 4 of this Convention,

2. Transit of a national, within the meaning of Article 6, of a country requested to grant transit may be refused.

3. Subject to the provisions of paragraph 4 of this Article, it shall be necessary to produce the documents mentioned in Article 12, paragraph 2.

4. If air transport is used, the following provisions shall apply:
   (*a*) when it is not intended to land, the requesting Party shall notify the Party over whose territory the flight is to be made and shall certify that one of the documents mentioned in Article 12, paragraph 2(*a*) exists. In the case of an unscheduled landing, such notification shall have the effect of a request for provisional arrest as provided for in Article 16, and the requesting Party shall submit a formal request for transit;
   (*b*) when it is intended to land, the requesting Party shall submit a formal request for transit.

5. A Party may, however, at the time of signature or of the deposit of its instrument of ratification of, or accession to, this Convention, declare that it will only grant transit of a person on some or all of the conditions on which it grants extradition. In that event, reciprocity may be applied.

6. The transit of the extradited person shall not be carried out through any territory where there is reason to believe that his life or his freedom may be threatened by reason of his race, religion, nationality or political opinion.

ARTICLE 22

PROCEDURE

Except where this Convention otherwise provides, the procedure with regard to extradition and provisional arrest shall be governed solely by the law of the requested Party.

ARTICLE 23

LANGUAGE TO BE USED

The documents to be produced shall be in the language of the requesting or requested Party. The requested Party may require a translation into one of the official languages of the Council of Europe to be chosen by it.

ARTICLE 24

EXPENSES

1. Expenses incurred in the territory of the requested Party by reason of extradition shall be borne by that Party.

2.   Expenses incurred by reason of transit through the territory of a Party requested to grant transit shall be borne by the requesting Party.

3.   In the event of extradition from a non-metropolitan territory of the requested Party, the expenses occasioned by travel between that territory and the metropolitan territory of the requesting Party shall be borne by the latter. The same rule shall apply to expenses occasioned by travel between the non-metropolitan territory of the requested Party and its metropolitan territory.

ARTICLE 25

DEFINITION OF 'DETENTION ORDER'

For the purposes of this Convention, the expression 'detention order' means any order involving deprivation of liberty which has been made by a criminal court in addition to or instead of a prison sentence.

ARTICLE 26

RESERVATIONS

1.   Any Contracting Party may, when signing this Convention or when depositing its instrument of ratification or accession, make a reservation in respect of any provision or provisions of the Convention.

2.   Any Contracting Party which has made a reservation shall withdraw it as soon as circumstances permit. Such withdrawal shall be made by notification to the Secretary-General of the Council of Europe.

3.   A Contracting Party which has made a reservation in respect of a provision of the Convention may not claim application of the said provision by another Party save in so far as it has itself accepted the provision.

ARTICLE 27

TERRITORIAL APPLICATION

1.   This Convention shall apply to the metropolitan territories of the Contracting Parties.

2.   In respect of France, it shall also apply to Algeria and to the overseas Departments and, in respect of the United Kingdom of Great Britain and Northern Ireland, to the Channel Islands and to the Isle of Man.

3.   The Federal Republic of Germany may extend the application of this Convention to the *Land* of Berlin by notice addressed to the Secretary-General of the Council of Europe, who shall notify the other Parties of such declaration.

4.   By direct arrangement between two or more Contracting Parties, the application of this Convention may be extended, subject to the conditions laid down in the arrangement, to any territory of such Parties, other than the territories mentioned in paragraphs 1, 2 and 3 of this Article, for whose international relations any such Party is responsible.

ARTICLE 28

RELATIONS BETWEEN THIS CONVENTION AND BILATERAL AGREEMENTS

1. This Convention shall, in respect of those countries to which it applies, supersede the provisions of any bilateral treaties, conventions or agreements governing extradition between any two Contracting Parties.

2. The Contracting Parties may conclude between themselves bilateral or multilateral agreements only in order to supplement the provisions of this Convention or to facilitate the application of the principles contained therein.

3. Where, as between two or more Contracting Parties, extradition takes place on the basis of a uniform law, the Parties shall be free to regulate their mutual relations in respect of extradition exclusively in accordance with such a system notwithstanding the provisions of this Convention. The same principle shall apply as between two or more Contracting Parties each of which has in force a law providing for the execution in its territory of warrants of arrest issued in the territory of the other Party or Parties. Contracting Parties which exclude or may in the future exclude the application of this Convention as between themselves in accordance with this paragraph shall notify the Secretary-General of the Council of Europe accordingly. The Secretary-General shall inform the other Contracting Parties of any notification received in accordance with this paragraph.

ARTICLE 29

SIGNATURE, RATIFICATION AND ENTRY INTO FORCE

1. This Convention shall be open to signature by the Members of the Council of Europe. It shall be ratified. The instruments of ratification shall be deposited with the Secretary-General of the Council.

2. The Convention shall come into force 90 days after the date of deposit of the third instrument of ratification.

3. As regards any signatory ratifying subsequently the Convention shall come into force 90 days after the date of the deposit of its instrument of ratification.

ARTICLE 30

ACCESSION

1. The Committee of Ministers of the Council of Europe may invite any State not a Member of the Council to accede to this Convention, provided that the resolution containing such invitation receives the unanimous agreement of the Members of the Council who have ratified the Convention.

2. Accession shall be by deposit with the Secretary-General of the

Council of an instrument of accession, which shall take effect 90 days after the date of its deposit.

ARTICLE 31

DENUNCIATION

Any Contracting Party may denounce this Convention in so far as it is concerned by giving notice to the Secretary-General of the Council of Europe. Denunciation shall take effect six months after the date when the Secretary-General of the Council received such notification.

ARTICLE 32

NOTIFICATIONS

The Secretary-General of the Council of Europe shall notify the Members of the Council and the Government of any State which has acceded to this Convention of:

(*a*) the deposit of any instrument of ratification or accession;

(*b*) the date of entry into force of this Convention;

(*c*) any declaration made in accordance with the provisions of Article 6, paragraph 1, and of Article 21, paragraph 5;

(*d*) any reservation made in accordance with Article 26, paragraph 1;

(*e*) the withdrawal of any reservation in accordance with Article 26, paragraph 2;

(*f*) any notification of denunciation received in accordance with the provisions of Article 31 and by the date on which such denunciation will take effect.

IN WITNESS WHEREOF the undersigned, being duly authorised thereto, have signed this Convention.

DONE at Paris, this 13th day of December 1957, in English and French, both texts being equally authentic, in a single copy which shall remain deposited in the archives of the Council of Europe. The Secretary-General of the Council of Europe shall transmit certified copies to the signatory Governments.

List of parties

AUSTRIA 21 May 69; CYPRUS 22 Jan 71; DENMARK 13 Sep 62; FINLAND 12 May 71; GFR 2 Oct 76; GREECE 29 May 61; IRELAND 2 May 66; ISRAEL 27 Sep 67; ITALY 6 Aug 63; LIECHTENSTEIN 28 Oct 69; LUXEMBOURG 18 Nov 76; NETHERLANDS 14 Feb 69; NORWAY 19 Jan 60; SPAIN 7 May 82; SWEDEN 22 Jan 59; SWITZERLAND 20 Dec 66; TURKEY 7 Jan 60

Schengen Accord

CONVENTION APPLYING THE SCHENGEN AGREEMENT OF 14 JUNE 1985, 19 JUNE 1990

. . .

Chapter 4

EXTRADITION

ARTICLE 59

1. The provisions of this Chapter are intended to supplement the European Convention of 13 September 1957 on Extradition as well as, in relations between the Contracting Parties which are members of the Benelux Economic Union, Chapter I of the Benelux Treaty on Extradition and Mutual Assistance in Criminal Matters of 27 June 1962, as amended by the Protocol of 11 May 1974, and to facilitate the implementation of these agreements.

2. Paragraph 1 shall not affect the application of the broader provisions of the bilateral agreements in force between Contracting Parties.

ARTICLE 60

In relations between two Contracting Parties, one of which is not a party to the European Convention on Extradition of 13 September 1957, the provisions of the said Convention shall apply, subject to the reservations and declarations made at the time of ratifying this Convention or, for Contracting Parties which are not parties to the Convention, at the time of ratifying, approving or accepting the present Convention.

ARTICLE 61

The French Republic undertakes to extradite, at the request of one of the Contracting Parties, persons against whom proceedings are being taken for offences punishable under French law by deprivation of liberty or under a detention order for a maximum period of at least two years and under the law of the requesting Contracting Party by deprivation of liberty or under a detention order for a maximum period of at least a year.

ARTICLE 62

1. As regards interruption of prescription, only the provisions of the requesting Contracting Party shall apply.

2. An amnesty granted by the requested Contracting Party shall not prevent extradition unless the offence falls within the jurisdiction of that Contracting Party.

3. The absence of a charge or an official notice authorizing proceedings, necessary only under the legislation of the requested Contracting Party, shall not affect the obligation to extradite.

ARTICLE 63

The Contracting Parties undertake, in accordance with the Convention and the Treaty referred to in Article 59, to extradite between themselves persons being prosecuted by the legal authorities of the requesting Contracting Party for one of the offences referred to in Article 50(1), or being sought by them for the purposes of execution of a sentence or detention order imposed in respect of such an offence.

ARTICLE 64

A report included in the Schengen Information System in accordance with Article 95 shall have the same force as a request for provisional arrest under Article 16 of the European Convention on Extradition of 13 September 1957 or Article 15 of the Benelux Treaty on Extradition and Mutual Assistance in Criminal Matters of 27 June 1962, as amended by the Protocol of 11 May 1974.

ARTICLE 65

1. Without prejudice to the option to use the diplomatic channel, requests for extradition and transit shall be sent by the relevant Ministry of the requesting Contracting Party to the relevant Ministry of the requested Contracting Party.

2. The relevant Ministries shall be;
- as regards the Kingdom of Belgium: the Ministry of Justice;
- as regards the Federal Republic of Germany: the Federal Ministry of Justice and the Justice Ministers or Senators of the Federal States;
- as regards the French Republic: the Ministry of Foreign Affairs;
- as regards the Grand Duchy of Luxembourg: the Ministry of Justice;
- as regards the Kingdom of the Netherlands: the Ministry of Justice.

ARTICLE 66

1. If the extradition of a wanted person is not obviously prohibited under the laws of the requested Contracting Party, that Contracting Party may authorize extradition without formal extradition proceedings, provided that the wanted person agrees thereto in a statement made before a member of the judiciary after being examined by the latter and informed of his right to formal extradition proceedings. The wanted person may have access to a lawyer during such examination.

2. In cases of extradition under paragraph 1, a wanted person who explicitly states that he will not invoke the rule of speciality may not revoke that statement.

2 United Nations resolutions

CONTENTS

RESOLUTION 731 (1992)

*Adopted by the Security Council at its 3033rd meeting,
on 21 January 1992*

The Security Council,

...

Reaffirming also its resolution 635 (1989) of 14 June 1989, in which it condemned all acts of unlawful interference against the security of civil aviation and called upon all States to cooperate in devising and implementing measures to prevent all acts of terrorism, including those involving explosives,

Recalling the statement made on 30 December 1988 by the President of the Security Council on behalf of the members of the Council strongly condemning the destruction of Pan Am flight 103 and calling on all States to assist in the apprehension and prosecution of those responsible for this criminal act,

Deeply concerned over the results of investigations, which implicate officials of the Libyan Government and which are contained in Security Council documents that include the requests addressed to the Libyan authorities by France ... the United Kingdom of Great Britain and Northern Ireland ... and the United States of America ... in connection with the legal procedures related to the attacks carried out against Pan American flight 103 and Union de transports aériens flight 772;

Determined to eliminate international terrorism,

1. *Condemns* the destruction of Pan American flight 103 and Union de tranports aériens flight 772 and the resultant loss of hundreds of lives;

2. *Strongly deplores* the fact that the Libyan Government has not yet responded effectively to the above requests to cooperate fully in establishing responsibility for the terrorist acts referred to above against Pan American flight 103 and Union de tranports aériens flight 772;

3. *Urges* the Libyan Government immediately to provide a full and effective response to those requests so as to contribute to the elimination of international terrorism;

4. *Requests* the Secretary-General to seek the cooperation of the Libyan Government to provide a full and effective response to those requests;

5. *Urges* all States individually and collectively to encourage the Libyan Government to respond fully and effectively to those requests;

6. *Decides* to remain seized of the matter.

RESOLUTION 748 (1992)

Adopted by the Security Council at its 3063rd meeting,
on 31 March 1992

The Security Council,

Reaffirming its resolution 731 (1992) of 21 January 1992,

Noting the reports of the Secretary-General,

Deeply concerned that the Libyan Government has still not provided a full and effective response to the requests in its resolution 731 (1992) of 21 January 1992,

. . .

Determining, in this context, that the failure by the Libyan Government to demonstrate by concrete actions its renunciation of terrorism and in particular its continued failure to respond fully and effectively to the requests in resolution 731 (1992) constitute a threat to international peace and security,

. . .

Acting under Chapter VII of the Charter,

1.   *Decides* that the Libyan Government must now comply without any further delay with paragraph 3 of resolution 731 (1992) regarding the requests contained in documents S/23306, S/23308 and S/23309;

2.   *Decides also* that the Libyan Government must commit itself definitively to cease all forms of terrorist action and all assistance to terrorist groups and that it must promptly, by concrete actions, demonstrate its renunciation of terrorism;

3.   *Decides* that, on 15 April 1992 all States shall adopt the measures set out below, which shall apply until the Security Council decides that the Libyan Government has complied with paragraphs 1 and 2 above;

4.   *Decides also* that all States shall:

(a) Deny permission to any aircraft to take off from, land in or overfly their territory if it is destined to land in or has taken off from the territory of Libya, unless the particular flight has been approved on grounds of significant humanitarian need by the Committee established by paragraph 9 below;

(b) Prohibit, by their nationals or from their territory, the supply of any aircraft or aircraft components to Libya, the provision of engineering and maintenance servicing of Libyan aircraft or aircraft components, the certification of airworthiness for Libyan aircraft, the payment of new claims against existing insurance contracts and the provision of new direct insurance for Libyan aircraft;

5. *Decides further* that all States shall:

(a) Prohibit any provision to Libya by their nationals or from their territory of arms and related material of all types, including the sale or transfer of weapons and ammunition, military vehicles and equipment, paramilitary police equipment and spare parts for the aforementioned, as well as the provision of any types of equipment, supplies and grants of licensing arrangements, for the manufacture or maintenance of the aforementioned;

(b) Prohibit any provision to Libya by their nationals or from their territory of technical advice, assistance or training related to the provision, manufacture, maintenance, or use of the items in (a) above;

(c) Withdraw any of their officials or agents present in Libya to advise the Libyan authorities on military matters;

6. *Decides* that all States shall:

(a) Significantly reduce the number and the level of the staff at Libyan diplomatic missions and consular posts and restrict or control the movement within their territory of all such staff who remain; in the case of Libyan missions to international organizations, the host State may, as it deems necessary, consult the organization concerned on the measures required to implement this subparagraph;

(b) Prevent the operation of all Libyan Arab Airlines offices;

(c) Take all appropriate steps to deny entry to or expel Libyan nationals who have been denied entry to or expelled from other States because of their involvement in terrorist activities;

7. *Calls upon* all States, including States not members of the United Nations, and all international organizations, to act strictly in accordance with the provisions of the present resolution, notwithstanding the existence of any rights or obligations conferred or imposed by any international agreement or any contract entered into or any licence or permit granted prior to 15 April 1992;

8. *Requests* all States to report to the Secretary-General by 15 May 1992 on the measures they have instituted for meeting the obligations set out in paragraphs 3 to 7 above;

9. *Decides* to establish, in accordance with rule 28 of its provisional rules of procedure, a Committee of the Security Council consisting of all the members of the Council, to undertake the following tasks and to report on its work to the Council with its observations and recommendations:

(a) To examine the reports submitted pursuant to paragraph 8 above;

(b) To seek from all States further information regarding the action taken by them concerning the effective implementation of the measures imposed by paragraphs 3 to 7 above;

(c) To consider any information brought to its attention by States concerning violations of the measures imposed by paragraphs 3 to 7 above and, in that context, to make recommendations to the Council on ways to increase their effectiveness;

(d) To recommend appropriate measures in response to violations of the measures imposed by paragraphs 3 to 7 above and provide information on a regular basis to the Secretary-General for general distribution to Member States;

(e) To consider and to decide upon expeditiously any application by States for the approval of flights on grounds of significant humanitarian need in accordance with paragraph 4 above;

(f) To give special attention to any communications in accordance with Article 50 of the Charter from any neighbouring or other State with special economic problems that might arise from the carrying out of the measures imposed by paragraphs 3 to 7 above;

10. *Calls upon* all States to cooperate fully with the Committee in the fulfilment of its task, including supplying such information as may be sought by the Committee in pursuance of the present resolution;

11. *Requests* the Secretary-General to provide all necessary assistance to the Committee and to make the necessary arrangements in the Secretariat for this purpose;

12. *Invites* the Secretary-General to continue his role as set out in paragraph 4 of resolution 731 (1992);

13. *Decides* that the Security Council shall, every 120 days or sooner should the situation so require, review the measures imposed by paragraphs 3 to 7 above in the light of the compliance by the Libyan Government with paragraphs 1 and 2 above taking into account, as appropriate, any reports provided by the Secretary-General on his role as set out in paragraph 4 of resolution 731 (1992);

14. *Decides* to remain seized of the matter.

RESOLUTION 883 (1993)

Adopted by the Security Council at its 3312th meeting,
on 11 November 1993

The Security Council,

Reaffirming its resolutions 731 (1992) of 21 January 1992 and 748 (1992) of 31 March 1992,

Deeply concerned that after more than twenty months the Libyan Government has not fully complied with these resolutions,

Determined to eliminate international terrorism,

Convinced that those responsible for acts of international terrorism must be brought to justice,

Convinced also that the suppression of acts of international terrorism, including those in which States are directly or indirectly involved, is essential for the maintenance of international peace and security,

Determining, in this context, that the continued failure by the Libyan Government to demonstrate by concrete actions its renunciation of terrorism, and in particular its continued failure to respond fully and effectively to the requests and decisions in resolutions 731 (1992) and 748 (1992), constitute a threat to international peace and security,

Taking note of the letters to the Secretary-General dated 29 September and 1 October 1993 from the Secretary of the General People's Committee for Foreign Liaison and International Cooperation of Libya (S/26523) and his speech in the General Debate at the forty-eighth session of the General Assembly (A/48/PV.20) in which Libya stated its intention to encourage those charged with the bombing of Pan Am 103 to appear for trial in Scotland and its willingness to cooperate with the competent French authorities in the case of the bombing of UTA 772,

Expressing its gratitude to the Secretary-General for the efforts he has made pursuant to paragraph 4 of resolution 731 (1992),

Recalling the right of States, under Article 50 of the Charter, to consult the Security Council where they find themselves confronted with special economic problems arising from the carrying out of preventive or enforcement measures,

Acting under Chapter VII of the Charter,

1. *Demands* once again that the Libyan Government comply without any further delay with resolutions 731 (1992) and 748 (1992);

2. *Decides*, in order to secure compliance by the Libyan Government with the decisions of the Council, to take the following measures, which shall come into force at 00.01 EST on 1 December 1993 unless the

Secretary-General has reported to the Council in the terms set out in paragraph 16 below;

3. *Decides* that all States in which there are funds or other financial resources (including funds derived or generated from property) owned or controlled, directly or indirectly, by:

(a) the Government or public authorities of Libya, or

(b) any Libyan undertaking,

shall freeze such funds and financial resources and ensure that neither they nor any other funds and financial resources are made available, by their nationals or by any persons within their territory, directly or indirectly, to or for the benefit of the Government or public authorities of Libya or any Libyan undertaking, which for the purposes of this paragraph, means any commercial, industrial or public utility undertaking which is owned or controlled, directly or indirectly, by

(i) the Government or public authorities of Libya,

(ii) any entity, wherever located or organized, owned or controlled by (i), or

(iii) any person identified by States as acting on behalf of (i) or (ii) for the purposes of this resolution;

4. *Further decides* that the measures imposed by paragraph 3 above do not apply to funds or other financial resources derived from the sale or supply of any petroleum or petroleum products, including natural gas and natural gas products, or agricultural products or commodities, originating in Libya and exported therefrom after the time specified in paragraph 2 above, provided that any such funds are paid into separate bank accounts exclusively for these funds;

5. *Decides* that all States shall prohibit any provision to Libya by their nationals or from their territory of the items listed in the annex to this resolution, as well as the provision of any types of equipment, supplies and grants of licensing arrangements for the manufacture or maintenance of such items;

6. *Further decides* that, in order to make fully effective the provisions of resolution 748 (1992), all States shall:

(a) require the immediate and complete closure of all Libyan Arab Airlines offices within their territories;

(b) prohibit any commercial transactions with Libyan Arab Airlines by their nationals or from their territory, including the honouring or endorsement of any tickets or other documents issued by that airline;

(c) prohibit, by their nationals or from their territory, the entering into or renewal of arrangements for:

(i) the making available, for operation within Libya, of any aircraft or aircraft components, or

    (ii) the provision of engineering or maintenance servicing of any aircraft or aircraft components within Libya;

(d) prohibit, by their nationals or from their territory, the supply of any materials destined for the construction, improvement or maintenance of Libyan civilian or military airfields and associated facilities and equipment, or of any engineering or other services or components destined for the maintenance of any Libyan civil or military airfields or associated facilities and equipment, except emergency equipment and equipment and services directly related to civilian air traffic control;

(e) prohibit, by their nationals or from their territory, any provision of advice, assistance, or training to Libyan pilots, flight engineers, or aircraft and ground maintenance personnel associated with the operation of aircraft and airfields within Libya;

(f) prohibit, by their nationals or from their territory, any renewal of any direct insurance for Libyan aircraft;

7. *Confirms* that the decision taken in resolution 748 (1992) that all States shall significantly reduce the level of the staff at Libyan diplomatic missions and consular posts includes all missions and posts established since that decision or after the coming into force of this resolution;

8. *Decides* that all States, and the Government of Libya, shall take the necessary measures to ensure that no claim shall lie at the instance of the Government or public authorities of Libya, or of any Libyan national, or of any Libyan undertaking as defined in paragraph 3 of this resolution, or of any person claiming through or for the benefit of any such person or undertaking, in connection with any contract or other transaction or commercial operation where its performance was affected by reason of the measures imposed by or pursuant to this resolution or related resolutions;

9. *Instructs* the Committee established by resolution 748 (1992) to draw up expeditiously guidelines for the implementation of paragraphs 3 to 7 of this resolution, and to amend and supplement, as appropriate, the guidelines for the implementation of resolution 748 (1992), especially its paragraph 5 (a);

10. *Entrusts* the Committee established by resolution 748 (1992) with the task of examining possible requests for assistance under the provisions of Article 50 of the Charter of the United Nations and making recommendations to the President of the Security Council for appropriate action;

11. *Affirms* that nothing in this resolution affects Libya's duty scrupulously to adhere to all of its obligations concerning servicing and repayment of its foreign debt;

12. *Calls upon* all States, including States not Members of the United Nations, and all international organizations, to act strictly in accordance with the provisions of the present resolution, notwithstanding the existence

of any rights or obligations conferred or imposed by any international agreement or any contract entered into or any licence or permit granted prior to the effective time of this resolution;

13. *Requests* all States to report to the Secretary-General by 15 January 1994 on the measures they have instituted for meeting the obligations set out in paragraphs 3 to 7 above;

14. *Invites* the Secretary-General to continue his role as set out in paragraph 4 of resolution 731 (1992);

15. *Calls again upon* all Member States individually and collectively to encourage the Libyan Government to respond fully and effectively to the requests and decisions in resolutions 731 (1992) and 748 (1992);

16. *Expresses its readiness* to review the measures set forth above and in resolution 748 (1992) with a view to suspending them immediately if the Secretary-General reports to the Council that the Libyan Government has ensured the appearance of those charged with the bombing of Pan Am 103 for trial before the appropriate United Kingdom or United States court and has satisfied the French judicial authorities with respect to the bombing of UTA 772, and with a view to lifting them immediately when Libya complies fully with the requests and decisions in resolutions 731 (1992) and 748 (1992); and *requests* the Secretary-General, within 90 days of such suspension, to report to the Council on Libya's compliance with the remaining provisions of its resolutions 731 (1992) and 748 (1992) and, in the case of non-compliance, *expresses* its resolve to terminate immediately the suspension of these measures;

17. *Decides* to remain seized of the matter.*

* See also Security Council resolution 1044 (1996).

3 Cases

CONTENTS

Nezar Nawat Mansour Hazi Hindwai

COURT OF APPEAL (The Lord Chief Justice, Mr Justice McCowan and Mr Justice Pill): 7 March 1988

Attempting to place device likely to destroy or damage aircraft – attempting to place explosives on passenger aircraft – potential loss of 370 lives – length of sentence.

Forty-five years imprisonment upheld on a man who attempted to place an explosive device on an aircraft, which would have exploded with the loss of 370 lives.

The appellant was convicted of attempting to place on an aircraft an explosive device likely to destroy or damage the aircraft, contrary to Aviation Security Act 1982. He had persuaded his girl friend, who was pregnant, to carry unwittingly a bag containing an explosive device onto an aircraft. If the device had exploded at the time set on the timing device, the aircraft would have been at 39,000 feet and 370 people would have been killed. Sentenced to 45 years imprisonment.

Held: the sentence was not a day too long.

Lord Lane CJ: On October 24, 1986 at the Central Criminal Court before Mars-Jones J. and a jury, this applicant, Nezar Nawat Mansour Hazi Hindawi, a Jordanian, was convicted of attempting to place on an aircraft a device likely to destroy or damage the aircraft, contrary to the Criminal Attempts Act 1981 and the Aviation Security Act 1982. He was sentenced to 45 years' imprisonment.

There were subsidiary counts to which he eventually pleaded guilty of possessing firearms and ammunition in respect of which he was sentenced to 18 months' imprisonment concurrent with each other and with the 45 years' imprisonment.

He now renews his applications for leave to appeal against conviction and sentence after refusal by the single judge.

The prosecution's case in brief – we shall have to go into it in a little more detail in a moment – was that on April 17 this applicant tried to smuggle a bag containing a large quantity of explosives and a timing and detonating device concealed in a calculator on to an El Al Boeing 747 aircraft, which was due to leave London Heathrow on a flight to Israel. The way in which it was alleged he had done that was to persuade his pregnant Irish girl friend to carry unsuspectingly that lethal cargo on to the aeroplane. There is no doubt that if that bag containing that explosive and that detonator had successfully been placed upon the aeroplane, it would, as was discovered from an examination of the timing device later, have exploded when the aircraft was some 39,000 feet probably over Austria, with the result of course that all the 370 people on the aeroplane would have been killed.

(*The Court refused leave to appeal against conviction.*)

This is an application for leave to appeal against the sentence of 45 years' imprisonment.

Put briefly, this was about as foul and as horrible a crime as could possibly be imagined. It is no thanks to this applicant that his plot did not succeed in destroying 360 or 370 lives in the effort to promote one side of a political dispute by terrorism.

In the judgment of this Court the sentence of 45 years' imprisonment was not a day too long. This application is refused.

R v Moussa Membar and Others

COURT OF APPEAL (Criminal Division): 23 May 1983

Lawton LJ: (Reading the judgment of the Court) Mr Blom-Cooper, we are all agreed that the first of your points is essentially a point of law, so this is an appeal as of right.

On 17th September, 1982, at the Central Criminal Court, after a trial before Mr Justice Woolf, these Appellants were convicted of hijacking contrary to Section 1(1) of the Hijacking Act, 1971. They were sentenced as follows. Moussa Membar, who was clearly the leader of the hijackers, to 8 years' imprisonment; Mohammed Abdallah to 6 years' imprisonment; Abdallah Abdallah also to 6 years' imprisonment; Mohammed Ahmed to 4 years' imprisonment; and Yassin Membar to 3 years' imprisonment. They now appeal on a point of law to this court. They also apply for leave to appeal against their sentences.

At about 17.20 (local time) on 26th February, 1982, a Tanzanian aircraft Boeing 737 set out from Mwanza airport for Dar es Salaam. That was an internal flight in Tanzania. After about half an hour, three men apparently carrying guns and a grenade, led by Moussa Membar who was the self-styled leader of a Tanzanian youth democracy movement, entered the flight deck and ordered the pilot to change course to Nairobi for refuelling. According to the pilot, a man called Mazula, Moussa Membar told him that the aim of his movement was to overthrow President Nyerere. He threatened to blow the plane up if the pilot did not do as he was told. Two passengers who had been on the flight deck and the co-pilot were man-handled back to the passenger cabin.

The passengers were ordered to hand over their possessions, raise their hands and keep their eyes closed. Throughout the flight the Appellants made further statements of their opposition to the Tanzanian government. The chief steward (Iddi) in the passenger cabin was hit in the chest by one of the group (probably Mohammed Abdallah), who also held a gun to Iddi's mouth. Iddi's arm was cut in the skirmish. Another one of the hijackers placed wires, apparently connected to explosive devices, around the cabin's emergency windows. The hostess was threatened by Mohammed Abdallah with what seemed to be a grenade and was hit by Abdallah Abdallah with the flat surface of a knife. The steward had a gun pressed against his neck and heard threats to shoot anyone who moved. Some male passengers were hit with the flat of a knife and one had what appeared to be a gun held to his face and was shown what appeared to be a grenade.

Yassin Membar, who appeared to be an ordinary passenger, was beaten in front of the passengers to ensure their obedience. That was a bit of play-acting, because Yassin Membar was a member of the hijacking gang This bit of play-acting had been decided upon before the plane left Mwanza as a way of showing that the gang meant business. Moussa Membar discovered a gun on the flight deck and its owner was made to load it.

At Nairobi the plane was refuelled and food was sent on board. Moussa Membar held his gun at the co-pilot's head while requests for fuel were made. In order to refuel, the pilot moved the plane on the instructions of the air traffic controller. After a few hours at Nairobi the plane set off to Jeddah on Moussa Membar's instructions. According to the stewardess, Moussa Membar stopped two of the group hitting passengers. They also threatened her with what appeared to be their weapons and then Moussa Membar calmed those members of the gang down. The plane was allowed to stop at Jeddah only for refuelling. Charts relating to Europe were sent on board. The plane left Jeddah at about 3.30 a.m. GMT on 27th February, 1982. The pilot was told to head for Rome by Moussa Membar who was handling the gun belonging to one of the passengers. Unfortunately, a shot was discharged into the rear of the co-pilot's seat and the bullet entered the co-pilot's back and lodged in his right groin. It was accepted by the prosecution that that was almost certainly an accident. The plane landed at Athens where the co-pilot was treated by a doctor and more fuel and food was taken on board.

The plane the set off for Great Britain and landed at 3 p.m. GMT on 27th February, at Stansted airport. A telephone connection was made and Moussa Membar made repeated demands to see an exiled Tanzanian, Oscar Kambona, and the Tanzanian High Commissioner. Fuel for any further flight was refused, but food was sent to the plane and the passengers spent the night on board.

On the following day, after Mr Kambona and another man had spoken to the group, the passengers were allowed to leave in small groups. The airport authorities and the police then took over the aircraft and the weapons, if they can be called such, were then collected. They were all found to be dummies. The so-called bombs or grenades were made of candles and wire; there was a wooden grenade; there were two so-called bombs made of wire and paper; there were three knives; there was one .38 revolver, which probably was taken from one of the passengers; and six rounds of .38 ammunition.

All the gang were arrested and they were interrogated. The interrogation is only relevant in the case of the Appellant, Yassin Membar. He was seen by a Detective Sergeant Judge. Yassin Membar did not speak English. An interpreter in Swahili had to be found. One was found and he was a man who had been in the Kenyan Police Force and was familiar with police procedures. In the course of that interview, Detective Sergeant Judge most unfortunately said to the interpreter something like: 'Tell him that he is required to answer some questions'. Detective Sergeant Judge should never in the circumstances have used the word 'required'.

The interpreter, however, told the judge at the trial within a trial which took place that he had not translated the word 'required' into Swahili. He has used a phrase which was consistent with the English translation of the caution in its proper form. He had at first been a little vague about the matter and said he did not really recollect, but he was pressed further in the course of his cross-examination and he ended by saying that he was sure that he had not translated the word 'required' and that he had used the proper form of caution.

Yassin Membar made a statement in Swahili which the interpreter took down in Swahili and subsequently translated into English. He said that he had written out the caution in Swahili at the head of the statement and in writing it out in Swahili he had used the proper words of the caution. Mr Justice Woolf, in deciding whether or not to admit Yassin Membar's statement, came to the conclusion that it was unfortunate that Detective Sergeant Judge had used the word 'required', but on the other hand he was equally satisfied that by the time the word 'required' had got into Swahili it was no longer in that imperative form and that Yassin Membar was cautioned in the ordinary way. As the essence of the matter was that the judge had to be satisfied that Yassin Membar had made a voluntary statement, it seems to us that he was justified on the evidence in coming to that conclusion. Accordingly, there is nothing in our judgment in the point which has been taken separately on behalf of Yassin Membar.

On the facts which I have stated, it would appear at first sight that this was an ordinary case of hijacking, clearly within the provisions of Section 1(1) of the Hijacking Act, 1971. Had it not been for the case which was put forward on behalf of the Appellants, it would have been a case which fell squarely within the provisions of that Section; but the case which was put forward on behalf of the Appellants was a surprising one. It came to this. The five Appellants were anxious to remove themselves and their families from Tanzania, because they felt that they were being oppressed by the government of that country. The problem for them was how to get out of Tanzania. The obvious way of getting out was by air, but to use that way they would have to pass through the usual kind of immigration control if they were going to get out by way of an international airline.

So the plan was worked out that they would get out by way of an aircraft on an internal service which they would hijack. But even hijacking was going to be very difficult, unless at least one member of the crew was willing to co-operate with them. According to Moussa Membar, who was the only one of the Appellants to give evidence, he collaborated with the commander of the plane who was the man Mazula. Mazula was willing to be of help, because he had come to the conclusion (so it was said) that his future in aviation lay more with Middle Eastern Airways than it did with the Tanzanian State Airways. On the other hand, equally clearly from his point of view and his future in aviation, he could not overtly collaborate with the gang in hijacking the aircraft.

What was worked out was this. Once the aircraft was in the air, that is to say in flight within the meaning of the Hijacking Act, 1971, he would indulge in a bit of play-acting and pretend to be overpowered by the threats of the gang, but would in fact be willing to fly the aircraft off its flight path from Mwanza to Dar es Salaam to Nairobi and thereon elsewhere in the world as the gang required. It was said by Moussa Membar in the course of his evidence that this was all part of the plan. The prosecution would have none of it. They put the case forward as being an ordinary straightforward case of hijacking.

The learned judge, when he came to sum up to the jury, had the task of deciding whether or not there could be a hijacking if the commander of the plane was co-operating with those who clearly wanted to take control of the plane. The argument which was put forward at the trial on behalf of the Appellants by Mr Blom-Cooper was this. Once the commander of the aircraft joined the conspiracy to take over the plane, there could not in law be a case of hijacking within the provisions of Section 1 of the Hijacking Act, 1971. Mr Blom-Cooper accepted that there might have been a number of other offences which the Appellants and the commander of the aircraft could have committed, but it would not have been an offence under Section 1(1) of the 1971 Act.

The basis of Mr Blom-Cooper's argument was this. The statute starts off in its long title by saying: 'An Act to give effect to the Convention for the Suppression of Unlawful Seizure of Aircraft; and for connected purposes'. The relevant convention is known as the Hague Convention which was signed by a large number of states on 16th December, 1970. The preamble to the convention is in these terms: 'Considering that unlawful acts of seizure or exercise of control of aircraft in flight jeopardize the safety of persons and property, seriously affect the operation of air services, and undermine the confidence of the peoples of the world in the safety of civil aviation; considering that the occurrence of such acts is a matter of grave concern; considering that, for the purpose of deterring such acts, there is an urgent need to provide appropriate measures for punishment of offenders; have agreed as follows:' Article 1 is in almost identical terms with the provisions of Section 1(1) of the 1971 Act.

Mr Blom-Cooper invited our attention to Article 9 of the convention which provides as follows: 'When any of the acts mentioned in Article 1(a) has occurred or is about to occur, Contracting States shall take all appropriate measures to restore control of the aircraft to its lawful commander or to preserve his control of the aircraft'. On the strength of that convention, Mr Blom-Cooper says that in 1971 if effect was to be given to the Hague Convention, an act of Parliament had to be passed which would reflect the primary concept behind the convention, namely that it is the safety of the aircraft in the air which has got to be protected and nothing else. Mr Blom-Cooper submitted that the convention had nothing to do with the unlawful deviation of aircraft from their flight schedule or anything of that kind.

He went on to submit that if the lawful commander of the aircraft is in control of it, then there cannot be a hijacking. From that he asked us to deduce that when the commander of an aircraft is in conspiracy with those who are clearly wanting the aircraft to be deflected from its scheduled flight path, then although other offences may be committed, it is not an offence of hijacking.

In the course of his submission, in answer to a question from the bench, Mr Blom-Cooper accepted that so far as the courts of England and Wales are concerned we are concerned solely with the way in which the intention of a convention is reflected in the words of the act of Parliament. If there are any ambiguities in the wording of the Act, then it is permissible to look at the terms of the convention with the object of attempting to solve the ambiguity. But, in our judgment, if there are no ambiguities in the Act of Parliament, the intention of the convention is irrelevant for the purposes of construction.

I turn now to the wording of the Hijacking Act 1971. It provides as follows: '1 (1) A person on board an aircraft in flight who unlawfully, by the use of force or by threats of any kind, seizes the aircraft or exercises control of it commits the offence of hijacking'. I need not read the rest of the Section. On a construction of that provision, in accordance with the ordinary canons of construction, the commander of an aircraft is a person on board it and he is on board it in flight as soon as the doors of the aircraft are shut. Clearly in this case, as the 'hijacking' took place half an hour after it had left Mwanza airport, the commander was a person on board the aircraft in flight.

What meaning should be given to the words: 'who unlawfully, by the use of force or by threats of any kind, seizes in the aircraft or exercises control of it'? When a commander of an aircraft in flight deviates from his course in collaboration with others on board who wish to seize the aircraft and take control of it, he must in our judgment be acting unlawfully, because the control of an aircraft in flight is primarily the control of the commander, but it is also the control of the air traffic controller. It was accepted on the evidence in this case that when this aircraft set off from Mwanza airport, it had only got a certain way along its scheduled flight path to Dar es Salaam under the control of the air traffic controllers at Mwanza airport. It had in fact passed out of the control of the air traffic controllers at Mwanza airport and had passed into the control of the air traffic controllers at Dar es Salaam airport when the 'hijacking' took place. It turned out on the evidence that although they had passed from one sphere of control into another sphere of control, there had not in fact been established any radio communication between the aircraft and Dar es Salaam airport at the material time.

The control of the air traffic controllers is of very great importance, because that control ensures that an aircraft in flight flies at an altitude which as far as is humanly possible avoids collisions with other aircraft. It was accepted in evidence that the commander of an aircraft has a duty not only to his employers who have appointed him commander, but to the air traffic control of the airports between which he is travelling to keep to the deposited flight schedule. If he departs from it, unless he had a reasonable and lawful excuse for doing so, he is doing something which is contrary, certainly in Great Britain, to the various regulations which affect air traffic control and to a limited extent in Tanzania to the local air traffic control regulations.

But over and above that in the circumstances of this case there was another factor. Passenger carrying aircraft on scheduled flights always have a co-pilot. He has various duties, one of which is to take charge of the aircraft if an emergency arises. No doubt, in ordinary contemplation the emergency is the sudden illness or indisposition of the commander of the aircraft. But it was clear from the evidence given in this case, including expert evidence given on behalf of the Appellants, that the co-pilot may have the duty of taking control in other circumstances, such as a marked deviation from the scheduled flight path. It would be his duty, so it was accepted, to query any marked deviation and if the commander persisted in a deviation which was a major deviation and not one merely to avoid a particular temporary emergency, for the co-pilot to do his best to keep the air traffic controller of the relevant area aware of what was happening.

On the facts of this case, it is clear that the Appellants did their best to separate the co-pilot from the commander; in other words, they were doing their best to ensure that the co-pilot could not do anything to control the commander if he decided to depart from his deposited flight schedule. That being so, the Appellants, if they were acting in collaboration with the commander (which was always denied by the commander) were doing something with the collaboration of the commander to ensure that the control of the aircraft would pass out of the hands of those who had a duty to control it, namely the co-pilot and the air traffic controllers.

It seems to us, therefore, that in those circumstances it is possible on the proper construction of this Section for a situation to arise for a commander of an aircraft to be a party with others to controlling his own aircraft by threats or force.

That being so, we turn now to the way in which this case was conducted. As I have already said, the defence case was that the commander was in collaboration with the five Appellants. Mr Justice Woolf had the task of deciding how to deal with this situation in his summing-up. He did so in this way. He started, at page 90 of the transcript, as follows: 'Now, I here touch upon what has been the real issue on the facts of the case, which counsel have conducted and argued before you. The prosecution contend that the captain of the aircraft only flew to Nairobi because of the threats that were made to him and that he was in no way a party to what was happening. If you come to the conclusion that you are sure the prosecution are right about that, then, members of the jury, although it is a matter for you, you may come to the conclusion that the only possible decision that you can come to on the facts of this case is that the prosecution have proved their case because of the matters which really are not in dispute.'

Mr Blom-Cooper has not queried that passage, but the learned judge went on to say: 'However, the defence argue that you should at least not be satisfied that the captain was not a party to what happened and you should at least consider that it may be the case that the captain was in agreement with what was happening and that an arrangement had been made beforehand whereby he made it clear at least to one defendant, and that defendant had made it clear to the others, that he would be in agreement to what was going to happen. Now, members of the jury, if you come to the conclusion that the captain may have been an agreeing party in that sense, that does not mean that you find the accused not guilty as a matter of course. Contrary to what was submitted to you by Mr Blom-Cooper, a captain can be a party to the hijacking of his own plane. If you come to the conclusion that the captain may have been involved, it will still be necessary for you to go on and consider whether or not these defendants exercised control of that aircraft by threats of violence to the crew and passengers and intended to do so.' He then went on to go through the evidence, inviting the jury's attention to the fact that the co-pilot undoubtedly had a duty to control the aircraft in certain circumstances.

No criticism has been made of the way he analysed the evidence relating to the duties of the co-pilot. The main submission has been that he was wrong in saying that the jury could still find the Appellants guilty, even though they may not have been sure that the commander of the aircraft was not a party to the conspiracy to hijack the plane. For the reasons which we have already given, it seems to us that on the proper construction of Section 1(1) of the 1971 Act, a commander of an aircraft, if he collaborates with those who are threatening and using force to the crew, can be a party to their controllling an aircraft. In those circumstances, in our judgment, Mr Justice Woolf was right and on the evidence there was ample evidence upon which the jury could convict.

Accordingly the appeal is dismissed.

We make one technical observation about this matter. When the indictment was first drafted and signed by the appropriate officer of the court, it was in these terms: 'The Appellants on the 27th day of February, 1982, whilst on board an Air Tanzanian Boeing 737 aircraft 5 HATC in flight between Mwanza, Tanzania and Stansted airports, unlawfully, by threats of causing injury to passengers and crew, exercised control of the said aircraft'. We have been told by Mr Wright, who appeared for the prosecution, that the indictment was amended at the outset of the trial by striking out the word 'Stansted, and putting in the words 'Dar es Salaam'. Unfortunately, nobody seems to have amended the indictment. We order it to be amended and it is to be regretted that the appropriate officer of the court did not ensure that the amendment was made at the trial.

So far as sentence is concerned, on the facts as I have recounted them, it seems to us that this was an ordinary case of hijacking. There was nothing unusual about it. As the Hague Convention says, these cases of hijacking are matters of grave concern and call for severe punishment, passengers are put in fear, very often a great deal of time is wasted, and public resources are wasted in the various countries dealing with a hijacking. It follows, therefore, that there was not anything wrong with these sentences at all, indeed some might take the view that they were on the lenient side.

But what has been urged upon us is that the court was entitled to and should have taken into consideration the motives which led these Appellants to do that which they did. Those motives, according to their version of them, were that they wished to avoid living in a state with what they considered to have an oppressive regime. In our judgment, it is difficult in these cases for courts to assess the motives and genuineness of people who indulge in this kind of criminal activity which is so grave from the public point of view. We do not go so far as to say that under no circumstances whatsoever should the courts take into account motives of this kind, but it is very dangerous for them to do so. If the motives are genuine, no doubt the Executive in this country will consider them when decisions have to be made about expelling people from this country who have come here without lawful permission.

For this court to start assessing the motives of people who say that they are fleeing from oppressive political regimes is imposing a duty on this court which it is almost impossible to perform adequately and which, if it is performed, may result in complications of an international character which are not the concern of this court but the concern of Her Majesty's Government.

In those circumstances, we are of the opinion that the applications for leave to appeal against sentence should be dismissed.

DISPOSITION:

Applications for Leave to appeal against sentence dismissed.

Lujambio Galdeano

Conseil d'Etat 25.9.1984

REQUÊTE de M. Lujambio Galdeano, tendant.

1° à l'annulation du décret du 23 septembre 1984 accordant son extradition comme suite à une demande des autorités espagnoles;

2° au sursis à l'exécution de ce décret;

Vu la convention franco-espagnole d'extradition signée le 14 décembre 1877; la convention de Genève du 28 juillet 1951, et le protocole signé à New York le 31 janvier 1967; la loi du 10 mars 1927; le code pénal; le code de procédure pénale; la loi du 25 juillet 1952; le décret du 2 mai 1953; la loi du 11 juillet 1979; la circulaire du 13 janvier 1983; l'ordonnance du 31 juillet 1945 et le décret du 30 septembre 1953; la loi du 30 décembre 1977;

CONSIDÉRANT que d'après la loi du 10 mars 1927, les décrets d'extradition sont pris après avis favorable de la chambre d'accusation; que cette disposition n'exclut pas un recours en cassation ouvert contre cet avis et fondé uniquement sur les vices de forme ou de procédure dont il serait entaché; qu'il en résulte que tout moyen de forme ou de procédure touchant à l'avis de la chambre d'accusation échappe à la compétence du Conseil d'Etat, saisi d'un recours contre le décret d'extradition, alors même qu'il n'aurait pas été articulé devant la Cour de cassation; qu'il n'appartient donc pas au Conseil d'Etat d'examiner les moyens de la requête mettant en cause la régularité externe de l'avis de la Chambre d'accusation de Pau; que le Conseil d'Etat doit, en revanche, se prononcer, d'une part sur les vices propres du décret d'extradition, et d'autre part, sur la légalité interne de la mesure d'extradition, au regard des lois et conventions internationales, afin de vérifier si, notamment d'après l'examen de l'affaire par la chambre d'accusation, le gouvernement a pu légalement décider que les conditions de l'extradition, pour celles des infractions qu'il retient, étaient réunies;

Sur les moyens concernant les vices propres du décret attaqué: – Cons., d'une part, qu'aux termes de l'article 22 de la Constitution, 'les actes du Premier ministre sont contresignés, le cas échéant, par les ministres chargés de leur exécution'; que l'exécution d'un décret d'extradition ne comporte nécessairement l'intervention d'aucune décision relevant de la compétence du ministre de l'intérieur et du ministre des relations extérieures; que dès lors et quelles que soient les mentions figurant dans son article d'exécution, le décret attaqué n'est pas entaché d'illégalité faute d'avoir été contresigné par lesdits ministres;

Cons., d'autre part, que contrairement à ce que soutient le requérant le décret attaqué est suffisamment motivé au regard de la loi du 11 juillet 1979;

Sur les moyens tirés de la violation de la convention franco-espagnole du 14 décembre 1877 et de la loi du 10 mars 1927: – Cons. qu'il ressort de l'article 1er de la loi du 10 mars 1927, que les dispositions de ladite loi ne sont applicables qu'en l'absence de traité ou sur les points qui n'ont pas été réglementés par un traité;

Cons. en premier lieu, qu'il résulte de l'article 2 de la convention franco-espagnole du 14 décembre 1877 que l'assassinat figure parmi les crimes donnant lieu à extradition; qu'aux termes du même article: 'Dans tous les cas . . . l'extradition ne pourra avoir lieu que lorsque le fait similaire sera punissable d'après la législation du pays à qui la demande a été adressée'; que, si le décret attaqué accorde l'extradition pour 'assassinats par groupes armés et organisés', cette incrimination se réfère à une infraction similaire au crime d'assassinat prévu et réprimé par les articles 296 et suivants du code pénal français: que la référence à l'existence de groupes armés et organisés ne modifie pas la qualification d'assassinat donnée à l'infraction;

Cons. qu'il ressort des pièces versées au dossier que, contrairement à ce que soutient le requérant, la notion d'infraction commise 'par groupes armés et organisés' a été introduite dans la législation pénale espagnole antérieurement aux faits reprochés;

Cons. en deuxième lieu qu'en vertu de l'article 3 de la convention franco-espagnole d'extradition: 'Aucune personne accusée ou condamnée ne sera livrée si le délit pour lequel l'extradition est demandée est considéré par la partie requise comme un délit politique ou un fait connexe à un semblable délit'.

Cons. qu'il est reproché à M. Lujambio Galdeano d'avoir pris part à 'des assassinats par groupes armés et organisés'; que la circonstance que ces crimes, qui ne constituent pas des infractions politiques par leur nature, auraient été commis dans le cadre d'une lutte pour l'indépendance du pays basque, ne suffit pas, compte tenu de leur gravité, à les faire regarder comme ayant un caractère politique; que le fait qu'ils auraient été commis alors que l'intéressé agissait dans le cadre de groupes armés et organisés n'est pas d'avantage de nature à donner un caractère politique aux infractions reprochées au requérant; que dès lors M. Lujambio Galdeano n'est pas fondé à soutenir que les auteurs du décret attaqué ont violé les dispositions de l'article 3 précité de la convention du 14 décembre 1877;

Cons., en troisième lieu, qu'il ne ressort pas des pièces du dossier que, dans les circonstances de l'affaire, l'extradition de M. Lujambio Galdeano ait été demandée par le Gouvernement espagnol dans un autre but que la répression d'infractions de droit commun; que le requérant n'est dès lors pas fondé à soutenir qu'elle aurait été demandée dans un but politique au sens de l'article 5 de la loi du 10 mars 1927, dont les règles complètent sur ce point les stipulations de la convention franco-espagnole d'extradition;

Sur les autres moyens de la requête: – Cons., d'une part que, contrairement aux allégations du requérant, le système judiciaire espagnol respecte les droits et libertés fondamentaux de la personne humaine, ainsi que l'exigent les principes généraux du droit de l'extradition;

Cons., d'autre part, qu'aux termes des dispositions du paragraphe F-2° de l'article 1er de la convention de Genève sur le statut des réfugiés: 'Les dispositions de cette convention ne seront pas applicables aux personnes dont on aura des raisons sérieuses de penser ... *b*) qu'elles ont commis un crime grave de droit commun en dehors du pays d'accueil avant d'y être admises comme réfugiés'; qu'eu égard à la gravité de l'infraction de droit commun qui lui est reprochée et au sérieux des présomptions qui pèsent sur lui, M. Lujambio Galdeano n'est pas fondé à se prévaloir de la qualité de réfugié au sens de la convention précitée pour soutenir qu'il ne pouvait être extradé;

Cons. que de tout ce qui précède il résulte que M. Lujambio Galdeano n'est pas fondé à demander l'annulation du décret attaqué; ... (rejet).

Klaus Croissant

Conseil d'Etat 7.7.1978

REQUÊTE du sieur Croissant (Klaus), tendant 1° à l'annulation d'un décret du 16 novembre 1977 accordant son extradition aux autorités fédérales allemandes, 2° au sursis de l'exécution dudit décret;

Vu la loi du 10 mars 1927; la convention de Genève du 28 juillet 1951 sur le statut des réfugiés, ensemble le protocole relatif au statut des réfugiés, signé à New-York du 31 janvier 1967; la convention franco-allemande du 29 novembre 1951; la Constitution du 4 octobre 1958; le décret du 27 février 1974; le code pénal; le code de procédure pénale; l'ordonnance du 31 juillet 1945 et le décret du 30 septembre 1953; la loi du 30 décembre 1977;

Sur le moyen tiré d'irrégularités dans la composition de la Chambre d'accusation: – CONSIDÉRANT que lorsque, conformément aux dispositions de l'article 16 de la loi du 10 mars 1927, la Chambre d'accusation donne un avis motivé sur une demande d'extradition, cette Chambre, exerçant alors une attribution administrative, siège dans la formation habituelle en laquelle elle exerce ses attributions judiciaires; qu'il n'est pas contesté qu'il en a été ainsi en l'espèce;

Cons. que, pour soutenir que la composition de la Chambre d'accusation, lors de l'examen de la demande d'extradition, serait irrégulière, le sieur Croissant conteste la légalité de la délibération de l'Assemblée générale de la Cour d'appel de Paris, en date du 5 octobre 1977, et de l'ordonnance du Premier Président de cette Cour en date du 6 octobre 1977, fixant la composition de cette Chambre; que s'agissant d'une juridiction de l'ordre judiciaire qui ne siège pas dans une composition particulière lorsqu'elle exerce des fonctions administratives, le requérant n'est pas recevable à mettre en cause, à l'occasion de l'exercice de ses fonctions, des décisions prises par l'autorité judiciaire pour assurer le fonctionnement du service public de la justice;

Sur le moyen tiré de ce que la Chambre d'accusation aurait violé les droits de la défense et méconnu l'étendue de ses pouvoirs: – Cons. que l'avis de la Chambre d'accusation mentionne que les présomptions qui se dégagent des éléments figurant au dossier 'ne peuvent être battues en brèche par la prétention de Croissant de considérer le système "info" comme un moyen d'organisation collective de la défense'; que la Chambre d'accusation s'est ainsi prononcée, pour l'écarter, sur la demande du sieur Croissant tendant à la production de nouvelles pièces destinées à démontrer que le système d'information qu'il lui est reproché d'avoir fait fonctionner n'était qu'un moyen légal d'organiser la défense de ses clients; qu'en rejetant cette demande, la Chambre d'accusation n'a ni violé les droits de la défense, ni méconnu l'étendue de ses pouvoirs;

Sur le moyen tiré de ce que le gouvernement a méconnu l'étendue de ses pouvoirs en se croyant lié par l'avis favorable de la Chambre d'accusation: – Cons. qu'il ressort des pièces versées au dossier que si, dès le mois d'octobre 1977, le gouvernement avait l'intention de se conformer en principe à l'avis de la Chambre d'accusation, cette position de principe n'impliquait pas que le gouvernement se soit à tort cru lié par un avis favorable à l'extradition et ait ainsi méconnu l'étendue des pouvoirs qu'il tient de l'article 18 de la loi du 10 mars 1927;

Sur le moyen tiré de ce que le gouvernement n'a pas procédé à un examen complet des circonstances de l'affaire: – Cons. qu'il résulte de l'instruction que le délai qui s'est écoulé entre la transmission de l'avis de la Chambre d'accusation et la signature du décret attaqué a été suffisant pour permettre au gouvernement, ainsi qu'il l'a fait, de procéder au vu de cet avis à un examen définitif et complet des circonstances de l'affaire;

Sur le moyen tiré de ce que le décret attaqué ne pouvait légalement être pris avant que la Cour de cassation ait statué sur le recours formé par le sieur Croissant contre l'avis de la Chambre d'accusation: – Cons. que, selon l'article 16 de la loi du 10 mars 1927, la Chambre d'accusation, lorsqu'elle donne son avis sur une demande d'extradition, statue sans recours; qu'il résulte de ces dispositions et de la nature même de cet avis, rendu dans le cours d'une procédure administrative, que les dispositions de l'article 569 du code de procédure pénale, qui prévoient qu'il est sursis à l'exécution de l'arrêt de la Cour d'appel pendant les délais du recours en cassation et, s'il y a eu recours, jusqu'au prononcé de l'arrêt de la Cour de cassation, ne sont pas applicables aux arrêts par lesquels la Chambre d'accusation donne son avis sur les demandes d'extradition; que, dès lors, le sieur Croissant n'est pas fondé à soutenir qu'en prenant le décret attaqué avant que la Cour de cassation se soit prononcée sur son recours contre l'avis de la Chambre d'accusation le gouvernement a violé les dispositions de l'article 569 du code de procédure pénale;

Sur le moyen tiré de la violation de l'article 33 de la Convention de Genève du 28 juillet 1951 sur le statut des réfugiés: – Cons. qu'en vertu des dispositions du paragraphe A 2 de l'article 1er de la Convention de Genève sur le statut des réfugiés et du paragraphe 2 de l'article 1er du protocole du 31 janvier 1967 relatif au statut des réfugiés 'le terme réfugié' s'appliquera à toute personne... qui, craignant avec 'raison d'être persécutée du fait de sa race, de sa religion, de sa nationalité, de son appartenance à un certain groupe social ou de ses opinions politiques... se trouve hors du pays dont elle a la nationalité et qui ne peut ou, du fait de cette crainte, ne veut se réclamer de la protection de ce pays';

Cons. que si le sieur Croissant s'est trouvé hors de la République fédérale d'Allemagne, pays dont il a la nationalité, il ne résulte pas des pièces versées au dossier qu'il n'ait pu se prévaloir de la protection de ce pays ou n'ait voulu, en raison des craintes de persécution qu'il aurait éprouvées 'avec raison' pour l'une des causes ci-dessus énumérées se réclamer de cette protection; que, dans ces conditions, il n'est pas fondé à se prévaloir de la qualité de réfugié au sens de cette disposition de la convention;

Sur le moyen tiré de ce que le mandat d'arrêt n'indiquerait pas la date des faits reprochés au sieur Croissant: – Cons. qu'il ressort des termes mêmes du mandat d'arrêt décerné le 15 juillet 1977 par le tribunal régional de Stuttgart que les faits pour lesquels l'extradition du sieur Croissant a été démandée ont été commis 'depuis 1972 et jusqu'au moins début 1976'; que, dès lors, le moyen manque en fait;

Sur le moyen tiré de ce que la demande d'extradition se fonderait sur une loi pénale allemande rétroactive et donc contraire à l'ordre public français: – Cons. que les modifications apportées à compter du 1er janvier 1975, à l'article 129 du code pénal allemand, qui selon le mandat précité sont applicables au sieur Croissant, n'ont pas affecté la définition de l'infraction réprimée par cet article; qu'elles se sont bornées à supprimer la surveillance de la police, dont la peine pouvait être assortie et à permettre de prononcer une amende au lieu des peines d'emprisonnement qui étaient seules prévues précédemment et qui sont demeurées inchangées; que ces dispositions nouvelles, moins sévères que celles auxquelles elles se sont substituées, étaient d'application immédiate; que, dès lors, le sieur Croissant n'est pas fondé à soutenir que l'ordre public français s'oppose à ce qu'il lui en soit fait application;

Sur le moyen tiré de ce que les faits reprochés au sieur Croissant ne sont pas punis par l'article 248 du code pénal d'une peine atteignant le minimum auquel l'extradition est subordonnée par l'article 3 de la Convention du 29 novembre 1951: – Cons. qu'aux termes de l'article 3 de la Convention précitée 'sont sujets à extradition: 1° les individus qui sont poursuivis pour des crimes ou délits punis par les lois des parties contractantes d'une peine d'au moins un an d'emprisonnement'; qu'il résulte clairement de cette disposition, rapprochée des autres dispositions du même article, que doivent être regardées comme étant punies d'une peine d'au moins un an d'emprisonnement les infractions pour lesquelles le maximum de la peine encourue est d'un an ou plus; que la peine prévue par l'article 248 du code pénal à l'égard des personnes qui, comme le sieur Croissant, sont habilitées par leurs fonctions à approcher les détenus est un emprisonnement de six mois à deux ans; que cette peine satisfait à la condition exigée par l'article 3 de la convention précitée; que, dès lors, le moyen ne saurait être accueilli;

Sur le moyen tiré de ce que les faits reprochés au sieur Croissant ne tombent pas sous le coup de l'article 267 du code pénal: – Cons. qu'aux termes de l'article 267 du code pénal 'sera puni de la réclusion criminelle à temps de cinq à dix ans quiconque aura sciemment et volontairement favorisé les auteurs des crimes prévus à l'article 265, en leur fournissant des instruments de crime, moyens de correspondance, logement ou lieu de réunion';

Cons. qu'il est reproché au sieur Croissant d'avoir fourni à des détenus poursuivis pour le crime d'association de malfaiteurs, prévu à l'article 265 du code pénal, non pas seulement, comme il le prétend, des moyens d'information, tels que livres, brochures ou notices, mais aussi des moyens de correspondance leur permettant de communiquer entre eux et avec des membres de leur organisation restés en liberté; que le requérant n'est, dès lors, pas fondé à soutenir que ces faits ne tombent pas sous le coup de l'article 267 du code pénal;

Sur le moyen tiré de la violation de l'article 4 de la Convention franco-alle-mande d'extradition du 29 novembre 1951: – Cons. qu'aux termes de l'article 4 de la Convention du 29 novembre 1951 'l'extradition ne sera pas accordée si l'infraction pour laquelle elle est demandée est considérée par la partie requise, d'après les circonstances dans lesquelles elle a été commise comme une infraction politique ou comme un fait commis pour préparer une telle infraction, l'exécuter, en assurer le profit, en procurer l'impunité';

Cons. qu'ainsi qu'il a été dit ci-dessus, il est reproché au sieur Croissant d'avoir fourni des moyens de correspondance à des détenus qui étaient poursuivis pour s'être associés dans le but de commettre des crimes contre les personnes et pour avoir effectivement commis plusieurs crimes de cette nature; que la circonstance que ces crimes, qui ne sont pas politiques par leur objet, auraient eu pour but, selon le mandat d'arrêt précité, 'de renverser l'ordre établi en République fédérale d'Allemagne' ne suffit pas, compte tenu de leur gravité, à les faire regarder comme ayant un caractère politique; que, si le sieur Croissant prétend qu'en ce qui le concerne il a agi dans le but de faire respecter les droits de la défense, ce mobile, à le supposer établi, n'est pas de nature à donner un caractère politique aux infractions qui lui sont reprochées et qui consistent dans une aide apportée par le sieur Croissant à des détenus, dont il était l'avocat en vue de leur permettre non pas d'assurer leur défense, mais de poursuivre leurs activités criminelles; que, dès lors, le requérant n'est pas fondé à soutenir qu'en accordant son extradition, les auteurs du décret attaqué ont violé les dispositions précitées de l'article 4 de la convention du 29 novembre 1951;

Sur le moyen tiré de la violation de l'article 5, 2° de la loi du 10 mars 1927: – Cons. qu'aux termes de l'article 1er de la Convention franco-allemande d'extradition du 29 novembre 1951, ratifiée en vertu de l'ordonnance du 17 décembre 1958, 'les parties contractantes s'engagent réciproquement à se livrer, selon les règles et sous les conditions déterminées par les articles suivants, les individus qui sont poursuivis . . . par les autorités judiciaires de l'Etat requérant'; qu'il résulte clairement de cette disposition qu'elle ne permet pas au Gouvernement français de subordonner l'extradition à des conditions autres que celles qui sont prévues par la convention; que, si l'article 1er de la loi du 10 mars 1927 dispose que cette loi s'applique aux points qui n'auraient pas été réglementés par les traités, cette disposition ne saurait prévaloir sur celles de la convention précitée, qui sont plus récentes et qui, en vertu de l'article 55 de la Constitution du 4 octobre 1958, ont une autorité supérieure à celle de la loi; que, dès lors, le sieur Croissant n'est pas fondé à se prévaloir des dispositions de l'article 5, 2° de la loi du 10 mars 1927 pour soutenir que le Gouvernement français ne pouvait légalement accorder son extradition aux autorités fédérales allemandes; . . . (rejet).

Picabea Burunza

Conseil d'Etat 27.10.89

REQUÊTE de M. Picabea Burunza tendant à l'annulation du décret du 28 juillet 1989 accordant son extradition aux autorités espagnoles;

Vu la Constitution; le code pénal; le code de procédure pénale; la convention européenne de sauvegarde des droits de l'homme et des libertés fondamentales du 4 novembre 1950; la convention de Genève du 28 juillet 1951 et le protocole signé à New-York le 31 janvier 1967; la convention européenne d'extradition du 13 décembre 1957; la loi n° 79–587 du 11 juillet 1979; l'ordonnance n° 45–1708 du 31 juillet 1945, le décret n° 53–934 du 30 septembre 1953 et la loi n° 87–1127 du 31 décembre 1987;

Sur la légalité externe du décret attaqué: – CONSIDÉRANT que le décret du 5 mai 1989 autorisant l'extradition de M. Picabea Burunza pour l'exécution du reliquat des peines prononcées à son encontre le 29 juin 1981 par le tribunal national de Madrid énumère les infractions pour lesquelles l'intéressé a été poursuivi et les condamnations dont il a fait l'objet, précise que les faits dont il a été reconnu coupable sont punissables en droit français et qu'ils n'ont pas un caractère politique et indique qu'il n'apparaît pas que ces condamnations aient été prononcées pour des considérations de race, de religion, de nationalité ou d'opinions politiques; que ce décret relève enfin que le quantum des peines prononcées répond aux exigences de l'article 2 de la convention européenne d'extradition du 13 décembre 1957; que ni l'omission du numéro des articles du code pénal français applicables aux infractions commises ni celle de la date de la demande du Gouvernement espagnol n'entachent la légalité du décret attaqué lequel satisfait, dès lors, aux exigences de l'article 3 de la loi du 11 juillet 1979;

Sur la légalité interne du décret attaqué: – Cons. que M. Picabea Burunza a été condamné pour assassinat, dépôt d'armes de guerre et vol; que la circonstance que les actes pour lesquels il a été condamné auraient été commis dans le cadre d'une lutte pour l'indépendance du Pays basque ne suffit pas, compte tenu de leur gravité, à les faire regarder comme ayant un caractère politique; qu'il n'apparaît pas que les poursuites aient eu lieu et que les peines aient été prononcées pour des considérations de race, de nationalité ou d'opinions politiques;

Cons. qu'il ne ressort pas des pièces du dossier que les condamnations pour l'exécution desquelles l'extradition de M. Picabea Burunza a été accordée n'aient pas été prononcées au terme d'une procédure contradictoire par une juridiction qui n'ait pas respecté les droits et libertés fondamentaux de la personne humaine ainsi que l'exigent les principes généraux du droit de l'extradition;

Cons. qu'il résulte de tout ce qui précède que M. Picabea Burunza n'est pas fondé à demander l'annulation du décret attaqué; . . . (rejet).

Bereciartua-Echarri

Conseil d'Etat 1.4.1988

REQUÊTE de M. Bereciartua-Echarri tendant:
1° à l'annulation du décret du 30 janvier 1987 accordant son extradition au Gouvernement espagnol,
2° au sursis à l'exécution de ce décret;
Vu la Constitution; la loi du 10 mars 1927; la convention de Genève du 28 juillet 1951, relative au statut des réfugiés, et le protocole signé à New York le 31 janvier 1967; la convention européenne d'extradition du 13 décembre 1957; la loi du 11 juillet 1979; l'ordonnance du 31 juillet 1945 et le décret du 30 septembre 1953; la loi du 30 décembre 1977;
Sans qu'il soit besoin d'examiner les autres moyens de la requête: –
CONSIDÉRANT qu'aux termes de l'article 1ᵉʳ A 2° de la convention de Genève du 28 juillet 1951 sur le statut de réfugié, la qualité de réfugié est reconnue à: 'toute personne . . . qui, craignant avec raison d'être persécutée du fait de sa race, de sa religion, de sa nationalité, de son appartenance à un certain groupe social ou de ses opinions politiques, se trouve hors du pays dont elle a la nationalité et qui ne peut ou, du fait de cette crainte, ne veut se réclamer de la protection de son pays';
Cons. qu'il ressort des pièces du dossier qu'à la date à laquelle a été pris le décret accordant aux autorités espagnoles l'extradition de M. Bereciartua-Echarri, ressortissant espagnol d'origine basque, pour des faits intervenus entre février 1979 et juin 1981, le requérant bénéficiait de la qualité de réfugié en vertu d'une décision du 21 juin 1973, maintenue par une décision du 30 juillet 1984 de la commission des recours des réfugiés, non contestée par le directeur de l'office français de protection des réfugiés et apatrides et devenue définitive;
Cons. que les principes généraux du droit applicables aux réfugiés, résultant notamment de la définition précitée de la convention de Genève, font obstacle à ce qu'un réfugié soit remis, de quelque manière que ce soit, par un Etat qui lui reconnaît cette qualité, aux autorités de son pays d'origine, sous la seule réserve des exceptions prévues pour des motifs de sécurité nationale par ladite convention; qu'en l'espèce, le Garde des sceaux, ministre de la justice, n'invoque aucun de ces motifs; qu'ainsi, et alors qu'il appartenait au gouvernement, s'il s'y croyait fondé, de demander à l'office français de protection des réfugiés et apatrides de cesser de reconnaître la qualité de réfugié à M. Bereciartua-Echarri, le statut de ce dernier faisait obstacle à ce que le gouvernement pût légalement décider de le livrer, sur leur demande, aux autorités espagnoles; que le décret attaqué est dès lors entaché d'excès de pouvoir;. . . (annulation du décret).

Garcia-Ramirez (José Carlos)

Cass Crim 21.9.1984

LA COUR,

Vu les mémoires produits;

Sur le premier moyen de cassation pris de la violation de l'article 593 du code de procédure pénale, ensemble violation des droits de la défense,

'en ce que l'arrêt attaqué ne se prononce pas sur la demande de renvoi présentée par le conseil du demandeur dans le mémoire régulièrement déposé devant la Chambre d'accusation;

'alors que, aux termes de l'article 593 du Code de procédure pénale, la Chambre d'accusation doit, à peine de nullité, se prononcer sur l'ensemble des demandes dont elle est saisie; que le silence de l'arrêt est d'autant plus grave que la demande de renvoi était justifiée par la circonstance que, pour l'audience du 8 août 1984, la défense n'avait pas encore, le 6 août précédent, reçu communication de la traduction des pièces du dossier;'

Attendu que dans un mémoire daté du 4 août 1984 et parvenu le 6 août au greffe de la Chambre d'accusation pour l'audience du 8 courant, le demandeur a sollicité 'le renvoi de l'affaire à une date ultérieure compte tenu de la brièveté des délais, de la complexité de la procédure et de sa non-traduction' non sans avoir cependant exposé les deux moyens de défense qu'il entendait développer, le premier 'tendant à démontrer qu'il devait être considéré comme un réfugié politique', le second que 'les infractions reprochées sont des infractions politiques et qu'en conséquence l'extradition était impossible en application de l'article 3 de la convention d'extradition franco-espagnole'; que l'énoncé même de ces griefs établit que Garcia-Ramirez José Carlos avait connaissance des faits exposés dans les pièces de la procédure jointes à la demande du Gouvernement espagnol;

Qu'ainsi il ne saurait être fait grief à l'arrêt attaqué de n'avoir pas spécialement répondu à la demande de renvoi du demandeur;

Qu'en effet une telle demande ne peut être considérée comme un chef péremptoire de défense, qu'aucune critique touchant la régularité formelle de la procédure n'a été soulevée, qu'au jour de l'audience la défense était en possession notamment de la traduction des pièces; qu'en statuant au fond à l'audience prévue, la Chambre d'accusation a implicitement mais nécessairement écarté tout renvoi estimant qu'elle était en mesure de rendre son avis sur l'extradition demandée sans pour autant porter atteinte aux droits de la défense compte tenu de l'argumentation développée par celui-ci devant les juges; que de surcroît Garcia-Ramirez José Carlos était informé depuis le 2 août 1984 du contenu des pièces servant de base à la demande d'extradition et rédigées dans sa langue natale, comme l'exige l'article 6 § 3 *a* et *b* de la convention européenne de sauvegarde des droits de l'homme et des libertés fondamentales;

D'où il suit que le moyen, recevable en la forme, ne saurait être accueilli;

Sur le deuxième moyen de cassation pris de la violation des articles 156, 157, 158, 159, 160 et 206 du code de procédure pénale, ensemble violation des droits de la défense,

'*en ce que l'arrêt attaqué a été rendu au vu des pièces de la procédure menée en Espagne à l'encontre du demandeur et dont la traduction figure au dossier;*

'*alors, d'une part, que cette traduction est nulle puisqu'elle n'a été ordonnée ni par la Chambre d'accusation, ni par aucune autre autorité judiciaire;*

'*alors, d'autre part, et en toute hypothèse, que cette traduction ne pouvait être faite que par des experts inscrits sur une liste ou, à tout le moins, en cas d'empêchement dûment constaté, par deux experts ayant prêté serment au préalable; qu'en l'espèce la traduction qui figure au dossier n'indique ni quel est ou quels sont son ou ses auteurs, ni quelle est sa ou leur qualité, ni s'il a ou s'ils ont prêté serment; qu'elle n'a donc aucune valeur légale et ne peut servir de base à la décision de la Chambre d'accusation;*'

Attendu que contrairement à ce que soutient le demandeur, aucune disposition de la loi du 10 mars 1927 n'impose la traduction des pièces de justice jointes à une demande d'extradition émanant d'un gouvernement étranger ni ne fixe les conditions de forme d'une éventuelle traduction;

Qu'il ne saurait être suppléé au silence de la loi en ayant recours aux dispositions des articles 156 et suivants du code de procédure pénale qui sont étrangers à la matière;

Que d'ailleurs le demandeur n'a pas déposé devant la Chambre d'accusation de conclusions tendant à voir désigner des experts au sens des articles précités pour procéder à une nouvelle traduction des pièces, se bornant, ainsi qu'il a été dit ci-dessus, à demander le renvoi de l'affaire, soutenant ne pas être en possession d'une traduction lors de la rédaction de son mémoire;

D'où il suit que le moyen, recevable en la forme, ne peut qu'être écarté:

Sur le troisième moyen de cassation pris de la violation de l'article 3 de la convention franco-espagnole d'extradition du 14 décembre 1877 et de l'article 5–2° de la loi du 10 mars 1927,

'*en ce que l'arrêt attaqué a donné un avis favorable à l'extradition du demandeur;*

'*alors qu'il résulte des propres énonciations de l'arrêt que les faits pour lesquels l'extradition a été demandée ont un caractère politique; que, dès lors, l'extradition du demandeur ne pouvait être accordée aux autorités espagnoles;*'

Attendu que ce moyen critique l'un des motifs de l'arrêt qui se rattache directement et sert de support à l'avis de la Chambre d'accusation sur la suite à donner à la demande d'extradition;

Que ce moyen est en conséquence irrecevable par application des dispositions de l'article 16 de la loi du 10 mars 1927;

Qu'il n'appartient donc pas à la Cour de Cassation de l'examiner:

Sur le quatrième moyen de cassation pris de la violation de l'alinéa 4 du Préambule de la Constitution du 27 octobre 1946, des articles 1er et 33 de la convention de Genève du 28 juillet 1951 relative au statut des réfugiés, ensemble des articles 2 et 5 de la loi du 25 juillet 1952 portant création de l'office français de protection des réfugiés et apatrides,

'*en ce que l'arrêt attaqué a considéré que le recours formé contre la décision implicite refusant de lui reconnaître la qualité de réfugié n'était pas suspensif, le demandeur ne pouvait se prévaloir dudit recours pour s'opposer à l'extradition;*

'*alors que, d'une part, le préambule de la Constitution de 1946 érige le droit d'asile en principe constitutionnel;*

'*et alors que, d'autre part, il résulte des stipulations de la convention de Genève du 28 juillet 1951 et des dispositions de la loi du 25 juillet 1952 que la décision, par laquelle il est statué sur une demande d'admission au statut de réfugié, a un caractère récognitif et rétroagit à la date d'entrée de l'intéressé sur le territoire français; que, dès lors, ladite convention interdisant par ailleurs l'extradition d'un réfugié vers son pays d'origine, la Chambre d'accusation ne pouvait émettre un avis favorable à la demande d'extradition présentée par l'Espagne à l'encontre du demandeur tant que la juridiction saisie de son recours ne s'était pas définitivement prononcée sur sa qualité de réfugié;*'

Attendu que le demandeur dans son mémoire produit devant la Chambre d'accusation a énoncé qu'il devait être considéré comme bénéficiant du statut de réfugié politique et qu'en conséquence 'l'extradition ne pouvait être prononcée contre lui';

Attendu que c'est à bon droit que les juges ont estimé qu'il était 'sans intérêt aux débats que l'intéressé prétende avoir élevé un recours contre le refus implicite de l'office français de protection des réfugiés et apatrides (OFPRA)' de lui reconnaître le statut de réfugié politique;

Qu'à les supposer exactes, les allégations de Garcia-Ramirez José Carlos ne sauraient constituer une exception préjudicielle à l'arrêt de la Chambre d'accusation dont celle-ci aurait méconnu la portée, dès lors, qu'en admettant que le demandeur puisse se prévaloir du statut de réfugié, l'article 33 de la convention de Genève du 28 juillet 1951 concerne seulement l'expulsion ou le refoulement, mesures administratives juridiquement différentes de l'extradition;

Qu'au surplus l'attribution de la qualité de réfugié a un caractère

recognitif et que le réfugié est celui qui entre dans l'application de l'article
1 A 2 de la convention de Genève et de l'article 1 § 2 du protocole du 31
janvier 1967 et non celui qui est titulaire d'un certificat délivré par
l'OFPRA;

Qu'enfin aux termes de l'article 5 de la loi du 25 juillet 1952 la saisine de
la commission de recours des réfugiés n'a d'effet suspensif que dans les cas
prévus à l'alinéa 2 *b* dudit article qui ne porte pas référence aux décisions
de refus de l'OFPRA;

D'où il suit que le moyen, recevable en ce qu'il critique les dispositions
de l'arrêt ayant implicitement refusé de surseoir à statuer ne saurait être
accueilli;

Sur le cinquième moyen de cassation pris de la violation des articles 9,
10 et 16 de la loi du 10 mars 1927, ensemble des articles 1ᵉʳ et 6 de la convention franco-espagnole d'extradition du 14 décembre 1877;

'en ce que l'arrêt attaqué vise "la demande d'extradition régulièrement
présentée le 9 juillet 1984 par le Gouvernement de l'Espagne ... en
vertu d'un mandat d'arrêt décerné le 10 juin 1981 par le juge d'instruction central de Madrid ...';

'alors que le Gouvernement espagnol n'a jamais présenté de demande
d'extradiction le 9 juillet 1984; qu'en effet, le seul document versé au
dossier et portant cette date est une pièce de procédure adressée
directement au ministre des relations extérieures et à "l'autorité judiciaire compétente française" par le juge d'instruction de Madrid, qui
n'avait aucune compétence pour demander l'extradition du demandeur;
que dès lors est nul l'arrêt attaqué qui ne vise pas la demande formée
par le Gouvernement espagnol;'

Attendu qu'il est fait grief à l'arrêt attaqué d'avoir visé 'la demande
d'extradition régulièrement présentée le 9 juillet 1984 par le Gouvernement
espagnol' alors que ledit gouvernement n'a jamais présenté de demande
d'extradition à cette date, le seul document figurant au dossier étant une
pièce de procédure adressée directement au ministre des relations
extérieures et à 'l'autorité judiciaire française' par l'un des juges d'instruction de Madrid qui n'avait aucune compétence pour demander l'extradition
du demandeur;

Mais attendu que s'il est exact que l'arrêt attaqué fait référence à une
demande d'extradition présentée le 9 juillet 1984 par le Gouvernement
espagnol, la Cour de Cassation est à même de s'assurer que conformément
aux prescriptions de la loi du 10 mars 1927 la demande d'extradition de
Garcia-Ramirez José Carlos a été transmise au ministre des relations
extérieures par l'ambassade d'Espagne le 30 juillet 1984 et vise l'arrêt de
mise en accusation et d'emprisonnement conditionnel du 1ᵉʳ octobre 1981
en exécution duquel le demandeur a été arrêté par les services de police
français et placé sous écrou extraditionnel;

D'où il suit que la référence à une demande du 9 juillet 1984 constitue une simple erreur matérielle sans portée sur la régularité formelle de la procédure d'extradition concernant le demandeur;

Qu'en conséquence le moyen ne saurait être retenu;

Et attendu que l'arrêté attaqué a été rendu par une chambre d'accusation compétente, régulièrement composée conformément aux dispositions du code de procédure pénale, et que la procédure est régulière;

REJETTE le pourvoi.

Décision no 86–213 DC du 3 septembre 1986

Le Conseil constitutionnel a été saisi, le 8 août 1986, par MM. Robert Schwint, Noël Berrier, Germain Authié, Albert Ramassamy, André Méric, Mme Cécile Goldet, MM. Louis Perrein, Gérard Delfau, Bernard Desbrière, Bernard Parmantier, Charles Bonifay, Michel Dreyfus-Schmidt, Jacques Bialski, René Régnault, Jules Faigt, Jean-Pierre Masseret, Jean Peyrafitte, Léon Eeckhoutte, Marcel Costes, Pierre Bastié, Philippe Madrelle, Michel Darras, Jean Geoffroy, Franck Sérusclat, Mme Geneviève Le Bellegou-Béguin, MM. Jean-Pierre Bayle, Guy Allouche, Tony Larue, Pierre Matraja, Michel Charasse, Mme Irma Rapuzzi, MM. Jacques Carat, André Delelis, Gérard Roujas, Roland Grimaldi, Maurice Pic, Gérard Gaud, Félix Ciccolini, Louis Longequeue, Marc Bœuf, Edouard Soldani, Marcel Bony, Robert Pontillon, Henri Duffaut, Pierre Noé, Bastien Leccia, Roger Rinchet, Claude Fuzier, William Chervy, Roland Courteau, Marcel Vidal, Lucien Delmas, André Rouvière, Michel Moreigne, Robert Guillaume, François Autain, Robert Laucournet, Georges Dagonia, Marc Plantegenest, Michel Manet, Marcel Debarge et Georges Benedetti, sénateurs, dans les conditions prévues à l'article 61, alinéa 2, de la Constitution, de la conformité à celle-ci de la loi relative à la lutte contre le terrorisme et aux atteintes à la sûreté de l'Etat.

Le Conseil constitutionnel,

Vu la Constitution;

Vu l'ordonnance no 58–1067 du 7 novembre 1958 portant loi organique sur le Conseil constitutionnel, notamment les articles figurant au chapitre II du titre II de la ladite ordonnance;

Le rapporteur ayant été entendu;

Considérant que les auteurs de la saisine demandent que 'les parties de l'article 1ᵉʳ et les articles 4, 5 et 6 de la loi relative à la lutte contre le terrorisme' soient déclarés contraires à la Constitution comme méconnaissant le principe de la légalité des délits et des peines, le principe de l'égalité devant la justice et le principe de la liberté individuelle;

Sur le moyen tiré de la méconnaissance du principe de la légalité des délits et des peines:

Considérant que les auteurs de la saisine relèvent que la loi soumise à l'examen du Conseil constitutionnel ne définit pas d'infractions spécifiques caractérisant les activités terroristes, mais que l'article 1ᵉʳ de la loi tend à soumettre à des règles particulières la poursuite, l'instruction et le jugement de diverses infractions déjà définies par le code pénal ou par des lois spéciales, lorsque ces infractions 'sont en relation avec une entreprise individuelle ou collective ayant pour but de troubler gravement l'ordre public par l'intimidation ou la terreur';

Considérant que, selon les auteurs de la saisine, il s'ensuivrait tout d'abord que les conditions d'application des règles particulières de poursuite, d'instruction et de jugement établies par la loi présentement examinée ne seraient pas déterminées par référence aux éléments constitutifs d'une ou plusieurs infractions définis de manière objective, mais par référence à l'élément purement subjectif que constitue le but poursuivi par l'auteur du ou des actes incriminés; qu'ainsi la loi méconnaitrait le principe constitutionnel de la légalité des délits et des peines formulé par l'article 8 de la Déclaration des droits de l'homme et du citoyen de 1789;

Considérant que les auteurs de la saisine indiquent que ce principe est encore plus gravement méconnu du fait que les conséquences attachées à la relation existant entre certaines infractions et une 'entreprise individu-elle ou collective ayant pour but de troubler gravement l'ordre public par l'intimidation ou la terreur' ne se limitent pas aux règles de poursuite, d'instruction ou de jugement, mais concernent aussi les peines applicables; qu'en effet, d'une part, aux termes de l'article 5 de la loi complétant l'arti-cle 44 du code pénal, l'existence d'une telle relation a pour effet de rendre les auteurs de ces diverses infractions passibles, outre les peines attachées à celles-ci, d'une peine d'interdiction de séjour d'un minimum de deux ans que le juge doit obligatoirement prononcer; que d'autre part, l'existence de la même relation rend applicable aux auteurs des infractions, aux termes de l'article 6 de la loi insérant dans le code pénal les articles 463–1 et 463–2, des dispositions prévoyant, sous certaines conditions, des exemptions ou des réductions de peine; qu'ainsi les articles 5 et 6 de la loi permettent, en violation du principe de la légalité des délits et des peines, que des peines, ainsi que des exemptions ou des réductions de peine soient prononcées sans que les infractions correspondantes aient été définies avec une précision suffisante;

Considérant que l'application des règles particulières posées par la loi tant en ce qui concerne la poursuite, l'instruction et le jugement qu'en ce qui a trait aux peines applicables est surbordonnée à deux conditions: d'une part, que les faits considérés soient constitutifs de certaines infrac-tions définies par le code pénal ou par des lois spéciales; d'autre part, que les infractions soient en relation avec une entreprise individuelle ou collective ayant pour but de troubler gravement l'ordre public par l'intimidation ou la terreur;

Considérant que la première condition fixée par la loi, qui renvoie à des infractions qui sont elles-mêmes définies par code pénal ou par des lois spéciales en termes suffisamment clairs et précis, satisfait aux exigences du principe constitutionnel de la légalité des délits et des peines; que, de même, seconde condition est énoncée en des termes d'une précision suffisante pour qu'il n'y ait pas méconnaissance de ce principe; qu'ainsi le premier moyen formulé par les auteurs de saisine ne saurait être retenu;

Sur le moyen tiré de ce que l'article 706–25 du code de procédure pénale violerait le principe d'égalité devant la justice:

Considérant que l'article 706–25 du code de procédure pénale, tel qu'il résulte de l'article 1er de la loi présentement examinée, dispose, s'agissant des infractions visées au nouvel article 706–16: 'Pour le jugement des accusés majeurs, la cour d'assises est composée conformément aux dispositions de l'article 698–6';

Considérant que l'article 698–6, premier alinéa, du code de procédure pénale est ainsi conçu: 'Par dérogation aux dispositions du titre 1er du livre II, notamment aux articles 240 et 248, premier alinéa, et sous réserve des dispositions de l'article 698–7, la cour d'assises prévue par l'article 697 est composée d'un président et de six assesseurs désignés comme il est dit aux alinéas 2 et 3 de l'article 248 et aux articles 249 à 253'; qu'il en résulte qu'elle ne comprend pas de jurés; que le 3° du deuxième alinéa du même article 698–6 écarte les dispositions des articles 359 et 360 imposant une majorité renforcée pour les décisions prises par une cour d'assises composée de magistrats et de jurés lorsqu'elles sont défavorables à l'accusé et leur substitue la règle de la majorité simple pour les mêmes décisions émanant de la cour d'assises ne comportant pas de jurés;

Considérant que les auteurs de la saisine font valoir tout d'abord que le nombre et la diversité des infractions visées à l'article 706–16 nouveau sont tels que le jugement de ces infractions par une cour d'assises ne comportant pas de jurés ne peut être regardé comme une simple exception au principe de l'intervention du jury en matière de crimes;

Considérant que les infractions criminelles énumérées à l'article 706–16 nouveau ne sont justiciables de la cour d'assises composée selon les termes de l'article 698–6 qu'autant qu'il est établi qu'elles sont en relation avec une entreprise individuelle ou collective ayant pour but de troubler gravement l'ordre public par l'intimidation ou la terreur; qu'ainsi, à s'en tenir au seul texte de l'article 706–16 nouveau, l'exception apportée au principe de l'intervention du jury a un caractère limité; que l'argument invoqué par les auteurs de la saisine manque par suite en fait;

Considérant que les auteurs de la saisine font valoir également qu'il n'existe pas dans l'intention même du législateur d'incriminations propres aux activités terroristes; que la poursuite ne peut concerner que des infractions déjà définies et réprimées par le code pénal ou par des lois spéciales; que, dès lors, rien ne saurait justifier au regard du principe d'égalité devant la justice que ces infractions soient jugées par des juridictions différentes selon qu'il est ou non prétendu qu'elles sont 'en relation avec une entreprise individuelle ou collective ayant pour but de troubler gravement l'ordre public par l'intimidation ou la terreur'; que, quelle que soit la variété de leurs mobiles, des infractions définies par les mêmes éléments constitutifs doivent être jugées par les mêmes juges et selon les mêmes règles;

Considérant qu'il est loisible au législateur, compétent pour fixer les règles de la procédure pénale en vertu de l'article 34 de la Constitution, de prévoir des règles de procédure différentes selon les faits, les situations et les personnes auxquelles elles s'appliquent, pourvu que ces différences ne procèdent pas de discriminations injustifiées et que soient assurées aux justiciables des garanties égales, notamment quant au respect du principe des droits de la défense;

Considérant que la différence de traitement établie par l'article 706–25 nouveau du code de procédure pénale entre les auteurs des infractions visées par l'article 706–16 nouveau selon que ces infractions sont ou non en relation avec une entreprise individuelle ou collective ayant pour but de troubler gravement l'ordre public par l'intimidation ou la terreur tend, selon l'intention du législateur, à déjouer l'effet des pressions ou des menaces pouvant altérer la sérénité de la juridiction de jugement; que cette différence de traitement ne procède donc pas d'une discrimination injustifiée; qu'en outre, par sa composition, la cour d'assises instituée par l'article 698–6 du code de procédure pénale présente les garanties requises d'indépendance et d'impartialité; que devant cette juridiction les droits de la défense sont sauvegardés; que, dans ces conditions, le moyen tiré de la méconnaissance du principe d'égalité devant la justice doit être écarté;

Sur les articles 706–23 et 702 du code de procédure pénale:

Considérant que les auteurs de la saisine soutiennent que la loi soumise à l'examen du Conseil constitutionnel porte atteinte à la liberté individuelle, d'une part, en raison de l'insuffisance des garanties données par l'article 706–23 du code de procédure pénale aux personnes faisant l'objet de mesures de garde à vue, d'autre part, en ce que les règles de poursuite, d'instruction et de jugement prévues par l'article 697 et par les nouveaux articles 706–17 à 706–25 du code de procédure pénale sont étendues par l'article 702 nouveau du code à des infractions relevant auparavant du droit commun sans qu'il soit d'ailleurs exigé qu'elles soient en relation avec une entreprise individuelle ou collective ayant pour but de troubler gravement l'ordre public par l'intimidation ou la terreur;

En ce qui concerne l'article 706–23 relatif à la garde à vue:

Considérant que l'article 706–23 du code de procédure pénale, tel qu'il résulte de l'article 1er de la loi présentement examinée, dispose: 'Pour l'application des articles 63, 77 et 154, si les nécessités de l'enquête ou de l'instruction relatives à l'une des infractions entrant dans le champ d'application de l'article 706–16 l'exigent, la garde à vue d'une personne majeure peut faire l'objet d'une prolongation supplémentaire de quarante-huit heures. Cette prolongation est autorisée, soit à la requête du procureur de la République, par le président du tribunal dans le ressort duquel s'exerce la garde à vue ou le juge délégué par lui, soit, dans les cas prévus par les articles 72 et 154, par le juge d'instruction. L'intéressé doit être présenté à l'autorité qui statue sur la prolongation préalablement à la décision. Dans le cas où la prolongation est décidée, un examen médical est de droit. Le procureur de la République ou, dans les cas prévus par les articles 72 et 154, le juge d'instruction est compétent pour désigner le médecin chargé de cet examen.';

Considérant que les auteurs de la saisine soutiennent que le respect de la liberté individuelle exigerait que, en cas de prolongation de quarante-huit heures de la garde à vue, la présentation de l'intéressé à un magistrat du siège et l'intervention d'un examen médical soient quotidiennes;

Considérant qu'il résulte de l'article 706–23 nouveau du code de procédure pénale que le champ d'application des dispositions critiquées concerne des enquêtes portant sur des infractions déterminées appelant, en raison de leur rapport avec une entreprise individuelle ou collective ayant pour but de troubler gravement l'ordre public par l'intimidation ou la terreur, des recherches particulières; que cet article exige que la prolongation de la garde à vue soit subordonnée à une décision du magistrat du siège auquel l'intéressé doit être présenté; qu'au surplus, est prescrite la surveillance médicale de la personne gardée à vue; que ces dispositions s'ajoutent aux garanties résultant des règles de portée générale du code de procédure pénale qui ont pour effet de placer sous le contrôle du procureur de la République la garde à vue ou qui exigent, conformément au dernier alinéa de l'article 64, un examen médical passé vingt-quatre heures si l'intéressé en fait la demande; que, dès lors, les dispositions de l'article 706–23 nouveau du code de procédure pénale ne méconnaissent pas l'article 66 de la Constitution;

En ce qui concerne l'article 4 de la loi modifiant l'article 702 du code de procédure pénale relatif aux atteintes à la sûreté de l'Etat:

Considérant que, dans sa rédaction issue de la loi n° 82–621 du 21 juillet 1982, l'article 702, alinéas 1er et 2, du code de procédure pénale dispose: 'En temps de paix, les crimes et délits contre la sûreté de l'Etat sont instruits et jugés par les juridictions de droit commun et selon les règles du présent code. Lorsque les fait poursuivis constituent un crime ou un délit prévu et réprimé par les articles 70 à 85 du code pénal ou une infraction connexe, la compétence est dévolue aux juridictions prévues et organisées par les articles 697 et 698–6'; c'est-à-dire respectivement par un tribunal de grande instance où sont affectés des magistrats spécialisés en matière militaire et par une cour d'assises composée exclusivement de magistrats;

Considérant que l'article 4 de la loi présentement examinée est ainsi conçu: 'Les deux premiers alinéas de l'article 702 du code de procédure pénale sont remplacés par l'alinéa suivant: "En temps de paix, les crimes et délits prévus par les articles 70 à 103 du code pénal, ainsi que les infractions connexes sont instruits, poursuivis et jugés conformément aux dispositions des articles 697 et 706–17 à 706–25."';

Considérant que le premier effet de ces nouvelles dispositions est de soumettre au jugement des juridictions prévues et organisées par les articles 697 et 698–6 les crimes et délits prévus et réprimés par les articles 86 à 103 du code pénal, c'est-à-dire les attentats, complots et autres infractions contre l'autorité de l'Etat et l'intégrité du territoire national, les crimes tendant à troubler l'Etat par le massacre ou la dévastation, les crimes commis par la participation à un mouvement insurrectionnel et les infractions prévues par les articles 100 et 103 du code pénal, alors que, dans l'état du droit résultant de la loi no 82–621 du 21 juillet 1982, ces règles de compétence juridictionnelle ne visaient, parmi les crimes et délits contre la sûreté de l'Etat, que ceux prévus aux articles 70 à 85, c'est-à-dire les crimes de trahison et d'espionnage et les autres atteintes à la défense nationale;

Considérant que le second effet des dispositions de l'article 4 de la loi présentement examinée est de rendre applicables à l'ensemble des infractions visées par les articles 70 à 103 du code pénal les règles relatives à la poursuite, à l'instruction et au jugement posées par les articles 706–17 à 706–25 nouveaux du code de procédure pénale;

Considérant que les auteurs de la saisine font valoir, à l'encontre des dispositions susanalysées, que l'extension des règles dérogatoires au droit commun posées par les articles 706–17 à 706–25 nouveaux du code de procédure pénale à toutes les infractions, même constitutives de simples délits d'imprudence, conduit, notamment en ce qui concerne l'application du régime de la garde à vue, à une violation du principe de la liberté individuelle;

Considérant que, ainsi qu'il a été dit ci-dessus, s'il est loisible au législateur de prévoir des règles de procédure pénale différentes selon les faits, les situations et les personnes auxquelles elles s'appliquent, c'est à la condition que ces différences ne procèdent pas de discriminations injustifiées et que soient assurées aux justiciables des garanties égales;

Considérant que les règles de composition et de procédure dérogatoires au droit commun qui trouvent, selon le législateur, leur justification dans les caractéristiques spécifiques du terrorisme ne sauraient, sans qu'il soit porté atteinte au principe d'égalité devant la justice, être étendues à des infractions qui ne présentent pas les mêmes caractéristiques et qui ne sont pas nécessairement en relation avec celles visées à l'article 706–16 nouveau du code de procédure pénale; que, dès lors, et sans qu'il soit besoin de statuer sur le moyen invoqué, l'article 4 de la loi, qui modifie l'article 702 du code de procédure pénale, est contraire à la Constitution;

Considérant qu'en l'espèce, il n'y a lieu pour le Conseil constitutionnel de soulever d'office aucune question de conformité à la Constitution en ce qui concerne les autres dispositions de la loi soumise à son examen,

Décide:

Art 1er. – L'article 4 de la loi relative à la lutte contre le terrorisme et aux atteintes à la sûreté de l'Etat est déclaré non conforme à la Constitution.

Art. 2. – Les autres dispositions de la loi ne sont pas contraires à la Constitution.

Art. 3. – La présente décision sera publiée au *Journal officiel* de la République française.

Délibéré par le Conseil constitutionnel dans ses séances des 2 et 3 septembre 1986.

Le président,
ROBERT BADINTER

4 Domestic legislation and official statements

CONTENTS

UNITED KINGDOM DOMESTIC LEGISLATION

The Tokyo Convention Act 1967

Enacted to give effect to the Tokyo Convention 1963. The Act also gives effect to certain provisions relating to piracy of the 1958 Geneva Convention on the High Seas.

The Suppression of Terrorism Act 1978

Enacted to give effect to the European Convention on the Suppression of Terrorsm. It also amends the law relating to the extradition of criminals and the obtaining of evidence for criminal proceedings outside the UK and confers jurisdiction in respect of certain offences committed outside the UK.

The Internationally Protected Persons Act 1978

Implements the Convention on the Prevention and Punishment of Crimes against Internationally Protected Persons 1973.

The Taking of Hostages Act 1982

Implements the International Convention against the Taking of Hostages.

The Hijacking Act 1971

Enacted to give effect to the Hague Convention for the Suppression of Unlawful Seizure of Aircraft. However, this Act has been repealed and its provisions replaced and consolidated in the **Aviation Security Act 1982**.

The Protection of Aircraft Act 1973

Enacted to give effect to the Montreal Convention for the Suppression of Unlawful Acts against the Safety of Civil Aviation. The Act also makes provision for the protection of aircraft, aerodromes and air navigation installations against acts of violence. It also amended certain provisions of the Hijacking Act. This Act was also repealed and its provisions replaced by the **Aviation Security Act 1982**.

The Aviation Security Act 1982

Consolidates the UK enactments on aviation security including the Hijacking Act and the Protection of Aircraft Act.

The Aviation and Maritime Security Act 1990

Gives effect to the Montreal Protocol for the Suppression of Unlawful Acts of Violence at Airports which supplements the Montreal Convention for the Suppression of Unlawful Acts against the Safety of Civil Aviation. It also gives effect to the Convention for the Suppression of Unlawful Acts against the Safety of Maritime Navigation and to the Protocol for the Suppression of Unlawful Acts against the Safety of Fixed Platforms Located on the Shelf which supplements that Convention.

LOI NO. 88–1020 DU 9 SEPTEMBRE 1986 RELATIVE
A LA LUTTE CONTRE LE TERRORISME ET AUX ATTEINTES
A LA SURETE DE L'ETAT

L'Assemblée nationale et le Sénat ont adopté,

Le Conseil constitutionnel a déclaré conforme à la Constitution,

Le Président de la République promulgue la loi dont la teneur suit:

Art, 1er, – Il est créé, après le titre XIV du livre IV du code de procédure pénale, un titre XV ainsi intitulé: 'Des infractions en relation avec une entreprise individuelle ou collective ayant pour but de troubler gravement l'ordre public par l'intimidation ou la terreur' et composé des articles 706–16 à 706–25 suivants:

'*Art. 706–16.* – Lorsqu'elles sont en relation avec une entreprise individuelle ou collective ayant pour but de troubler gravement l'ordre public par l'intimidation ou la terreur, sont poursuivies, instruites et jugées selon les règles du présent code, sous réserve des dispositions du présent titre, les infractions définies par:

'1° Les articles 257–3, 265 à 267, 295 à 298, 301, 303 à 305, 310, 311, les troisième (2°) et quatrième (3°) alinéas de l'article 312, les articles 341 à 344, 354, 355, 379, les troisième à septième alinéas de l'article 382, l'article 384, le premier alinéa de l'article 400, les deuxième à cinquième alinéas de l'article 434, les articles 435 à 437 et 462 du code pénal;

'2° L'article 3 de la loi du 19 juin 1871 qui abroge le décret du 4 septembre 1870 sur la fabrication des armes de guerre;

'3° L'article 6 de la loi n° 70–575 du 3 juillet 1970 portant réforme du régime des poudres et substances explosives;

'4° L'article 38 et, en ce qui concerne les armes et munitions des première et quatrième catégories, les articles 31 et 32 du décret-loi du 18 avril 1939 fixant le régime des matériels de guerre, armes et munitions;

'5° Les articles 1er et 4 de la loi n° 72–467 du 9 juin 1972 interdisant la mise au point, la fabrication, la détention, le stockage, l'acquisition et la cession d'armes biologiques ou à base de toxines;

'6° Les articles 16 et 17 de la loi du 15 juillet 1845 sur la police des chemins de fer.

'Les dispositions du présent articles sont également applicables aux infractions connexes.

. . .

V. – Les contrats d'assurance de biens ne peuvent exclure la garantie de l'assureur pour les dommages résultant d'actes de terrorisme ou d'attentats commis sur le territoire national. Toute clause contraire est réputée non écrite.

Un décret en Conseil d'Etat définira les modalités d'application du présent paragraphe.

Art. 10. – La présente loi sera applicable aux faits commis postérieurement à son entrée en vigueur.

La présente loi sera exécutée comme loi de l'Etat.

Fait à Paris, le 9 septembre 1986.

Par le Président de la République:
FRANÇOIS MITTERAND

DECLARATION RELATIVE AU TERRORISME
INTERNATIONAL ADOPTEE A TOKYO LE 5 MAI 1986

'1) Nous, les chefs d'Etat et de gouvernement des sept principales démocraties et les représentants de la Communauté européenne réunis à Tokyo, réaffirmons avec force notre condamnation du terrorisme international sous toutes ses formes, de ses complices et de ceux, y compris les gouvernements, qui le commanditent ou le soutiennent.

'Nous exprimons notre horreur face à l'augmentation du niveau de ce terrorisme depuis notre dernière rencontre, et en particulier du recours, flagrant et cynique, qui y est fait en tant qu'instrument de politique gouvernementale. Le terrorisme n'a aucune justification. Il se développe uniquement par le biais de moyens méprisables, qui ignorent les valeurs de la vie humaine, de la liberté et de la dignité. Il doit être combattu sans relâche et sans compromission.

'2) Reconnaissant que le combat sans relâche contre le terrorisme est une tâche que la Communauté internationale, dans son ensemble, se doit d'entreprendre, nous nous engageons à déployer un maximum d'efforts dans la lutte contre cette plaie.

'Le terrorisme doit être combattu avec efficacité par une action résolue, tenace, discrète et patiente, combinant des mesures nationales et une coopération internationale.

'Par conséquent, nous exhortons toutes les nations partageant nos vues à collaborer avec nous, notamment dans des forums internationaux tels que l'Organisation des Nations Unies, l'Organisation internationale de l'aviation civile et l'Organisation maritime internationale, mettant à profit leur expertise afin d'améliorer et d'étendre les contre-mesures contre le terrorisme et contre ceux qui le commanditent ou le soutiennent.

'3) Nous, les chefs d'Etat et de gouvernement, convenons d'intensifier l'échange d'information dans les forums appropriés sur les menaces ou menaces potentielles découlant d'activités terroristes et de ceux qui les commanditent ou les soutiennent, ainsi que sur les moyens de les prévenir.

'4) Nous prescrivons les mesures suivantes, qui sont ouvertes à tout gouvernement concerné, en vue de priver les terroristes internationaux de l'occasion et des moyens de mettre à exécution leurs plans et objectifs, d'identifier et de décourager leurs auteurs.

'Nous avons décidé d'appliquer ces mesures, dans le cadre du droit international et de nos propres juridictions, à l'encontre de tout Etat qui est l'évidence impliqué dans le terrorisme international, soit en le commanditant soit en le soutenant, et, en particulier, à l'encontre de la Libye, jusqu'à ce que l'Etat concerné renonce à sa complicité avec le terrorisme ou au soutien envers lui.

'Ces mesures sont:

'– Refus d'exporter des armes à destination d'Etats qui commanditent ou soutiennent le terrorisme;

'– Limitations strictes de la taille des missions diplomatiques et consulaires, et autres organismes officiels à l'étranger, d'Etats qui sont impliqués dans de telles activités;

'– Contrôle des déplacements des membres de ces missions et organismes et, le cas échéant, réduction draconienne, voire fermeture, de ces missions et organismes;

'– Refus d'autorisation d'entrée à toute personne, y compris au personnel diplomatique, qui a été expulsée ou interdite (de séjour) dans un quelconque de nos Etats pour avoir été soupçonnée d'être impliquée dans le terrorisme international, ou qui a été condamnée pour terrorisme;

'– Amélioration des procédures d'extradition en stricte conformité avec les législations nationales en vigueur pour faire juger ceux qui sont responsables de tels actes de terrorisme;

'– Renforcement des dispositions et procédures d'immigration et d'obtention de visa à l'égard des ressortissants des Etats qui commanditent ou soutiennent le terrorisme;

'– Coopération bilatérale et multilatérale la plus étroite possible entre la police, les organismes chargés de la sécurité et autres autorités concernées, dans la lutte contre le terrorisme;

'– Chacun de nous s'est engagé à œuvrer dans les instances internationales appropriées auxquelles nous appartenons pour faire en sorte que des mesures analogues soient acceptées et appliquées par le plus grand nombre possible de gouvernements;

'– Nous maintiendrons une étroite coopération pour faire avancer les objectifs énumérés dans cette déclaration et examiner des mesures complémentaires. Nous convenons de rendre plus efficace la Déclaration de Bonn de 1978 dans la lutte contre toutes les formes de terrorisme touchant à l'aviation civile. Nous sommes prêts à encourager, tant sur le plan bilatéral que multilatéral, l'adoption de nouvelles mesures par les organisations internationales ou instances compétentes pour combattre le terrorisme international sous toutes ses formes'.

LES GROUPES ET SOUS-GROUPES DU COMITE EXECUTIF DE SCHENGEN

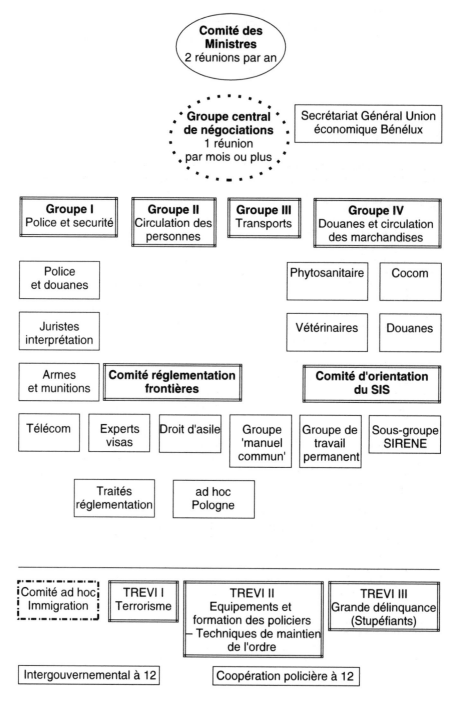

Index